Praise for

Entangling Vines

"A magnificent book. The old vines still hold."
—from the foreword by Nelson Foster, coauthor of *The Roaring Stream*

"A masterpiece. It will be our inspiration for ten thousand years."
—Robert Aitken, author of *The Gateless Barrier*

"A wonderful book, a book to take if you are planning to be shipwrecked
on a desert island; it is a book I open every day, and teach from every day.
It is surprising, lucid, scholarly, alive, unassuming, and it goes deep."
—John Tarrant, author of *Bring Me the Rhinoceros and Other Zen Koans
That Will Save Your Life*

"This book summons us into a dynamic immediacy with life itself."
—Wendy Egyoku Nakao, abbot of the Zen Center of Los Angeles

"An excellent translation of an important collection."
—Taigen Leighton, in *Japanese Journal of Religious Studies*

Entangling Vines

宗門葛藤集

A CLASSIC COLLECTION OF
Zen Koans

Translated and annotated by
Thomas Yūhō Kirchner

Foreword by Nelson Foster
Introduction by Ueda Shizuteru

Wisdom Publications, Inc.
199 Elm Street
Somerville, MA 02144 USA
www.wisdompubs.org

Library of Congress Cataloging-in-Publication Data for the hardcover edition is as follows:
Shūmon kattōshū. English.
Entangling vines: Zen koans of the Shūmon kattōshū / translated and annotated by Thomas Yūhō Kirchner; foreword by Nelson Foster; introduction by Ueda Shizuteru.—First Wisdom edition.
    pages cm
Previously published: Saga Tenryuji: Tenryu-ji Institute for Philosophy and Religion, 2004.
Includes bibliographical references and index.
ISBN 1-61429-077-6 (cloth: alk. paper)
1. Rinzai (Sect)—Quotations, maxims, etc. 2. Koan. I. Kirchner, Thomas Yūhō, translator, writer of added commentary. II. Title.
BQ9367.S5813 2013
294.3'927—dc23

                    2012037699

ISBN 978-1-61429-615-7   eBook ISBN 978-1-61429-096-4

23 22 21 20 19
5 4 3 2 1

Cover art by Phil Pascuzzo. Cover design by Gopa&Ted2. Set in Minion Pro and Nanzan Minion Pro fonts 10.5pt/12.6pt.
Typesetting for this book was done by Thomas Yūhō Kirchner.

Printed in the United States of America.

Please visit fscus.org.

Contents

Foreword by Nelson Foster 1
Introduction by Ueda Shizuteru 7
Translator's Preface 15
Preface to the Wisdom Edition 25
Conventions and Abbreviations 29

Entangling Vines, Part 1

Case 1	二祖安心	Pacifying the Mind of the Second Patriarch 33
Case 2	六祖衣鉢	The Sixth Patriarch's Robe and Bowl 33
Case 3	五祖他奴	Wuzu's "Someone's Servants" 34
Case 4	雲門須彌	Yunmen's "Mount Sumeru" 35
Case 5	馬祖即心	Mazu's "This Very Mind" 35
Case 6	趙州放下	Zhaozhou's "Drop It!" 35
Case 7	兜率三關	Doushuai's Three Barriers 36
Case 8	靈雲見桃	Lingyun Sees Peach Blossoms 36
Case 9	趙州柏樹	Zhaozhou's "Juniper Tree" 37
Case 10	黃龍三關	Huanglong's Three Barriers 38
Case 11	瑞巖主人	Ruiyan's "Master" 39
Case 12	趙州勘婆	Zhaozhou Sees Through an Old Woman 39
Case 13	郎中地獄	Langzhong's "Hell" 40
Case 14	長生混沌	Changsheng's "Chaos" 41
Case 15	孤峰不白	One Peak Is Not White 42
Case 16	牛過窗櫺	An Ox Goes through a Lattice Window 43
Case 17	乾峰三種	Qianfeng's "Three Types of Sickness" 43
Case 18	山谷木犀	Shangu's Sweet-Olive Blossoms 44
Case 19-1	香嚴上樹	Xiangyan's "Up a Tree" 45
Case 19-2	大慧樹上	Dahui's "Up a Tree" 46
Case 20	雲門屎橛	Yunmen's "Dry Piece of Shit" 46
Case 21	雲門蘇盧	Yunmen's "*Sulu*" 46
Case 22-1	德山托鉢	Deshan Carries His Bowls 47
Case 22-2	密庵意旨	Mian's "True Meaning" 48
Case 23	馬祖西江	Mazu's "West River" 48

Case 24   不入涅槃   Not Entering Nirvana   49
Case 25   石霜竿頭   Shishuang's "Top of a Pole"   49
Case 26   香嚴擊竹   Xiangyan's Sound of a Bamboo   49
Case 27   心隨萬境   The Mind Turns with Its Surroundings   50
Case 28-1   倩女離魂   Qiannu and Her Spirit   51
Case 28-2   虛堂頌古   Xutang's Verse   51
Case 29   雲門露字   Yunmen's "Exposed"   52
Case 30   密庵沙盆   Mian's "Brittle Bowl"   52
Case 31   國師三喚   The National Teacher Calls Three Times   53
Case 32   懶安有句   Lan'an's "Being and Nonbeing"   54
Case 33   南泉鎌子   Nanquan's Sickle   57
Case 34   百丈野狐   Baizhang's Wild Fox   57
Case 35   關山賊機   Kanzan's "Works like a Thief"   59
Case 36   二僧捲簾   Two Monks Roll Up Bamboo Shades   59
Case 37   虛空爲紙   Use the Empty Sky for Paper   59
Case 38   賢女屍林   The Wise Women in the Mortuary Grove   60
Case 39   漂墮鬼國   Drifting to the Land of the Demons   60
Case 40   秀才造論   A Scholar Writes a Treatise   61
Case 41   室內一燈   The Lamp in the Room   62
Case 42   心身共捨   Cast Aside Both Mind and Body   62
Case 43   達磨不來   Bodhidharma Didn't Come to China   63
Case 44   丹霞燒佛   Danxia Burns a Buddha Image   64
Case 45   寤寐恒一   Asleep or Awake, At All Times Be One   64
Case 46-1   趙州無字   Zhaozhou's "Wu"   65
Case 46-2   無字之頌   A Verse on Zhaozhou's "Wu"   65
Case 46-3   中峰無字   Zhongfeng's Eight-Word Question on "Wu"   66
Case 46-4   大慧無字   Dahui's "Wu"   66
Case 46-5   僧未問佛   Before the Monk Asked about Buddha Nature   66
Case 46-6   古德透徹   Penetrate It Thoroughly   67
Case 47   佛直祖曲   Buddha Straight, Ancestors Crooked   67
Case 48   女子出定   A Woman Comes Out of Samadhi   67
Case 49   水上行話   East Mountain Walks on the Water   68
Case 50   法華禪定   Lotus Samadhi   68
Case 51   大通智勝   The Buddha of Great Universal Wisdom Excellence   68
Case 52   黃龍念讚   Huanglong's "Sutra Chanting"   69
Case 53   馬祖塩醬   Mazu's "Salt and Sauce"   69
Case 54   柏樹托鉢   Juniper Tree, Carrying Bowls   70
Case 55   張公喫酒   Mr. Zhang Drinks Wine   70
Case 56   鼓山伽陀   Gushan's Gāthā   71
Case 57   一失人身   To Lose a Human Birth   71

Case 58	首山此經	Shoushan's "This Sutra" 71
Case 59	興化打中	Xinghua's "Hold to the Center" 72
Case 60	潙山水牯	Guishan's "Water Buffalo" 73
Case 61	古帆未掛	The Sail Has Yet to Be Hoisted 74
Case 62	洞山三斤	Dongshan's "Three Pounds of Hemp" 74
Case 63	南堂異類	Nantang's "Other Realms" 74
Case 64	無功德話	No Merit 75
Case 65	千尺井中	A Man in a Thousand-Foot Well 75
Case 66	大梅梅子	Damei's "Plum Pit" 76
Case 67	法燈未了	Fadeng Is Not Yet Finished 77
Case 68	南泉油糍	Nanquan's Fried Dumplings 77
Case 69	無鬚鎖子	A Springless Lock 78
Case 70	外道六師	The Six Non-Buddhist Teachers 78
Case 71	芭蕉拄杖	Bajiao's Staff 79
Case 72	世尊未說	The Buddha Never Preached 80
Case 73	圜悟禍門	Yuanwu's "Gate of Misfortune" 80
Case 74	莫妄想話	Drop Deluded Thought 80
Case 75	錯用心話	Misusing the Mind 81
Case 76	仰山枕子	Yangshan's Headrest 81
Case 77	三佛夜話	The Three Buddhas' Night Talk 82
Case 78	馬祖翫月	Mazu's Moon Viewing 82
Case 79	佛不知有	The Buddhas Don't Know It 83
Case 80	臨濟孤峰	Linji's "Solitary Peak" 83
Case 81	語默離微	Speech and Silence 84
Case 82	仰山白槌	Yangshan's Gavel 85
Case 83	六祖風幡	The Sixth Patriarch's Banner in the Wind 86
Case 84	五家評商	Comments on the Five Houses 86
Case 85	百草頭話	All the Plants 87
Case 86	願空諸有	Know the Emptiness of All That Exists 88
Case 87	女子定答	Why the Woman Came Out of Samadhi 89
Case 88	見色明心	To See Form and Enlighten the Mind 89
Case 89	別峰相見	A Meeting on Another Mountain 90
Case 90	南泉水牯	Nanquan's "Water Buffalo" 91
Case 91	雲門三句	Yunmen's Three Statements 91
Case 92	薰風自南	A Fragrant Breeze from the South 91
Case 93	百丈開田	Baizhang's New Paddy 92
Case 94	華嚴心喻	The *Avataṃsaka Sutra*'s Simile of the Mind 92
Case 95	運庵反衣	Yun'an Returns the Vestment 93
Case 96	讚六祖偈	A Verse in Praise of the Sixth Patriarch 94
Case 97	一子出家	When Someone Is Ordained 94

Case 98   圜悟投機   Yuanwu's Enlightenment Verse 94
Case 99   夾山境話   Jiashan's Surroundings 95
Case 100   袈裟裏鞋   Straw Sandals in My Vestment 96
Case 101   夾山掘坑   Jiashan Digs a Hole 96
Case 102   朝聞夕死   Hear in the Morning, Die in the Evening 97
Case 103   平常是道   Ordinary Mind Is the Way 97
Case 104   井楼請救   Calling for Help from the Well Tower 98
Case 105   路逢死蛇   A Dead Snake in the Road 98
Case 106   慈明行心   Ciming's Practice 100
Case 107   大燈三問   Daitō's Three Questions 100
Case 108   維摩金粟   Vimalakīrti, the Golden-Millet Tathāgata 100
Case 109   胡子無鬚   The Barbarian Has No Beard 101
Case 110   心不是佛   Mind Is Not Buddha 101
Case 111   清税孤貧   Qingshui, Poor and Alone 102
Case 112   維摩丈室   Vimalakīrti's Ten-Foot-Square Room 102
Case 113   佛性三轉   Foxing's Three Turning-Phrases 103
Case 114   世尊初生   When the Buddha Was Born 103
Case 115   南泉失火   Nanquan Loses the Fire 104
Case 116   溈山摘茶   Guishan Picks Tea 105
Case 117   百丈不食   Baizhang's "No Eating" 105
Case 118   南嶽說似   Nanyue's Explanation 106
Case 119   洛浦供養   Luopu's "Offerings" 106
Case 120   雲門一曲   Yunmen's Tune 107
Case 121   趙州救火   Zhaozhou's "Put Out the Fire!" 107
Case 122   黃檗烏藤   Huangbo's Staff 107
Case 123   濟下三評   Comparing Three Students of Linji 108
Case 124   世尊蓮目   The World-Honored-One's Lotus Eyes 110
Case 125   東西密付   The Secret Transmission from West to East 111
Case 126   孔子一變   Confucius's "Changes" 111
Case 127   治生商業   Earning a Living and Producing Things 111

Entangling Vines, Part 2

Case 128   德山燒疏   Deshan Burns His Commentaries 113
Case 129   洞山地神   Dongshan and the Earth Spirit 114
Case 130   興化罰錢   Xinghua Levies a Fine 114
Case 131   麻谷手巾   Magu and the Hand-Cloth 115
Case 132   疎山壽塔   Shushan's Memorial Tombstone 116
Case 133   塡王思佛   King Udayana Thinks of the Buddha 117
Case 134   首山竹篦   Shoushan's Stick 118
Case 135   世尊拈華   The World-Honored-One Holds Up a Flower 119

Case 136	迦葉刹竿	Mahākāśyapa's Temple Flagpole 119
Case 137	廣慧罪業	Guanghui's "Evil Karma" 119
Case 138	乾峰一路	Qianfeng's "Single Road" 121
Case 139	南嶽磨塼	Nanyue Polishes a Tile 121
Case 140	兜率荔支	Doushuai's Lychees 122
Case 141	佛境魔境	Realm of the Buddha, Realm of Mara 124
Case 142	松源三轉	Songyuan's Three Turning-Phrases 126
Case 143	虛堂三問	Xutang's Three Questions 126
Case 144	大燈三轉	Daitō's Three Turning-Phrases 127
Case 145	南泉住庵	Nanquan Living in a Hermitage 127
Case 146	慈明榜字	Ciming's Signpost 128
Case 147	慈明盆水	Ciming's Bowl of Water 129
Case 148	鐘声七條	Putting on Your Vestment at the Sound of the Bell 130
Case 149	微細流注	Subtle Flow 130
Case 150	法雲示衆	Fayun Addresses the Assembly 130
Case 151	仰山撲鏡	Yangshan Smashes a Mirror 131
Case 152	雲門舉令	Yunmen's Sermon 132
Case 153	陳操登楼	Chen Cao in a Tower 132
Case 154	婆子燒庵	An Old Woman Burns Down a Hermitage 132
Case 155	別有生涯	A Different Way of Doing Things 133
Case 156	一言駟馬	One Word and a Four-Horse Team 134
Case 157	法身喫飯	The Dharmakāya Eats Food 134
Case 158	虛堂兩字	Xutang's "Words" 134
Case 159	臨濟三句	The Three Statements of Linji 135
Case 160	華嚴法界	The *Avataṃsaka Sutra*'s Dharma Realms 136
Case 161	洞山夏末	Dongshan's "End of the Training Period" 137
Case 162	曹山大海	Caoshan's "Great Sea" 138
Case 163	毘婆尸頌	The Verse of Vipaśyin 138
Case 164	雲門失通	Yunmen Loses His Powers 139
Case 165	殃崛産難	Aṅgulimāla and the Difficult Delivery 139
Case 166	巖頭渡子	Yantou the Ferryman 140
Case 167	麻谷鋤草	Magu Digs Up Weeds 141
Case 168	皓月償債	Haoyue's "Paying Debts" 141
Case 169	大燈鐵話	Daitō's "Iron" 142
Case 170	佛教祖意	Buddha's Teaching, Bodhidharma's Intention 142
Case 171	末後評頌	Comment and Verse on the Final Word 143
Case 172	慈明執爨	Ciming Tends the Hearth 144
Case 173	慈明虎聲	Ciming and the Tiger's Roar 144
Case 174	慈明脫履	Ciming Takes Off a Shoe 145
Case 175	關山本有	Kanzan's "Inherently Perfect Buddha" 146

Case 176   臨濟赤肉   Linji's "Hunk of Red Flesh" 146

Case 177   臨濟四境   Linji's Four Realms 147

Case 178   臨濟四喝   Linji's Four Shouts 148

Case 179   一喝商量   One Shout Remains 148

Case 180   臨濟主句   Linji's "Host and Guest" 149

Case 181   四賓主話   The Four Guest-Host Relationships 149

Case 182   百丈再參   Baizhang Goes to See Mazu Again 150

Case 183-1   慈明連喝   Ciming's Consecutive Shouts 152

Case 183-2   虛堂幽谷   Xutang's Dark Valley 152

Case 184   興化兩遭   Xinghua's Two Waves of the Hand 153

Case 185   南院啐啄   Nanyuan's "Pecking and Tapping" 153

Case 186   虛堂拄杖   Xutang's Staff 155

Case 187   臨濟築拳   Linji Delivers a Blow 155

Case 188   洞山三頓   Dongshan's "Three-Score Blows" 158

Case 189   慈明論棒   Ciming Asks about the Three-Score Blows 159

Case 190   州勘庵主   Zhaozhou Checks Two Hermits 160

Case 191   瑯琊先照   Langye's "Perception First" 160

Case 192   臨濟栽松   Linji Plants Pines 161

Case 193   百丈說了   Baizhang's "Already Explained" 162

Case 194   德山行棒   Deshan Uses His Stick 163

Case 195   臨濟瞎驢   Linji's "Blind Ass" 164

Case 196   張拙看經   Zhang Zhuo Sees the Sutra 165

Case 197   南方一棒   The Staff of the South 165

Case 198   文殊來參   Mañjuśrī Visits 166

Case 199   一拳拳倒   To Knock Down with One Blow 166

Case 200   雪峰打僧   Xuefeng Strikes a Monk 167

Case 201   善財採藥   Sudhana Gets Some Medicine 168

Case 202   投子答佛   Touzi Answers "Buddha" 169

Case 203   雲門喚遠   Yunmen Calls Attendant Chengyuan 169

Case 204   楞嚴轉物   The Śūraṅgama Sutra's "Turning Things Around" 170

Case 205   守廓跛鼈   Shoukuo's "Lame Nag" 170

Case 206   長沙翫月   Changsha Enjoys the Moon 171

Case 207-1   臨濟洗脚   Linji Washes His Feet 172

Case 207-2   松源上堂   Songyuan Takes the High Seat 172

Case 208   臨濟四料   Linji's Four Positions 173

Case 209   陸亙笑哭   Lu Gen's Laughing and Crying 173

Case 210   臨濟四用   Linji's Four Functions 174

Case 211   乾峰舉一   Qianfeng's "Take Up the One" 174

Case 212   文殊起見   Mañjuśrī Gives Rise to Views 174

Case 213   徹翁遺誡   Tettō's Admonitions 175

Case 214   無邊刹境   The Infinite Realms   175
Case 215   樂天問法   Letian Asks about the Dharma   175
Case 216   浮盃答婆   Fubei Answers a Woman   176
Case 217   色即是空   Form Is Emptiness   176
Case 218   臨濟教化   Linji Asks for Alms   177
Case 219   趙州爐話   Zhaozhou's "Talk around the Fireside"   177
Case 220   潙山攀米   Guishan Picks Up a Grain of Rice   177
Case 221   常侍看毬   Changshi Watches a Polo Game   178
Case 222   福田惡道   No Merit, Evil Realms   179
Case 223   清浄本然   Pure Original Nature   180
Case 224   荒草不鋤   An Uncut Weed Patch   180
Case 225   金翅鳥王   The Garuḍa King   181
Case 226   折半裂三   Split in Two, Torn in Three   182
Case 227   斎僧功德   The Merit of Donating Food to the Sangha   182
Case 228   瑯琊洪鐘   Langye's "Great Bell"   183
Case 229   法無二法   In the Dharma There Is No Duality   183
Case 230   菩提宿將   A Veteran General of the Dharma Assembly   184
Case 231   莊嚴三昧   Flower Adornment Samadhi   185
Case 232   一切放下   Let Go of Everything   185
Case 233   擊動法鼓   Sound the Dharma Drum   186
Case 234   心地含種   The Mind-Ground Contains the Seeds   186
Case 235   空空法界   The Dharma Realm of the Emptiness of Emptiness   187
Case 236   一法若有   If a Single Dharma Exists   188
Case 237   補陀巖上   Atop Mount Putuo   189
Case 238   圓相因起   The Origin of the Circle-Figures   189
Case 239   宏智四借   Hongzhi's Four "Uses"   191
Case 240   生解未分   After Birth and Before Discrimination   192
Case 241   智不到處   Where Wisdom Cannot Reach   192
Case 242   古德大死   An Ancient Worthy's "Great Death"   192
Case 243   慧覺無罪   Huijue's "No Sin"   192
Case 244   宏智八句   The Eight Phrases of Hongzhi   192
Case 245   踏著不嗔   To Be Stepped On without Anger   193
Case 246   月夜斷索   A Piece of Rope on a Moonlit Night   194
Case 247   憲宗問光   Xianzong Asks about the Light   194
Case 248   大王来也   The Great King Has Come   195
Case 249   路逢達道   Responding to a Wayfarer on the Road   195
Case 250   黃檗禮佛   Huangbo Bows to a Buddha Image   196
Case 251   那吒析肉   Prince Nata Tears His Flesh   196
Case 252   隱峰推車   Yinfeng Pushes a Wheelbarrow   197
Case 253   關山罵僧   Kanzan Scolds a Monk   197

Case 254   許老胡知   I Accept That the Old Barbarian Knows 197

Case 255   十智同眞   Ten Realizations, Same Reality 198

Case 256   天皇恁麼   Tianhuang's "Like This" 199

Case 257   夾山法身   Jiashan's "Dharmakāya" 200

Case 258   茶陵投機   Chaling's Enlightenment Verse 201

Case 259   白雲未在   Baiyun's "Still Lacking" 201

Case 260   太宗擎鉢   Taizong Holds a Bowl 201

Case 261   斷百思想   Stop All Thoughts 202

Case 262   趙州石橋   Zhaozhou's Stone Bridge 202

Case 263   佛早留心   A Buddha Long Ago Set His Mind 203

Case 264   洞山果子   Dongshan's Fruit 203

Case 265   長慶拄杖   Changqing's Staff 203

Case 266   僧被蛇齩   A Monk Is Bitten by a Snake 204

Case 267   國師水梡   The National Teacher's Water Bowl 204

Case 268   三界輪廻   Moving through the Three Realms 205

Case 269   明眼落井   A Clear-Eyed Person Falls into a Well 206

Case 270-1   首山綱宗   Shoushan's Principles of the Teaching 206

Case 270-2   拖泥帶水   Filthy, Stagnant Water 207

Case 271   撲落非他   The Sound of the Wood Isn't Separate from Me 207

Case 272   南泉遷化   Nanquan's Death 208

Reference Materials

Biographical Notes 213

Chart of Names in Pinyin 287

Chart of Names in Wade-Giles 293

Chart of Names in Japanese 299

Bibliography 305

Index 313

About the Translator 339

Foreword

THIS BOOK OFFERS "ENTANGLING VINES," but who would want them and what for? The phrase suggests tough, jungly vegetation that will trip you up, snag you in its rope-like sinews, and hold you captive. As a title, it seems calculated to put off all but the boldest or most foolhardy readers, signaling that exploration of these pages will be a struggle—arduous, exhausting, possibly futile altogether. It invites risk-takers, curiosity seekers, and especially, perhaps, people driven to get to the bottom of life's biggest questions. Shall we count you in?

As the subtitle makes clear, the vines threatening to tie us up here are koans, the famously enigmatic little stories of Zen tradition. The liveliness and strangeness of koans—the humor and inscrutability of their repartee, their unorthodox treatment of Buddhist doctrine, the indifference they exhibit to logic or social convention, their frequent eruption into hitting and hollering, their broad expressive range, from crudeness to banality to poetry of great subtlety and beauty—have made them intriguing to people of diverse cultures ever since they emerged as a feature of Zen's Chinese precursor, Chan, some nine centuries ago.

Understanding has lagged far behind interest, unfortunately. In attempting to characterize koans, popular writers commonly resort to the words *puzzles* and *riddles*, which are so inaccurate as to be positively misleading. Academic specialists fare little better with such arid definitions as "pedagogical tools for religious training." Zen masters, who seem supremely qualified to explain the nature and working of koans, typically deflect requests for such information, declaring words inadequate to do justice to the phenomenon. Try a koan and see for yourself, they say.

Which brings us back to the entanglement under consideration—yours. Entanglement in koans takes two basic forms, one of them praised in Chan and Zen tradition, the other deplored, even ridiculed. The latter is a fascination with koans that remains merely literary or intellectual. The tradition doesn't reject such pursuits wholesale; indeed, it possesses an extraordinarily rich literature, and many of its great figures have demonstrated nimbleness and delight in the life of the mind. Zen has always insisted, however, that other interests be subordinated to practice and awakening, and it deploys a set of vivid metaphors to emphasize the absurdity and fruitlessness of a Zen student entering the thickets of analysis and interpretation before experiencing insight: heading east when you want to go west, scratching your shoe when your foot itches, beating the cart instead of the horse.

The approved form of entanglement with koans involves thorough, sustained absorption in one koan at a time, in the hope that it will eventually resolve in a deeply liberating realization. Before the process runs its course, however, engaging a koan in this fashion often feels tedious or even torturous—every bit as constricting and exasperating as the title metaphor implies—and the bonds grow still tighter if one thrashes around mentally in the effort to get loose. So whoever originally applied the phrase "entangling vines" to koans undoubtedly deserves a prize for Truth in Advertising (Medieval Chinese Division). It wasn't a private effort, though; institutionally, for centuries Chan and Zen have stressed the hardship of working with koans, promoting images of the process even more painful to contemplate than getting snarled in a web of creepers. The most cringe-inducing of these liken koan study to nightmares at the dining table—gnawing on an iron bun, eating the putrid mash left after the fermentation of alcohol, lapping up the shit and piss of bygone sages, swallowing a red-hot iron ball that can't be disgorged.

Despite such repulsive warnings, generations of Zen practitioners—male and female, lay and monastic, dauntless or terrified—have undertaken koan work and survived to verify its joys and lasting benefits as well as its intermittent miseries. Most descriptions of the process attribute the difficulty of koans to their deliberate thwarting of rationality. By this account, koans function as efficient traps for logical thought because the masters of old designed them expressly for that purpose. While it's true that logic rarely produces significant insight into a koan, the notion that koans are explicitly intended to impede logic doesn't hold up.

Centuries ago, the annals of Chan tell us, a monk questioned his distinguished master about the sayings of his predecessors, asking, "Did the buddhas and ancestral teachers have the intention of tricking people or not?" The master's reply holds for Buddhist texts of all kinds but fits koans particularly well:

> Tell me, do rivers and lakes have any intention of obstructing people? Although rivers and lakes have no intention of obstructing people, still people can't cross them, so they become barriers from a human standpoint. Although ancestral teachers and buddhas had no intention of tricking people, right now people can't go beyond them, so ancestral teachers and buddhas trick people after all.

Rather than presuming that koans were created to confound us, we would do well to take them at face value, as good-faith attempts to present the Dharma, the wisdom of the Buddha, in a straightforward, perhaps striking, manner. Many events in everyday life surprise and confuse us, after all, though no one intends them to; we simply don't understand them or even know how to understand them. From this perspective, it seems utterly unremarkable that a koan—a few words cherished for illuminating reality in a profound way—would go over our heads on first encounter (and maybe for quite a while afterward). Koans often perplex the monastics and laypeople who appear in them, and evidence abounds that they've perplexed innumerable monks, nuns, and laypeople who've pondered them as well. You're baffled by them? Big deal. Join the crowd.

Beyond the qualities that have made koans a challenge in any age lie obstacles of a more mundane sort. Readers of this book can't help being hampered by the fact that an enormous gulf of time, language, history, and worldview separates us from the original parties to its content—both the people who speak and act in its koans and those who later transcribed, edited, compiled, and published them. While the latter surely had posterity in mind as they went about their tasks, they had to speak to their culture in its own terms. Even if they could have imagined readers like you and me, they couldn't possibly have tailored their texts to suit modern minds.

Judging it infeasible to bridge this culture gap, some Asian teachers whose own training centered on traditional koans have chosen to set them aside when instructing Westerners, instead improvising koans free of exotic references. Other masters, determined to transmit the legacy of koan study intact, have strived to help non-Asian practitioners cross the cultural gulf. This effort has sometimes led them to minimize cultural differences and assert dubiously universal human qualities and "archetypes," and it has inevitably necessitated more or less detailed exposition of distinctively Asian elements that crop up in the koan stories.

Entangling Vines presents a lesser problem in this regard than earlier and better-known koan casebooks such as the *Gateless Barrier* and *Blue Cliff Record*, for it dispenses with all the embellishments that complicate and enrich those collections. Even so, most readers would be lost without the exemplary assistance that Thomas Kirchner provides in this translation, elucidating as he does every contextual feature that would obscure the basic sense of its koans. Luckily for us, he works from both sides of the cultural divide, coupling scholarly expertise and long years as a Zen priest in Japan with a keen awareness of Westerners' needs deriving from his American upbringing. Besides rendering the text into English with great care, he has supplied the Chinese graphs for convenient comparison, generously annotated terms and allusions that would escape most of us otherwise, and furnished biographical information on every identifiable figure who appears herein.

Thus equipped, in most instances even a newcomer to Zen can readily discern the literal meaning of these koans and get a sense of their players, but engagement with a koan only starts there. What ensues will depend on a number of factors: your background in Zen practice and in koan training particularly, the character of the specific koan under consideration, your teacher's guidance, and so on. In general, however, the process involves finding one's way into the koan, imaginatively inhabiting the situation that it describes and exploring the metaphors and images it uses. Out of this reconnoitering comes an awareness of which point or points in the koan require clarification. Then the hard work begins. To promote full absorption in the koan and penetration of each point, many masters advocate the use of a *huatou* (話頭, J., *watō*), a word or brief phrase that stands in for the full koan and that, with enough determination and practice, you can learn to carry in the midst of daily life and even in sleep, as well as during periods of formal, seated practice (zazen).

From this, it should be apparent that we're talking about complete immersion in the koan, an absorption that crosses supposed boundaries between the physical, emotional, psychological, and mental aspects of our lives. Although reason doesn't play a prominent role in this process, it can't be excluded; as engagement with the koan deepens, a type of inquiry develops that doesn't privilege one faculty over another. It often comes as a surprise to Westerners that inquiry of this nature is bodily as much as anything else and that, accordingly, expressions such as "working on a koan" don't boil down to euphemisms for thinking hard. Rather, they signify total commitment to the koan without trying to wring meaning from it. Its resolution can't be forced. One can only trust the process and carry on, however long it may take. Such is the degree of entanglement that koan study calls for.

At no small risk of oversimplification, perhaps we can say that koan work amounts, in the long run, to passing through a koan as a set of words and reanimating the realization from which those words sprang. The experience of resolving a koan has the quality of seeing with your own eyes what its originator must have seen in order to formulate them that way. One has the feeling not of matching wits with some faraway sage but of an intimate, immediate meeting of minds, a variation on the "mind-to-mind transmission" that Chan and Zen have noisily proclaimed and celebrated. A well-known Chinese master of the thirteenth century went so far as to declare that a breakthrough on his preferred koan would enable you to meet its author personally and "walk hand in hand with the generations of ancestral masters, truly knitting your eyebrows with theirs, seeing with the same eyes and hearing with the same ears."

How this could occur no one can tell. I suppose neuroscientists may hope to document it with their imaging devices, but such an event is rare enough even in serene temple circumstances that the chances of its taking place under laboratory conditions become hopelessly small. To say, as I just did, that resolving a koan entails "reanimating" a prior realization actually attributes too much agency to the practitioner and too little to the koan. I might just as well say that the ancient realization encapsulated in the koan enlivens us practitioners. A phrase favored by the illustrious master Hakuin Ekaku conveys the mutuality of the process: "Mind illuminates old teachings; old teachings illuminate mind."

The preceding overview of koan work derives all but entirely from the lineage of Chan and Zen known in Japan as the Rinzai sect. The other major strain of Japanese Zen, the Sōtō sect, for centuries institutionally disavowed and criticized koan practice, but that's started to change in recent years. Research demonstrating a long and proud heritage of koan work in their own school has prompted some Sōtō leaders in the United States and elsewhere to begin experimenting with ways to revive it. *Entangling Vines* may prove helpful in this endeavor, for it contains follow-up koans, often referred to as "checking questions," omitted by earlier koan collections. Masters use these secondary koans to test students' realization and prod them to further insights.

The Sōtō sect historically has denigrated koan practice chiefly on the grounds that it can become delusory in its own right, hooking people on a quest for buddha nature—a quest to grasp the ungraspable and gain what nobody lacks. This criticism, trenchant as it is, doesn't diminish in any regard the benefit countless Chan and Zen practitioners past and present have received from koan work, but it does point up a third form of entanglement with koans perhaps more dangerous than the pair described above. Frequently koans cling for a while after resolving, as practitioners' understandable elation and feeling of accomplishment morph into smugness and obsession with "passing koans." If this tendency isn't soon scotched, it can easily toughen into private arrogance and condescension and, even more lamentably, sometimes results in exaggerated public attention to kenshō (realization experiences) and koan study per se. Old Chan worthies called this getting bound with a golden chain, since attachment to liberation has brought merely a glorified sort of enslavement.

Consider yourself warned. *Entangling Vines* is a magnificent book, subject to serious and consequential misuse. If you feel drawn to investigation of koans, get yourself a reliable guide—a Zen master of good reputation who's done protracted, close training in a lineage with a history of koan work—and throw yourself into it headlong. The old vines still hold.

Nelson Foster

NELSON FOSTER is a Dharma heir of Diamond Sangha founder Robert Aitken and succeeded him at its Honolulu temple. He now teaches mainly at Ring of Bone Zendo in the Sierra Nevada foothills, making periodic visits to the East Rock Sangha in New England.

Introduction

THE KOAN COLLECTION *Shūmon kattōshū* 宗門葛藤集 has found an able translator in Thomas Kirchner, a ten-year veteran of Zen monastic life and presently the caretaker of Rinsen-ji, the subtemple that serves as the Founder's Hall of Tenryū-ji in Kyoto. In translating this work, one of the most important texts for Japanese Rinzai koan studies, Kirchner worked closely with Rev. Hirata Seikō (1924–2008), the former Chief Abbot of the Tenryū-ji branch of Rinzai Zen and former master of Tenryū-ji monastery.

Born in the state of Maryland in 1949, Kirchner left the United States in 1969 for a junior-year-abroad program at the International Division of Waseda University in Tokyo. There he studied Japanese culture and religion, and practiced the martial art of *kyūdō* (Japanese archery). His first encounter with a Zen master was with ninety-five-year-old Katō Kōzan Rōshi (1876–1971), the priest of a small temple in the mountains west of Tokyo and one of the greatest Zen teachers of that generation. Through this connection he later met Kōzan Rōshi's successor, Tsukada Kōun Rōshi (1898–1985), priest of the temple Shōan-ji in Nagano Prefecture, where Kirchner moved in early 1971 to begin formal Zen practice.

Kirchner's encounter with these two exceptional teachers determined the course of his subsequent training. In the Spring 1996 issue of the journal *Zen Bunka*, Kirchner briefly described his stay under Kōun Rōshi. I find it a particularly evocative picture of his early contact with Zen, so I reproduce it here in full:

> On the weekends I used to attend the meditation retreats at Katō Kōzan's temple Toku'un-in, located deep in a valley where two rivers joined. It was on one of these visits that I first met Tsukada Kōun Rōshi.
>
> Every autumn, as the Japanese maples started to redden, Kōun Rōshi and several of his students would visit Toku'un-in to pay their respects to Kōzan Rōshi. On these occasions meditation would be cancelled, and everyone would gather around a large table for an informal dinner in honor of the visitors. Kōun Rōshi, seventy-two years old at the time, had none of the mysterious air that I once associated with Zen masters. He was a plain man, looking rather like an old farmer, with a gaze that was open, yet penetrating and perceptive.

Those at the table asked me if there was anything I wished to ask Kōun Rōshi. As it was, a question had been on my mind for some time. I had come to Japan on a student visa for my junior-year-abroad program with Waseda, and had remained after the program to begin Zen practice. To support myself I was working as an English teacher, an activity that my visa status did not, strictly speaking, allow. Full honesty with oneself is central to Zen practice, I felt, and yet in order to practice Zen I was having to lie. I asked Kōun Rōshi what I should do in such a situation. He immediately replied, with a good-natured laugh, "In a situation like that, you should be completely honest about telling the lie."

My plan had been to live at Toku'un-in from January 1971, but when I arrived at the temple soon after the New Year's holiday it became obvious that Kōzan Rōshi's failing health would make that impossible. The people there recommended that I stay instead with Kōun Rōshi at Shōan-ji, saying they would notify him of my coming. The next morning I went to the nearby town of Itsukaichi and boarded a local train for Nagano Prefecture, high in the mountains of central Japan. At about seven o'clock in the evening, after several transfers and a few extended stops at snow-covered rural stations, each one colder than the last, I finally arrived at Nakagomi, the town nearest Shōan-ji. A twenty-minute bus ride took me to the foot of the long stone path leading up to the temple through a grove of giant cryptomeria trees. The moonlight, reflected by the snow, cast a pale glow over the winter landscape.

Reaching the temple, I noticed lights on in the room next to the entrance hall, and called out in greeting. Kōun Rōshi had not, it turned out, received word of my coming, but if he and his wife were surprised to see a shaven-headed foreigner standing in their entranceway they did not show it. My request to stay was accepted without so much as a raised eyebrow. Thus began my half-year stay under this unusual master.

Every day Kōun Rōshi would rise with us at four-thirty in the morning for an hour of zazen in the piercing cold of the meditation hall. After seating himself he would lean forward and strike his own shoulders several times with his short warning-stick (*keisaku*), as if to spur himself on to greater efforts. Zazen was followed by private *sanzen* instruction, then about thirty or forty minutes of sutra chanting in the main hall. At the end of the formal sutra service Kōun Rōshi would take a few sticks of lighted incense out on the porch, raise them toward the morning sky in his wrinkled hand, and read a few short sutras.

Kōun Rōshi read the sutras with an unusual rhythm. Katō Kōzan Rōshi once called him a *tanuki* (a racoon-like animal with a trickster reputation), and, sure enough, whenever anyone tried to follow his rhythm Kōun Rōshi would subtly change it.

But, *tanuki* though he may have been, Kōun Rōshi had no deceit. There was a deep integrity about him; at that time I was full of unrealistic ideals about Zen, enlightenment, and Zen masters, yet nothing that Kōun Rōshi said or did during the entire time I was there betrayed those ideals, or seemed in any way dishonest or false.

Unusually for a Zen master, he was something of a philosopher, a man who enjoyed discussing ideas and who had a gift for explaining complex problems in simple terms. No matter how abstract or theoretical a question I would ask, he always had a concrete reply that somehow cut through to the core of the issue. Never in these discussions did I sense any impatience—he would explain until I was satisfied, however long that took. The master also put great value on *samu* 作務, manual labor. The best jobs for Zen monks were weed-pulling and emptying the toilets, he said, and even at his age he would help with those chores.

Later, after I left Nagano and began formal monastic life, I would sometimes return to Shōan-ji during the off-season. No matter what my doubts and questions were at the time, merely being with Kōun Rōshi for a few days was enough to dispel them.

The rōshi remained in good health until the end of his life. According to his wife, one evening he said "I'll rest now," and went to bed. That night he died in his sleep. He was eighty-eight years old.

Desiring to experience formal monastic life, in June 1971 Kirchner entered Shōfuku-ji monastery in Kobe as a lay monk and trained there for three years under Yamada Mumon Rōshi (1900–1988). In 1974 he was ordained and given the name Shaku Yūhō 釋 雄峯, and soon afterward entered Kenchō-ji monastery in Kamakura as an *unsui* (a formal Zen training monk). He remained at Kenchō-ji under Minato Sodō Rōshi (1912–2006) until 1978, when he left monastic life for several years to complete his college studies. After receiving a B.A. in Buddhist studies from Ōtani University in 1981, he resumed his training under Sodō Rōshi, who had in the meantime moved to Kennin-ji monastery in Kyoto.

In 1984, after three years at Kennin-ji, Kirchner left the *unsui* life and moved to the Daitoku-ji subtemple Hōshun-in. Returning to his academic studies, he received a masters degree in Buddhist studies from Otani University and in education from Temple University (Japan). In 1992 he accepted the position of copyeditor at the Nanzan Institute for Religion and Culture at Nanzan University in Nagoya, and he worked there for six years on the Institute's journals and monographs. During this period he lived near the Sōtō Zen temple Tokurin-ji, where every morning he tended a large vegetable garden before heading to work. Following a health breakdown in 1997 he resigned his position and returned to Kyoto, where, in addition to his duties as caretaker of the Tenryū-ji subtemple Rinsen-ji, he works at the International Research Institute for Zen Buddhism at Hanazono University.

Kirchner's varied life experiences, including monastic training, meditation, academic research, and professional translation and editing, can be seen as part of his overall practice of Zen. These elements have now come together to make the *Kattōshū* available to the English-speaking world.

The *Shūmon Kattōshū*

The *Shūmon kattōshū* is one of the few major koan texts to have been compiled in Japan. The name of the compiler (or compilers) is unknown. So, too, is the date of compilation, but the fact that the first printed version appeared in the year 1689 makes it, at the very latest, a work of the early Tokugawa period (1600–1868).

Most of the 272 cases that constitute the *Kattōshū* were taken from Chinese koan collections popular in Japan, like the *Wumen guan* 無門關 (Gateless Gate), *Blue Cliff Record* 碧巖錄, *Record of Linji* 臨濟錄, *Record of Equanimity* 從容錄, and *Record of Xutang* 虛堂錄, as well as biographical literature like the *Jingde-Era Record of the Transmission of the Lamp* 景德傳燈錄 and *Compendium of the Five Lamps* 五燈會元.

An intriguing additional feature, however, is the presence of eight koans of Japanese origin. Case 61 features the Japanese monk Nanpo Jōmyō 南浦紹明 (1235–1309), who studied in China and transmitted the lineage of Xutang Zhiyu 虛堂智愚 (1185–1269); Cases 107, 144, 169, and 225 feature Shūhō Myōchō 宗峰妙超 (1282–1338), the successor of Nanpo; Cases 35, 225, and 253 feature Kanzan Egen 關山慧玄 (1277–1360), the chief Dharma heir of Shūhō and the founder of Myōshin-ji 妙心寺; Case 213 features Tettō Gikō 徹翁義亨 (1295–1369), Shūhō's successor at Daitoku-ji; and Case 225 features Musō Soseki 夢窓疎石 (1275–1351), a contemporary of Kanzan Egen and the founding priest of Tenryū-ji. The "ancient worthy" mentioned in Case 170 may also have been Musō Soseki. Hakuin Ekaku 白隱慧鶴 (1686–1769), the great reviver of the Japanese Rinzai school, appears in Case 199 of the present *Kattōshū* text, although this is a later accretion that does not appear in the first edition, published when Hakuin had just been born.

With the exception of Musō, the Japanese masters who appear are all associated with the Ōtōkan 應燈關 lineage, the Japanese Rinzai teaching line starting with Nanpo Jōmyō, Shūhō Myōchō, and Kanzan Egen, and continuing through the generations of their successors (the name Ōtōkan derives from the *ō* 應 of Daiō Kokushi 大應國師 [Nanpo's honorary title], the *tō* 燈 of Daitō Kokushi 大燈國師 [Shūhō's title], and the *kan* 關 of Kanzan Egen 關山慧玄). The text's design, too, follows that of a koan collection by Shūhō entitled *Daitō's One*

Hundred and Twenty Cases 大燈百二十則. It is nearly certain, therefore, that the *Kattōshū* was compiled by priests of the Ōtōkan lineage. The ascendancy of this school (all present-day Rinzai masters belong to it) secured the position of the *Kattōshū* in the Rinzai koan training system, a position strengthened by each of the text's successive printings during the seventeenth, nineteenth, and twentieth centuries.

The *Kattōshū*, then, took form in accordance with the special character and approach of the Japanese Rinzai Zen school. The compilers—most likely a series of masters who selected and rearranged its contents in response to the practical needs of their students—created an anthology especially suited for use in koan-oriented Zen meditation practice.

The first distinctive feature of the collection is the large number of koans it contains. Its 272 cases far outnumber the 48 cases of the *Wumen guan*, the 100 cases of the *Blue Cliff Record*, and the 100 cases of the *Record of Equanimity*. A text with this number and variety of koans would provide ample material for a master as he worked with a student over the years, examining and refining the Zen experience first from one standpoint, then from another. Kajitani Sōnin (1914–95), former chief abbot of Shōkoku-ji and author of an annotated, modern-Japanese translation of the *Kattōshū*, commented that "herein are compiled the basic Dharma materials of the koan system" (1982, "Kaidai" 解題). And, in fact, most of the central koans in the present Rinzai koan curriculum are contained in this work.

Another distinctive feature of the *Kattōshū* is that, unlike the *Wumen guan* and *Blue Cliff Record*, the koans are presented "bare," with no introductions, commentaries, or verses. This, too, may be seen as a result of the text's development within the context of active Zen training: the straightforward structure of the koans tends to give them added force and immediacy, emphasizing the point that the koan is asking the student to address. The vitality of this approach is certain to bring home to English-speaking readers the fact that the question each koan confronts us with is the same as the question that Zen as a whole confronts us with, which, at the deepest level, is the question that life itself confronts us with.

Although Kirchner began the *Kattōshū* translation as a personal project, when the text's many difficulties became apparent he turned to Tenryū-ji's Hirata Seikō Rōshi for advice. Hirata met with Kirchner several times a month over the course of a year and a half to clarify the Chinese readings and discuss approaches to translating the koans themselves. Hirata's two principal Dharma heirs, Sasaki Yōdō and Yasunaga Sodō, joined the seminars on a number of occasions.

Both Sasaki and Yasunaga are, like Hirata, striving to find Zen's place in the modern world even as they maintain the classical Zen tradition. Sasaki,

Hirata's successor as master of Tenryū-ji monastery, is a graduate of Kyoto University, where he studied modern academic Buddhology under Kajiyama Yūichi (1925–2004). Sasaki is the author of a book on Tenryū-ji's founder Musō Soseki, and he is at present the leading authority on this figure.

Yasunaga, following completion of his training under Hirata, established an international Zen center at his temple, Shōun-ji, and joined the faculty of Hanazono University in Kyoto as a professor of Zen studies. He is also active in the East-West Spiritual Exchange, a program of interreligious dialogue between Buddhist and Christian monks and nuns.

The participation of these three masters, deeply versed in both traditional Zen practice and modern academic thought, helped lay a solid foundation for the readings and interpretations of the *Kattōshū* koans.

During the past several decades linguists specializing in Tang and Song Chinese have identified many inaccuracies in the traditional Japanese readings of the Chinese Zen literature, the implication being that these mistaken readings have led to misunderstandings of the texts themselves. This challenge to traditional Japanese Zen is one that must be taken seriously—if the texts are to be used at all, they obviously must be read in a manner that is linguistically correct. This is doubly true when translation is involved.

Nevertheless, merely reading a text in a philologically correct way does not guarantee that one understands the text's message. The reading of any work invariably involves interpretation, and that, in turn, inevitably brings up questions of the depth and horizon of that interpretation. This is particularly true in the case of Zen texts, where the surface meaning of the words does not always directly convey the intention of the author or speaker. The paradoxical result is that readings which are correct from a linguistic point of view can suggest interpretations that are misleading, and vice versa. This is one of the most intriguing aspects of Zen literature.

The question of how to read a text in a philologically sound way does not always correspond to the question of how to read a text in a way that yields the text's true intention (a way of reading that, in Zen, implies an almost *physical* process, in which the problem addressed by the text is recognized as one's own personal problem). Zen has produced many texts, and Zen without texts is not Zen. Yet texts in and of themselves are also not Zen. Zen *encompasses* texts; that which the texts cannot express is approached *through* the texts, then experienced *beyond* the texts. Mere knowledge of the term "original face," for example, does not mean that one truly knows what the term is pointing to.

The people most familiar with the use of texts in Zen training are the *shike*, the masters at the Zen training monasteries. During the one-on-one encounters between master and disciple known as *sanzen*, koans like those in the *Kattōshū* are given to the monk in the form of questions or problems that the monk must respond to. These questions are presented in the form of language, and the responses, too, are expressed in the form of language (including body language and silence). Yet the trajectory that connects these two linguistic endpoints is not itself a step-by-step progression of words. There occurs during the deep samadhi of zazen a leap that separates and yet simultaneously bridges the language of the question and the language of the response. This process may be characterized as one of "from language, into language," with the inquiry emerging *from* words and the response emerging *into* words.

In this "from language, into language" dynamic lies the true significance of "text" in Zen practice. At the same time, the text represents a form of invitation to and guidance in experiencing this movement "from language, into language."

This dynamic continues another step in the case of the present translation: "from Sino-Japanese, into English." Here too a leap out of language and back into language was required. The synergistic action of this double leap has given birth to a new text, one that emerges into the world of English less influenced than the original text by the outlook of Japanese culture.

In this way, translation can be a valuable approach to the re-creation of a new, more direct expression of Zen. *Entangling Vines* had its origins in the discussions between three forward-looking Japanese Zen masters and an experienced Zen monk from America. It is my hope that it will not be seen simply as an English translation of the *Shūmon kattōshū*, but as an important text in its own right.

Ueda Shizuteru

UEDA SHIZUTERU, Professor Emeritus at Kyoto University, specializes in the philosophy of religion. His areas of interest include Christian mysticism, Buddhist thought, and Kyoto School philosophy. He is a longtime practitioner of Zen meditation.

Translator's Preface

THERE ARE IN ZEN two texts known as the *Shūmon kattōshū*. One, alternatively referred to as the *Kuzō kattōshō* 句雙葛藤鈔, is a voluminous anthology of phrases used in former times as a source for capping phrases, the words and verses from Chinese literature with which students demonstrated and refined their understanding of koans. The other *Kattōshū*—the subject of the present translation—is a collection of koans used in Japanese Rinzai Zen training. Though little known outside Zen circles, this *Kattōshū* is one of the more important of the koan collections. Every Rinzai Zen practitioner who advances in koan work must, sooner or later, examine this text.

Different teaching lines appear to use it in different ways. Some employ it from the early stages of koan training, combining *Kattōshū* koans with those from better-known works like the *Wumen guan*, *Blue Cliff Record*, and the *Record of Linji*. Others use it at a more advanced stage, subsequent to work with the other koan collections. According to monastic friends who have worked extensively with the *Kattōshū* as an advanced-level text, the emphasis—even more than in the other collections—is on eliminating the last attachments to dualistic thought. The koans are thus often approached in ways quite unexpected even to experienced Zen students. As one monastic friend commented, "If there's anything you can say about the *Kattōshū* koans, it's that your first response is certain to be wrong."

This enigmatic quality of the *Kattōshū* extends to its very origins. The text is known to be a medieval Japanese work, but no one knows exactly who compiled it or when. Koans from Chinese sources predominate, but here and there cases involving Japanese masters appear, with one (Case 61) featuring a Japanese monk (Nanpo) and his Chinese master (Xutang). Even the wording can be quite enigmatic; in the course of translating the text I found that requests to Zen masters for paraphrases of especially obscure passages often resulted in widely varying responses, depending on the individual master's sense of what the koan might be asking.

The title, *Shūmon kattōshū*, may be translated as, simply, "The Zen-school koan collection," since the most common contemporary usage of the word *kattō* 葛藤 in Zen is as a synonym for "koan." The word has a long and interesting history, however. The first character, 葛 *katsu*, means "kudzu," the tough vine infamous among farmers in the American South for its invasive vigor. The second character, 藤 *tō*, means "wisteria," another tough and vigorous vine but one known also for the beauty of its white or lavender flowers. Together the characters 葛藤 came to indicate entanglements, complications, difficulties, or struggles—the image comes to mind of vines ensnaring a person's feet as he makes his way across a field.

This sense of "things that ensnare" was adopted in Chinese Zen Buddhism as a natural metaphor for kleśa, the hindrances that impede people's search for liberation and bind them to the cycle of birth and death. In Zen the term quickly took on the connotation of the specific difficulties and impediments resulting from attachments to words and concepts. Appearances in the Tang-dynasty Zen literature, such as in the *Record of Linji* and the *Recorded Sayings of Muzhou* 睦州語錄, suggest that the word was used both in this sense and as a disparaging synonym for the verbal exchanges (*mondō* 問答) by which Zen monks induced awakening or tested each other's understanding.

Later, with the rise of koan Zen in the Song dynasty, *kattō* came to indicate not only words as impediments but also words as expedient devices to help bring the student to enlightenment; hence the connection with koans. The term thus took on the dual nuance, both positive and negative, so often seen in Zen terminology. Zen as a tradition may not be *based* on words and letters, but it does use, even *need*, words and letters to help precipitate that awakening which transcends language. Koan work, of course, is the prime example of this approach. As Prof. Ueda Shizuteru writes in his Introduction, the dynamic of koan training "may be characterized as one of 'from language, into language,' with the inquiry emerging *from* words and the response emerging *into* words."

The *Kattōshū* itself is a large work in terms of the number of koans it contains: with 272 cases, it is several times the size of collections like the *Wumen guan* and the *Blue Cliff Record*. Yet as a publication it is relatively small. Presenting just the koans themselves and lacking pointers, commentaries, and verses, it fills only forty-five leaves in the wood-block print edition commonly used by Zen monks.

As mentioned by Prof. Ueda, most of the material in the *Kattōshū* originally comes from the Chinese Zen literature, with a few koans of Japanese origin. Among the Chinese sources are the *Wumen guan*, with which it shares, in full or in part, forty-five cases; the *Blue Cliff Record*, with which it shares, in full or in part, forty-six cases; and the *Record of Linji*, with which it shares sixteen cases, for a total of one hundred and six. With eight of these cases overlapping between either the *Blue Cliff Record* and the *Wumen guan* or the *Blue Cliff Record* and the *Record of Linji*, a total of ninety-nine of the *Kattōshū* koans derive from the text's more famous predecessors in the Rinzai Zen literature.

The remaining Chinese koans come from a broad range of materials, including the *Record of Xutang* 虛堂錄, the *Recorded Sayings of the Ancient Worthies* 古尊宿語錄, the *Jingde-Era Record of the Transmission of the Lamp* 景德傳燈錄, the *Essential Materials from the Zen School's Successive Lamp Records* 宗門聯燈會要, and the *Compendium of the Five Lamps* 五燈會元.

Although it is unknown who compiled the *Kattōshū*, several unusual features of the collection tell us much about its origins. The first of these features is the prevalence of cases involving the master Xutang Zhiyu 虛堂智愚 (1185–1269). Xutang, although a significant figure in the history of Chinese Zen, is not typically classed with such giants as Nanquan Puyuan 南泉普願 (748–835), Linji Yixuan 臨濟義玄 (d. 866), Zhaozhou Congshen 趙州從諗 (778–897), and Yunmen Wenyan 雲門文偃 (864–949). Yet Xutang appears in seventeen *Kattōshū* cases, as many as Nanquan, and nearly as many as Zhaozhou (twenty-three) and Yunmen (also twenty-three). Furthermore, Xutang often serves in the role of commentator, giving him, in effect, the final say on the words and actions of other masters. Few other figures are accorded this authority.

Xutang's presence assumes even greater significance when one takes into account the fact that five of the six Japanese masters appearing in the standard *Kattōshū* text—Nanpo Jōmyō 南浦紹明 (1235–1309), Shūhō Myōchō 宗峰妙超 (1282–1338), Kanzan Egen 關山慧玄 (1277–1360), Tettō Gikō 徹翁義亨 (1295–1369), and Hakuin Ekaku 白隱慧鶴 (1686–1769)—are in Xutang's direct teaching line. (The sixth master and sole exception is Musō Soseki 夢窓楚石 [1275–1351], an illustrious priest in another lineage and a contemporary of Shūhō Myōchō and Kanzan Egen.) Nanpo was Xutang's student and successor, and transmitted the lineage to Shūhō; Shūhō, in turn, transmitted it to Kanzan and Tettō; and Hakuin (known in the West as the creator of the famous "sound of one hand" koan) was the great revitalizer of the lineage in Japan's early modern era. Taken together, these features strongly suggest compilation of the *Kattōshū* within the teaching line of Xutang's Japanese successors, known as the Ōtōkan lineage (for an explanation of the derivation of the name Ōtōkan, see the Introduction, page 10).

Further evidence of Ōtōkan involvement is provided by the actual koans selected for inclusion in the collection. In a detailed study of the historical background of the *Kattōshū*, Andō Yoshinori of Komazawa Women's University traces a likely process of development starting with the *Daitō hyakunijissoku*, a collection of 120 koans with comments by Shūhō Myōchō (Andō 2002). The two lineages stemming from Shūhō—the Daitoku-ji school under Tettō and the Myōshin-ji school under Kanzan—further developed Shūhō's koan system in their literature of secret koan records (*missan roku* 密参録), all of which predate the earliest edition of the *Kattōshū*.

Andō, comparing the contents of the various *missan roku* collections,

shows that the text he labels *Hekizen hekigo* 碧前碧後 var. A, associated with
the Tōkai 東海 lineage of the Myōshin-ji school, contributes 153 koans to the
Kattōshū, well over half of the total cases. Moreover, Cases 2–73 of the *Kattōshū*
are arranged in the same order as they appear in the "Hekizen," the first fascicle
of the *Hekizen hekigo*, while Cases 128–95 appear in the same order as they do
in the "Hekigo," the second fascicle. The remaining koans are largely taken
from a class of koan texts known as the *kinshishū* 金屎集 (golden turd collections), which are also associated with the Tōkai lineage, being an outgrowth of
the *Hekizen hekigo* var. A material.

Andō's research thus points to the development of the *Kattōshū* as part of
a process of koan systematization occurring in the Myōshin-ji school's Tōkai
lineage. To the Tōkai-lineage materials the *Kattōshū* compilers added a small
number of koans from other traditions, such as Tettō's Daitoku-ji school (e.g.,
Case 213) and the Sōtō school (e.g., Cases 239 and 244).

As noted in the Introduction, the earliest known edition of the *Kattōshū*
was that of 1689; Andō lists the dates and publishers of the various editions as
follows:

1689 (Genroku 元禄 2): Yamatoya Jūzaemon 大和屋重左衛門
1858 (Ansei 安政 5):   Kyōto Ryūshiken 京都柳枝軒
1859 (Ansei 安政 6):   Tanbaya Eisuke 丹波屋榮助
1886 (Meiji 明治 19): Yano Muneo 矢野宗男, ed.
1890 (Meiji 明治 23): Unkyō Chidō 雲嶠智道, ed.
1914 (Taishō 大正 3): Unkyō Chidō, ed., Shimada Shunpo 島田春浦
1916 (Taishō 大正 5): *Zudokko*, Shōhen 『塗毒鼓』正編, Fujita Genro
                       藤田玄路, ed.
1950 (Shōwa 昭和 25): *Zudokko*, Shōhen, Fujita Genro, ed.
1982 (Shōwa 昭和 57): *Shūmon kattōshū* 『宗門葛藤集』, Kajitani Sōnin
                       梶谷宗忍, trans. and annot.

The Genroku edition of 1689 was somewhat shorter than the Ansei edition of 1858, containing only 254 cases, of which six are duplicates that appear
in both fascicles of the book. Altogether the Ansei edition contains thirty-one
koans not found in the Genroku version. Six of these koans are replacements
for the duplicates; when carving the new woodblocks the Ansei editors carefully replaced the second occurrence of the repeated cases with different koans
consisting of exactly the same number of lines, thus preserving as much as possible the original Genroku layout. Other additions included koans that neatly
filled the spaces (even of a single line) that had been left blank in the Genroku
edition.

The nearly 170-year gap between the Genroku-era first edition (1689) and
Ansei-era second edition (1858), followed by numerous editions and reprint-
ings, is intriguing. Although the sudden popularity of the text from the mid-

nineteenth century may owe in part to the emergence of established publishing houses and improvements in printing technology, Andō (2002, p. 9) argues that it primarily reflects the upsurge of interest in Zen from late in the Tokugawa era (1600–1868) through the middle of the Shōwa era (1925–89).

Another and perhaps more pertinent explanation, however, may lie in the establishment and rapid development of the modern Rinzai monastic system during the nineteenth and early twentieth centuries. The Rinzai training monasteries—known as *senmon dōjō* 專門道場 or *sōdō* 僧堂—were established and taught almost entirely by masters in the Myōshin-ji school's Hakuin lineage, which by the Shōwa period included all Japanese Rinzai teachers. The coincidence of the *Kattōshū*'s new popularity and the ascendancy of the Hakuin lineage provides further evidence of the text's roots in the Myōshin-ji tradition.

Indeed, the *Kattōshū* as it appeared in its complete form in 1858 can rightly be considered a product of the Hakuin school, particularly since several of the koans newly included in the Ansei edition (e.g., Case 259, "Baiyun's 'Still Lacking,'" and Case 272, "Nanquan's Death") are considered pivotal in Hakuin Zen koan training (Andō 2011, p. 158). The importance of the text in the Rinzai monastic koan system is indicated by its inclusion in the *Poison-Painted Drum* 塗毒鼓, a compendium of essential materials for Rinzai koan study published by Kennin-ji.

That the *Kattōshū*, despite its popularity within the Rinzai monastic world, remains relatively unknown outside of that world may be attributed to several factors, most relating to the textual difficulty of the collection itself. As mentioned above, many of the cases are expressed in extremely obscure Chinese; this is particularly true of those involving the Chinese master Xutang Zhiyu. Although the general thrust of these koans is usually apparent (which is generally sufficient for koan work, where a pivotal phrase or two is often all that is at issue), on a sentence-by-sentence level the meaning is often quite unclear. Compounding the problem is the lack in the Inzan lineage—one of the two main branches of Hakuin Zen—of an oral tradition regarding many of the koans. Although monks in the Takujū lineage (the other main branch) usually go over the entire text in the course of their training, Inzan masters inform me that in their tradition only about one-third of the koans are used.

I suspect that these are among the reasons that Zen masters seldom take up the *Kattōshū* as a subject for Zen lectures and writings, choosing instead better-known and better-researched texts like the *Wumen guan*, *Blue Cliff Record*, and *Record of Linji*. This paucity of commentary has meant that, although an interested reader can easily obtain books on most of the important Zen texts, almost no literature exists on the *Kattōshū*. Of the nine editions listed above, all but one are simply presentations of the Chinese koan texts, without amplification. The sole exception, Kajitani's *Shūmon kattōshū*, provides the only scholarly research on the work. Privately published in 1982 by Kajitani's temple, Shōkoku-ji, it offers the original text, the *kakikudashi* (Sino-Japanese rendering), Kajitani's Japanese translation and interpretive commentary, and annotation on persons and terminology.

It was thus to Kajitani's book that I turned first when I started my English translation in 1999. Before describing my own efforts, however, I should first mention two partial translations that provided me with much valuable help and encouragement during the early stages of the project. First, Burton Watson, retired professor of Columbia University and one of the finest translators of Chinese and Japanese literature, generously shared with me his translations of those *Kattōshū* cases taken up by Yoshida Shōdō Rōshi, Chief Abbot of Kenchō-ji, in his lectures on this text (among the very few lecture series on the *Kattōshū*). Second, Victor Sōgen Hori, a fellow Zen monk in Japan during the 1970s and 1980s and now professor of Japanese religions at McGill University in Montreal, provided his translations of those *Kattōshū* koans he had examined during the course of his own monastic training. His translations were in part based on earlier renditions by Walter Nowick, a Zen student at Daitoku-ji during the 1950s and 1960s and the retired teacher at Moonspring Hermitage in Surry, Maine.

These preliminary materials provided me with much-needed momentum as I turned to Kajitani's 650-page *Shūmon kattōshū* for more in-depth analysis and commentary. I originally considered doing a straight translation of Kajitani's book, but it did not prove to be entirely suitable for that purpose. The work contains a number of problematic readings and scribal errors, and the commentary, although of course an acceptable expression of Kajitani's own viewpoint, does not necessarily accord with the way other masters would regard the koans.

Since over a third of the *Kattōshū* koans are also found in the *Wumen guan*, *Blue Cliff Record*, and *Record of Linji*, the first place I turned to for "second opinions" was the excellent research and commentary on these works found in the Japanese Zen literature. For the *Wumen guan*, the extensive and detailed commentaries of Yamada Mumon (1976), Katō Totsudō (1939–40, vols. 13–15), Yamamoto Genpō (1960), Iida Tōin (1913), and others were especially helpful. For the many, often quite difficult, koans taken from the *Blue Cliff Record*, the studies of Katō (1939–40, vols. 1–12) and Yamada (1985) were indispensable, as they are among the few works that examine not just the *Blue Cliff Record*'s main cases and verses but also the lengthy commentaries. For the *Record of Linji*, the studies by Asahina (1968), Yamada (1997), and Yanagida (1972) were very useful, although the excellent English translations of this work by Ruth Fuller Sasaki (1975, 2009) and Burton Watson (1993a) lessened the need for extensive research in the Japanese literature. The translations of those *Kattōshū* koans taken from the *Record of Linji* are largely based on the 2009 Sasaki edition.

Other valuable English translations were found in the works of Zenkei Shibayama (1974), Robert Aitken (1990), and J. C. Cleary (1999) for the *Wumen guan*, Thomas Cleary and J. C. Cleary (1977), and Thomas Cleary (1998) for the *Blue Cliff Record*. The *Kattōshū* also quotes from a broad spectrum of other Chinese sources, ranging from classics like the Confucian *Analects*, to Buddhist sutras like the *Vimalakīrti Sutra*, to Zen texts like Huangbo's *Essentials on the Transmission of Mind* 傳心法要 and Yongjia's *Song of Enlightenment* 證道歌. For these, lucid translations were provided by the works of Arthur Waley (1938), John Blofeld (1958, 1962), Robert Thurman (1976), Sheng-yen (1987, 1997), and others.

After researching what I was able to in the Japanese and English literature, I was still faced with a large amount of difficult text for which little reference material was available. For help with this I turned to Hirata Seikō, Chief Abbot of Tenryū-ji. Rev. Hirata, whose background in Zen practice, Western philosophy, and foreign languages made him particularly qualified for the task, generously agreed to meet for weekly study sessions, during which we would discuss traditional readings and the general intent of the koans. Later, as described in detail by Prof. Ueda in his Introduction, monthly seminars were arranged at the Tenryū-ji Institute for Philosophy and Religion with Rev. Hirata, myself, and Hirata's two Dharma heirs, Sasaki Yōdō and Yasunaga Sodō. As a result of this cooperative effort a preliminary translation was finished by the summer of 2003.

However, a number of questions still remained regarding the most difficult passages; the cryptic comments and verses of Xutang Zhiyu were generally the problem. Valuable help with these was provided by Dōmae Sōkan 道前宗閑, priest of the small Kyoto temple Fukujō-ji and an old friend from my monastic years at Kenchō-ji and Kennin-ji. Rev. Dōmae, translator and annotator of a recently published study of the *Tales from the Land of Locust-Tree Tranquility* 槐安国語, Hakuin's notoriously difficult commentary on the *Record of Daitō* 大燈錄 (Hakuin 2003), combines a deep knowledge of Zen arcana with expertise in the extensive database of primary and secondary Zen sources compiled by the Institute for Zen Studies in Kyoto. With his help I was finally able to come up with workable translations for the *Kattōshū*'s more difficult passages. Especially valuable in this respect was Dōmae's familiarity with the unpublished commentaries of the great Myōshin-ji scholar-monk Mujaku Dōchū 無著道忠 (1653–1744), whose *Cultivating the Record of Xutang* 虛堂錄犂耕 provides detailed analyses of Xutang's writings.

Inevitably, over the course of the translation process a fair amount of note material accumulated. Despite a personal preference for lengthy annotation (one of the features I like most about Miura and Sasaki's classic *Zen Dust*), I tried to limit the notes to information essential for understanding the koans on a literary level (understanding them in the context of koan training is, of course, an entirely different matter). In several cases, however, the obscurity of the text or the ambiguity of the terms and images made it necessary to include interpretive material, some of it rather detailed. In other cases, I was unable to resist including what is little more than interesting background information; often this is material that, important or not, is presented in virtually all Zen lectures on the koan in question. Again, I would like to emphasize that such comments do not constitute "answers" to the koans in question (they would certainly not be accepted as such by a competent Zen master) but rather interpretations of what the koan is asking.

It should be kept in mind, too, that such interpretations are in no way absolute. One lesson that was particularly impressed upon me in the course of translating this text was that there are various ways of viewing and working with these koans. A metaphor, for example, may be interpreted one way by a certain teacher and in quite a different way by another. Thus, although I have tried as much as possible to eliminate outright errors of translation, I cannot claim to have eliminated "errors" of interpretation.

The painstaking task of checking the first English translation was begun by my friend Wayne Yokoyama of Hanazono University, who examined the manuscript for stylistic and grammatical errors, and who offered a number of creative alternatives to my translations. He also had many valuable suggestions on matters of book design and layout. Later, after the manuscript had been revised, he proofread the entire text several times.

Burton Watson agreed to check the manuscript for Chinese readings, in the course of which he caught a number of inconsistencies and textual errors, and suggested smoother wordings for several of my translations. Liang Xiaohong, a Chinese Buddhist scholar associated with Nanzan University in Nagoya, kindly took time from her busy schedule to examine the Pinyin readings in the Biographical Notes and Name Chart sections.

When the translation was finally more or less complete, Nelson Foster, a Dharma heir of the American Zen master Robert Aitken and teacher at the Honolulu Diamond Sangha and Ring of Bone Zendo, closely examined and commented upon the entire manuscript. His professional editing skills resulted in a much more tightly and suitably worded manuscript, and his keen Zen eye caught a number of questionable readings and interpretations. He also looked over my often overgenerous annotation, separating that which was genuinely useful from that which was unnecessary and distracting.

A final check of the translations was made by Victor Hori, who identified further dead weight in the annotation, suggested alternatives for overly abstract terminology, and used his deep knowledge of the Zen literature (gained through his experience in translating the Zen phrase anthologies for his excellent book *Zen Sand*, 2003) to suggest alternative renditions of a number of particularly difficult expressions.

Much of the research and editorial work for the *Kattōshū* was carried out at the International Research Institute (IRIZ) at Hanazono University, where I am employed as an associate researcher. For this and much other invaluable support I must offer especial thanks to Nishimura Eshin, President of Hanazono University; Okimoto Katsumi, Director of the IRIZ; and Yoshizawa Katsuhiro, chief researcher at the Institute.

Toga Masataka, secretary general of Tenryū-ji and executive director of the Institute for Zen Studies, has throughout the years provided unfailing support for this translation. It is thanks to his firm but good-natured pressure in setting clear deadlines that *Entangling Vines* is being published now and not at some ever-receding time in the future. Important roles in the translation, editing, and publication of this work were also played by many others at the Institute for Zen Studies, especially Maeda Naomi and Nishimura Egaku.

Finally, I would like to thank my teacher, Harada Shōdō Rōshi; Priscilla Daichi Storandt; and the rest of the community at Sōgen-ji for their steady interest in the project, their trial use of preliminary versions, and their feedback on points of difficulty. This was of inestimable help in maintaining momentum and bringing *Entangling Vines* to completion.

To these and many other people who contributed to this translation in ways both direct and indirect, I owe a deep debt of gratitude. Their cooperation was essential in helping me produce as accurate a translation as possible at this time; responsibility for any remaining errors lies entirely with me.

Thomas Yūhō Kirchner
Rinsen-ji, Kyoto

Preface to the Wisdom Edition

N OT LONG AFTER the Tenryū-ji Institute for Philosophy and Religion published the hardcover edition of *Entangling Vines* in 2004, Wisdom Publications generously agreed to consider issuing an American paperback edition. Toga Masataka, secretary general of Tenryū-ji, immediately supported this idea, asking only that the Tenryū-ji Institute first be allowed to deplete its stock of hardcover copies. Permission for publishing the paperback edition was granted in the spring of 2010.

It was a long wait, but in many ways the timing was fortuitous. In the years since the hardcover edition appeared a number of corrections have been suggested by readers (in particular Edmund Skrzypczak, former editor of *Monumenta Nipponica*), and I myself have reconsidered the wording of a number of the translations. More importantly, though, my chief Japanese collaborator on the 2004 edition, Dōmae Sōkan, published in 2010 his own extensively annotated modern Japanese edition of the *Shūmon kattōshū*, inspired in part by his work on the English *Entangling Vines*.

In the course of investigating the original sources for the koans I consulted him about, Dōmae realized that the *Kattōshū* in its present form shows many of the same sort of accretions and scribal errors found in virtually all texts transmitted through the centuries via handwritten (or hand-carved) copies. In several cases entire sentences had been lost, obscuring the original meaning of the passages. Errors of this type are now easier to discover and rectify, owing to the nearly complete digital library of Zen literature presently available through the Chinese Buddhist Electronic Text Association and elsewhere. This library also facilitates the task of comparing the various usages of difficult expressions in order to clarify the meaning of passages that in the past have confounded even Zen masters.

The results of Dōmae's labors, with restored koans, modern Japanese translations, and copious notes, was published in March 2010, under the title *Kōteibon Shūmon kattōshū* 校訂本宗門葛藤集 (Zen school koan collection: Revised edition). This volume is certain to become required reading for all serious Japanese Rinzai monks. The timely appearance of Dōmae's book meant that revisions for the Wisdom paperback edition of *Entangling Vines* could go well beyond the mere correction of typos, etc. With Dōmae's book as my primary resource I was able not only to correct errors but also to retranslate a number of the koans, sometimes with significant changes in the meaning. An example of how different the final results sometimes were is the enlightenment poem appearing in the koan "Xiangyan's Sound of a Bamboo." The translation in the 2004 edition of *Entangling Vines*, based on Kajitani's interpretation, is:

> A single "tock!"—all knowledge forgotten
> No need for further study and practice.
> Daily activities proclaim the Ancient Way.
> No more falling into passive stillness.
> Wherever I go I leave no trace;
> In the world I forget proper conduct.
> Everywhere Masters of the Way
> Speak of this as the highest function.

The revised version is:

> A single "tock"—all prior knowledge forgotten
> This is *not* the result of practice—
> Daily activities proclaim the Ancient Way.
> No more falling into passive stillness.
> Wherever I go I leave no trace;
> In all situations my actions are free.
> Everywhere masters of the Way
> Speak of this as the highest function.

Similarly, the existing notes have been considerably rewritten and a number of new notes added on the basis of information provided by Dōmae. The research contained in these notes must therefore be credited largely to Dōmae; I served primarily as his appreciative translator.

Dōmae also uncovered interesting new information on the historical development of the *Kattōshū* when he examined the Genroku edition—the original edition of 1689—at the National Diet Library in Tokyo. As noted in the Translator's Preface, he discovered that this edition was significantly different from the Ansei edition of 1858, containing considerably fewer cases and showing such signs of textual immaturity as the repetition of several koans in both the first and second sections. Prof. Andō Yoshinori, on whose study of the *Kattōshū* I relied in my original Preface, revised his analysis in line with Dōmae's research when he published his *Chūsei Zenshū ni okeru kōan no kenkyū* (Koans in the Medieval Zen School) in 2011. I, too, have emended my historical comments in the Preface to reflect this new material.

I have also followed Dōmae's lead in renumbering the koans in accordance with the system used in the standard *Kattōshū* text. In contrast to Kajitani, who assigns separate numbers to all of the entries in the text, the editors of the standard text considered a number of the koans to be subsidiary to the immediately preceding koans and thus left them unlisted in the table of contents. Although Dōmae does list them, he assigns the same number to the koan and its subsidiary (or subsidiaries), distinguishing the two by adding a "1" to the main case and a "2" to the subsidiary. Thus there are Cases 19-1 and 19-2, 22-1 and 22-2, 28-1 and 28-2, and 207-1 and 207-2. The largest number of subsidiaries, five, are those connected with "Zhaozhou's 'Wu,'" with "Zhaozhou's 'Wu'" itself numbered 46-1 and the subsidiaries numbered 46-2, 46-3, etc. Certain other koans treated by Kajitani as single koans (such as 183 and 270) actually consist of two sections: the main case followed by the comments of the master Xutang Zhiyu. These koans are returned to their divided form by Dōmae; thus we have Cases 183-1 / 183-2 and 270-1 / 270-2.

In the original text the koan "Buddha Straight, Ancestors Crooked" is located immediately after "Zhaozhou's 'Wu.'" However, since "Buddha Straight, Ancestors Crooked" is followed by the five koans subsidiary to "Zhaozhou's 'Wu,'" Dōmae felt it appropriate to relocate it after these five, another decision in which I have followed his lead.

The final result is a numbering system that is somewhat more complicated than the system in the 2004 edition of *Entangling Vines*, but that more accurately represents the true relationship between the respective koans.

Other changes include expanded biographies of a number of the masters in the Biographical Notes, partly in response to comments by readers that they particularly enjoyed this part of the book. The need for a full index was also mentioned by readers, and quickly became apparent to me, too, as I searched, often futilely, for koans whose titles I couldn't recollect or obscure items of information buried in the footnotes. The index in the present edition will, I hope, help alleviate these and other problems, despite the difficulties inherent in indexing what is, in effect, a collection of anecdotes and stories.

Nelson Foster, Dharma heir of Robert Aitken Roshi and teacher at the Ring of Bone Zendo, whose insightful advice contributed greatly to the 2004 edition, graciously agreed to provide a foreword for this Wisdom edition. Foster's essay, focusing on the often misunderstood issue of what it means to work with koans as part of meditation practice, sets the right tone for a book intended as an aid for traditional Rinzai Zen training.

Finally, I would like to express my appreciation to Josh Bartok, senior editor at Wisdom Publications, and the rest of the Wisdom staff for their generous help in making this new edition possible.

Thomas Yūhō Kirchner
Rinsen-ji, Kyoto

Conventions and Abbreviations

$E_{NTANGLING}$ V_{INES} is intended primarily as an aid to English-speaking practitioners of Zen meditation in the Japanese Rinzai tradition. Although I have attempted to produce a book that meets at least minimal academic standards, it is not essentially a scholarly work, and the academic apparatus is consequently not overly elaborate. Sources for the koans, when identified at all, are generally limited to the other well-known koan collections that are presently available in English translation, such as the *Wumen guan, Blue Cliff Record*, and *Record of Linji*. Annotation is, as much as possible, strictly factual in nature; interpretive material, although often unavoidable, has in most cases been kept to a minimum in order not to limit the usefulness of a koan in practice situations.

The Chinese text used in the present translation is based on the version prepared by the International Research Institute for Zen Buddhism and available from the Institute's website. This text was then collated with Dōmae Sōkan's 2010 edition and corrected when necessary.

The biographies in the lengthy Biographical Notes section are chiefly for the purpose of providing context for the koans (they also provided an opportunity to translate a number of extra koans). Thus the entries do not attempt to present the latest scholarly research on the masters mentioned, but rather summarize the traditional accounts of the masters' lives and teachings, as such accounts are generally what is most relevant when working with the koans. Readers who wish to know more about Zen history from an academic point of view should refer to the excellent studies by scholars such as Philip Yampolsky, John R. McRae, Peter N. Gregory, and Dale S. Wright.

Generally speaking, everyone whose name appears in a koan, no matter how minor his or her role, is given an entry in the Biographical Notes; when such a person's name appears in the text notes or in the biographical entry for another person it is italicized and no Chinese characters or dates are provided (these are given in the biographical entry itself). People who appear *only* in the text notes or in the biographical entries of other people do not (with a few notable exceptions) receive biographical entries of their own; Chinese characters and dates are provided for these figures when they are mentioned.

The Bibliography consists primarily of works I consulted during the course of translating the *Kattōshū*. It is thus a highly selective list; a complete listing of Japanese and Western-language Buddhist works related in some way to the *Kattōshū* would constitute a small book in itself.

Sanskrit Buddhist terminology is treated as much as possible as accepted English vocabulary. Words that are now generally known to English readers familiar with Eastern thought, such as "samsara" and "samadhi," appear un-italicized and without diacritical marks. Words that are less familiar, such as "dharmakāya" or "nirmāṇakāya," are unitalicized but retain diacritical marks, as do proper nouns. The titles of texts are sometimes given in translation and sometimes not, depending upon which form I felt more likely to be familiar to readers. For example, the title of the *Wumen guan* is given in its Chinese form, while that of the *Biyan lu* is given in English as the *Blue Cliff Record*.

I have tried to keep capitalization to a minimum, partly in agreement with the present trend in publishing toward lowercasing, and partly because usages like "Truth," "Nothingness," and "the Absolute" suggest the existence of a kind of Neoplatonist realm of (capitalized) Buddhist Reality separate from (lowercased) everyday reality. I have, however, followed the Wisdom house style in capitalizing "dharma" when it refers to the Buddhist teachings or universal truth and lowercasing it when it refers to phenomena. Similarly, the word "way" is capitalized when it serves as a translation of "Tao," since "way" as "Tao," if not capitalized, can often be taken to mean "method" or "manner." Terms like "buddha" and "tathagata" are capitalized when referring to Śākyamuni or other specific persons but lowercased when used as general nouns.

The following abbreviations were adopted:

C. Chinese

J. Japanese

T *Taishō shinshū daizōkyō* 大正新脩大藏經
(Buddhist canon published in the Taishō era)

X *Shinsan Dainihon Zokuzōkyō* 卍新纂大日本續藏經
(Revised supplement to the Japanese Buddhist canon)

REEPR *The Rider Encyclopedia of Eastern Philosophy and Religion.*
London: Rider, 1989.

ZGDJ *Zengaku daijiten* 禪學大辭典 (Zen studies dictionary),
ed. Komazawa Daigakunai Zengaku Daijiten Hensansho
駒沢大學内禪學大辭典編纂所. Tokyo: Taishūkan, 1985.

ZGJI *Zengo jii* 禪語字彙 (Zen glossary), ed. Imai Fukuzan 今井福山
and Nakagawa Shūan 中川澁庵. Tokyo: Hakurinsha, 1935.

ZGJT *Zengo jiten* 禅語辞典 (Zen lexicon), ed. Iriya Yoshitaka 入矢義高
and Koga Hidehiko 古賀英彦. Kyoto: Shibunkaku, 1991.

Entangling Vines

宗門葛藤集

Part 1

Case 1   二祖安心   *Pacifying the Mind of the Second Patriarch*[1]

二祖慧可、問達磨大師云、某心未安、乞師安心。師云、將心來與汝
安。祖云、覓心不可得。師云、與汝安心竟。

Huike, the Second Patriarch, said to Bodhidharma, "My mind is not yet at
rest. Master, I implore you, set my mind to rest."

The master replied, "Bring your mind here and I'll set it to rest for you."

Huike said, "I've searched for my mind, but am unable to find it."

"There," said the master, "I've set your mind to rest."

    1. Also *Wumen guan* 41, Main Case. For background material on this koan see
Huike in the Biographical Notes.

Case 2   六祖衣鉢   *The Sixth Patriarch's Robe and Bowl*[1]

六祖因明上座趁至大庾嶺。祖見明至、即擲衣鉢於石上云、此衣表
信、可力爭耶、任君將去。明遂舉之、如山不動。踟蹰悚慄。明云、
我來求法、非爲衣也。願行者開示。祖云、不思善不思惡、正與麼
時、那箇是明上座父母未生已前本來面目。明當下大悟、遍體汗流。
泣淚作禮問云、上來密語密意外、還更有意旨否。祖曰、我今爲汝說
者、即非密也。汝若返照自己面目、密却在汝邊。明云、某甲雖在黃
梅隨衆、實未省自己面目。今蒙指授入處、如人飲水冷暖自知。今行
者即是某甲師也。祖云、汝若如是、則吾與汝同師黃梅、善自護持。

The senior monk Huiming pursued Huineng, the Sixth Patriarch, to Dayu
Peak. Huineng, seeing him come, put the robe and bowl on a rock and said,
"This robe represents faith. How can it be taken by force? You may have it."

    Huiming tried to pick it up, but, like a mountain, it couldn't be moved.
Shaken and frightened, Huiming said, "I came in search of the Dharma, not
for the sake of the robe. Lay brother,[2] please instruct me."

Huineng said, "Think not of good, think not of evil. At this very moment, what is your original face before your father and mother were born?"[3]

At that moment Huiming was deeply enlightened, and his entire body flowed with sweat. With tears in his eyes, he bowed and asked, "Is there any meaning still more profound than the hidden meaning and words you have just imparted to me?"

"There's nothing hidden about what I have revealed," replied Huineng. "If you turn your own light inward and illuminate your original face, what is hidden is within yourself."

Huiming said, "Although I practiced with the assembly under Hongren, I had yet to realize my original face. Now that you have shown the way in, I'm like one who has tasted water and knows for himself whether it's cold or warm. You, lay brother, are now my teacher."

Huineng replied, "If that's how it is with you, then you and I are equally the disciples of Hongren. Take good care of yourself!"[4]

1. Also *Wumen guan* 23, Main Case. For background material on this koan, see *Huineng* and *Huiming* in the Biographical Notes. The word 衣, translated here as "robe" for the sake of simplicity, actually referred in ancient China not to the monk's robe but to the 袈裟, a clerical garment used primarily in ceremonies (see Case 95, note 1, for more detail).

2. A lay brother 行者 was, in China, a nonordained worker in a monastery. Huineng is said to have been the first Chinese lay brother. In Japan the term was applied to people, both ordained and nonordained, who were engaged in caring either for the senior clergy or for the temple buildings.

3. The translation of this line follows the interpretation of Japanese Zen. The Chinese text can also be translated, "What was your original face before your father and mother gave birth to you?"

4. This statement, 善自護持, is usually interpreted in Japanese Zen to mean "Maintain well this teaching you have received."

Case 3   五祖他奴   Wuzu's "Someone's Servants"[1]

東山演禪師示衆曰、釋迦彌勒、猶是渠奴、且道、渠是阿誰。

Wuzu Fayan of Mount Dong said to the assembly, "Even Śākyamuni and Maitreya are merely someone's servants.[2] Tell me, who is it?"

1. Also *Wumen guan* 45, Main Case.
2. Śākyamuni is the historical buddha; Maitreya is the buddha of the future. See *Śākyamuni* and *Maitreya* in the Biographical Notes.

Case 4   雲門須彌   *Yunmen's "Mount Sumeru"*

雲門因僧問、不起一念時、還有過也無。門云、須彌山。

A monk asked Yunmen Wenyan, "Is anything amiss when not a single thought arises?"

Yunmen replied, "Mount Sumeru!"[1]

1. In Indian cosmology Mount Sumeru is the enormous mountain at the center of each world-system in the universe. The mountain stretches from 84,000 *yojana* below the surface of the sea to 84,000 *yojana* above it (a *yojana* is variously defined as between six and fifteen kilometers in length). The god Indra resides on its summit in Trāyastrimśa Heaven, and the four heavenly kings dwell on its four sides. It is surrounded by seven concentric golden mountain ranges, each separated by a sea of fresh water. Beyond these is a saltwater ocean containing the four continents of our world-system: Pūrvavideha to the east, Aparagodānīya to the west, Uttarakuru to the north, and Jambudvīpa (the human realm) to the south of Sumeru. Surrounding the entirety are two ranges of iron mountains.

Case 5   馬祖即心   *Mazu's "This Very Mind"*[1]

明州大梅山法常禪師、問馬祖云、如何是佛。祖云、即心即佛。後有
僧又問、如何是佛。祖云、非心非佛。

Damei Fachang of Ming Province asked Mazu Daoyi, "What is buddha?"
Mazu answered, "This very mind is buddha."
Later another monk asked Mazu, "What is buddha?"
The master replied, "Not mind, not buddha."

1. The first question-and-answer exchange forms *Wumen guan* 30, Main Case; the second forms *Wumen guan* 33, Main Case. For a follow-up see *Damei Fachang* in the Biographical Notes.

Case 6   趙州放下   *Zhaozhou's "Drop It!"*[1]

嚴陽尊者問趙州、一物不將來時如何。州云、放下著。者云、已是一
物不將來、放下這什麼。州云、恁麼則擔取去。者於言下大悟。

Yanyang Shanxin asked Zhaozhou Congshen, "If I come with nothing, what then?"

"Drop it!" replied Zhaozhou.

"But I've come with nothing," answered Yanyang. "How can I drop it?"

"Then go on carrying it!" said Zhaozhou. At this Yanyang was deeply enlightened.

1. Also *Record of Equanimity* 57, Main Case.

Case 7   兜率三關   *Doushuai's Three Barriers*[1]

兜率悦和尚、設三關問學者、撥草參玄、只圖見性、即今上人性在甚
處。識得自性、方脱生死。眼光落地時、作麼生脱。脱得生死、便知
去處、四大分離、向甚麼處去。

Doushuai Congyue devised three barriers to test his students:

Pulling weeds and exploring the mystery are solely for the purpose of seeing your true nature.[2] So, right now, where is your true nature?

If you realize your true nature, you escape birth-and-death. So as the light in your eyes dims,[3] how do you escape?

When you escape birth-and-death, you know where you go. So as your four elements separate,[4] where do you go?

1. Also *Wumen guan* 47, Main Case.

2. "Pulling weeds" refers either to clearing a path to call upon a teacher, or to removing obstructive thoughts and delusions. "The mystery" translates 玄; "dark" is the original sense of the word, but it came to indicate, in Taoism and later in Zen, "the hidden," "the mysterious," or "the abstruse principle."

3. That is, as you approach death.

4. The four great elements—earth, water, fire, and air—signify the various components of the body, with earth representing the solid elements, water the liquid elements, fire the life energies, and air the bodily movements. Thus the separation of the four elements signifies the total dissolution of the physical body.

Case 8   靈雲見桃   *Lingyun Sees Peach Blossoms*

福州靈雲志勤禪師、因見桃花悟道。有頌云、三十年來尋劍客、幾回
葉落又抽枝。自從一見桃花後、直至如今更不疑。後舉似溈山。山
曰、從緣入者、永不退失。汝善護持。玄沙聞云、諦當甚諦當、敢保
老兄猶未徹在。雲門云、說甚徹不徹、更參三十年。後來、大川濟和
尚上堂、僧出舉前頌問、大川答云、作賊人心虛。

Lingyun Zhiqin of Fuzhou was enlightened upon seeing the blossoms of a peach tree. In a verse he said:

> For thirty years I sought a sword-master.[1]
> How many times have leaves fallen and new buds appeared?
> But ever since seeing the peach blossoms,
> From then till now I have never doubted again!

Later he related this verse to his master, Guishan Lingyou. Guishan said, "Those who enlighten through circumstances[2] never regress. Take good care of yourself!"

When Xuansha Shibei heard about this, he said, "Lingyun may well have been right, but I'll guarantee that his understanding was incomplete."[3]

Wuzu Fayan[4] said, "You talk of complete and incomplete? Thirty more years of training!"

Later, during a lecture, a monk asked Dachuan Puji about the verse. Dachuan said, "A thief has no peace of mind."[5]

1. "Sword-master" 劍客 indicates a master of the Way, one who wields the sword of wisdom that cuts the root of delusion, "the sword that freely gives life or takes it away."

2. "Those who enlighten through circumstances" translates 從緣入者, which refers to those who reach enlightenment not through the teachings of a master but spontaneously through the functioning of the senses.

3. This can be a statement of either praise or blame, but in this case it is one of praise. Xuansha later sent Lingyun a laudatory verse.

4. The *Kattōshū* has Yunmen Wenyan as the speaker here, but this exchange is found not in Yunmen's records but in those of Wuzu Fayan.

5. This may be a statement either of praise or censure.

Case 9   趙州柏樹   *Zhaozhou's "Juniper Tree"*[1]

趙州因僧問、如何是祖師西來意。州云、庭前柏樹子。僧云、和尚莫
將境示人。州云、我不將境示人。僧云、如何是祖師西來意。州云、
庭前柏樹子。後來法眼問覺鐵觜云、承聞、趙州有柏樹子話是否。觜
云、先師無此話、莫謗先師。眼云、眞獅子兒能獅子吼。

A monk once asked Zhaozhou Congshen, "What is the meaning of Bodhidharma's coming from the West?"[2]

Zhaozhou answered, "The juniper tree in front of the garden."[3]

The monk replied, "Master, don't teach me using external objects."

Zhaozhou said, "I'm not teaching you using external objects."

The monk asked, "What is the meaning of Bodhidharma's coming from the West?"

Zhaozhou answered, "The juniper tree in front of the garden."

Afterward Fayan Wenyi asked Jue Tiezui, "I heard that your teacher, Zhaozhou, spoke of a juniper tree. Is this true?"

Jue Tiezui replied, "My late teacher never said such a thing—don't slander him!"

Fayan commented, "A true lion's cub gives a good lion's roar!"

1. Zhaozhou and the monk's initial exchange forms *Wumen guan* 37, Main Case, and the *Record of Equanimity* 47, Main Case.

2. "What was the meaning of Bodhidharma's coming from the West?" is a standard question in Zen, meaning, in effect, "What is the essence of Zen?" What was it, in other words, that Bodhidharma wished to transmit when he made the long, dangerous trip from India to China? (In China, India was regarded as "the West," since travelers came from the west over the Silk Road.)

3. The type of tree mentioned, the 柏, is often translated as "oak," but the Chinese character 柏 actually refers to a type of juniper tree. The reading of "oak," *kashiwa*, for this character is a Japanese one. Harada Shōdō Rōshi has commented in conversation that the uselessness of the Chinese juniper tree for lumber or nearly any other purpose lends added meaning to Zhaozhou's reply.

Case 10   黄龍三關   *Huanglong's Three Barriers*[1]

黃龍禪師、問隆慶閑禪師云、人人有箇生緣處、如何是汝生緣處。對曰、早晨喫白粥、至今又覺飢。又問、我手何似佛手。對曰、月下弄琵琶。又問、我脚何似驢脚。對云、鷺鷥立雪非同色。師每以此三語問學者、莫能契其旨。天下叢林、目爲三關。纔有酬者、師無可否、斂目危坐。人莫涯其意。延之又問其故。師云、已過關者、掉臂徑去。安知有關吏。從吏問可否、此未透關者也。

Huanglong Huinan asked Longqing Qingxian, "Everyone has their own native place. What is your native place?"

Longqing answered, "Early this morning I had some rice gruel, and now I feel hungry again."

"How does my hand resemble a buddha's hand?" Huanglong asked.

"Playing a lute in the moonlight,"[2] Longqing answered.

"How does my leg resemble a donkey's leg?" he asked.

Longqing answered, "A snowy egret stands in the snow, but their colors are not the same."[3]

Huanglong always presented students with these three statements, but no one could come up with a satisfactory response. Monks everywhere called them the Three Barriers of Huanglong. Even with the few who gave answers, the master would neither agree nor disagree but only sit there in formal posture with eyes closed. No one could fathom his intent. When the layman Fan Yanzhi asked the reason for this, Huanglong replied, "Those who have passed through the gate shake their sleeves and go straight on their way. What do they care if there's a gatekeeper? Those who seek the gatekeeper's permission have yet to pass through."

1. Huanglong's questions are also found in the postscript to the *Wumen guan*.
2. An image for equality in the midst of distinction.
3. An image for distinction in the midst of equality.

Case 11   瑞巖主人   *Ruiyan's "Master"*[1]

瑞巖彦和尚、每日自喚主人公、復自應諾。乃云、惺惺著、喏。他時
異日、莫受人瞞、喏喏。

Every day Ruiyan Shiyan would call to himself, "Master!"
   "Yes!" he would answer himself.
   "Be wide awake!" he would say.
   "Yes!"
   "Whatever the time, whatever the day, never be misled by others!"
   "Yes! Yes!"

1. Also *Wumen guan* 12, Main Case.

Case 12   趙州勘婆   *Zhaozhou Sees Through an Old Woman*[1]

臺山路上、有一婆子。凡有僧問、臺山路向甚麼處去。婆云、驀直
去。僧纔行三五步、婆云、好箇師僧、又恁麼去。後有僧舉似趙州。
州云、待我去爲你勘過這婆子。明日便去亦如是問、婆亦如是答。州
歸謂眾云、臺山婆子、被我勘破了也。

An old woman lived by the road to Mount Tai.[2] A monk asked her, "What is the road to Mount Tai?"
   "Straight ahead," the woman said.

When the monk had walked a few steps the woman remarked, "Such a good monk, yet off he goes!"

Later a monk mentioned this to Zhaozhou Congshen. Zhaozhou said, "I'll go check this old woman for you."

The next day Zhaozhou went and asked the woman the same question, and she answered in the same way. Zhaozhou returned and said to the assembly, "I've seen through that old woman of Mount Tai."

1. Also *Wumen guan* 31, Main Case.

2. Mount Tai 臺, more properly referred to as Mount Wutai 五臺, is located in Shanxi, not far from the city of Zhaozhou, where Zhaozhou Congshen lived. Mount Tai has long been identified with the "Mount Clear-and-Cool" mentioned in the *Avataṃsaka Sutra* as the dwelling place of Mañjuśrī, the bodhisattva of wisdom. It is regarded as the most sacred of the four Buddhist mountains in China, the others being Mount Putou 破頭, sacred to Avalokiteśvara; Mount Jiuhua 九華, sacred to Kṣitigarbha; and Mount Emei 蛾眉, sacred to Samantabhadra. Mount Tai, as the mountain sacred to Mañjuśrī, represents the realm of "straight ahead" absolute equality, while Mount Emei, as sacred to Samantabhadra, represents the more convoluted relative world of duality.

Case 13   郎中地獄   *Langzhong's "Hell"*

崔郎中問趙州、從上大善知識、還墮地獄也無。州云、老僧末上落。

中云、已是大善知識、爲甚還落地獄。州云、我若不墮、爭得救郎中。

Cui Langzhong asked Zhaozhou Congshen, "Do enlightened teachers ever fall into hell?"[1]

"I'll be the first to go there,"[2] replied Zhaozhou.

"But you're an enlightened teacher," said Langzhong. "Why would you fall into hell?"

"If I didn't fall into hell, how could I help you?" Zhaozhou answered.

1. The text of the *Kattōshū* has 從上諸聖、還墮地獄也無, "Have sages ever fallen into hell?," but in the original sources for this koan the text reads 大善知識 (great enlightened teachers) or 和尚 (reverend priest); e.g., x 68:82b; x 80:93c.

"Enlightened teacher" 善知識 is a translation of the Sanskrit *kalyāṇamitra* (lit., "good and wise friend" or "worthy friend"), a Buddhist term referring to someone who helps others on the path to enlightenment. It is used in various meanings depending upon the context, and thus has been rendered in several ways in the present translation.

2. The standard *Kattōshū* text has 驀上落, "[They] go there straightaway," but

the original sources all have 老僧未上入, with 老僧, "the old monk," indicating Zhaozhou himself. The 驀上 of the standard *Kattōshū* text is a scribal error for the identically pronounced 未上, which has the nuance of going somewhere before anyone else.

Case 14 長生混沌 *Changsheng's "Chaos"*

長生問靈雲、混沌未分時如何。雲云、露柱懷胎。生云、分後如何。
雲云、如片雲點太清。生云、未審太清還受點也無。雲不答。生云、
恁麼則含生不來也。雲亦不答。生云、直得純清絕點時如何。雲云、
猶是眞常流注。生云、如何是眞常流注。雲云、似鏡長明。生云、向
上還有事也無。雲云、有。生云、作麼生是向上事。雲云、打破鏡
來、與汝相見。長生問、混沌未分時、含生何來。師云、如露柱懷胎。

Changsheng asked Lingyun Zhiqin, "What about the time of primordial chaos,[1] before any differentiation?"

Lingyun answered, "A pillar conceives."[2]

Changsheng said, "What about after differentiation?"

Lingyun responded, "It is like a wisp of cloud marking the Great Pure Sky."[3]

Changsheng asked, "Does the Great Pure Sky accept this mark or not?"

Lingyun didn't say anything.

Changsheng continued, "If that were so, living beings would not come forth."

Again Lingyun didn't say anything.

Changsheng continued, "How about when there's only absolute purity and all stains are avoided?"

Lingyun replied, "That would closely resemble the pure realm of enlightenment."[4]

"What is it to 'closely resemble the pure realm of enlightenment'?"

"It is like the infinite luminosity of a mirror," said Lingyun.

"Is there, then, a transcendence even of this?"[5] asked Changsheng.

"There is," replied Lingyun.

"What is this transcendence?" Changsheng asked.

Lingyun said, "Smash the mirror, then you and I can meet."[6]

[Changsheng then asked, "At the time of primordial chaos, before any differentiation, from where do living beings come?"

Lingyun answered, "A pillar conceives."][7]

1. "The time of primordial chaos" 混沌未分 is the time before the differentiation of yin and yang, the two fundamental forces that are said in Chinese philosophy to generate all phenomena into existence.

2. "Pillar" 露柱 (lit., "exposed pillar") usually means a pillar not hidden in the architecture of a building; it may also indicate an independently standing pillar, column, or obelisk. The term is often used in Zen to signify no-mind or the unconscious.

3. "Great Pure Sky" 大清 (lit., "the great purity") refers to the vast emptiness of a clear sky. The term can also indicate the Way.

4. The phrase "closely resemble the pure realm of enlightenment" translates 眞常流注, which, in Dōmae's reading, refers to the ālaya-vijñāna, the eighth and deepest consciousness according to the Yogācāra school's philosophy of the mind. It is known as the seed or storehouse consciousness since the karmic seeds of an individual's existence are stored there. Upon purification the ālaya-vijñāna transforms into the Great Perfect Mirror Wisdom, which perceives all things in their suchness.

5. "Transcendence" 向上事 indicates supreme realization—the transcendence even of enlightenment, the emptying even of śūnyatā.

6. The Japanese Zen master *Hakuin Ekaku* often stressed the need to shatter the Great Perfect Mirror Wisdom of the storehouse consciousness in order to attain true enlightenment.

7. The final two sentences, following "Smash the mirror, then you and I can meet," are not found in the original texts (e.g., T 47:1007a).

Case 15   孤峰不白   *One Peak Is Not White*

僧問曹山云、雪覆千山、爲甚麼孤峰不白。山云、須知異中異。僧
云、如何是異中異。山云、不墮諸山色。

A monk asked Caoshan Benji, "Snow covers a thousand mountains. Why is one peak not white?"

Caoshan said, "You should recognize 'distinction within distinction.'"[1]

The monk asked, "What is 'distinction within distinction'?"

Caoshan said, "Not falling into being the color of the other mountains."

1. Dōmae comments that 'distinction within distinction' 異中異 is one of the series of four relationships between the world of equality and the world of discrimination. The others are distinction within equality 同中異, equality within distinction 異中同, and equality within equality 同中同. Distinction within distinction refers to true individuality, the absolute separation of self and other.

Case 16　牛過窓櫺　*An Ox Goes through a Lattice Window*[1]

五祖演禪師曰、譬如水牯牛過窓櫺、頭角四蹄都過了、因甚麼尾巴過
不得。

Wuzu Fayan said, "It's as though a water buffalo is passing through a lattice window.[2] Its head, horns, and legs have all gone through. Why can't its tail go through?"

　　1. Also *Wumen guan* 38, Main Case. This koan was identified by *Hakuin Ekaku* as one of the eight "difficult to penetrate" (J., *nantō* 難透) koans.
　　2. The original Chinese can mean either "passing through" or "passing by." Most Rinzai masters prefer the former, for the sake of emphasis.

Case 17　乾峰三種　*Qianfeng's "Three Types of Sickness"*

乾峰和尚上堂曰、法身有三種病二種光、須是一透過、始解穩坐地。
雲門出眾云、庵内人爲甚麼不知庵外事。峰呵呵大笑。門云、猶是學
人疑處。峰云、子是什麼心行。門云、也要和尚相委悉。峰云、直須
恁麼穩密、始解穩坐地。門云、喏喏。

Yuezhou Qianfeng went to the hall and said, "The dharmakāya[1] has three types of sickness and two types of light.[2] Only after passing through these can one sit in peace."
Yunmen Wenyan stepped forward from the assembly and asked, "Why is the fellow in the hut unaware of what's going on outside?"
Qianfeng gave a hearty laugh.
Yunmen said, "Your student is still dissatisfied."
Qianfeng asked, "What's on your mind?"
Yunmen said, "I'd like you to be completely clear on this."
"Yes, only when one is careful and thorough can one truly sit in peace," Qianfeng replied.
"Exactly!" Yunmen agreed.

　　1. The dharmakāya is one of the "three bodies" of a buddha proposed by the Mahayana doctrine of the trikāya, which categorizes buddha's absolute and relative aspects. The three bodies are:
　　Dharmakāya: the absolute body of buddha; buddha as truth itself, as the essence of wisdom. The dharmakāya is typically represented by Vairocana Buddha.
　　Saṃbhogakāya: the "reward" or "recompense" body, received as a reward for fulfilling the vows undertaken while the buddha was still a bodhisattva. The saṃbhogakāya is typically represented by Amitābha Buddha.

Nirmāṇakāya: the body assumed by a buddha when appearing in the world to bring enlightenment to others. The nirmāṇakāya is typically represented by the historical buddha, Śākyamuni.

2. The "three types of sickness and two types of light" are interpreted in various ways. One interpretation is that found in *Record of Equanimity* 11, in which the three types of sickness are:

i. Missing the way prior to arrival 未到走作: to be caught in the realm of the relative, unable to attain the state of enlightenment.

ii. Attachment after arrival 已到住著: to attain the state of enlightenment but then cling to this state as though it were something substantial.

iii. Liberation free of all conditions 透脫無依: to attain the realm of liberation (not dwelling inwardly in śūnyatā, nor clinging outwardly to phenomena) but then to cling to this state of nondependence.

The two types of light correspond to aspects of (i), above.

The ZGDJ explains the three types of sickness in the same way as the *Record of Equanimity*. It defines the "two types of light" as:

i. Subtle delusions that arise on the subjective level 能取光.
ii. Subtle delusions that arise on the objective level 所取光. (977a)

An alternate way of interpreting the three types of sickness is simply to see them as the three poisons: attachment, aversion, and ignorance.

Similarly, the two types of light may be seen as: the light of samadhi 禪光, that is, the light of undifferentiated truth, associated with Mañjuśrī; and the light of wisdom 智光, the light of differentiated functioning in the world, associated with Samantabhadra.

Case 18   山谷木犀   *Shangu's Sweet-Olive Blossoms*

山谷一日、參晦堂和尚。堂云、所公諳書中有一兩句。仲尼曰、以吾
爲隱乎二三子、吾無隱乎你。甚與宗門事恰好也。公知之麼。云、不
知。時晦堂與山谷山行之次、天香滿山。堂問曰、公聞木犀花香麼。
云、聞。堂曰、吾無隱乎你。山谷忽悟去也。經兩月後、庭堅參死心
禪師。死心一拶曰、心長老死學士死、燒爲兩堆灰。恁麼時向什麼處
相見。庭堅擬議無如何。後在黔南道中畫寢、及覺不覺忽悟、得死心
用處。從是得大自在之三昧。

One day the poet Shangu was visiting Huitang Zuxin. Huitang said, "You know the passage in which Confucius says, 'My friends, do you think I'm hiding things from you? In fact, I am hiding nothing from you.'[1] It's just the same with the Great Matter of Zen. Do you understand this?"

"I don't understand," Shangu replied.

Later, Huitang and Shangu were walking in the mountains where the air was filled with the scent of the sweet-olive blossoms. Huitang asked, "Do you smell the fragrance of the blossoms?"

Shangu said, "I do."

Huitang said, "You see, I'm hiding nothing from you."

At that moment Shangu was enlightened.

Two months later he visited Sixin Wuxin. Sixin greeted him and said, "I'll die and you'll die and we'll end up burnt into two heaps of ashes. At that time, where will we meet?"

Shangu tried to respond but couldn't come up with anything. Later, while on the road to Qiannan, he awoke from a nap and suddenly understood Sixin's intent. Thereafter he attained the samadhi of perfect freedom.

1. *Analects* 7:23.

Case 19-1　香嚴上樹　*Xiangyan's "Up a Tree"*[1]

香嚴智閑禪師云、如人上樹、口啣樹枝、手不攀枝、脚不踏樹。樹下
有人問西來意、不對即違他所問、若對又喪身失命。正與麼時、作麼
生對。有虎頭上座云、上樹即不問、未上樹請和尚道。師呵呵大笑。

雪竇云、樹上道即易、樹下道即難。老僧上樹、致將一問來。

Xiangyan Zhixian said, "It's as though a person were up a tree, hanging from a limb by his teeth and unable to grab a branch with his hands or touch the trunk with his feet. Someone under the tree asks, 'What is the meaning of Bodhidharma's coming from the West?' If the person doesn't reply, he fails the questioner; if he does reply, he loses his life. In such a situation, how would you respond?"

The senior monk Hutou said, "I don't care about climbing the tree. Please say something, Master, about before the tree was climbed!"

The master gave a hearty laugh.

Regarding this, Xuedou Chongxian commented, "It's easy to speak when up a tree, hard to speak beneath it. This old monk[2] will climb a tree. Bring me a question!"

1. The first paragraph appears as *Wumen guan* 5, Main Case.
2. Referring to Xuedou himself.

Case 19-2 大慧樹上 *Dahui's "Up a Tree"*

大慧杲禪師、問空東山云、香嚴樹上意旨如何。山云、好對春風唱
鷓鴣。

Dahui Zonggao[1] asked Dongshan Huikong, "What is the meaning of Xiang-yan's 'Up a Tree'?"

Dongshan replied, "Let's sing 'Partridge' to the spring breeze!"[2]

1. Although the *Kattōshū* identifies the questioner as *Wan'an Daoyan*, all other sources for this koan identify him as *Dahui Zonggao*.

2. The partridge 鷓鴣 is a southern Chinese bird that symbolizes feelings of homesickness. Here "partridge" refers to the title of a song, about which a famous Tang poem says, "If guests from South of the River are present, do not sing 'Partridge' to the spring breeze" (*Complete Tang Poems* 全唐詩 675), since the song causes melancholy in people from that region. Dongshan's reply is based on this line, though it expresses the same feeling in a paradoxical fashion.

Some masters interpret this line to mean, "Dongshan replied, 'Wonderful! [Xiangyan] sang "Partridge" to the spring breeze!'"

Case 20 雲門屎橛 *Yunmen's "Dry Piece of Shit"*[1]

僧問雲門、如何是佛。門云、乾屎橛。

A monk asked Yunmen Wenyan, "What is buddha?"

Yunmen answered, "A dry piece of shit."[2]

1. Also *Wumen guan* 21, Main Case.

2. Certain scholars of Tang-dynasty slang interpret this term, 乾屎橛, to mean a bamboo stick used in place of toilet paper; recent opinion tends toward the translation above. Needless to say, in either case the intention of the term is the same.

Case 21 雲門蘇盧 *Yunmen's "Sulu"*

雲門示眾云、平地上死人無數、出得荊棘林者好手。時有僧出云、恁
麼則堂中第一座有長處也。門云、蘇盧蘇盧。

Yunmen Wenyan addressed the assembly, saying, "The level plain is strewn with corpses; only those who pass through the thorn forest are true adepts."[1]

At that moment a monk stepped forth and said, "If that's the case, then the head monk of the hall has true skill."

"*Sulu, sulu!*"[2] said Yunmen.

1. "The level plain" represents dead-sitting, do-nothing Zen. "The thorn forest" is a metaphor for the teaching devices of a true Zen master.

2. Dōmae describes *sulu, sulu* 蘇盧蘇盧 as a mantra meaning "come forth, come forth," intended to summon the aid of the buddhas and bodhisattvas. Other sources see it as an incantation for driving off demons.

Case 22-1   德山托鉢   *Deshan Carries His Bowls*[1]

雪峰在德山會下作飯頭。一日、齋晚。德山托鉢下至法堂。峰云、鐘未鳴鼓未響、這老漢托鉢向什麼處去。山無語低頭歸方丈。雪峰舉似巖頭。頭云、大小德山不會末後句。山聞令侍者喚至方丈、問云、汝不肯老僧那。頭密啓其意。山至來日上堂、與尋常不同。頭於僧堂前、撫掌大咲曰、且喜此老漢會末後句。他後天下人、不奈他何。雖然如是、只得三年活。果三年化去。

Xuefeng Yicun was serving as cook in the assembly under Deshan Xuanjian. One day lunch was late. When Deshan came down to the hall carrying his bowls, Xuefeng asked him, "The bell and drum [announcing mealtime] have not yet sounded. Where are you heading with your bowls, old fellow?"

Deshan silently bowed and returned to his quarters.

When Xuefeng told Yantou Quanhuo about this, Yantou commented, "Even Deshan, great as he is, doesn't know the final word."[2]

Hearing of this, Deshan had his attendant summon Yantou. "You don't approve of me?" he asked.

Yantou secretly revealed his purpose to him. The next day Deshan's lecture was not the same as usual. Yantou went to the front of the monks' hall. Clapping and laughing, he said, "How wonderful that the old fellow has grasped the final word. After this no one in the world can do anything to him. Even so, he has only three years left to live."

Three years later Deshan died.

1. Also *Wumen guan* 13, Main Case, and *Blue Cliff Record* 51, Commentary on the Main Case.

2. "Final word" 末後句 means, literally, "the word after the end," the word beyond all words. For the significance of the "final word," see Cases 72, 140, and 171.

Case 22-2   密庵意旨   *Mian's "True Meaning"*

僧問密庵傑和尚、德山托鉢意旨如何。庵云、無意旨。曰、因什麼托
鉢下僧堂。庵云、要行便行要坐便坐。

A monk asked Mian Xianjie, "What is the meaning of 'Deshan Carries His
Bowls'?" The master answered, "No meaning."

"Then why," asked the monk, "did Deshan carry his bowls down to the
monks' hall?"

"If he wants to go, he goes; if he wants to sit, he sits,"[1] Mian replied.

1. A passage of similar meaning is found in the *Record of Linji*:

Conforming with circumstances as they are, [a true follower of the Way] exhausts
his past karma; accepting things as they are he puts on his clothes; when he wants
to walk he walks, when he wants to sit he sits; he never has a single thought of seeking buddhahood. Why is this so? A man of old said: "If you seek buddha through
karma-creating activities, buddha becomes the great portent of birth-and-death."
(Sasaki 2009, p. 171)

Case 23   馬祖西江   *Mazu's "West River"*[1]

龐居士參馬祖便問、不與萬法爲侶者、是什麼人。祖云、待你一口吸
盡西江水、即向你道。士豁然大悟、作頌曰、十方同聚會、箇箇學無
爲。此是選佛場、心空及第歸。

Layman Pang Yun called upon Mazu Daoyi and asked, "Who is it that
doesn't keep company with the ten thousand things?"

Mazu answered, "I'll tell you when you swallow the water of the West
River in a single gulp."

At that moment Pang was deeply enlightened. He composed a verse:

All in the ten directions are of the same assembly,
Each and every one learning nondoing.[2]
This is the place where buddha is chosen.[3]
Mind empty, exam passed, I've returned home.

1. Also *Blue Cliff Record* 42, Commentary on the Main Case.

2. Another possible translation is "From the ten directions we've equally
gathered together, each of us learning that there's nothing to do."

3. Another possible translation is "This is the place where buddhas are selected."
The original Chinese term, 選佛場, is sometimes used in Zen as a synonym for
"meditation hall."

Case 24   不入涅槃   *Not Entering Nirvana*

文殊所說摩訶般若曰、清淨行者不入涅槃。破戒比丘、不墮地獄。

In the *Mahāprajñā Sutra Preached by Mañjuśrī* it says, "Virtuous practitioners do not enter nirvana; precept-breaking monks do not fall into hell."[1]

> 1. T 8:728b. The Japanese Zen master Hakuin once commented on this koan
> with the following verse: "Silent ants pull at a dragonfly's wing; young swallows
> rest side by side on a willow branch. Silk-growers' wives, pale in face, carry
> their baskets; village children with pilfered bamboo shoots crawl through a
> fence." After hearing this verse, two monks who had completed their training
> under the great Zen master Kogetsu Zenzai 古月禪材 (1667–1751) decided to
> train again under Hakuin.

Case 25   石霜竿頭   *Shishuang's "Top of a Pole"*[1]

石霜和尚云、百尺竿頭、如何進步。

Shishuang asked, "How would you step forward from the top of a hundred-
foot pole?"

> 1. A fuller version of this koan appears in *Wumen guan* 46, Main Case. The
> speaker is believed to be *Shishuang Chuyuan*, although the koan is found in
> neither his records nor those of *Shishuang Qingzhu*. In *Record of Equanimity* 79
> the speaker is *Changsha Jingcen* (see Biographical Notes), and a similar koan is
> found in the section on Changsha in the Song-dynasty biographical collection
> *Compendium of the Five Lamps* 五燈會元.

Case 26   香嚴擊竹   *Xiangyan's Sound of a Bamboo*[1]

香嚴智閑禪師、一日、芟除草木。因以瓦礫擊竹作聲、廓然省悟。乃
述頌曰、一擊忘前知、更不假修治。動容揚古路、不墮悄然機。處處
無蹤跡、聲色忘威儀。諸方達道者、咸言上上機。

One day Xiangyan Zhixian was cutting weeds when he knocked a piece of
tile against a bamboo. Hearing the sound, Xiangyan was suddenly enlightened. He composed a verse:

> A single "tock"—all prior knowledge forgotten
> This is not the result of practice—

Daily activities proclaim the Ancient Way.
No more falling into passive stillness.[2]
Wherever I go I leave no trace;
In all situations my actions are free.[3]
Everywhere masters of the Way
Speak of this as the highest function.[4]

1. For background material on this case, see *Xiangyan Zhixian* in the Biographical Notes.

2. The original Chinese, 悄然機, generally refers to a state of sadness but in Zen is interpreted to mean a quietistic state.

3. Literally, "In [the realm of] sound and form I forget all I do," with "the realm of sound and form" 聲色 signifying the phenomenal world. 聲色 can also indicate the worldly passions, though in Buddhism this is a minor usage. "All I do" 威儀 is literally "proper conduct," the monk's dignified deportment in the four "postures" of walking, standing, sitting, and lying.

4. "Highest function" translates 上上機, with 上上 referring to beings of the highest potential. In the Zen context the sentence can be seen to mean "to function perfectly in accordance with the Way."

Case 27   心隨萬境   *The Mind Turns with Its Surroundings*

第二十二祖、摩拏羅尊者、傳法偈曰、心隨萬境轉、轉處實能幽。隨流認得性、無喜亦無憂。眞淨克文拈云、可恁麼不可恁麼。

Manora, the twenty-second Indian ancestor, said in his transmission verse:

The mind turns with its surroundings,
A turning that is truly profound.[1]
Perceive mind's nature within this flow,
And there is neither joy nor sorrow.

Zhenjing Kewen[2] commented on this verse, saying, "It's like this, yet it isn't like this."

1. "Truly profound" translates 幽, which can also mean "dark," "silent," or "mysterious."

2. The original text has Langye Huijue 瑯瑘慧覺, but none of the source materials on this master contain this koan. It is, however, found in the "Discourses" 上堂 section of the *Record of Zhenjing* 眞淨錄.

Case 28-1   倩女離魂   *Qiannu and Her Spirit*[1]

五祖演禪師、問僧云、倩女離魂、那箇是眞底。

Wuzu Fayan asked a monk, "Qiannu and her spirit were separated.[2] Which was the real Qiannu?"

1. Also *Wumen guan* 35, Main Case.

2. The tale of Qiannu was a popular Tang-dynasty story, found in such sources as the *Extensive Record of the Era of Great Peace* 太平広記. Qiannu 倩女 was in love with a young man named Wang Zhou 王宙, whom she had known since childhood and who fully returned her affection. However, when a promising young government official asked for the hand of the beautiful Qiannu in marriage, her father quickly agreed to the advantageous match. Zhou, deeply distressed, could not bear to live nearby with Qiannu married to another man, so he decided to travel upriver to start a new life. The night he departed, however, he heard someone behind him. When he looked to see who it was, he was overjoyed to find that Qiannu had followed him. The two decided to proceed onward to the region of Shu 蜀, where they settled, married, and had two children. Qiannu could not forget her parents, however, so after five years she and Zhou decided to return to their hometown to ask her father's forgiveness for their rash act. Upon arriving, Zhou proceeded alone to Qiannu's home to explain the situation. Greeted warmly by Qiannu's father, Zhou said that he and Qiannu had run off together, but that they were now married and living comfortably with two children. The father, greatly astonished, replied that his daughter had been there in his house for the entire five years, though ill and incapable of speaking. Zhou, visiting the sick woman's room, saw that it was indeed Qiannu. He thereupon led her father to the river, where the other Qiannu, his wife, was waiting with their two children. They returned to the house, and, as they approached, the sick Qiannu left her bed and came to meet them. Seeing the married Qiannu, she smiled and walked toward her, and suddenly the two women merged, becoming one person.

Case 28-2   虛堂頌古   *Xutang's Verse*

虛堂、倩女離魂頌云、行弔先桃苅、喪車後紙錢。老胡門下客、寧可入黄泉。

Xutang Zhiyu composed a verse on "Qiannu and Her Spirit":

> In front of the cortege, peach branches and reed brooms;
> Behind the hearse, paper money.
> We disciples of the Old Foreigner—
> Why would we enter the Realm of the Dead?[1]

1. Mujaku: Brooms made of peach branches and reeds preceded funeral processions to symbolically sweep away misfortune. Special paper money was burnt or strewn after the hearse as an offering to the deities of death, in order to ensure a safe passage to a good afterlife for the deceased. "The Old Foreigner" is Śākyamuni. Mujaku comments that discussing the true and the false from the standpoint of Qiannu and her spirit as separate forms will lead one straight into the realm of death. If even secular people exorcize the evil and inauspicious at the time of death, why should buddha-disciples who have thoroughly seen through the realm of samsara ever have to enter the unhappy land of the dead?

Case 29   雲門露字   *Yunmen's "Exposed"*

僧問雲門、殺父殺母、向佛前懺悔。殺佛殺祖、向甚麼處懺悔。門云、露。

A monk asked Yunmen Wenyan, "If you kill your father and mother, you can repent in front of the buddhas. If you kill the buddhas and ancestors, where can you repent?"[1]

Yunmen said, "Exposed!"[2]

1. See also *Record of Linji*, Discourse 18: "Whatever you encounter, either within or without, slay it at once. On meeting a buddha slay the buddha, on meeting an ancestor slay the ancestor, on meeting an arhat slay the arhat, on meeting your parents slay your parents, on meeting your kinsman slay your kinsman, and you attain emancipation. By not cleaving to things, you freely pass through" (Sasaki 2009, pp. 22, 236).

2. This is an example of Yunmen's "one-word barriers." "Exposed!" 露 denotes something that, just as it is, is fully revealed in all of its truth and immediacy.

Case 30   密庵沙盆   *Mian's "Brittle Bowl"*

天童密庵咸傑禪師、一日、應庵問、如何是正法眼。密曰、破沙盆、應領之。雙杉元禪師、戒行嚴潔、住秀之天寧。小參舉、應庵華因問密庵、如何是正法眼。庵云、破沙盆、拈云、者些說話、如丫叉路口、多年一條爛木頭、風吹日炙。道印文在什麼處。五陵公子少年時、得意春風躍馬蹄。不惜黃金作彈子、海棠花下打黃鸝。元和尚爲甚別不提唱、唯拈古詩一篇。

One day Ying'an Tanhua asked Mian Xianjie of Tiantong, "What is the True Eye of the Dharma?"[1]

Mian answered, "A brittle bowl."[2]

Ying'an accepted this reply.

Shuangshan Yuan was a strict observer of the precepts who lived at Tianning temple in Xiushuixian. One day during an informal Dharma talk he mentioned this exchange between Ying'an and Mian, commenting, "Such stories are like a broken signpost, wind-bleached, sun-scorched, and long abandoned by a fork in a road. Tell me, what was written [on this signpost]?" [He recited a verse:]

> When the princes of Wuling were young
> They danced their horses and reveled in the spring breeze;
> With no thought of expense they made pellets of gold
> And shot at nightingales under flowering trees.

Why didn't Shuangshan lecture on Mian's words, but simply recite an old poem?

1. "The True Eye of the Dharma" refers to the eye of enlightenment that can discern the true nature of the Dharma.

2. "A brittle bowl" translates 沙盆, a type of bowl that was fired from clay containing sand and that was therefore easily cracked or broken. In the *Record of Xuefeng* 雪峰録 the term is used to represent the human body.

Case 31   國師三喚   *The National Teacher Calls Three Times*[1]

南陽忠國師、三喚侍者。侍者三應諾。國師云、將謂吾辜負汝、元來
却是汝辜負吾。

The National Teacher Nanyang Huizhong called to his attendant three times. Three times his attendant answered.

The National Teacher said, "I've always thought I let you down, but actually it's you who have let me down."[2]

1. Also *Wumen guan* 17, Main Case.

2. "Let you down" and "let me down" translate 辜負汝 and 辜負吾, respectively. The word 辜負 has many nuances—"betray," "go against," "oppose," "transgress against," etc.—and is rendered in different ways by different masters depending upon their sense of the koan.

Case 32   懶安有句   *Lan'an's "Being and Nonbeing"*[1]

福州長慶懶安和尚、示衆云、有句無句、如藤倚樹。疎山聞得道、
我有一轉語、要去問者老子。夏罷遂入閩見懶安和尚。又謂之潙山
和尚。裴相國帥閩、自潙山請住長慶。疎山到彼、值師泥壁次、疎
山便問。有句無句、如藤倚樹、是和尚語否。潙山云、是。疎山
云、忽然樹倒藤枯、句歸何處。潙山放下泥盤、呵呵大笑歸方丈。
疎山云、某甲三千里外、賣却布單、特爲此事來。和尚爲甚不與某
甲說。潙山云、侍者將錢來、與者矮闍黎去。他日有獨眼龍、爲汝
點破去在。(疎山)後到明招擧前話。招云、潙山頭正尾正、只是不
遇知音。疎山云、忽然樹倒藤枯、句歸何處。招云、更使潙山咲轉
新。疎山當下有省。乃云、潙山元來咲中有刀。後來大慧禪師、在
圓悟會裡、悟遂令居擇木堂、作不釐務侍者、每日同士大夫入室。
圓悟只擧有句無句、如藤倚樹。大慧纔開口、悟便道不是。如是將
半年。一日同趙表之、方丈藥石次、(大慧)把箸在手、忘了喫飯。
圓悟顧師而語表之曰、只這漢參得黃楊木禪也。師遂引狗看熱油鐺爲
喻。圓悟曰、只這便是金剛圈栗棘蓬。居無何扣圓悟曰、聞和尚嘗
問五祖此話、不知記其答否。圓悟笑而已。師云、若對人天衆前問、
今豈無知者耶。圓悟乃云、向問有句無句如藤倚樹時如何。祖云、描
也描不成、畫也畫不就。又問、忽遇樹倒藤枯時如何。祖云、相隨來
也。師聞擧乃抗聲曰、某甲會也。圓悟曰、只恐你透公案不得。云、
請和尚擧。圓悟遂擧。師出語無滯。圓悟曰、今日方知吾不汝欺也。
遂著臨濟正宗記、以付之、俾掌記室、分座訓徒。

Changqing Lan'an of Fuzhou addressed the assembly, saying, "'Being' and 'nonbeing' are like vines clinging to a tree."[2]

Shushan Guangren, hearing of this, said, "I have a turning-phrase[3] for that old man—I must call on him." So at the end of the training period he went to the province of Min to visit Changqing Lan'an, who was also known as Guishan Lan'an because he came from Guishan [in Hunan] to become priest of Changqing Temple at the invitation of Layman Pei Xiu, who was governor of Min at the time.

When Shushan arrived, Lan'an was plastering a wall. Shushan asked, "'Being and nonbeing are like vines clinging to a tree.' Did you say that?"

"Yes," Lan'an replied.

"If suddenly the tree falls and the vines wither," Shushan said, "where do 'being' and 'nonbeing' go?"

Lan'an threw down his plaster tray and gave a loud laugh, then started for his quarters. Shushan said, "I've sold my possessions and traveled three thousand *li* here for the sake of this matter! Why won't you give me an explanation?"

Lan'an said to his attendant, "Bring some money and give it to this little monk."[4] Then he turned to Shushan and said, "There's a one-eyed dragon who will set you right on this matter someday."

Later, Shushan went to Mingzhao Deqian [who was blind in one eye] and related the above story. Mingzhao said, "Lan'an's the real thing from head to toe, only he's never met a true friend."

Shushan asked, "If suddenly the tree falls and the vines wither, where do 'being' and 'nonbeing' go?"

Mingzhao responded, "That would make Lan'an laugh again!"

At that moment Shushan was awakened, and said, "There was a dagger in Lan'an's laughter right from the very start."

Later, Dahui Zonggao, while still a student under Yuanwu Keqin, was placed in the attendants' quarters and given the position of attendant-without-duties. Every day Yuanwu would have him come to his room for instruction, just like the officials who were Yuanwu's lay students. All Yuanwu ever said was, "'Being' and 'nonbeing' are like vines clinging to a tree." Whenever Dahui opened his mouth to respond Yuanwu would cut him off, saying, "That's no good."

Nearly half a year went by in this way. One day while Yuanwu was having dinner with the official Zhao Biaozhi, Dahui, chopsticks in hand, forgot to eat his rice.

Yuanwu looked over at Dahui, then turned to Zhao and said, "This fellow is practicing boxwood Zen."[5]

Dahui explained to Yuanwu that he felt like a dog eyeing a frypan of hot food.[6] Yuanwu replied, "This is [hard to penetrate and hard to grasp,] like a vajra or a chestnut burr."[7]

Later Dahui went to Yuanwu and said, "I heard that you once asked Wuzu about 'being' and 'nonbeing.' Do you remember the master's answer?" In reply Yuanwu only laughed.

Dahui said, "Since you asked in front of the assembly, surely even now there is someone who remembers."[8]

Yuanwu replied, "When I asked about the statement, 'Being and nonbeing are like vines clinging to a tree,' Wuzu answered, 'Try to describe it, and it cannot be described; try to portray it, and it cannot be portrayed.' When I asked, 'What if the tree suddenly falls and the vines wither?' Wuzu said, 'They come down together!'"[9]

When Dahui heard this story he cried, "I've got it!"

Yuanwu said, "I fear you haven't thoroughly penetrated this koan."

Dahui said, "Please, Master, question me in any way you wish." Yuanwu proceeded to question him, and Dahui replied without hesitation.

Yuanwu said, "Today you see that I haven't deceived you." He then conferred upon Dahui the *Record of the True School of Linji*,[10] designated him secretary, and had him lecture to the other monks.

1. The first section of this koan appears as *Record of Equanimity* 87, Main Case.

2. The words translated as "being" and "nonbeing" are 有句 and 無句, respectively. The character 句 generally means "word" or "phrase," but here it has little meaning in itself, so that 有句 and 無句 refer simply to 有 ("being," form, the phenomenal aspect of reality) and 無 ("nonbeing," emptiness, the noumenal aspect of reality).

When Changqing says, "'Being' and 'nonbeing' are like vines clinging to a tree," he means that being and nonbeing are mutually dependent. Shushan's question, "If the tree suddenly falls and the vines wither, where would 'being' and 'nonbeing' go?" inquires about going beyond being and nonbeing, existence and nonexistence, phenomenon and noumenon.

3. A "turning-phrase" 一轉語 is a word or phrase of deep significance that either reveals the depth of understanding of the speaker or precipitates understanding in the listener at a critical moment in that person's practice. In the former sense, the word "turning" indicates the presentation of a different aspect of one's understanding; in the latter sense, "turning" expresses the fundamental "turnabout" that occurs upon awakening.

4. Shushan Guangren was apparently quite short in stature. See *Shushan Guangren* in the Biographical Notes.

5. The boxwood tree is said to be extremely slow-growing, and even to shrink during leap years. "Boxwood Zen" often refers to the Zen of students who, though slow to awaken, are earnest and unswerving in their practice.

6. The image is one of being unable either to partake of something or to let it go, just as a dog is unable to eat food that is too hot yet is unwilling to leave it behind.

7. A vajra is a legendary Indian weapon used by the deities; circular in shape, it is said to be capable of destroying anything. A chestnut burr cannot be grasped because of its spines.

8. That is, "Since you asked in public, there is no reason to refrain from telling me Wuzu's answer."

9. The original Chinese, 相隨來也, is open to various interpretations depending on the context. zGDJ has "to understand what the master has said"; zGJT has "to imitate someone or follow his or her lead."

10. The *Record of the True School of Linji* 臨濟正宗記 is a text compiled by Yuanwu that stresses the importance of the true lineage of Linji Zen and recognizes Dahui as a genuine lineage holder. It was presented to Dahui in 1129, four years after his major awakening, when Dahui was forty years of age.

Case 33　南泉鎌子　*Nanquan's Sickle*

南泉在山作務次、僧問、南泉路向何處去。泉拈起鎌子云、我者茅鎌
子、買得三十錢。僧云、不問茅鎌子、南泉路向何處去。泉云、我使
得甚快也。

Once when Nanquan Puyuan was working in the mountains a monk asked
him, "Which way is the road to Nanquan?"

Nanquan held up his sickle and said, "I bought this sickle for thirty
coins."

The monk said, "I didn't ask about the sickle. Which way is the road to
Nanquan?"

Nanquan said, "I can use this—it's so sharp!"[1]

1. Or, "I've tried this and it cuts very well!"

Case 34　百丈野狐　*Baizhang's Wild Fox*[1]

百丈山大智禪師、凡參次、有一老人、常隨衆聽法。衆退老人亦退。
忽一日不退。師遂問、面前立者復是何人。老人云、某甲非人也。於
過去迦葉佛時、曾住此山。因學人問、大修行底人、還落因果也無。
某甲答他云、不落因果。後五百生墮野狐身。今請和尚代一轉語、貴
脫野狐身。遂問、大修行底人、還落因果也無。師云、不昧因果。老
人於言下大悟、作禮云、某甲已脫野狐身、遂住在山後。敢告和尚、
乞依亡僧事例。師令維那白槌告衆曰、食後送亡僧。大衆言議、一衆
皆安、涅槃堂又無病人、何故如是。食後只見、師領衆至山後巖下、
以拄杖指出一死野狐、乃依法火葬。師至晚上堂、舉前因緣。黃檗便
問、古人錯祇對一轉語、五百生墮野狐身、轉轉不錯、合作箇什麽。
師云、近前來與你道。檗遂近前與師一掌。師拍手笑曰、將謂胡鬚
赤、更有赤鬚胡。

Whenever Baizhang Huaihai lectured an old man would sit with the
assembly and listen to the teachings. When the assembly left, so would the
old man. Then one day the old man remained, and the master asked him,
"Who are you, standing there in front of me?"

The old man said, "I am not human. Long ago, in the time of Kāśyapa
Buddha,[2] I was the abbot living on this mountain. A student asked whether
people of true practice are subject to cause and effect. I said, 'They are not

subject to cause and effect.' For this I have been reborn as a fox for five hundred lifetimes. Please, I request of you a turning-phrase so that I may be freed from this fox's body." He then asked, "Are people of true practice subject to cause and effect?"

The master answered, "They are not confused about cause and effect."[3]

At these words the old man was deeply enlightened. He bowed and said, "I am now free of the fox's body, which is lying on the other side of the mountain. I beseech you, perform for me the service for a deceased monk."

The master had the duty-monk strike the gavel and announce to the community that there would be a service for a dead monk after the meal.[4] The monks wondered about this among themselves, since everyone was well and no one had been sick in the infirmary.

After the meal the master led the group to the foot of a cliff on the other side of the mountain, where he pointed out a dead fox with his staff. He then cremated it in accordance with the rule.

That evening the master took the high seat and explained the day's events. Thereupon Huangbo asked, "Because the old man gave a mistaken answer he was reborn as a fox for five hundred lifetimes; what would have happened to him if his answer hadn't been wrong each time?"

The master said, "Come close and I'll tell you." Huangbo went up and gave the master a slap.

The master clapped his hands and said, "I thought I was a red-bearded foreigner, but here's someone who's even more of a red-bearded foreigner!"[5]

1. Also *Wumen guan* 2, Main Case.

2. Kāśyapa Buddha was the fourth of the Seven Buddhas of the Past. The seven were: (1) Vipaśyin, (2) Śikhin, (3) Viśvabhū, (4) Kāśyapa, (5) Krakucchanda, (6) Kanakāmuni, and (7) Śākyamuni (the historical buddha).

3. The original Chinese is a double negative, which is a strong emphasizer, so that the meaning is, in effect, "People of true practice are crystal clear about cause and effect."

4. The duty-monk 維那 is the monk in charge of supervising the work and job assignments at the monastery. The term combines 維, an abbreviation of 綱維, "supervisor," and 那, the last syllable of the Chinese transliteration of *karma-dāna* (羯磨陀那), the Sanskrit term for the monk who filled the same position in Indian Buddhist monasteries.

5. The term "red-bearded foreigner" has several connotations. In certain contexts it refers to Bodhidharma; here, the commentaries generally agree, the meaning is "bandit" or "thief," terms that, in the paradoxical manner of Zen, constitute high praise.

Case 35   關山賊機   *Kanzan's "Works like a Thief"*

關山和尚曰、柏樹子話、有賊之機。

Kanzan Egen said, "The koan 'Zhaozhou's "Juniper Tree"'[1] works like a thief."

    1. See Case 9.

Case 36   二僧捲簾   *Two Monks Roll Up Bamboo Shades*[1]

清涼大法眼、因僧齋前上參次、眼以手指簾。時有二僧、同去捲簾。
眼云、一得一失。

When the monks had gathered in the hall before the midday meal to hear Fayan Wenyi, the master pointed to the bamboo shades. At this, two monks went and rolled them up, both in the same manner. Fayan said, "One got it, one missed."

    1. Also *Wumen guan* 26, Main Case.

Case 37   虛空爲紙   *Use the Empty Sky for Paper*

五祖演禪師示衆云、若有人虛空爲紙、大海爲硯、須彌爲筆、如何書
得祖師西來(意)五字。若書得西來意五字、老僧展坐具禮拜你。

Wuzu Fayan said, "Using the empty sky for paper, the sea for an inkwell, and Mount Sumeru for a brush,[1] how would you write the words, 'The meaning of the Patriarch's coming from the West?' If any of you can do this, I will spread my sitting cloth and bow before you."[2]

    1. In Indian cosmology, Mount Sumeru is the Universal Mountain. See Case 4, note 1.

    2. The sitting cloth (Skt. *niṣīdana*) is one of the few articles that a monk is allowed to possess. Originally used for sitting, it is now in East Asia used primarily during ceremonies, when monks spread it on the floor or on a cushion to make their prostrations to the Buddha. It is employed in a similar way to show respect for an eminent monk; thus "to spread one's sitting cloth" is synonymous with "to express respect or admiration for." See Cases 123, note 5, and 131.

Case 38   賢女屍林   *The Wise Women in the Mortuary Grove*

世尊。因七賢女遊屍陀林。一女指屍謂諸娣云、屍在這裡、人向甚處
去。中有一姉云、作麼作麼。諸娣諦觀、各各契悟。

Once, at the time of the Buddha, seven wise women were taking a walk
through a mortuary grove. One pointed to a corpse and asked the others,
"The corpse is here, but where has the *person* gone?"

One of the other women asked, "How about it? How about it?"

The other women all saw clearly, and each attained enlightenment.[1]

1. Also *Blue Cliff Record* 55, Commentary on the Main Case. This story is found
in several sutras, e.g., the *Sutra of the Seven Women* 七女經 (T 14:556). Seven
princesses who followed the Dharma asked one day to leave the palace and walk
among the burial mounds. When the king asked why, they replied that beautiful
sights and delicious flavors ultimately bring no benefit, but that death is something
everyone must face. They left the palace and walked among the corpses, and each
wrote a verse on the reality of death. This drew the admiration of Indra, who said
he would give them anything they wished. One woman asked to be born in a tree
without roots, branches, or leaves; one asked to be born in a formless place prior
to ying and yang; and another asked to be born in a mountain valley that didn't
echo even when shouted into. Indra said it was beyond even his power to grant
these wishes, so the women went to study under Kāśyapa Buddha.

Case 39   漂墮鬼國   *Drifting to the Land of the Demons*

于頔相公問紫玉、如何是黑風吹其船舫、漂墮羅刹鬼國。師云、于頔
這客作漢、問恁麼事作什麼。于當時失色。師指云、祇這箇便是漂墮
羅刹鬼國。于聞已信受。

The minister Yu Di asked Ziyu Daotong, "What is meant by 'A fierce wind
blew a ship off course and set it drifting toward the land of the rakṣasas'?"[1]

The master replied. "Yu Di, you miserable lackey! Why do you ask something like *that*?"

Yu Di's face turned white. The master pointed to him and said, "You have
just drifted to the land of the rakṣasas."

Yu Di took this teaching to heart.

1. A line from the *Lotus Sutra*; T 9:56c; see Watson 1993b, p. 299. A rakṣasa is
a demon that devours human beings. For background material on this koan, see
Yu Di in the Biographical Notes.

Case 40　秀才造論　*A Scholar Writes a Treatise*

昔有秀才、造無鬼論。成纔放筆、忽一鬼現身、斫手謂秀才曰、你
爭奈我何。五祖演道、我當時若見、便以手作鵓鳩觜向伊道、谷谷
呱。南堂靜曰、秀才雖知無鬼、而不知鬼之所以無。五祖先師雖知鬼
之所以無、而不能掃蹤滅跡。若是大隋即不然。待他斫手道你　爭奈
我何、只向道、閻。直饒是大力鬼王、也教伊頭破作七分、如阿梨樹
枝。且道、是那箇閻字。(汝道無我、䫇)

A scholar[1] once wrote a treatise denying the existence of spirits. The moment
he finished and laid down his brush a spirit appeared before him, saluted,
and then demanded, "So, scholar, what are you going to do about *me*?"

Wuzu Fayan commented, "If I had seen the demon, I would have put my
hands in front of my mouth like the beak of a *bo* dove and cried, 'Coo!
Coo!'"[2]

Nantang said, "Though the scholar knew there are no spirits, he didn't
know *why* there are none. Though Wuzu knew why there are no spirits,
he couldn't remove the traces and erase the tracks. I wouldn't have done
it that way. When the spirit appeared, saluted, then demanded what I
intended to do, I'd have looked at him and shouted, '*Yan!*'[3] Even if the
spirit was the great, powerful Demon-King himself, I'd have cleaved his
skull into seven pieces, like the branch of an *arjaka* tree.[4] Tell me, then,
what is this word *yan*?"

"You said I don't exist. *Ni!*"[5]

1. The scholar was Yuan Zhan 阮瞻 (210–63), mentioned in the Chinese historical text *Chronicles of the Shin Dynasty* 晋書 49.

2. On clear days the male *bo* dove 鵓鳩 is said to call out to female doves, and
on rainy days to chase them away with cries that become more rapid. Wuzu
Fayan was imitating the dove's rapid calls, "Coo! Coo!" as a form of spell to
drive away the demon.

3. *Yan* 閻 here may refer to Yanmo 閻魔 (Skr., Yama; J., Enma), the greatest of
the demons, who is lord of the underworld and judge of the dead. He is regarded
in Buddhism as an alternate manifestation of the bodhisattva Kṣitigarbha.

4. This image comes from the *Lotus Sutra*, "Chapter on Dhāraṇī" (陀羅尼
品): "If there are those who fail to heed our spells / and trouble and disrupt the
preachers of the Law, / their heads will split into seven pieces / like the branches
of the *arjaka* tree" (Watson 1993b, p. 311). The word translated as "branch" 枝 is
thought to refer in the Chinese *Lotus Sutra* to the tree's flower, which is said to
break into seven pieces when touched.

5. This final sentence, 汝道無我䫇, does not appear in the original text, the
Comprehensive Record of the Lamp 普燈錄, although it does appear in subsequent

sources like the *Compendium of the Five Lamps*. The last word, *ni* 聻, is employed in Zen either as a term of sharp challenge or inquiry, or as the equivalent of a shout, in order to jolt students' minds out of mistaken perceptions and awaken them to the reality of the moment just as it is.

Although irrelevant to this koan, interesting background information on the word 聻 is found in Morohashi, where it is noted that in China spirits were thought to become 聻 when they died. Just as humans are terrified of spirits, so are spirits terrified of 聻. Thus writing the character 聻 on a piece of paper and pasting it above the entrance to a household was believed to keep all spirits away (9:233).

Case 41   室内一燈   *The Lamp in the Room*

香林遠禪師、僧問、如何是室内一盞燈。遠云、三人證龜作鼈。

A monk asked Xianglin Chengyuan, "What is the single lamp in the room?"[1]
Xianglin replied, "If three people testify to it, a terrapin becomes a softshell."

1. The flame represents prajñā wisdom; the single oil lamp burning in the room thus represents the unending lightning flash that must never be extinguished.

Case 42   心身共捨   *Cast Aside Both Mind and Body*

黄檗運禪師示衆云、内外身心、一切共可捨。凡人多不肯空心、恐落
於空。不知自心本空。愚人除事不除心、智者除心不除事。菩薩心如
虚空、一切共捨、所作福德、皆不貪著。然捨有三等。内外身心、一
切俱捨。猶如虚空無所取着。然後方應物、能所皆忘、是爲大捨。
若一邊行道布德、一邊旋捨、無希望心、是爲中捨。若廣修衆善、有
所希望、聞法知空、遂乃不着、是爲小捨。大捨如火燭在前、更無迷
悟。中捨如火燭在傍、或明或暗。小捨如火燭在後、不見坑穽。（故）。

Huangbo Xiyun said to the assembly

Inner and outer, body and mind—all must be discarded. Most people are unwilling to empty their minds, fearing they will fall into emptiness; little do they realize that mind itself is empty from the start. The foolish eliminate things but do not eliminate thought; the wise eliminate thought but do not eliminate things. Bodhisattvas have minds like empty space—they have let go of everything and have no attachments, even to the merit they have made. Furthermore, there are three levels of renunciation. Great renunciation is when inner and outer, body and mind, have all been cast aside and, like empty space, have no place for attachment; after this, one follows the situation and responds to circumstances, with both subject and object forgotten. Middling renunciation is when one follows the Way and accumulates merit even as one immediately abandons it and retains no attachments. Small renunciation is when one does all sorts of good deeds in the hope of gaining merit but relinquishes such attachments upon hearing the Dharma and realizing that all is empty. Great renunciation is like having a flame in front of you: no longer is there either delusion or enlightenment. Middling renunciation is like having a flame at your side: there are times of light and times of darkness. Small renunciation is like having a flame behind you: you cannot see the pitfalls in front of you.[1]

1. From Huangbo's *Essentials of Transmitting the Mind* 傳心法要. See also Blofeld 1958, pp. 48–49.

Case 43   達磨不來   *Bodhidharma Didn't Come to China*

福州玄沙備禪師、因雪峰呼爲頭陀。每見之曰、再來人也、何不徧參
去。對云、達磨不來東土、二祖不往西天。雪峰然之。

Xuefeng Yicun called Xuansha Shibei of Fuzhou a true ascetic,[1] and, whenever he saw him, said, "You're a reborn sage![2] Why don't you go on pilgrimage to study Zen?"

In response Xuansha said, "Bodhidharma didn't come to China, the Second Patriarch didn't go to India."[3] Xuefeng accepted this answer.

1. The term "a true ascetic" translates 頭陀, which is a transliteration of the Sanskrit *dhūta*, someone who has abandoned all attachments to food, shelter, and clothing and singlemindedly pursues the Way.

2. "A reborn sage" 再來人, lit., "one who has come again," refers to a reborn buddha, bodhisattva, or great sage.

3. Xuansha's comment refers to the fact that during his training he decided to leave his native Fujian and study with masters in other parts of China. As he reached the pass that connects the mountain-ringed province of Fujian with the rest of China, he stumbled and hurt his toe. At that moment he was deeply enlightened, and exclaimed, "Bodhidharma didn't come to China, the Second Patriarch didn't go to India!" He thereupon turned around and returned to Fujian. See also Case 113.

Case 44   丹霞燒佛   *Danxia Burns a Buddha Image*

丹霞然禪師、嘗到洛京慧林寺值天寒。遂於殿中取木佛燒火向。院主
偶見呵責云、何得燒我木佛。師以杖撥灰云、吾燒取舍利。主云、木
佛安有舍利。師云、既無舍利、更請兩尊再取燒之。院主自〔後〕眉鬚
墮落。

Once when Zen master Danxia Tianran was staying at the temple Huilin si in the capital on a very cold day he took a wooden buddha image from the buddha hall, set it on fire, and warmed himself by the flames.

The temple supervisor happened to see this and scolded Danxia, saying, "How can you burn my wooden buddha!"

Danxia stirred the ashes with his staff and said, "I'm burning it to get the holy relics."[1]

The supervisor replied, "How could there be relics in a wooden buddha?"

"If there are no relics," Danxia answered, "then please give me the two attendant images to burn."

Later the supervisor's eyebrows fell out.[2]

1. "Holy relics" (Skt. *śarīra*) refers to the relics of a buddha or sage that remain after cremation and are sometimes said to be indestructible, gem-like substances.

2. Someone's eyebrows falling out is the traditional consequence of falsely preaching the Dharma.

Case 45   寤寐恒一   *Asleep or Awake, At All Times Be One*

首楞嚴經曰、寤寐恒一。

In the *Śūraṅgama Sutra* it is written, "Asleep or awake, at all times be one."[1]

1. T 19:151c. The quote is a slightly idiosyncratic reading of a line in the sutra. The full passage reads:

> Ananda, when a good person who has been practicing samadhi has reached the end of the aggregate of cognition, the usual cognitive processes involved in dreaming will disappear from his mind. *For him there will no longer be any difference between waking and sleeping.* His awareness will be as luminous, as empty, and as still as a cloudless sky. Images of gross external objects will no longer appear before him as objects of cognition. He will view all the phenomena in the world—the mountains, the rivers, and everything else—as mere reflections that briefly appear in a clear mirror, leaving nothing behind….Only the true essence of consciousness remains. (Buddhist Text Translation Society, 2009, p. 429; the italics are mine)

Case 46-1   趙州無字   *Zhaozhou's "Wu"*[1]

趙州、因僧問、狗子還有佛性也無。州云、無。僧云、一切衆生皆
有佛性、狗子爲什麼却無。州云、爲伊有業識性在。又有僧問、狗
子還有佛性也無。州云、有。僧云、既有爲甚却撞入這箇皮袋裡。
州云、爲他知而故犯。

A monk asked Zhaozhou Congshen, "Does a dog have buddha nature?"
Zhaozhou answered, "*Wu!*" [No!]
The monk replied, "All sentient beings have buddha nature.[2] Why would
a dog not have it?"
Zhaozhou said, "Because it has karmic consciousness."[3]
Another monk asked, "Does a dog have buddha nature?"
Zhaozhou answered, "*Yu!*"[4] [Yes!]
The monk replied, "If it has, why then is it still stuffed into a bag of skin?"
"Because though it knows, it deliberately transgresses," said Zhaozhou.

1. The first two sentences form *Wumen guan* 1, Main Case. The entire koan is
found in *Record of Equanimity* 18, Main Case.
2. The teaching that all sentient beings have buddha nature is one primarily
associated with the *Nirvana Sutra* (T 12:402c and elsewhere).
3. "Karmic consciousness" translates 業識性 (Skt. *karma vijñāna*), the deluded
consciousness that arises through the workings of fundamental ignorance.
4. The character 有 is read *you*, but to avoid confusion with the English "you"
it is rendered here as *yu*.

Case 46-2   無字之頌   *A Verse on Zhaozhou's "Wu"*

婺州義烏稠巖了贇禪師、題無字頌云、趙州狗子無佛性、萬疊青山藏
古鏡。赤脚波斯入大唐、八臂那吒行正令。

Zen master Chouyan Liaoyun of Wuzhou wrote the following verse on the
koan "*Wu*":
Zhaozhou's "A dog has no buddha nature,"
Endless blue mountains hide in the ancient mirror.[1]
Barefoot Persians enter the land of China,[2]
Eight-armed Nalakūvara follows the true teaching.[3]

1. "Endless blue mountains" is a synonym for all of phenomenal existence; the
ancient mirror represents buddha nature.

2. This line is sometimes translated "The barefoot Persian enters the land of China," with "the barefoot Persian" interpreted as a reference to Bodhidharma. There is, however, nothing to indicate that this is the actual meaning of the expression. Dōmae notes that Zen sources such as the *Zen Phrase Lexicon* 宗門 方語 identify the entire line as a Chinese expression meaning "to act ostentatiously or foolishly."

3. *Nalakūvara* is a Buddhist tutelary deity possessed of enormous strength; see Biographical Notes. The term "true teaching" 正令 generally refers to the Buddhadharma; in Zen it indicates more specifically the "separate transmission outside the teachings." "Implementing the true teaching" 正令當行 refers to the use of the shout, stick, and other methods by which the separate transmission is revealed. Dōmae comments that the verse compares the functioning of Zhaozhou's *Wu* koan to the delusion-crushing intensity of the guardian deity Nalakūvara.

Case 46-3   中峰無字   *Zhongfeng's Eight-Word Question on "Wu"*

中峰本和尚曰、趙州因甚道箇無字。謂之中峰八箇字。或謂之因 甚道話。

Zhongfeng Mingben asked, "What was the reason that Zhaozhou said '*Wu*'?"

This is called "The eight-word question of Zhongfeng" or "The question of why he said what he did."

Case 46-4   大慧無字   *Dahui's "Wu"*

大慧曰、趙州無字祇麼舉。

Dahui Zonggao said, "Just work diligently on Zhaozhou's '*Wu*.'"

Case 46-5   僧未問佛   *Before the Monk Asked about Buddha Nature*

古人云、此僧未問佛性、趙州未答無時如何。

A man of old[1] said, "Before the monk asked about buddha nature, before Zhaozhou answered '*Wu!*'—what about then?"

1. It is unknown who the "man of old" is.

Case 46-6　古徳透徹　*Penetrate It Thoroughly*

古徳云、透徹看。

An ancient worthy said,[1] "Penetrate it thoroughly!"[2]

　1. It is unknown who the "ancient worthy" is.
　2. "It" refers to Zhaozhou Congshen's "*Wu*."

Case 47　佛直祖曲　*Buddha Straight, Ancestors Crooked*[1]

佛說直、祖師爲甚麼唱曲。

The Buddha's teaching was straight. Why do the ancestors sing such a crooked tune?

　1. This koan is placed immediately after Case 46-1 in the original *Kattōshū* text. However, since the subsequent five cases all deal with the koan "Zhaozhou's *Wu*," I have followed Dōmae in placing the six *Wu* koans together and situating this koan immediately afterward.

Case 48　女子出定　*A Woman Comes Out of Samadhi*[1]

昔文殊至諸佛集處、值諸佛各還本處。惟有一女人、近彼佛坐、入於
三昧。文殊乃白佛言、何此女人得近佛坐、而我不得。佛告文殊、汝
但覺此女、令從三昧起、汝自問之。文殊遶女人三迊、鳴指一下、乃
托至梵天。盡其神力而不能出。世尊云、假使百千文殊、亦出此女人
定不得。下方過四十二億河沙國土、有罔明菩薩、能出此女人定。須
臾罔明大士、從地湧出禮拜佛。佛勅罔明。却至女人前、鳴指一下。
女人於是從定而立。

Long ago Mañjuśrī went to a gathering of buddhas as they were returning to their own domains. However, one woman remained sitting in samadhi near the seat of Śākyamuni Buddha.

　Mañjuśrī asked Śākyamuni, "Why can this woman stay close to the Buddha's seat when I cannot?"

　Śākyamuni replied, "Just wake the woman up, bring her out of samadhi, and ask her yourself."

Mañjuśrī circled the woman three times, snapped his fingers once, and raised her into the Brahma Heaven. But even after employing all of his supernatural powers he was unable to bring her out of samadhi.

Śākyamuni then said, "Even a hundred thousand Mañjuśrīs would not be able to bring this woman out of samadhi. Down below, past as many worlds as there are grains of sand in four billion two hundred million Ganges Rivers, there is a bodhisattva named Delusion who will be able to bring her out."[2] At that moment Delusion emerged from out of the ground and paid homage to Śākyamuni. Then, as instructed by the Buddha, he went before the woman and snapped his fingers once. At this she emerged from samadhi.

1. Also *Wumen guan* 42, Main Case. For a related koan, see Case 87.

2. "Delusion" is a translation of "Wangming" 罔明, a name synonymous with 無明 or 無知, "ignorance." In contrast to Mañjuśrī, the bodhisattva of perfect enlightenment, Delusion is a low-level bodhisattva.

Case 49   水上行話   *East Mountain Walks on the Water*

僧問雲門、如何是諸佛出身處。門曰、東山水上行。

A monk questioned Yunmen, "What is the place from which all buddhas come?"

Yunmen replied, "East Mountain walks on the water."

Case 50   法華禪定   *Lotus Samadhi*

法華曰、深入禪定、見十方佛。

In the *Lotus Sutra* it is written, "Deeply entering samadhi, see the buddhas of the ten directions."[1]

1. *Lotus Sutra*, "Chapter on Peaceful Practices" (安樂行品); T 9:39c.

Case 51   大通智勝   *The Buddha of Great Universal Wisdom Excellence*[1]

法華經曰、大通智勝佛、十劫坐道場。佛法不現前、不得成佛道。

In the *Lotus Sutra* it is written, "The Buddha of Great Universal Wisdom Excellence sat in the place of enlightenment for ten kalpas, but the Buddhadharma did not manifest to him, and he could not attain the Buddha-way."[2]

1. A fuller version of this koan appears as *Wumen guan* 9, Main Case.

2. This passage is from the *Lotus Sutra*, "Chapter on the Phantom City" 化城喻品 (T 9:26a; 160c). It is of interest to note that, according to the *Lotus Sutra* account, at the end of the ten kalpas the Buddha of Great Universal Wisdom Excellence sat on a throne made for him by the gods of the Brahma Heaven and, after ten more kalpas, attained Supreme Perfect Enlightenment. Following this he taught the Dharma, from one level to the next, until he reached the highest level, that of the *Lotus Sutra*.

Case 52   黃龍念讚   *Huanglong's "Sutra Chanting"*

黃龍和尚、住黃檗時、室中每舉曰、鐘樓上念讚、床脚下種菜。勝首座下一轉語道、猛虎當路坐。他便退黃檗與他住、自居積翠庵。

When Huanglong Huinan was residing on Mount Huangbo, he would say to monks in the *sanzen* room, "Up in the bell tower, reciting sutras; down by the meditation bench, raising vegetables."[1]

The head monk Sheng[2] gave a turning-phrase, saying, "A fierce tiger sits in the middle of the road."[3]

At this Huanglong retired, turning his position as master of the monastery over to Sheng and going to live at the Jicui Hermitage.

1. This line describes the daily monastic routine of ritual practice, meditation, and manual labor.

2. "Head monk Sheng" is *Huangbo Weisheng*.

3. A saying that indicates a person one can't heedlessly walk by, a person whom even the buddhas and ancestors can't approach.

Case 53   馬祖塩醬   *Mazu's "Salt and Sauce"*

馬祖既得法、直往江西、建立宗旨。一日、讓和尚曰、道一在江西說法。總不見持箇消息來。遂囑一僧云、汝去待他上堂、即問作麼生。看他道甚麼記取來。其僧依教去、見上堂、便出問作麼生。祖云、自從胡亂後三十年、不曾少鹽醬喫。讓然之。

After Mazu Daoyi received the Dharma from Nanyue Huairang, he went to Jiangxi and there spread the teachings of the Zen school.

One day Huairang said, "Daoyi is in Jiangxi teaching the Dharma, but there's been no word from him." He therefore said to one of the monks, "Go to Mazu's place, wait until he gives a lecture, then ask, 'How is it?' Remember what he says, then come and tell me."

The monk did as instructed, waiting for a lecture and then asking Mazu, "How is it?"

Mazu replied, "In the thirty years[1] since I left confusion behind,[2] I've never lacked for salt or sauce."

Huairang praised this reply.

1. The *Kattōshū* has "twenty years," but in the original sources (e.g., the *Discourses of Chan Master Dahui* 大慧普說; T 47:871a) the number is thirty. The text has been changed accordingly.

2. "Left confusion behind" is an attempt to translate the term 胡亂. Mujaku explains that the word 胡 means "barbarian" and 亂 refers to the turbulence that followed the barbarians' incursions, during which the Chinese would hurriedly leave their cities. From this the compound 胡亂 came to indicate a state of confusion. "Since I left confusion behind" implies "since I entered the Way"; in Buddhism it is said, "In food and clothing there is no mind that seeks the Way, but in the mind that seeks the Way there are food and clothing."

Case 54   柏樹托鉢   *Juniper Tree, Carrying Bowls*

趙州柏樹子與德山托鉢、是同是別乎。

"Zhaozhou's 'Juniper Tree'" and "Deshan Carries His Bowls"[1]—are these koans the same or are they different?

1. See Cases 9 and 22-1.

Case 55   張公喫酒   *Mr. Zhang Drinks Wine*

古人云、張公喫酒李公醉。

A man of old said, "Mr. Zhang drinks wine, Mr. Li gets drunk."[1]

1. "Mr. Zhang drinks wine, Mr. Li gets drunk" is a line from a popular song of the early Tang dynasty. Yunmen quotes it in his *Extensive Record* (T 47:558c).

Case 56   鼓山伽陀   *Gushan's Gāthā*

鼓山珪云、十年海上覓冤讐、不得冤讐未肯休。芍藥花開菩薩面、梭
欏葉散夜叉頭。

Gushan Shigui said, "For ten years at sea I have sought my enemy; until I find my enemy I cannot rest."[1]

> Blossoming peony flowers, like bodhisattvas' faces;
> Scattered palm fronds, like demons' heads.[2]

1. "Enemy" translates 冤讐, which can indicate either an enemy or a lover. In Zen it is used to indicate a true teacher or the original face.

2. Dōmae comments that both the bodhisattvas' faces and the demons' heads are aspects of the formless original face.

Case 57   一失人身   *To Lose a Human Birth*

梵網經云、一失人身、萬劫不復。

The *Brahma Net Sutra* says, "Lose your human birth once, and you may not regain it for ten thousand kalpas."[1]

1. T 24:1003a. The entire passage reads:

If we do not fear transgressions, it is difficult to develop a wholesome mind. Therefore, the sutras contain this teaching: Do not regard a minor misdeed as inconsequential. In time, drops of water may fill a large vessel. Offenses committed in a moment may result in eons of suffering in the hells. Once the human life is lost, it may not be regained for myriads of lifetimes. Youth is like a galloping horse. Our life is more fleeting than the waters of a mountain stream. Today we are alive; tomorrow, who knows? Let each of us practice diligently and singlemindedly. (Sutra Translation Committee of the United States and Canada 2000)

Case 58   首山此經   *Shoushan's "This Sutra"*

首山念禪師、僧問、一切諸佛皆自此經出、如何是此經。師云、低聲
低聲。僧云、如何受持。師云、不污染。

A monk asked Shoushan Shengnian, "The buddhas all issue from this sutra; what sutra is it?"[1] The master said, "Speak softly! Speak softly!"[2]

"How am I to receive and maintain this?" the monk asked.

"Never defile it!" answered the master.

1. In the *Diamond Sutra* one finds the sentence: "All the Dharmas of the buddhas and of the supreme and perfect enlightenment of the buddhas derive from this sutra" (T 8:749b). *Blue Cliff Record* 97, Commentary on the Main Case, remarks as follows:

> Fayan [Wenyi] said realizing buddhahood is called upholding the [*Diamond Sutra*]. The scripture says, "All buddhas, and the teaching of the complete enlightenment of all buddhas, come from this scripture." But tell me, what do you call "this scripture"? Is it the actual text?… [People nowadays] don't realize it all arises from their own original minds. (Cleary 1998, pp. 425, 427)

2. "Speak softly, speak softly" translates 低聲低聲, literally "low voice, low voice." The implied meaning is "speak quietly or people will hear." When speaking of the truth, be sure that your words are quiet enough not to reach the ears of those incapable of understanding them correctly (ZGDJ: 879c).

Case 59   興化打中   *Xinghua's "Hold to the Center"*

興化獎禪師、因僧問、四方八面來時如何。師云、打中間底。僧便禮
拜。師云、山僧昨日赴箇村齋、途中遇一陣狂風暴雨、向古廟裡避得
過。應庵華云、眾中商量道、向古廟裡避得過、是空劫已前自己。又
道、便是他安身立命處、殊不知興化腰纏十萬貫、騎鶴下揚州。

A monk asked Xinghua Cunjiang, "What should one do when things come from every direction?"

The master said, "Hold to the center."[1]

The monk bowed.

The master then said, "Yesterday, as I was on my way to a dinner in the village, I was caught in a sudden storm with heavy rain and violent wind, so I headed for an old shrine and found shelter."

Ying'an Tanhua commented, "The assembly considered the matter and said, 'Taking shelter in an old mausoleum refers to the self that precedes the Kalpa of Emptiness,[2] or to the place where Xinghua attained peace of mind and fully realized his original nature.' Little did they know that Xinghua, his purse filled with one hundred thousand in cash, mounted a crane and went down to Yangzhou."[3]

1. The verb "hold" in the sentence "Hold to the center" translates 打, a word that originally means "strike" or "hit" but that can be used in a wide variety of ways, e.g., 打酒, "to buy alcohol," 打水, "to draw water," 打草, "to cut weeds," 打車, "to make a cart," etc. (ZGDJ: 780b). Thus other possible translations are "Aim for the center," "Strike at the center," etc.

2. The Kalpa of Emptiness 空劫 is the kalpa that lies between the destruction of one universe and the formation of the next.

3. The implication of "going down to Yangzhou" is not entirely clear. The city of Yangzhou 揚州 had a well-known pleasure quarter. Morohashi, however, mentions an old tale that may provide relevant background information. A group of men were discussing their wishes. One man said that he would like to become governor of Yangzhou, another that he would like to have plenty of money, and another that he would like to fly on the back of a crane. Thereupon another man said, "So if someone slung a hundred thousand in cash from his waist, got on a crane, and flew off to Yangzhou, then he would fulfill all of these wishes at once" (5:319b–c).

Case 60   潙山水牯   *Guishan's "Water Buffalo"*

潙山祐禪師、示衆云、老僧百年後、向山下檀越家、作一頭水牯牛、
於左脇下書五字。云、潙山僧某甲。此時、若喚作潙山僧、又是水牯
牛、喚作水牯牛、又云潙山僧某甲。且道、喚作甚麼即得。仰山出禮
拜而去。

Guishan Lingyou addressed the assembly, saying, "When this old monk's one hundred years are finished, I'll be reborn as a water buffalo at the believer's house by the foot of the mountain.[1] On the water buffalo's lower left flank will be written the five characters 潙山僧某甲, 'Monk So-and-so of Mount Gui.' If you call it a monk from Mount Gui, it's still a buffalo, and if you call it a buffalo, it's still a monk of Mount Gui. So tell me then, to get it right, what should you call it?"

Yangshan Huiji stepped forward, bowed, and walked away.

1. See also Case 63, "Nantang's 'Other Realms,'" and Case 90, "Nanquan's 'Water Buffalo.'" In Rinzai Zen koan training the present koan and "Nanquan's 'Water Buffalo'" are linked.

It was also said in ancient China that those who died with unpaid debts were reborn as water buffaloes at the creditor's household. The characters of the dead person's name would often appear on the animal; the person's descendants would then buy the animal, paying off the debt.

Case 61　古帆未掛　*The Sail Has Yet to Be Hoisted*

僧問巖頭、古帆未掛時如何。頭云、小魚吞大魚。云、掛後如何。頭
云、後園驢喫草。虛堂問南浦、曰、古帆未掛時如何。浦云、蟭螟眼
裡五須彌。堂云、掛後如何。浦云、黃河向北流。

A monk asked Yantou Quanhuo, "How about when the old sail has yet to be hoisted?"

Yantou replied, "A small fish swallows a big fish."[1]

The monk said, "How about after it's been hoisted?"

Yantou said, "A donkey grazes in the back garden."

Later Xutang asked Nanpo Jōmyō, "How about when the old sail has yet to be hoisted?"

Nanpo said, "Five Mount Sumerus in the eye of a gnat."[2]

Xutang continued, "How about after it's been hoisted?"

Nanpo said, "The Yellow River flows north."[3]

    1. ZGDJ: An expression representing the transcendence of the dichotomy between large and small, active and passive.

    2. ZGJI: Same meaning as 1, above.

    3. The Yellow River actually flows east.

Case 62　洞山三斤　*Dongshan's "Three Pounds of Hemp"*[1]

僧因問洞山、如何是佛。山云、麻三斤。

A monk asked Dongshan Shouchu, "What is buddha?"

Dongshan answered, "Three pounds of hemp."[2]

    1. Also *Wumen guan* 18, Main Case; *Blue Cliff Record* 12, Main Case.

    2. Dōmae: The conceptual explanation that three pounds of hemp represents the amount of material in the Buddha's robe misses the point.

Case 63　南堂異類　*Nantang's "Other Realms"*

南堂十辨驗云、須向異類中行。

In his ten admonitions,[1] Nantang Yuanjing says, "Work actively in the other realms."[2]

1. Nantang's ten admonitions are:

1) have faith that there is a separate teaching transmitted outside the sutras;
2) gain a clear understanding of this separate transmission;
3) know the unity of the "Dharma-teaching of the sentient" 有情説法 and the "Dharma-teaching of the nonsentient" 無情説法;
4) see original nature as clearly as viewing it in the palm of your hand, and be calm and steadfast in spirit;
5) possess the discerning eye of the Dharma;
6) leave no traces, like a bird flying through the air;
7) be proficient in both doctrine and practice;
8) destroy the false and reveal the true;
9) manifest great functioning;
10) work actively in the other realms of existence.

2. The six realms of existence in Buddhist cosmology are those of: (1) the heavenly beings, (2) human beings, (3) asuras, (4) animals, (5) pretas or hungry ghosts, and (6) hell-dwellers. Precedents for Nantang's admonition to continue working in different realms of existence are seen in Case 60 ("Guishan's 'Water Buffalo'") and Case 90 ("Nanquan's 'Water Buffalo'").

Case 64   無功德話   *No Merit*[1]

達磨大師、見梁武帝。帝問、朕起寺度僧。有何功德。磨云、無功德。

When Bodhidharma met Emperor Wu of the Liang, the emperor asked, "I have founded temples and ordained monks. What merit have I gained from these acts?"

Bodhidharma answered, "No merit."

1. For a fuller version of this episode, see *Blue Cliff Record* 1, Commentary on the Main Case.

Case 65   千尺井中   *A Man in a Thousand-Foot Well*[1]

性空禪師、僧問、如何是祖師西來意。師云、若人在千尺井中、不假
寸繩出得此人、即答汝西來意。僧云、近日湖南暢和尚出世、亦爲人
東語西話。師乃喚沙彌寂子、拽出這死屍看。仰山後舉似耽源、如何
出得井中人。源云、咄、癡漢、誰在井中。仰山不契、後又問潙山、
如何出得井中人。山乃召云、慧寂。寂應諾。山云、出了也。寂後住
仰山、常舉前話、示衆云、我於耽源處得體、潙山處得用。

A monk asked Shishuang Xingkong, "What is the meaning of the Patriarch coming from the West?"

The master answered, "Let's say there's a man in a thousand-foot well. Get him out without using any rope, and I'll answer you about the meaning of the Patriarch's coming from the West."

The monk said, "But in Hunan now there's a priest named Chang who freely explains all sorts of things to people."[2]

Thereupon Xingkong summoned the novice Jizi [Yangshan Huiji][3] and said, "Get this corpse out of here."

Later Huiji asked Danyuan Yingzhen, "How would one get the man out of the well?"

Danyuan retorted, "Dolt! Blockhead! Who's in a well!?"

Huiji didn't understand, and later put the same question to Guishan Lingyou. Guishan called out, "Huiji!"

"Yes," Huiji answered.

"There, he's out of the well!" said Guishan.

Later, when Huiji lived on Mount Yang, he would always tell this story to the assembly, saying, "I grasped what it *is* at Danyuan's place, I grasped how it *works* at Guishan's."

1. See *Blue Cliff Record* 18, Commentary on the Main Case.

2. The monk is asking, "Other priests are willing to explain—why aren't you?" "Freely explains all sorts of things" translates 東語西話, literally, "Talks to the east and talks to the west."

3. Yangshan Huiji was at that time a novice studying under Xingkong, with the name Jizi 寂子.

Case 66   大梅梅子   *Damei's "Plum Pit"*

龐居士、因問大梅常和尚、久聞大梅、未審、梅子熟未也。師云、何
處著觜。居士云、百雜碎。師展手云、我還核子來。居士無語。

Layman Pang asked Damei, "I've long heard about the Great Plum.[1] Is the fruit ripe yet?"

The master said, "What's there to peck at?"

Layman Pang said, "I've chewed it to bits!"

The master held out his hand and said, "Then give me the pit."

Layman Pang said nothing.

1. The name "Damei" 大梅 means "big plum."

Case 67　法燈未了　*Fadeng Is Not Yet Finished*[1]

法燈示衆云、本欲深藏巖嶽隱遁過時。奈清涼老人有未了公案、出來
與他了却。時有僧出問、如何是未了公案。燈便打云、祖禰不了、殃
及兒孫。

Qingliang Taiqin said to the assembly, "At first I intended to pass my time secluded deep in the mountains, but, troubled by the unfinished koan of Old Man Qingliang,[2] I emerged and am now completing it for him."

At this a monk came forward and asked, "What is this unfinished koan?"

Taiqin struck the monk and said, "What the ancestors fail to finish brings misfortune to the descendants."[3]

1. "Fadeng" is the honorary title of *Qingliang Taiqin*.
2. Old Man Qingliang 清涼老人 refers to *Fayan Wenyi*, who was Taiqin's teacher.
3. This translation follows the ZGJT. The line is also found in *Blue Cliff Record* 55, Verse; Cleary translates it as "What the ancestors do not complete becomes the burden of the descendants" (1998, p. 266). The ZGJI interprets the sentence to mean, "If one fails to honor one's ancestors, misfortune befalls one's descendants."

Case 68　南泉油糍　*Nanquan's Fried Dumplings*

南泉願禪師、一日、不赴堂。侍者請赴堂。師云、我今日在莊上喫油
糍飽。者云、和尚不曾出入。師云、汝去問莊主。者方出門、忽見莊
主歸、謝和尚到莊喫油糍。

One day Nanquan Puyuan did not go to the hall to eat. When he was urged to do so by his attendant, Nanquan said, "Today I stopped in at the temple estate[1] and had some fried dumplings, so I'm satisfied."

"But you haven't gone out all day," replied the attendant.

"Then go ask the manager of the estate," said Nanquan.

Just as he was leaving the gate, the attendant saw the manager on his way home. The manager asked him to thank Nanquan for stopping by to have some fried dumplings.

1. "Estate" translates 莊, which refers in this case to a landed estate owned by the temple.

Case 69   無鬚鎖子   *A Springless Lock*

石霜諸禪師、僧問、如何是和尚深深處。師曰、無鬚鎖子兩頭搖。

A monk asked Shishuang Qingzhu, "The master's most profound depth—what is it like?"

The master replied, "A springless lock opens at both ends."[1]

1. The word 鎖子, also written 鏁子, means "lock." The character 鬚 indicates the spring in the lock's mechanism that opens the lock when the key is turned. A lock without a spring 無鬚鎖子 is thus an unopenable lock, which represents the hidden and ineffable buddha-mind. This buddha-mind opens, however, at the two poles of life-and-death, being-and-nonbeing, etc.

Case 70   外道六師   *The Six Non-Buddhist Teachers*

大珠和尚、因維摩座主問、經云、彼外道六師等、是汝之師。因其出家、彼師所墮、汝亦隨墮。其施汝者、不名福田。供養汝者、墮三惡道。謗於佛毀於法、不入衆數、終不得滅度。汝若如是、乃可取食。今請禪師、明爲解說。珠云、迷徇六根者、號之爲六師。心外求佛、名爲外道。有物可施、不名福田。生心受供、墮三惡道。汝若能謗於佛者、是不着佛求。毀於法者、是不着法求。不入衆數者、是不着僧求。終不得滅度者、智用現前。若有如是解者、便得法喜禪悦之食。

A lecturer on the *Vimalakīrti Sutra* questioned Dazhu Huihai, saying, "In the sutra it is written:

> The six non-Buddhist teachers are your masters. Follow them in renouncing the household life, and when they fall into error you, too, follow them into error. Those who make offerings to you receive no merit; those who make donations to you fall into the three evil realms.[1] Slander the Buddha, vilify the Dharma, do not join the Sangha, and, finally, fail to attain nirvana. If this is the way you are, then you can receive food.[2]

Meditation Master, please clarify the meaning of this passage for me."

Dazhu responded, "Those who, in delusion, follow the six senses are called 'the six teachers'; those who seek buddha outside the mind are called 'non-Buddhist.' If one makes offerings out of abundance, one receives no merit; if one receives donations with some purpose in mind, one falls into the three evil realms.

"If you slander the Buddha, then you seek nothing from the Buddha; if you vilify the Dharma, then you seek nothing from the Dharma; if you do not enter the Sangha, then you seek nothing from the Sangha; if in the end you fail to attain the realm of emancipation, then wisdom and its function are manifested right in front of you.

"If you understand the passage in this way, then you have attained the feast of joy in the Dharma and delight in samadhi."

1. The three evil realms 三惡道 are those of the animals, pretas (hungry ghosts), and hell-dwellers.

2. *Vimalakīrti Sutra*, "Disciples" chapter (T 14:540b–c). It should be noted that the *Vimalakīrti Sutra* passage as quoted in the koan is actually an abridged version of the actual text:

> Subhuti, if without seeing the Buddha or listening to his Law you are willing to take those six heretical teachers, Purana Kashyapa, Maskarin Goshaliputra, Samjayin Vairatiputra, Ajita Keshakambala, Kakuda Katyayana, and Nirgrantha Jnatiputra, as your teachers, leave the household life because of them, and follow them in falling into the same errors they fall into, then you will be worthy to receive food.
>
> Subhuti, if you can subscribe to erroneous views and thus never reach the "other shore" of enlightenment; if you can remain among the eight difficulties and never escape from difficulty, and can make common cause with earthly desires and remove yourself from a state of purity; if when you attain the samadhi of nondisputation you allow all living beings to attain the same degree of concentration; if those who give you alms are not destined to gain good fortune thereby, and those who make offerings to you fall into the three evil paths of existence; if you are willing to join hands with the host of devils and make the defilements your companion; if you can be no different from all these devils and these dusts and defilements; if you can bear hatred toward all living beings, slander the Buddhas, vilify the Law, not be counted among the assembly of monks, and in the end never attain nirvana—if you can do all this, then you will be worthy to receive food. (Watson 1997, pp. 42–43)

Case 71   芭蕉拄杖   *Bajiao's Staff*[1]

芭蕉和尚示衆云、你有拄杖子、我與你拄杖子。你無拄杖子、我奪你
拄杖子。[眞淨和尚云、你有拄杖子、我奪你拄杖子。你無拄杖子、
我與你拄杖子]。虛堂愚拈云、請各放下者拄杖子。且道、三轉語、
還有優劣也[無]。擊拂子。

Bajiao Huiqing said to the assembly, "If you have a staff, I'll give you a staff; if you have no staff, I'll take the staff away."

Zhenjing Kewen said, "If you have a staff, I'll take the staff away; if you have no staff, I'll give you a staff."[2]

Xutang Zhiyu commented, "Each of you, throw this staff away." He then said, "Now tell me, are any of these three turning-phrases better than the others?" He swished his whisk through the air.

1. The first part of this koan comprises *Wumen guan* 44, Main Case.
2. This line is missing in the present text of the *Kattōshū* but has been added in accordance with the original text, found in the *Record of Xutang* 9.

Case 72　世尊未說　*The Buddha Never Preached*[1]

世尊、臨入涅槃、文殊請佛再轉法輪。世尊咄云、吾四十九年住世、
未嘗說一字。汝請吾再轉法輪、是［吾］曾轉法輪耶。

As the Buddha was about to enter Parinirvāṇa, Mañjuśrī asked him to turn the wheel of the Dharma one more time. The Buddha admonished him, saying, "For forty-nine years I have dwelt in the world, but I've yet to preach a single word. You ask me to turn the wheel of the Dharma once again, but have I ever turned the wheel of the Dharma?"

1. See also *Blue Cliff Record* 28, Commentary on the Verse.

Case 73　圜悟禍門　*Yuanwu's "Gate of Misfortune"*

圜悟勤禪師、僧問、如何是佛。師曰、口是禍門。

A monk asked Yuanwu Keqin, "What is buddha?"
Yuanwu replied, "The mouth is the gate of misfortune."[1]

1. This expression is found in the *House Sayings of Confucius* 孔子家語 3:11.

Case 74　莫妄想話　*Drop Deluded Thought*[1]

汾州無業國師、凡有請問、但云莫妄想。

Whenever Fenzhou Wuye was asked a question, he would simply say, "Drop deluded thought!"

1. Also *Blue Cliff Record* 19, Commentary on the Main Case.

Case 75   錯用心話   *Misusing the Mind*

天童應庵華禪師、上堂云、參禪人切忌錯用心。悟明見性是錯用
心、成佛作祖是錯用心、看經講教是錯用心、行住坐(座)臥是錯用
心、[喫粥]喫飯是錯用心、屙屎送尿是錯用心、一動一靜一往一來是
錯用心。[更有一處錯用心]、歸宗不敢與諸人說破。何故。一字入公
門、九牛牽不出。

Ying'an Tanhua of Tiantong took the high seat and said, "Practitioners of Zen must be careful to avoid misusing the mind.

"To attain enlightenment and see self-nature—this is misusing the mind.

"To attain buddhahood and become a master—this is misusing the mind.

"To study the sutras and expound the teachings—this is misusing the mind.

"To walk, to stand, to sit, to lie down—this is misusing the mind.

"To [eat gruel and] eat rice—this is misusing the mind.

"To shit and to piss—this is misusing the mind.

"To move, to be still, to go, to come—this is misusing the mind.

"[There's one more misuse of the mind, but] I won't explain it, because 'once a word enters a government office, nine oxen cannot pull it out.'"[1]

1. Words in brackets are from the original text of the koan in the *Compendium of the Five Lamps* 五燈會元.

Case 76   仰山枕子   *Yangshan's Headrest*

僧問仰山、法身還解說法也無。山云、我說不得、別在一人說得。僧
曰、說得底人在什麼處。山推出枕子。溈山聞乃云、寂子用劍刃上事。

A monk asked Yangshan Huiji, "Can the dharmakāya expound the Dharma?"[1]

"I'm not able to expound it," replied Yangshan, "but there is someone else who can."

"And where is this person who can expound it?" asked the monk.

Yangshan pushed forward his headrest.

When Guishan Lingyou heard of this, he commented, "Yangshan strikes with a keen blade!"[2]

1. For "dharmakāya," see Case 17, note 1.

2. The sword blade is a metaphor for the wisdom that cuts through thought and discrimination to reveal original nature.

Case 77 三佛夜話 *The Three Buddhas' Night Talk*[1]

五祖演、三佛侍於一亭上夜話。及歸燈已滅。演於暗中曰、各下一轉
語。佛鑑曰、彩鳳舞丹霄。佛眼曰、鐵蛇橫古路。佛果曰、看脚下。
演曰、滅吾宗者乃克勤爾。

One evening, as Wuzu Fayan's three disciples Fojian Huiqin, Foyan Qingyuan, and Foguo Keqin were attending Wuzu at an inn, they and the master
talked so late that, when it came time to leave, the lamps were already out. In
the darkness Wuzu said, "Each of you, give me a turning-phrase."

Fojian said, "A radiant phoenix dances in the sky."[2]

Foyan said, "An iron snake lies across the ancient road."[3]

Foguo said, "Watch where you step!"[4]

Wuzu commented, "Only Foguo will destroy my teachings!"[5]

    1. The name of the koan derives from the fact that the three important disciples
of Wuzu Fayan appearing in this case all have names which contain the character
fo 佛 (buddha): "Fojian" 佛鑑 (Buddha Mirror), "Foyan" 佛眼 (Buddha Eye), and
"Foguo" 佛果 (Buddha Fruit; Foguo is another name for *Yuanwu Keqin*).

    2. An auspicious omen. (ZGJI)

    3. The road has gone to ruin; travelers can't pass through. (ZGJI)

    4. The expression Foguo uses, 看脚下, is frequently written on boards and
placed in the entrance halls of Zen temples as a reminder to remain always aware.

    5. An expression of the highest praise. See also Case 195.

Case 78 馬祖翫月 *Mazu's Moon Viewing*

百丈海、西堂藏、南泉願、侍馬祖翫月次、祖曰、正恁麼時如何。堂
曰、正好供養。丈云、正好修行。南泉拂袖便去。祖云、經入藏、禪
歸海、惟有普願獨超物外。

Once Baizhang Huaihai, Xitang Zhizang, and Nanquan Puyuan were
attending Mazu as they viewed the autumn moon. Mazu asked them what
they thought of the occasion.

Xitang said, "It's ideal for a ceremony."

Baizhang said, "It's ideal for training."

Nanquan shook his sleeves and walked away.[1]

Mazu said, "Zhizang has gained the teachings, Huaihai has gained the
practice, but Puyuan alone has gone beyond all things."[2]

1. To shake one's sleeves expresses scorn or may alternatively indicate leave-taking. See Cases 124, 183-1, and 207-2 for other examples.

2. Mazu's rejoinder is partly a play on words involving the names of Xitang Zhizang 西堂智藏 and Baizhang Huaihai 百丈懷海. The first two lines of his comment can be read, "Teachings enter the library 藏 (for 智藏); practice returns to the sea 海 (for 懷海)."

Case 79 佛不知有 *The Buddhas Don't Know It*[1]

僧問、南泉道、三世諸佛不知有、狸奴白牯却知有。爲甚麼三世諸佛
不知有。長砂云、未入鹿苑時、猶較些子。僧云、狸奴白牯、爲甚麼
却知有。長砂云、汝爭怪得伊。

A monk said, "Nanquan Puyuan said that the buddhas of the past, present, and future don't know it,[2] but cats and oxen do know it. Why is it that the buddhas of the past, present, and future don't know it?"

Changsha Jingcen said,[3] "They were better off before entering the Deer Park."[4]

"Why is it that cats and oxen do know it?"

"How could you possibly doubt that they would?" answered Changsha.

1. Nanquan's comment comprises *Record of Equanimity* 69, Main Case.

2. "Know it" translates 知有, a phrase that some commentators interpret as "to know what is" or "to know existence or being (Skt. *bhava*)" but that in Zen generally implies "to know enlightenment, buddha nature, the original face."

3. The *Kattōshū* has the monk addressing Nanquan, and Nanquan answering. The exchange has been altered here in accordance with the original version in the *Compendium of the Five Lamps*, where it appears in the chapter on Changsha Jingcen, with the monk quoting a statement by Nanquan.

4. The Deer Park is where the Buddha, after his awakening under the Bodhi Tree, gave his first sermon and gained his first disciples.

Case 80 臨濟孤峰 *Linji's "Solitary Peak"*[1]

臨濟上堂云、一人在孤峰頂上、無出身之路、一人在十字街頭、亦無
向背。那箇在前、那箇在後。不作維摩詰、不作傅大士。珍重。

Linji took the high seat in the hall and said, "One man is atop a solitary peak with nowhere further to go. One man is at a busy crossroads, distinguishing neither front nor back. Which one is ahead, which one is behind?[2] Don't take one to be Vimalakīrti and the other to be Fu Dashi.[3] Take good care of yourselves."

1. Also *Record of Linji*, Discourse 7.

2. Other translations include: "One person is on top of a solitary peak and has no path by which to leave. One person is at the busy crossroads and has neither front nor back. Which is ahead, which is behind?" (Sasaki 2009, p. 6); "One person is sitting on top of a lonely mountain peak, yet he has not removed himself from the world. One person is in the middle of the city streets, yet he has no likes and dislikes. Now which one is ahead? Which one is behind?" (Watson 1993a, p. 17); "One person is up on the summit of a solitary peak with no way to come forth. One person is at the crossroads and neither faces nor turns away from [the passing scene]. Which is in front, which is behind?" (Cleary 1999, p. 14).

Most interpretations of this passage contrast practice in the mountains with practice in the marketplace; Yamada comments that the man on the peak and the man at the crossroads are one and the same, as dead to the self when preaching among the crowds as when meditating in solitude (1976, p. 163).

3. The line can also be rendered, "Don't do like Vimalakīrti, don't do like Fu Dashi," meaning, "Don't be silent like Vimalakīrti, don't try to explain things like Fu Dashi." For background material on Vimalakīrti and Fu, see their entries in the Biographical Notes.

Case 81 語默離微 *Speech and Silence*[1]

風穴和尚、因僧問、語默涉離微。如何通不犯。穴云、長憶江南三月
裡、鷓鴣啼處百花香。

Fengxue Yanzhao was asked by a monk, "Speech and silence partake of both transcendence and functioning, so how can we proceed without transgressing?"[2]

Fengxue answered, "I always remember Jiangnan in the third month, partridges calling amid all the flowers so fragrant."[3]

1. Also *Wumen guan* 24, Main Case.

2. "Transcendence and functioning" translates 離微, a term first used by the fifth-century Chinese monk *Sengzhao*. The word 離 (lit., "separate" or "removed") indicates the world of the noumenal, separate from all forms, names, and phenomena; 微 (lit., "subtle" or "fine") indicates the mysterious and infinitely subtle functioning of this absolute truth in the world of phenomena. Thus 離微 denotes absolute, transcendent reality and its manifestations in the realm of things. The

questioner is saying, in other words, "Express the ultimate through silence, and you're limited to the noumenal. Express it in words, and you're limited to the phenomenal. So how can one function in true freedom without erring on either side?" Yamada (1976, p. 200) comments that 離 represents the return-to-the-source of zazen; 微 represents activity in the world. Speech offends against transcendence; silence offends against function. How then can we combine both aspects? See also Shibayama's detailed discussion (1974, pp. 176–77).

3. Fengxue's reply is identified by many annotators as a quote from the great Tang poet Du Fu 杜甫 (712–70), but these lines are not found in any of the poet's extant works. Dōmae suggests that the poem may have been written by Fengxue, who was himself from the Jiangnan region.

Case 82 仰山白槌 *Yangshan's Gavel*[1]

仰山和尚、夢見往彌勒處、安第二座。有一尊者白槌云、今日當第二
座說法。乃起白槌云、摩訶衍法離四句絕百非、諦聽諦聽。

In a dream Yangshan Huiji went to the place of Maitreya Bodhisattva and was assigned the second seat. One of the venerable monks there struck a gavel and said, "Today the person in the second seat will lecture on the Dharma."

Yangshan rose, struck the gavel, and said, "The Mahayana teaching transcends the four propositions and the one hundred negations.[2] Listen carefully! Listen carefully!"[3]

1. Also *Wumen guan* 25, Main Case, where Yangshan was assigned the third seat rather than the second seat.

2. The four propositions and the one hundred negations are formulations in Indian logic. The four propositions are identity, difference, being, and nonbeing. The one hundred negations comprise the sum total of the various ways in which these propositions may interrelate. Each proposition may be affirmed, negated, both affirmed and negated, or neither affirmed nor negated, resulting in four. This applies to all four of the original propositions, resulting in sixteen. These sixteen exist in the three worlds of past, present, and future, resulting in forty-eight. These forty-eight have either arisen or are about to arise, resulting in ninety-six. To the ninety-six are added the original four, resulting in one hundred. Since all are hypothetical and thus non-actual, they are referred to as negations.

3. "Listen carefully! Listen carefully!" translates 諦聽諦聽, which in the standard *Kattōshū* text is mistakenly rendered as 諦當諦當 ("This is true, this is true!").

Case 83   六祖風幡   *The Sixth Patriarch's Banner in the Wind*[1]

六祖大師、因風颺剎幡。有二僧對論。一僧云、幡動。一僧曰、風動。
往復曾未契理。祖云、不是風動、不是幡動、仁者心動。二僧悚然。

The Sixth Patriarch saw a banner flapping in the wind. Two monks were arguing, one saying that the banner was moving, the other that the wind was moving. They argued back and forth and were unable to agree.

The Sixth Patriarch said, "It isn't the banner that moves, nor is it the wind that moves. It's your minds that move." The two monks were astonished.

1. Also *Wumen guan* 29, Main Case.

Case 84   五家評商   *Comments on the Five Houses*

五祖演、因僧問、如何是臨濟下事。演云、五逆聞雷。如何是雲門
下。曰、紅旗閃爍。如何是曹洞下。曰、馳書不到家。如何是溈仰
下。曰、斷碑橫古路。如何是法眼下。曰、巡人犯夜。

A monk asked Wuzu Fayan, "What about the Linji school?"

The master said, "Mortal offenders hear the thunder."[1]

"What about the Yunmen school?"

The master said, "Scarlet banners flutter."[2]

"What about the Caodong school?"

The master said, "Messages are sent but never reach the house."[3]

"What about the Guiyang school?"

The master said, "A broken monument across an old road."[4]

"What about the Fayan school?"

The master said, "A night watchman breaks the curfew."[5]

1. "Mortal offenders" translates 五逆, people who have committed the five deadly sins of Buddhism: killing one's father, killing one's mother, killing an arhat, shedding the blood of a buddha, and destroying the harmony of the sangha. Such offenders were regarded as incapable of ever attaining enlightenment; according to the ZGJI, they were said to be struck dead by lightning and consigned immediately to hell.

Since Wuzu uses this term in conjunction with the Linji school, it is instructive to examine Linji's creative interpretation of a slightly different version of the five deadly sins, found in Discourse 22 of the *Record of Linji*:

Someone asked, "What is the karma of the five heinous crimes?" The master said,

"Killing the father, slaying the mother, shedding the blood of a buddha, destroying the harmony of the sangha, and burning the scriptures and images—this is the karma of the five heinous crimes."

"What is meant by 'father'?" The master said, "Avidyā is the father. When the place of arising or extinguishing of a single thought in your mind is not to be found, as with a sound reverberating throughout space, and there is nothing anywhere for you to do—this is called 'killing the father.'"

"What is meant by 'mother'?" The master said, "Covetousness is the mother. When a single thought in your mind enters the world of desire and seeks covetousness, but sees that all dharmas are only empty forms, and [thus] has no attachment anywhere—this is called 'slaying the mother.'"

"What is meant by 'shedding the blood of a buddha'?" The master said, "When in the midst of the pure Dharma realm you haven't in your mind a single reasoning thought, and [thus] pitch blackness pervades everywhere—this is called 'shedding the blood of a buddha.'"

"What is meant by 'destroying the harmony of the sangha'?" The master said, "When a single thought in your mind truly realizes that the bonds and enticements of the passions are like space with nothing upon which to depend—this is called 'destroying the harmony of the sangha.'"

"What is meant by 'burning the sutras and images'?" The master said, "When you see that causal relations are empty, that mind is empty, and that dharmas are empty, and [thus] your single thought is decisively cut off and, transcendent, you've nothing to do—this is called 'burning the sutras and images.'" (Sasaki 2009, p. 30)

2. ZGJI: Scarlet banners flutter in the distance, like cloud-dragons glimpsed in the mist.

3. ZGJI: Words and phrases point toward the truth but do not reach it. Room is left for the essential matter.

4. ZGJI: On an old, broken monument lying across a seldom-traveled road, the inscription is faint and only the clear-eyed can read it. Mujaku: All are puzzled.

5. ZGJT: In order to apprehend those who are out after the curfew, it is necessary for the watchman himself to break the curfew. As with Mujaku's traditional interpretation, "the watchman steals at night," the implication is that, in order to transcend words and letters, words and letters are used.

Case 85   百草頭話   *All the Plants*

會元第三、云、龐居士問靈照女云、古人曰、明明百草頭、明明祖師
意。汝如何會。女云、老老大大、作這箇語話。士曰、汝又作麽生。
云、明明百草頭、明明祖師意。士咲之。

According to the *Compendium of the Five Lamps*, fascicle 3, Layman Pang asked his daughter Lingzhao, "A man of old said, 'Clear, clear, in all of the plants;[1] clear, clear, is the intention of the ancestors.'[2] How do you understand this?"

"Again you speak of such things, old man though you are,"[3] replied Lingzhao.

"Well, how do you understand it?" the layman persisted.

"Clear, clear, in all of the plants; clear, clear, is the intention of the ancestors," she said.

At this the layman laughed.

1. This clause, 明明百草頭, is often translated, "Clear, clear, the tips of the plants," but Dōmae comments that in this case the character 頭 lacks its usual meaning of "head" or "tip," and simply signifies something to the effect of "regarding..." or "the matter of...."

It is unknown who the man of old is.

2. That is, the intention of the ancestors (what the ancestors sought to awaken people to) is clearly manifested even in the plants.

3. The standard *Kattōshū* text has 老老大大莫作這箇說話, "You shouldn't talk of such things, old man that you are"; this has been changed in accordance with the original text as it appears in the *Record of Layman Pang*: 老老大大作這箇語話 (x 69:134b).

Case 86   願空諸有   *Know the Emptiness of All That Exists*

于頔公、問龐居士疾次、士謂之曰、但願空諸所有、慎勿實諸所無。
好住。世間皆如影響。

When Prefect Yu Di came to inquire about Layman Pang's illness, Pang said to him, "I ask only that you know the emptiness of all that exists, and be careful not to take as real all that does not exist. Be well. Life in the world is like shadows and echoes."[1]

1. The *Recorded Sayings of Layman Pang* has the following passage between the two episodes given in *Kattōshū* Case 85 and Case 86.

The Layman was about to die. He spoke to Lingzhao, saying: "See how high the sun is and report to me when it's noon." Lingzhao quickly reported, "The sun has already reached the zenith, and there's an eclipse." While the Layman went to the door to look out, Lingzhao seated herself in her father's chair and, putting her palms together reverently, passed away. The Layman smiled and said: "My daughter has anticipated me." He postponed [his going] for seven days. (Sasaki, Iriya, and Fraser 1971, p. 75)

Case 87 女子定答 *Why the Woman Came Out of Samadhi*

虛堂、因僧問、文殊是七佛之師、因甚出女子定不得。師云、家鬼作
崇。僧云、罔明是下方聲聞、因甚却出得。師云、半幅全封。

A monk asked Xutang, "Mañjuśrī was the teacher of the Seven Buddhas.[1]
Why was he unable to bring the woman out of samadhi?"[2]

Xutang answered, "Because he was obstructed by his household spirits."[3]

The monk continued, "And why was Delusion, a low-level śrāvaka,[4] able
to make her emerge?"

"A half-sheet of paper is just right for wrapping,"[5] replied the master.

1. For the Seven Buddhas of the Past, see Case 34, note 2.

2. See Case 48.

3. Mujaku: Household spirits 家鬼 are ancestral spirits that generally work for
the benefit of their descendants, but occasionally their actions hurt the family
fortunes. In the present case, "household spirits" refers to Mañjuśrī's wisdom,
which put him so far above the level of the disciple that he was unable to help
her out of samadhi.

4. A śrāvaka ("voice-hearer") is a student who follows the teachings of the Buddha in order to attain nirvana. In Mahayana śrāvakas were criticized as concerned
only with their own salvation rather than with the liberation of all beings.

5. Mujaku: Just as small objects are more easily wrapped with small pieces
of paper than with large ones, so less mature students are often best helped by
bodhisattvas near their own level.

In the standard text of the *Kattōshū* this line is written 半幅全封, with 愊 ("sincerity") an obvious scribal error for 幅 ("a piece of paper").

Case 88 見色明心 *To See Form and Enlighten the Mind*[1]

雲門上堂云、作麼生是聞聲悟道、見色明心。擧起[手]曰、觀音菩薩
將錢來買餬餅。放下手曰、元來祇是饅頭。

Yunmen took the high seat and said, "What is it to hear sound and realize
the Way; to see form and enlighten the mind?"[2]

Raising his hand, Yunmen said, "Avalokiteśvara Bodhisattva brings
money and buys a sesame rice-cake." Lowering his hand, he said, "Actually,
it's a dumpling."[3]

1. Also *Record of Equanimity* 82.

2. For examples of enlightenment experiences precipitated by seeing forms

and hearing sounds, see Case 8, "Lingyun Sees Peach Blossoms," and Case 26, "Xiangyan's Sound of a Bamboo."

3. Yunmen apparently regarded sesame rice-cakes as a great delicacy; they are mentioned nineteen times in the *Comprehensive Record of Yunmen* 雲門廣錄. Dumplings were a plain, everyday type of food.

Yunmen's raised arm and lowered arm are usually interpreted to indicate, respectively, the realm of the transcendent and the realm of the relative. The arm gesture is believed to have its origin in the *Avataṃsaka Sutra* story of Sudhana's visit to Bhishmottaranirghosha, the eighth of the fifty-three teachers in the "Entry into the Realm of Reality" chapter. Bhishmottaranirghosha raises his hand and touches Sudhana's head, showing him the infinite worlds of the buddhas, beyond all bounds of space and time. Bhishmottaranirghosha then lowers his hand, and Sudhana is once again in the everyday world, standing in front of the bodhisattva.

Case 89   別峰相見   *A Meeting on Another Mountain*[1]

教中說、妙峰孤頂德雲比丘、從來不下山。善財去參、七日不逢。一日、却在別峰相見。及乎見了、却與他說一念三世一切諸佛、智慧光明、普見法門。圜悟云、德雲既不下山、因什麼却在別峰相見。若道他下山、教中說、德雲比丘、從來不曾下山、常在妙峰孤頂。到這裡、德雲與善財、的的在那裡。

In a sutra[2] it is written that Bhikku Meghaśri dwelt on the summit of Wondrous Mountain and never came down. Sudhana went to meet him but could not find him even after a week. One day, however, he encountered him on the peak of another mountain. After they met, the bhikku explained that a moment of thought penetrates the three worlds, manifested the wisdom-light of the myriad buddhas, and spoke of the unobstructed perception of the infinite buddha-lands.

Yuanwu Keqin commented, "If Meghaśri never came down from the peak of Wondrous Mountain, how then could he have met Sudhana on another mountain? You may say that he did leave the mountain, but it is written in the sutra that he never descended from the summit of Wondrous Mountain and was always there. So where exactly were Meghaśri and Sudhana?"

1. Also *Blue Cliff Record* 23, Commentary on the Main Case.
2. The sutra referred to is the *Avataṃsaka Sutra*, where Bhikku Meghaśri appears as the first of the fifty-three teachers Sudhana calls upon in the "Entry into the Realm of Reality" chapter.

Case 90   南泉水牯   *Nanquan's "Water Buffalo"*

趙州諗禪師、問南泉曰、知有底人、向甚處去。泉云、山前檀越家作
一頭水牯牛去。州云、謝師指示。泉云、昨夜三更月到窓。

Zhaozhou Congshen asked Nanquan Puyuan, "A person who knows it[1]—where should he go [when he dies]?"

Nanquan answered, "He should become a water buffalo at the believer's house by the foot of the mountain."

"Thank you, teacher, for this instruction," Zhaozhou said.

Nanquan said, "Last night at midnight the moonlight shone on the window."

1. See Case 79, note 2.

Case 91   雲門三句   *Yunmen's Three Statements*[1]

雲門三句、函蓋乾坤、截斷衆流、隨波逐浪。

The three statements of Yunmen:

It covers heaven and earth, like a lid on a box.
It severs all flows.
It rides the waves and sails the swells.[2]

1. Also *Blue Cliff Record* 90, Commentary on the Main Case. The third statement, 隨波逐浪, is also found in *Blue Cliff Record* 8, Introduction.

2. There are various interpretations of the three statements. The most generally accepted is that offered by the ZGDJ, which sees the statements as descriptive of the workings of a true Zen master:

The master's functioning perfectly fits that of the student;
The master cuts off the thoughts and delusions of the student;
The master matches his guidance to the capacities of the student and presses those capacities to the limit. (77a)

Case 92   薰風自南   *A Fragrant Breeze from the South*

徑山大慧杲禪師、一日聞圜悟陞堂、舉、僧問雲門、如何是諸佛出身
處。門曰、東山水上行。天寧即不然、忽有人問、如何是諸佛出身
處、只向他道、薰風自南來、殿閣生微涼。大慧言下便悟去。

One day Dahui Zonggao of Mount Jing heard Yuanwu Keqin say from the high seat:

> A monk asked Yunmen, "What is the place from which all buddhas come?"
>
> Yunmen replied, "East Mountain walks on the water."[1]
>
> But I wouldn't have said that. If someone were to ask me, "What is the place from which all buddhas come?" I would simply say:
>
> > A fragrant breeze blows from the south,
> > Giving rise in the palace to a refreshing coolness.[2]

At these words Dahui was greatly enlightened.[3]

1. See Case 49, above.

2. Yuanwu quotes from a famous poem by Liu Gongquan 柳公權 (778–865), a Tang-dynasty official known for his calligraphy and poetry. The verses were Liu's response to two lines presented by Emperor Wenzong 文宗 (809–40) in a linked-verse contest: "People suffer from the burning heat, but I always love the summer days."

3. This was only a partial awakening. For a description of Dahui's full enlightenment, see Case 32.

Case 93   百丈開田   *Baizhang's New Paddy*

洪州百丈山涅槃和尚、一日、謂僧云、汝與我開田了、我爲汝說大
義。僧開田了歸、請師說大義。師乃展開兩手。

Baizhang Weizheng (Niepan) of Hongzhao said to the monks, "If you clear a new rice paddy for me, I will explain to you the Great Principle."

After clearing the new paddy, the monks returned and asked the master to explain the Great Principle. The master held out his two hands.[1]

1. Baizhang indicates that there was nothing to impart, outside of the monks' act of clearing the paddy itself.

Case 94   華嚴心喻   *The* Avataṃsaka Sutra's *Simile of the Mind*

華嚴曰、心如工畫師、作種種五陰。一切世間中、莫不從心造。

In the *Avataṃsaka Sutra* it is written, "The mind is like an artist, ceaselessly producing the five skandhas.[1] In all the world, there is nothing that is not produced by the mind."[2]

1. The five skandhas are the transitory "aggregates" that constitute all physical, mental, and other elements in the phenomenal world. The five skandhas are:

1) form (*rūpa*);
2) sensation (*vedanā*);
3) perception (*saṃjñā*);
4) mental formations, particularly volition (*saṃskāra*);
5) consciousness (*vijñāna*).

2. T 9:465c. The verse in the *Avataṃsaka Sutra* reads, "The mind is like a painter / Who paints the five skandhas in all their forms; / In all of the worlds that exist; / There's nothing it doesn't create."

Case 95 運庵反衣 *Yun'an Returns the Vestment*

運庵、反松源衣之頌曰、老巖不負靈山記、颺下金襴如弊屣。

Regarding Yun'an Puyan's return of Baiyun Shouduan's vestment[1] to his teacher Songyuan Chongyue, [Beijian Jujian] wrote in praise:

> Venerable Puyan, true to Śākyamuni's transmission of the Dharma to Mahākāśyapa on the Vulture Peak,[2]
> Rejected the brocade vestment like a pair of worn-out sandals.[3]

1. "Vestment" translates 衣, which presently indicates a monk's robe but which in ancient China referred to the 袈裟, a large, rectangular clerical garment used in East Asian Buddhism. Worn around the body and over the ordinary robe, with the left shoulder covered and the right shoulder exposed, it corresponds to the original Buddhist robe of India, and thus symbolizes monkhood. It is generally worn only during rituals or, in some traditions, during meditation.

2. This refers to the Buddha's transmission of the Dharma to Mahākāśyapa on the Vulture Peak. See Case 135.

3. Songyuan Chongyue, nearing the end of his life, attempted to transmit the vestment of *Baiyun Shouduan*, his ancestor in the Dharma, to his disciple Yun'an, who was about to return to his home province, Siming. Yun'an, however, refused to accept it (though he did accept a portrait of Songyuan). The scene was reminiscent of Linji's refusal of Baizhang's backrest and armrest:

> One day [Linji] took his leave of Huangbo. Huangbo asked, "Where are you going?" "If I don't go to Henan, I'll return to Hebei," replied Linji. Huangbo hit at him. Linji seized Huangbo and gave him a slap. Laughing heartily, Huangbo called to his attendant, "Bring me the backrest and armrest that belonged to my late teacher Baizhang." "Attendant, bring me some fire!" cried Linji. "Be that as it may, just take them with you. In the future you'll sit on the tongue of every man on earth," said Huangbo. (Sasaki 2009, p. 47)

Case 96   讚六祖偈   *A Verse in Praise of the Sixth Patriarch*

圓悟禪師、讚六祖云、稽首曹溪眞古佛、八十生爲善知識。

Yuanwu Keqin said in praise of the Sixth Patriarch, "I prostrate myself before the true Old Buddha of Caoxi;[1] for eighty lives he was reborn as a wise friend and teacher."[2]

1. Caoxi 曹溪 was where the Sixth Patriarch resided.
2. For "wise friend and teacher," see Case 13, note 1.

Case 97   一子出家   *When Someone Is Ordained*

一子出家、九族生天、目連母因甚墮地獄。

When someone is ordained, nine generations of ancestors are reborn in the heavenly realms.[1] Why then did Maudgalyāyana's mother fall into hell?[2]

1. The statement that when a person is ordained nine generations of ancestors gain rebirth in heaven is found in several Zen texts, e.g., the *Record of Dongshan* (T 47:516b), but does not appear in any sutra in the Taishō Canon.
2. See also *Maudgalyāyana* in the Biographical Notes. The case draws upon the story that Maudgalyāyana, with his divine eye (one of his supernatural powers), saw his mother suffering in the realm of the hungry ghosts. Wishing to help her, he, together with the entire Buddhist community, made offerings.

Case 98   圓悟投機   *Yuanwu's Enlightenment Verse*

圓悟和尚、投機偈曰、金鴨香消錦繡帷、笙歌叢裡醉扶歸。少年一段
風流事、只許佳人獨自知。

In his enlightenment verse,[1] Yuanwu Keqin wrote:
> The fragrance of the golden-duck censer fades in the brocade curtains;
> Singing to the sound of a flute, I'm led home, drunk.[2]
> The deepest refinement of the youth
> Is for the lover alone to know.[3]

1. Enlightenment verses 投機 are traditionally written by Zen students to express the gist of their realization.
2. Dōmae notes that the phrase 醉扶歸, translated here as "I'm led home, drunk," is also the title of an ancient Chinese song.

3. According to *Compendium of the Five Lamps* 19, this poem was inspired by a verse Yuanwu heard from his teacher, *Wuzu Fayan*. A government official called upon Wuzu and asked what characterized the Zen school. Wuzu answered that a general sense of what it is about could be gained from the following poem: "I try to express my feelings but I am not able / Here in this back chamber I convey my sadness / By repeatedly calling my maid Little Jade, for no other reason / Than to have my man hear my voice."

"My man" refers to the lover of the young woman who wrote the poem. One day, seeing him near her residence, she wished to let him know that she was there. Careful of her reputation, however, she repeatedly called out to her maid Little Jade, for no other purpose than to let her lover hear her voice and make him aware of her presence.

Case 99 夾山境話 *Jiashan's Surroundings*

僧問夾山、如何是夾山境。山云、猿抱子歸青嶂後、鳥啣花落碧巖
前。法眼後大悟云、我二十年錯作境話會。

A monk asked Jiashan Shanhui, "What are Jiashan's surroundings?"[1]
Jiashan answered:

> Monkeys clasping their young return beyond the purple peaks
> Birds with flowers in their beaks alight in front of the blue cliff.[2]

Later Fayan Wenyi had a deep insight and commented, "For twenty years I misunderstood this story about Jiashan's surroundings."

1. "Surroundings" translates 境, a word with various meanings—"physical surroundings," "boundary," "circumstances," "stage," "state of mind"—that no single English term can adequately cover; here the meanings of "physical surroundings" and "state of mind" are both implied. In addition, the name Jiashan refers not only to Jiashan Shanhui the master but also to the mountain Jiashan 夾山, on which the master's monastery was located and from which the master derived his name. Thus the monk's question can signify not only "What are the natural surroundings of the monastery on Jiashan?" but also "What is Master Jiashan's state of mind?" The interrelation of these two meanings is evident in Chinese owing to the strong tendency in Zen to see the dharmakāya as manifested not only in the human mind but also in the phenomena of the natural world (this tendency was particularly strong in the Fayan school, the lineage founded by *Fayan Wenyi*, the master commenting above on Jiashan's verse). Master Jiashan's reply, too, reflects these profoundly meaningful ambiguities.

2. This verse was the inspiration for the title of the *Blue Cliff Record*, compiled by *Yuanwu Keqin* when he resided at Jiashan Shanhui's temple, Lingquan yuan.

Case 100   袈裟裏鞋   *Straw Sandals in My Vestment*[1]

僧問投子宗道者、如何是道者家風。者云、袈裟裏草鞋。僧云、不
審、意旨如何。者云、赤脚下桐城。

A monk asked Wayfarer Touzi Fazong, "What is your style of practice?"
Fazong replied, "Straw sandals in my vestment."
"What does that mean?" asked the monk.
"I go down to Tongcheng[2] in my bare feet," answered Fazong.[3]

1. Also *Blue Cliff Record* 58, Commentary on the Main Case.
2. Tongcheng was the town at the foot of the mountain on which Touzi's monastery was located.
3. Yamada: "Fazong's Zen is spontaneous, natural, and unaffected. Walking barefoot, he relies on neither the Dharma nor material things" (1985, 6:292–93).

Case 101   夾山掘坑   *Jiashan Digs a Hole*

夾山云、我二十年住此山、未曾舉著宗門中事。有僧問、承和尚有
言、二十年住此山、未曾舉著宗門中事、是否。山云、是。僧便掀倒
禪床。山休去。至明日普請掘一坑、令侍者請昨日問話僧來。山云、
老僧二十年、只說無義語、今請上座打殺老僧埋向坑中。若不打殺老
僧、上座自著打殺、埋此坑中。其僧束裝潛去。

Jiashan said, "I have lived on this mountain for twenty years but have never spoken of the Central Matter of our school."
A monk asked, "I heard that you claim never to have spoken of the Central Matter of our school in the twenty years you have been living on this mountain. Is this true?"
Jiashan replied, "It is."
Thereupon the monk pulled Jiashan off his seat. Jiashan retired.
The next day Jiashan ordered a pit to be dug, then told his attendant to summon the monk who had raised the question the day before. Jiashan said to him, "For the past twenty years, I have spoken nothing but nonsense. Please, venerable monk, beat me to death and bury me in this pit. If you cannot beat this old monk to death, then beat yourself to death and be buried." The monk gathered his belongings and secretly departed.[1]

1. Mujaku: The monk left not out of fear but because he rejected Jaishan's way of doing things; in this sense his silent departure was no different from his pulling

Jiashan off his seat. But he failed to understand Jiashan's attempt to guide him. If, when Jiashan challenged him to "beat yourself to death and be buried in this pit," the monk had raised his fist and retorted, "Let's see you bury *this*!" Jiashan would have given him the highest seat in the meditation hall.

Case 102   朝聞夕死   *Hear in the Morning, Die in the Evening*

夫子曰、朝聞道夕死可矣。

Confucius said, "Hear of the Way in the morning, die content in the evening!"[1]

1. *Analects* 4:8.

Case 103   平常是道   *Ordinary Mind Is the Way*[1]

南泉、因趙州問、如何是道。泉云、平常心是道。州云、還可假趣向否。泉云、擬向即乖。州云、不擬爭知是道。泉云、道不屬知不屬不知。知是妄覺、不知是無記。若眞達不疑之道、猶如大虛廓然洞豁。豈可強是非也。州於言下大悟。

Zhaozhou Congshen asked Nanquan Puyuan, "What is the Way?"
Nanquan said, "Ordinary mind is the Way."[2]
Zhaozhou asked, "Can we deliberately strive toward this?"
Nanquan said, "To strive is to diverge from it."
Zhaozhou said, "Without striving, how can we know the Way?"
Nanquan said, "The Way has nothing to do with knowing or not-knowing. 'Knowing' is delusion, 'not-knowing' is vacuity.[3] If you truly attain the Way-without-doubt, it is vast and boundless like open space. How can it be thought of in terms of right and wrong?"
At these words Zhaozhou was deeply enlightened.

1. Also *Wumen guan* 19, Main Case.
2. In his *Records* Mazu states:

> What is ordinary mind? Ordinary mind is without striving, without 'right' or 'wrong,' without grasping or rejection, without extinction or permanence, without 'sacred' or 'profane'.... Just as you're doing now, walking standing, sitting, lying, responding appropriately to all beings—all this is the Way.

3. "Vacuity" translates 無記, indicating a lack of content or function. Other possible translations include "oblivion" and "blankness."

Case 104   井楼請救   *Calling for Help from the Well Tower*

趙州、一日、在南泉時、在井樓上打水。見泉過乃抱定柱懸一脚云、
相救相救。泉遂於蹈梯上打云、一二三四五。師便下樓具威儀上方丈
云、適來謝和尚相救。虛堂代云、老僧不著便。

Zhaozhou Congshen, while a monk in the assembly under Nanquan Puyuan, was on the well tower one day drawing some water. Seeing Nanquan pass by, he grabbed a pillar, let one of his legs hang into the well, and shouted, "Save me! Save me!"

Nanquan hit the tower ladder and said, "One, two, three, four, five."

Zhaozhou thereupon came down from the tower. Putting on his robes, he went up to Nanquan's quarters and said, "Thank you for helping me a moment ago."

Xutang, commenting in place of Nanquan, said, "This old monk blundered."[1]

1. Xutang's comment expresses what he thought Nanquan should have said in response to Zhaozhou; "this old monk" would be Nanquan's way of referring to himself. The original Chinese expression for "blundered," 不著便, can be interpreted in many ways; depending upon the context, it can mean "unlucky," "at a loss," "inconvenient," or even "the message did not get through." The present translation follows Mujaku, who comments that in Xutang's view Nanquan should not have said "One, two, three, four, five." Mujaku sees the meaning of 不著便 as similar to that of the expression 得便宜是落便宜: to think that one has succeeded, only to find that one has failed (*Blue Cliff Record* 66, Verse).

ZGJT interprets 得便宜是落便宜 as, "To gain an advantage is to be trapped by advantage" (p. 352).

Case 105   路逢死蛇   *A Dead Snake in the Road*

夾山云、路逢死蛇莫打殺、無底籃子盛將歸。虛堂頌云、擔板漢、没
拘束。餓死首陽山、誓不食周粟。

Jiashan said, "If you find a dead snake in the road, don't kill it. Take it home in a bottomless basket."[1]

Xutang commented in a verse,

This board-carrier can't be restrained.[2]
Though he may starve to death on Mount Shouyang,
He's vowed never to eat the grain of Zhou.[3]

1. This statement by Jiashan is taken from a koan involving Jiashan and his student Fori Benkong 佛日本空 (n.d.), found in fascicle 13 of the *Compendium of the Five Lamps*:

> Fori, then sixteen and training under Jiashan after receiving transmission from *Yunju Daojian*, took tea one day to the monks at work in the fields. As he approached he rattled the teacups.
>
> When Jiashan looked at him, Fori said, "Monks cultivating the fields can use three or four cups of strong tea."
>
> Jiashan replied, "You have filled up the tea jug, but how many cups do you have in the basket?"
>
> Fori answered, "I have filled up the tea jug, but there's not a single cup in the basket." He proceeded to distribute tea to the monks, then commented, "Master, the assembly is hoping for a word from you."
>
> Jiashan responded, "If you find a dead snake in the road, don't kill it. Take it home in a bottomless basket."
>
> Fori commented, "If you hold a charm that illuminates the night, how many dawns would you see?"
>
> Jiashan said, "Monks! There's a true man here! Knock off work and go back to the monastery [to rest]!"
>
> They stopped work and went back. From that time on the community held Fori in the highest regard.

2. ZGJT: A "board-carrier" 擔板漢 is a person carrying a large plank on his shoulder, so that he is able to see in only one direction. The term usually indicates someone with a narrow way of viewing things, though it sometimes indicates firm determination. According to Mujaku, in this case it has the former meaning and refers to Jiashan.

3. The verse alludes to the story of the brothers Boyi 伯夷 and Shuqi 叔齊, recorded in the *Records of the Grand Historian* 史記. Boyi and Shuqi were princes of the state of Guzhu 孤竹 during the final years of the Yin dynasty (ca. 1500–1000 BCE). When the king died he bequeathed his realm to Shuqi, the younger but more able of the two brothers. Shuqi, however, would not accept the throne, as he refused to place himself above his elder brother Boyi. Boyi, for his part, also turned down the succession as he could not disobey the will of his father. Both brothers therefore left the kingdom.

Later, King Wu of Zhou 周武王 overthrew Di Xin 帝辛, the last king of the Yin dynasty, an act of disloyalty that the brothers refused to condone, even though the king had been an exceptionally evil ruler. They retired to live in the mountains as hermits, and finally starved to death on Mount Shouyang 首陽 rather than eat the food of a dynasty that had come into power through violence.

Mujaku: In this verse Xutang is saying that Jiashan is stuck in the realm of nothingness separate from the world of phenomena and will end up starving to death.

Case 106   慈明行心   *Ciming's Practice*

慈明、平生、以事事無礙行心、凡聖所不能測。

Ciming Chuyuan was always free and unrestricted in spirit.[1] No one could tell whether he was foolish or wise.

1. Ciming [Shishuang Chuyuan] is remembered in Zen for his often unconventional behavior (see, for example, Cases 147 and 174); the present koan draws on this image of the great master.

"Free and unrestricted" translates 事事無碍, which literally means "the unobstructed interpenetration of all things," a concept from the Huayan Buddhist doctrine of the four realms of the universe. These realms are:

i. the realm of phenomena 事法界,

ii. the realm of principle 理法界,

iii. the realm of the unobstructed and mutual interpenetration of principle and phenomena 理事無礙法界,

iv. the realm of the unobstructed and mutual interpenetration of phenomena and phenomena 事事無礙法界.

For the Huayan doctrine of the four realms, see also Case 160.

Case 107   大燈三問   *Daitō's Three Questions*

大燈國師云、如何是透脱一路、如何是身心不二、如何是因果。

National Teacher Daitō asked:

What is the single path to liberation?
What is nonduality of body and mind?
What is cause-and-effect?[1]

1. For cause-and-effect, see also Case 34.

Case 108   維摩金粟   *Vimalakīrti, the Golden-Millet Tathāgata*[1]

僧問雲居簡禪師、維摩是過去金粟如來、因甚在釋迦如來會下聽法。
簡曰、不是他爭人我。

A monk asked Yunju Daojian, "In a past life, Vimalakīrti was the Golden-Millet Tathāgata.[2] Why then did he study the Dharma as a disciple of Śākyamuni?"
Yunju replied, "Because he had no notions of self to contest."[3]

1. Also *Blue Cliff Record* 84, Commentary on the Verse.

2. The claim that in a past life Vimalakīrti was the Golden-Millet Tathāgata is not found in any extant sutra, although certain ancient masters, such as Jizang 吉藏 (549–623), identify it as originating in the *Essentials of Contemplation Sutra* 思惟三昧經. The earliest extant source is Wang Jin's 王巾 *Toutou Temple Stele Inscriptions* 頭陀寺碑文, fascicle 59.

3. The *Blue Cliff Record* has:

> Yunju said, "He didn't pit himself against others." Someone who is greatly liberated has nothing to do with becoming a buddha or not becoming a buddha. If you say such a one practices to attain buddhahood, this has even less to do with it. (Cleary 1998, pp. 372–73)

Case 109   胡子無鬚   *The Barbarian Has No Beard*[1]

水庵、示眾曰、西天胡子、因甚無鬚。

Shui'an Shiyi[2] asked the assembly, "Why does the barbarian from the West have no beard?"[3]

1. Also *Wumen guan* 4, Main Case.

2. The identification of the speaker in both the *Wumen guan* and the *Kattōshū* as *Huo'an Shiti* is an error; in the original biographical materials this statement is found in the entry for *Shui'an Shiyi*.

3. "The barbarian" is usually identified as Bodhidharma, who was known for his thick beard. Yamada comments that, in denying a known fact, this koan resembles a story about *Dongshan Liangjie*. Dongshan, while still a young boy studying at the local temple, was asked to recite the *Heart Sutra*. Coming to the phrase, "[There are] no eyes, no ears, no nose, no tongue, no thought," he stopped and asked, "But I do have eyes, ears, nose, and tongue. Why then does the sutra say that I don't?" The priest, recognizing the boy's ability, sent him for further study to the Zen master Wuxie Lingmo 五洩靈默 (747–818) (1976, pp. 37–38).

Case 110   心不是佛   *Mind Is Not Buddha*[1]

南泉、示眾云、心不是佛、智不是道。

Nanquan Puyuan said, "Mind is not buddha, wisdom is not the Way."

1. Also *Wumen guan* 34, Main Case. See also Case 5, above.

Case 111　清税孤貧　*Qingshui, Poor and Alone*[1]

曹山和尚、因僧問曰、清税孤貧、乞師賑濟。山云、税闍梨。税應
諾。山云、青原白家三盞酒、喫了猶道未濕唇。

The monk Qingshui said to Caoshan, "Master, I'm poor and alone. Please assist me."

Caoshan said, "Monk Qingshui!"

"Yes?" Qingshui responded.

Caoshan said, "You have had three cups of the best wine of Qingyuan,[2] and yet you claim not to have wet your lips."[3]

1. Also *Wumen guan* 10, Main Case.

2. Qingyuan was the region in which Caoshan was born and was famous for its fine wine.

3. Yamada comments that in Buddhism salvation is not "Knock and it shall be opened, seek and you shall find" but the realization that "though you knock not, it is already open; though you seek not, it is already found" (1976, p. 83).

Case 112　維摩丈室　*Vimalakīrti's Ten-Foot-Square Room*[1]

圜悟云、維摩乃過去古佛、亦有眷屬。助佛宣化、具不可思議辨才、
有不可思議境界、有不可思議神通妙用。於方丈室中容三萬二千獅
子寶座、與八萬大衆亦不寬狹。且道、是什麼道理。喚作神通妙用得
麼。且莫錯會。

Yuanwu Keqin said, "Vimalakīrti, who in the ancient past was a buddha,[2] possessed a family and helped Śākyamuni in his teaching. He had wondrous eloquence, wondrous perception, wondrous functioning, and wondrous powers. Inside his ten-foot-square room he placed thirty-two thousand jeweled-lion thrones and hosted an assembly of eighty thousand in perfect comfort.

"Tell me, what does this mean? Can one attribute it to the wondrous functioning of his supernatural powers? Don't get the wrong idea!"

1. Also *Blue Cliff Record* 84, Commentary on the Main Case. For background material on this case, see *Vimalakīrti* in the Biographical Notes.

2. In the ancient past, Vimalakīrti had been the Golden-Millet Tathāgata 金粟如來. See Case 108.

Case 113　佛性三轉　*Foxing's Three Turning-Phrases*

> 佛性禪師三轉語曰、向上一路、千聖共行、調達因甚入地獄。達磨不
> 來東土、二祖不往西天、玄沙因甚趯破脚指頭。打破虛空底人、向甚
> 麼處安著。

Gulin Qingmao (Zen Master Foxing) gave three turning-phrases:

> If all sages practice the single path to true enlightenment together, why
> did Devadatta fall into hell?[1]
> "Bodhidharma didn't come to China; the Second Patriarch didn't go to
> India." What, then, of Xuansha Shibei's stumbling and hurting his toe?[2]
> Those who have broken through the void—where can they rest?

1. The question refers to the legend that Devadatta (Śākyamuni's cousin who attempted to usurp the Buddha's position as head of the sangha, caused schisms in the sangha, and made several attempts on Śākyamuni's life) fell into hell while still alive. See *Devadatta* in the Biographical Notes.

It is of interest to note that, outside this koan, the statement "all sages practice the single path to true enlightenment together" 向上一路千聖共行 does not occur in the Zen literature. Rather, the position taken by Zen is that "the sages have never transmitted the single road to enlightenment" 向上一路千聖不傳 (e.g., Panshan Baoji 盤山寶積; x 80:77b). *Mian Xianjie* goes so far as to say, "Though a thousand sages join hands and travel the single path to enlightenment together, all will surely fall into hell" (x 80:441c).

2. The comment and question refer to the episode from Xuansha Shibei's biography, mentioned also in Case 43, in which Xuansha was leaving his native Fujian on pilgrimage to visit masters in other parts of China. As he reached the top of the mountain pass at the border of Fujian he stumbled and injured his toe, the pain of which precipitated a deep enlightenment experience. Xuansha thereupon exclaimed, "Bodhidharma didn't come to China, the Second Patriarch didn't go to India!" He then turned around and returned to Fujian.

Case 114　世尊初生　*When the Buddha Was Born*

> 世尊初生下、一手指天、一手指地、七步周行、目顧四方云、天上天下
> 唯我獨尊。雲門拈云、我當時若見、一棒打殺、與狗子令喫却。貴要天
> 下大平。瑯琊覺云、雲門可謂、將此身心奉塵刹、是則名爲報佛恩。

When the Buddha was born, he pointed to the sky with one hand and to the
earth with the other. He then walked seven steps in a circle, looked in each

of the four directions, and said, "Above the heavens and below, I alone am the Honored One."[1]

Yunmen commented, "If I'd seen the Buddha say that, I would have killed him with a blow of my staff and fed him to the dogs. It's important that the world be at peace."

Langye Huijue commented, "Yunmen, with body and mind, served the infinite worlds. This is known as requiting the benevolence of the Buddha."[2]

1. These are the first two lines of the Buddha's "birth verse," which he recited, according to legend, after his birth from his mother's side in the Lumbinī Grove. The full verse reads:

> Above the heavens and below,
> I alone am the Honored One.
> The triple world is full of suffering;
> It is I who will relieve it.

The source of the verse in this form appears to be the *Miscellany of the Mūlasarvāstivāda Vinaya* 根本說一切有部毘奈耶雜事 (T 24:298a), although the similar verse "In all of the worlds, I alone am the Honored One" 一切世間 唯我 獨尊 appears in the *Sutra of the Collection of the Original Acts of the Buddha* 佛 本行集經 (T 3:699a).

2. "Requiting the benevolence of the Buddha" is an expression from the *Śūraṅgama Sutra*: "At the *Śūraṅgama* assembly, Ānanda praised the Buddha, saying, 'With my whole heart I will serve all beings throughout the universe.' This is called 'requiting the benevolence of the Buddha'" (T 19:119b).

It is noteworthy that the expression "whole heart" 深心 (lit., "deep mind"), found in the *Śūraṅgama Sutra* and other sutras, is often changed to "body and mind" 身心 when quoted in Zen materials such as the present koan.

Case 115   南泉失火   *Nanquan Loses the Fire*

僧問南泉、端居丈室、將何指示人。泉云、昨夜三更失却牛、天曉起
來失却火。

A monk asked Nanquan Puyuan, "As you formally sit in your quarters,[1] how do you guide people?"

Nanquan replied, "Last night at midnight I lost the ox; this morning as dawn arrived I lost the fire."[2]

1. This refers to the master sitting in his room receiving monks for *sanzen* instruction. The exchange related here occurred just after Nanquan's installation as abbot of the monastery.

2. ZGJI: "Midnight" and "ox" are metaphors for darkness (equality); "dawn" and "fire" are metaphors for light (duality). Thus Nanquan has forgotten both equality and duality.

Case 116　潙山摘茶　*Guishan Picks Tea*

潙山與仰山摘茶次、潙云、終日只聞子聲、不見子形。仰遂撼茶樹。
潙云、子只得其用、不得其體。［仰曰、未審、和尚如何。潙良久］。
仰云、和尚只得其體、不得其用。潙云、放子三十棒。

One day Guishan Lingyou was picking tea with Yangshan Huiji. Guishan said, "All day long I've heard your voice but haven't seen your form."[1]

Yangshan shook the tea bush. Guishan commented, "You have the function but you don't have the essence."

"How about the master?" Yangshan replied. Guishan remained silent.[2]

"You have the essence but you don't have the function," Yangshan responded.

"I spare you thirty blows of my staff," said Guishan.

1. The word 聲, translated here as "voice," is interpreted by some masters to be the sound of Yangshan's tea-picking.

2. This line has been added to the *Kattōshū* text on the basis of the original version in *Compendium of the Five Lamps* 9.

Case 117　百丈不食　*Baizhang's "No Eating"*

百丈云、一日不作、一日不食。

Baizhang Huaihai said, "A day of no work—a day of no eating."[1]

1. Baizhang Huaihai was known for the importance he placed on physical work as part of Zen monastic practice (see *Baizhang Huaihai* in the Biographical Notes; for another koan on the place of labor in Zen, see Case 93). The inclusion of labor as a central element of the monastic lifestyle was a radical departure from Indian Buddhist monasticism, in which labor (for which the Sanskrit word is "karma") was strictly forbidden. Farming was particularly proscribed, as it involved not only the production of karma but also the unavoidable taking of sentient life during the processes of cultivation.

Case 118　南嶽說似　*Nanyue's Explanation*

六祖、因問南嶽讓和尚云、甚處來。讓云、嵩山安國師處來。祖云、
恁麼來物是誰。讓經八年、方下語云、說似一物即不中。祖云、還假
修證否。讓云、修證則不無、染污則不得。

The Sixth Patriarch asked Nanyue Huairang where he had come from.

"From the place of National Teacher Songshan Hui'an," said Huairang.

The Sixth Patriarch asked, "And *who* is it that has come?"

Only after eight years could Huairang respond. He said, "Any explanation is off the mark."[1]

The master asked, "Does it involve practice and realization?"

Huairang said, "Although practice and realization are not uncalled-for, it has never been defiled."[2]

1. Waddell translates this as "The moment I said it was 'this' I'd miss the mark completely" (1984, p. 130).

2. Although practice and realization are almost always part of the path for those who awaken, the mind that one awakens to is undefiled from the start.

Case 119　洛浦供養　*Luopu's "Offerings"*

洛浦、因僧問、供養百千諸佛、不如供養一箇無心道人。未審、百千
諸佛有何過、無心道人有何德。浦云、一片白雲橫谷口、幾多歸鳥夜
迷巢。

A monk asked Luopu Yuan'an, "A single follower of the Way free of thought is more worthy of offerings than a hundred thousand buddhas.[1] What is the failing of the buddhas, and what is the merit of the follower of the Way?"

Luopu answered, "A wisp of white cloud blocks the mouth of the valley; many returning birds cannot find their nests in the night."[2]

1. This statement has its source in the *Sutra in Forty-two Sections* 四十二章經, section 11. The passage reads in part:

> Offering food to a single pratyekabuddha surpasses offering food to one billion arhats. Offering food to a single buddha of the three periods of time surpasses offering food to ten billion pratyekabuddhas. Offering food to a single person of no-thought, no-abiding, no-cultivation, and no-attainment surpasses offering food to a hundred billion buddhas.

2. The ZGJI comments: "Deluded students who seek outside themselves even-

tually have no place to return." Conversely, the *Zen Phrase Lexicon* 句双葛藤鈔 says: "The valley is a no-minded wayfarer; the returning birds are mind and thoughts—fine it is that they lose their way."

Case 120   雲門一曲   *Yunmen's Tune*

雲門、僧問、如何是雲門一曲。門曰、臘月二十五。

A monk asked Yunmen, "What is Yunmen's tune?"[1]

Yunmen answered, "The twenty-fifth day of the twelfth month."[2]

1. The monk is asking, "What is Yunmen's teaching?," playing off the fact that "Yunmen" was the name of an ancient Chinese song.

2. The twenty-fifth day of the twelfth month is the end of the year. Regarding such interpretations, however, Dōmae quotes *Blue Cliff Record* 27, Commentary on the Main Case:

> If you seek Yunmen's meaning in his words you have already gone wrong. There are among Yunmen's statements many which people enjoy interpreting conceptually. If one understands him intellectually, one must mourn for one's descendants.

Case 121   趙州救火   *Zhaozhou's "Put Out the Fire!"*

趙州到黄檗。檗見來便閉却門。州於法堂内把火云、救火救火。檗便出擒住云、道道。州云、賊過後張弓。

When Zhaozhou Congshen called upon Huangbo, Huangbo saw him coming and shut the door.

Zhaozhou went to the Dharma Hall, where, torch in hand, he shouted, "Put out the fire! Put out the fire!"

Huangbo came out and grabbed him. "Speak! Speak!" he demanded.

Zhaozhou replied, "That's drawing the bow after the thief has left!"

Case 122   黄檗烏藤   *Huangbo's Staff*

黄檗、對臨濟施六十烏藤。

Huangbo gave Linji sixty blows with his staff.[1]

1. See Case 187.

Case 123 濟下三評 *Comparing Three Students of Linji*

光明藏鎮州三聖院慧然禪師章、寶曇曰、臨濟之門有寶壽三聖興化、
猶馬祖之門有百丈南泉歸宗也。百丈似馬祖而有氣力、歸宗似馬祖
而絶豪邁、南泉似馬祖而絶恢廓。以是知、寶壽似臨濟而篤實、三聖
似臨濟而駿發、興化似臨濟而困粹。篤實在青天喫棒處、打胡釘鉸
處見。駿發在召寂子打香嚴處、推倒德山、滅却正法眼藏處見。困粹
在紫羅帳裡撒眞珠、與面前橫兩遭處見。雖然各得其一、猶爲百世臨
濟、況得其全。豈不爲千萬世臨濟哉。愚常恨、棒喝不施於今世而臨
濟之道微。豈後之學者、力有所不能堪。抑其師之有所未盡其旨。如
人飲水冷暖自知、。興化一瓣香、自艱艱辛苦得之。所以盛大。

In the "Zen Master Huiran of Sansheng Temple" chapter of the *Treasury of Bright Light*, Juzhou Baotan says:

The disciples Baoshou Zhao, Sansheng Huiran, and Xinghua Cunjiang under Linji were much like the disciples Baizhang Huaihai, Guizong Zhichang, and Nanquan Puyuan under Mazu.

Baizhang resembled Mazu in his strength of character; Guizong resembled Mazu in his depth of talent; and Nanquan resembled Mazu in his greatness of mind. In the same way, Baoshou resembled Linji in his sincerity, Sansheng resembled Linji in his keenness, and Xinghua resembled Linji in his subtlety and depth.

The sincerity of Baoshou is seen in how he applied the staff to the clear blue sky,[1] and in how he struck Rivet-and-Shears Hu.[2] The keenness of Sansheng is seen in his exchange with Yangshan Huiji,[3] and also in the way he struck Xiangyan,[4] pushed over Deshan,[5] and extinguished Linji's True Dharma Eye.[6] The subtlety and depth of Xinghua is seen in his scattering of pearls in the purple-curtained room,[7] and in the way he waved his hand two times in front of the monk's face.[8] Though they each gained but a single of the master's qualities, still Linji's Zen has lasted a hundred generations. If all his qualities were grasped, how could Linji's Zen fail to flourish for a thousand or ten thousand generations?

What always troubles me is that if the stick and shout are not applied to the present generation, Linji's Dharma will decline. Why should there be anything that later generations cannot do if they but make the effort? The problem is that their teachers have not yet fully penetrated Linji's Dharma. It is like drinking water and knowing for oneself whether it is cold or warm. Xinghua's stick of incense[9]—this was gained through hardship and effort. Therefore Linji's Dharma flourishes.

1. A monk asked, "When there's not a cloud for ten thousand miles, what then?" Baoshou answered, "The clear sky should taste the staff!" The monk said, "What offense has the clear sky committed?" Baoshou struck him (*Compendium of the Five Lamps*, "Baoshou").

2. Rivet-and-Shears Hu (Hu Dingjiao) called upon Baoshou Zhao.[a] Baoshou said, "I've long heard about Rivet-and-Shears Hu. Is that you?"[b] "Yes," Hu answered. Baoshou asked, "Can you can drive a rivet into the void?" Hu replied, "Break it open, master, and bring it here!" Baoshou struck him. Hu didn't accept this. Baoshou said, "In the future, a talkative monk will clarify this matter for you." Hu later visited Zhaozhou and told him of this conversation. Zhaozhou asked, "Why were you hit by Baoshou?" Hu said, "I don't know what my error was." Zhaozhou said, "You couldn't even deal with this one split seam! How could you ask Baoshou to break open the void and bring it to you?" Hu was silent. Zhaozhou then said, "Just rivet shut that split seam." At these words Hu had an understanding (*Blue Cliff Record* 48, Commentary).

    a. Hu Dingjiao's name, 胡釘鉸, derived from the fact that he was a tinker (釘 means "nail" or "rivet," 鉸 means "scissors" or "shears").

    b. Hu was well known in China as a poet before starting his Zen study.

3. Sansheng Huiran arrived at Yangshan Huiji's place. Yangshan asked him, "What is your name?" Sansheng answered, "Huiji." Yangshan said, "Huiji is *my* name." Sansheng replied, "My name is Huiran." Yangshan laughed heartily (*Compendium*, "Sansheng").

4. Sansheng went to Xiangyan Zhixian's place. Xiangyan asked, "Where did you come from?" Sansheng answered, "From Linji." Xiangyan said, "Did you bring Linji's shout?" Sansheng hit Xiangyan in the mouth with his sitting cloth (*Compendium*, "Sansheng").

5. Sansheng went to Deshan Xuanjian's place and started to spread his sitting cloth [to pay obeisance]. Deshan said, "Don't spread your napkin—we don't have even leftover soup and spoiled rice." Sansheng said, "Even if you did, there's no place to put it." Deshan struck him. Sansheng grabbed Deshan's staff and pushed him onto the meditation platform. Deshan laughed heartily (*Compendium*, "Sansheng").

6. See Case 195.

7. Xinghua addressed the assembly, "I hear shouts in the front corridor and shouts in the back quarters. All of you, don't make blind shouts or wild shouts. Even if you shouted me up into the sky I'd come back down, and though I might not have a breath of air in me I'd revive and say, 'That's still not enough!' Why? Because I have yet to scatter pearls for you inside the purple-curtained room." (*Compendium*, "Xinghua"; "scattering pearls for you inside the purple-curtained room" indicates Xinghua's revealing his deepest understanding in the *sanzen* room.)

8. See Case 184.

9. Following Linji's death, Xinghua studied further under his fellow student Sansheng, from whom, he said, he learned the meaning of Linji's "host" and "guest." He then studied under Dajue, another of Linji's Dharma successors. When he inquired about the Dharma, Dajue threatened him with a beating. At this Xinghua

awoke to the deep meaning of the severe beatings Linji had received at the hand of his teacher Huangbo (see Case 187).

Xinghua later said that, had he stopped with Sansheng's teaching, his understanding would have been incomplete; under Dajue, he attained true realization. Nevertheless, at the ceremony in the Dharma Hall when Xinghua assumed the abbacy of a monastery and held up a stick of incense to announce whose successor he was, he said, "Elder brother Sansheng was too far above[a] me to merit this stick of incense; elder brother Dajue was too liberal.[b] It is best, therefore, that I offer it to my late teacher Linji."

> a. "Too far above" translates 孤, which usually means "solitary" or "lonely," but which in this case has a nuance of grandeur, like a solitary peak standing above all others.
>
> b. "Liberal" translates 賒, which has a variety of meanings, including "to buy or sell on credit," "to treat," "to stretch," "distant," "lenient," "loose," and "gentle." Here the meaning probably corresponds to "lenient," although it is difficult to define the exact sense in which the word is being used.

Case 124 世尊蓮目 *The World-Honored-One's Lotus Eyes*

風穴上堂云、世尊以青蓮目顧視大眾。乃曰、正恁麼時、且說箇甚麼。道不說而說、又是埋沒先聖。且道、說箇甚麼。念法華乃拂袖下去。穴擲下拄杖歸方丈。侍者隨後請益曰、念法華因甚麼不祇對和尚。穴曰、念法華會去也。

Fengxue Yanzhao went to the hall and said, "The World-Honored-One looked upon the assembly with his blue-lotus eyes."[1]

Then he asked, "At that moment, what was the Buddha teaching? If you say he was teaching by not teaching, you are slighting the Old Sage. So tell me, what was he teaching?"[2]

At this, Shoushan Shengnian shook his sleeves and left.

Fengxue threw down his staff and returned to his quarters. His attendant, following after him, asked, "Why didn't Shengnian answer you?"

"Because Shengnian understood," replied Fengxue.

1. "Blue-lotus eyes" 青蓮目 are one of the thirty-two marks of a buddha. In the Zen school the term "blue-lotus eyes" has come to mean eyes able to discern the true from the false. This case is the same in intent to Case 135, "The World-Honored-One Holds Up a Flower."

2. For background material, see *Shoushan Shengnian* in the Biographical Notes.

Case 125   東西密付   *The Secret Transmission from West to East*

竺土大僊心、東西密相付。作麼生是密付底。

The true mind of the Great Sage of India was secretly transmitted from west to east.[1] What was it that was secretly transmitted?

1. This statement comes from the "In Praise of Identity" 參同契 (T 51:2076), a short poem by *Shitou Xiqian*.

Case 126   孔子一變   *Confucius's "Changes"*

齊一變至於魯、魯一變至於道。道一變至何處。

With one change, Qi could attain to the level of Lu; with one change, Lu could attain to the Tao. With one change, to what would the Tao attain?[1]

1. Based on *Analects*, "Yong Ye 雍也" [6:24]. Qi and Lu were ancient Chinese countries.

Case 127   治生産業   *Earning a Living and Producing Things*

法華曰、治生産業、皆與實相、不相違背。

In the *Lotus Sutra* it is written, "Earning a living and producing things—these activities are all in accord with the true Dharma."[1]

1. This paraphrases a line from "The Teacher of the Law" chapter 法師功德品 of the *Lotus Sutra*:

> If good men or good women accept and uphold this sutra after the Thus Come One has entered extinction, if they read it, recite it, explain and preach it, or transcribe it, they will acquire twelve hundred mind benefits.... If they should expound some text of the secular world or speak on matters of government or those relating to wealth and livelihood, they will in all cases conform to the correct Law. (T 9:50a; Watson 1993b, p. 263)

Part 2

Case 128　德山燒疏　*Deshan Burns His Commentaries*[1]

龍潭信禪師、因德山侍立抵夜。師云、更深、子何不下去。山遂珍重
揭簾而出。見外面黑、却回云。門外黑。師乃點紙燭度與山。山擬
接。師便吹滅。山當下大悟作禮。師云、[子]見箇甚麼道理。山云、
某甲從今日去、不疑天下老和尚舌頭也。師至明日上堂告衆云、可
中有箇漢、牙如劍樹、口似血盆、一棒打不回頭、他時向孤峰頂上、
立吾道去在。山遂取平日疏鈔、於法堂前[將一炬火]提起云、窮諸玄
辨、若一毫致於大虛、竭世樞機、似一滴投於巨壑。將疏鈔便燒却、
禮辭而去。

Once, when Deshan Xuanjian had attended Longtan Chongxin until late in
the evening, Longtan said, "It is late. Why don't you go now?"

Deshan bid his teacher good night and raised the screen to leave. Seeing
how black the night was, however, he turned back and said, "It is dark outside." Longtan lit a paper torch[2] and offered it to Deshan, but just as Deshan
was about to take it the master blew it out. At that moment Deshan was deeply
enlightened. He bowed to Longtan, who asked, "What truth have you seen?"

Deshan replied, "From now on I'll never doubt the words of venerable
priests anywhere."

The next day Longtan took the high seat in the hall and said, "If there's
someone with fangs like a row of swords and a mouth like a bowl of blood,
who doesn't look back though hit with a stick, some day he'll climb to the
top of a solitary peak and there establish our Way."

Afterward Deshan took the commentaries he had been studying and,
holding a torch in front of the Dharma Hall, said, "Though one masters
the profoundest doctrines, it's like casting a single hair into the great void.
Though one accomplishes the world's most important tasks, it's like throwing a drop of water into the vast ocean." He then set fire to his commentaries, bowed to Longtan, and left.

1. Also *Wumen guan* 28, Main Case; *Blue Cliff Record* 4, Commentary on the Main Case.

2. A paper torch 紙燭 is a cord of twisted, oiled paper used as a taper.

Case 129　洞山地神　*Dongshan and the Earth Spirit*[1]

洞山和尚、一生住院、土地神覓他蹤跡不見。一日、廚前抛撒米麪。

洞山起心曰、常住物色、何得作踐如此。土地神遂得一見、便禮拜。

Though Dongshan Liangjie spent his life at the temple, the local earth spirit,[2] search though he might, couldn't locate so much as a trace of him.

Then one day Dongshan noticed some grain scattered on the ground in front of the kitchen. He became angry and said, "How could community supplies be wasted like this!"

At that moment the earth spirit finally detected him and paid him homage.

1. Also *Blue Cliff Record* 97, Commentary on the Verse.

2. Local earth spirits 土地神 are the tutelary deities of a particular region. In East Asian Zen monasteries these spirits are usually honored in a small "earth-spirit shrine" 土地堂.

Case 130　興化罰錢　*Xinghua Levies a Fine*

興化獎禪師、一日謂克賓維那云、汝不久爲唱導之師。賓云、我不入這保社。師云、你會了不入、不會了不入。賓云、總不恁麼。師便打云、克賓維那、法戰不勝、罰錢設饡飯。次日、興化入堂、白槌云、克賓維那、法戰不勝、罰錢五貫、設饡飯一堂、仍須出院。賓後出世、住太行山嗣興化。

One day Xinghua Cunjiang said to Taihang Kebin, the duty-monk,[1] "Soon you will become a teacher who guides others."

"I won't join that bunch!" answered Kebin.

"You won't join because you have fully understood, or you won't join because you haven't fully understood?" asked Xinghua.

"It's got nothing to do with any of that!" replied Kebin.

Thereupon Xinghua struck him and said, "Duty-monk Kebin lost a Dharma-battle. You must pay a fine to buy a rice-and-vegetable dinner."

The next day Xinghua entered the hall, struck the gavel, and said, "Duty-monk Kebin failed to win a Dharma-battle. He must pay a fine of five strings of cash, with which the assembly will be treated to a rice-and-vegetable dinner. Then he must leave the monastery."

Kebin left and went to live on Mount Taihang, and later succeeded to Xinghua's teachings.[2]

1. For "duty-monk," see Case 34, note 4.

2. A monk would announce whose successor he was only upon assuming the position of abbot at an official temple. See, e.g., Case 123, note 9.

Case 131   麻谷手巾   *Magu and the Hand-Cloth*

麻谷、一日紙帳内坐。以手巾蓋頭。披雲入見、便作哭聲、良久出去
法堂、繞禪床一匝再來。谷去却手巾而坐。雲云、死中得活、萬中
無一。谷下床作抽坐具勢。雲近前把住曰、前死後活、你還甘否。谷
云、甘即甘、阿師堪作什麼。雲推開云、知道你前言不副後語。

One day Magu Baotie was sitting inside a paper curtain,[1] his head covered with a hand-cloth.[2] Piyun entered, saw this, and gave a mournful cry. After a moment he went out to the Dharma Hall, circled the meditation seat once, then went again to where Magu was. Magu had removed the cloth and was sitting.

Piyun said, "Not one in ten thousand gains life within death!"

Magu came down from his seat and started to spread his sitting cloth.[3] Piyun stepped forward, grabbed him, and demanded, "A moment ago you were dead, now you've came back to life—are you alright with that?"

"I'm alright, though it's of no consequence to me."[4]

Piyun pushed him away and said, "I see. But what you said first doesn't match what you said next."[5]

1. Paper curtains were used as windbreaks on cold days.

2. Mujaku: A hand-cloth 手巾 was a small cloth placed over the face of the corpse at the wake. Magu sitting with this on his head signifies death; sitting without it signifies life.

3. A sign of respect. See Case 37, note 2.

4. Mujaku: The term 阿師 usually refers to the other person, but here it represents the speaker, that is, Magu.

5. What Magu said first is his statement "I'm alright"; what he said next is his statement "Though it's of no consequence to me." Mujaku: Piyun sees that Magu is beyond life and death.

Case 132 疎山壽塔 *Shushan's Memorial Tombstone*[1]

撫州疎山仁禪師、因主事僧、爲師造壽塔了、來白師。師曰、汝將幾
錢與匠人。僧云、一切在和尚。師云、爲將三文與匠人好、爲將兩文
與匠人好、爲將一文與匠人好、若道得與吾親造壽塔。其僧茫然。羅
山時在大庾嶺住庵。後有僧、到大嶺舉似前話。嶺云、還有人道得
麼。僧云、未有人道得。嶺云、你歸舉似疎山道。若將三文與匠人、
和尚此生決定不得塔。若將兩文與匠人、和尚與匠人共出一隻手。若
將一文與匠人、帶累匠人眉鬚墮落。僧回舉似疎山。師具威儀、遙望
大嶺、禮拜讚歎云、將謂無人。大庾嶺有古佛、放光射至此間。雖然
也是臘月裡蓮花。大嶺聞得云、我與麼道、早是龜毛長數尺。

The head monk came and told Shushan Guangren that construction of the master's memorial tombstone was finished. Shushan asked the monk, "How much money will you give the mason?"

"I will leave that entirely to you," the monk replied.

The master asked, "Is it best to give the mason three coins, is it best to give him two coins, or is it best to give him one coin? If you're able to answer, that indeed would be the finest memorial tombstone you could build for me." The monk was dumbfounded.

At that time Luoshan Daoxian was living in a hermitage on Dayu Peak. One day a monk went to the mountain and told Luoshan of the conversation between Shushan and the head monk.

"Has anyone been able to say anything?" asked Luoshan.

"As yet, no one," replied the monk.

"Then," said Luoshan, "go back and tell Shushan that if he gave the mason three coins he would never get a memorial tombstone in his entire life; if he gave him two coins, he and the mason would work on the tombstone together; if he gave him one coin, he and the mason would both lose their eyebrows."[2]

The monk went back and gave the message to Shushan. The master assumed a dignified manner, gazed toward Dayu Peak, bowed, and said, "I thought there was no one who could say anything, but on Dayu Peak is an old buddha emitting a brilliant light that reaches even to here. Nonetheless, this is a case of a lotus blooming in the twelfth month."[3]

Upon hearing of Shushan's words, Luoshan said: "I would have said, 'The tortoise's tail hairs are already several feet longer.'"[4]

1. "Memorial tombstone" translates 壽塔, a gravestone erected by monks or nuns prior to their death.

2. "Coin" translates 文, a small unit of money. Yoshizawa (2003, p. 136) com-

ments: "Three coins" signifies "smearing oneself with mud and drenching oneself with water," that is, adjusting the level of one's teaching to the capacity of lower level learners. "Two coins" signifies the secondary principle (verbal or relative explanation), employed as an upāya to guide middle-level learners. "One coin" signifies the transcendent principle, employed to guide learners of the highest capacity. For "losing one's eyebrows," see Case 44, note 2.

3. "A lotus blooming in the twelfth month" is a metaphor for something exceedingly rare, impossible, or fabulous.

4. "Tortoise's tail hairs" is a metaphor for something that does not exist.

Case 133   塡王思佛   *King Udayana Thinks of the Buddha*

南泉、一日、喚院主。主應諾。師云、佛九十日在切利天、爲母說
法。優塡王思佛。請目連運神通三轉攝匠人。往彼彫佛像。只彫得三
十一相。爲甚麼梵音相彫不得。主便問、如何是梵音相。師云、賺殺
人。古德頌云、紫金光聚照山河、天上人間意氣多。曾勅文殊領徒
衆、毘耶城裡問維摩。

One day Nanquan Puyuan called, "Head monk!"

"Yes!" the head monk replied.

Nanquan said, "During the time that the Buddha was in the Trāyastrimśa Heaven[1] preaching the Dharma to his mother, King Udayana missed him and decided to ask Maudgalyāyana for help.[2] Maudgalyāyana employed his supernatural powers three times to transport a sculptor to the Trāyastrimśa Heaven. The sculptor was able to represent thirty-one of the Buddha's thirty-two distinguishing characteristics;[3] why wasn't he able to represent the characteristic of the Noble Voice?"

"What is the Noble Voice?" asked the head monk.

"Deceiving people!"[4] Nanquan answered.

An ancient worthy commented in verse:

The Buddha's radiance illumines mountains and rivers;
The heavens and the earth are filled with his virtue.
He once told Mañjuśrī to lead a great assembly of disciples
To visit Vimalakīrti in Vaiśālī."[5]

1. In Buddhist cosmology, Trāyastrimśa Heaven (the Heaven of the Thirty-three Deities) is the second of the heavens in the realm of desire, located on a plateau atop Mount Sumeru. In the center is the palace of the god Indra, and at each of the four cardinal directions is a mountain where eight deities reside.

2. King Udayana is said to have been the king of Kauśāmbī and a great

devotee of the Buddha. According to the *Zengyi ahan jing* 增一阿含經 28, when the Buddha ascended to the Trāyastrimśa Heaven to preach the Dharma to his deceased mother, King Udayana missed him so much that he had an image of the Buddha carved. When the Buddha returned from Trāyastrimśa Heaven the king showed him the image, which the Buddha praised as an excellent upāya for teaching. This image is traditionally said to have been the first buddha image made and to have eventually been enshrined at Seiryō-ji in Kyoto. In fact, images of the Buddha were not made until several centuries after the Buddha's death.

3. The thirty-two distinguishing characteristics 三十二相 are the primary physical marks of a buddha and a cakravartin (wheel king; see Case 146, note 6), the difference being that a buddha possesses eighty secondary characteristics that a cakravartin lacks. Lists of the characteristics differ to some extent; for the version found in the *Mahāvyutpatti*, see Hurvitz 1980, pp. 353–55.

4. Dōmae: "People are deceived that some special 'Noble Voice' exists." *Shoushan Shengnian*, when asked what the Noble Voice was, responded, "Donkeys bray, dogs bark" (x 80:233b).

5. A reference to the *Vimalakīrti Sutra*, in which an enormous multitude of beings, led by Mañjuśrī, visit Vimalakīrti in his ten-foot-square chamber. See *Vimalakīrti* in the Biographical Notes. The "ancient worthy" is *Xutang Zhiyu*.

Case 134   首山竹篦   *Shoushan's Stick*[1]

汝州首山省念禪師、因拈竹篦示衆云、汝等諸人、若喚作竹篦即觸、
喚不作竹篦即背。汝諸人、且喚作什麼。時葉縣省和尚、在會下、乃
近前擘得、折作兩截、抛向階下却云、是什麼。師云、瞎。大慧禪師
拈云、速道速道。

Shoushan Shengnian of Ruzhou held up his stick[2] and said to the assembly, "Everyone, call this a stick and you violate its name;[3] say it's not a stick and you deny what it is. So, everyone, what do you call it?"

The priest Shexian Guixing, who at the time was studying under Shoushan, went up and seized the stick, broke it in half, and threw the pieces under the altar. "What's this?" he asked.

Shoushan said, "Blind!"

Commenting on this story, Dahui said, "Quick, speak! Quick, speak!"

1. Also *Wumen guan* 43, Main Case.

2. A master's stick 竹篦 is a short staff of about two to three feet in length and curved like a small bow. It is carried by a master as a badge of office and sometimes used in the *sanzen* room.

3. In ancient China it was taboo to say a person's true personal name.

Case 135   世尊拈華   *The World-Honored-One Holds Up a Flower* [1]

世尊在靈山會上、拈華示衆。此時人天百萬、悉皆罔措。獨有金色頭
陀、破顏微笑。世尊言、吾有正法眼藏、涅槃妙心、實相無相、微妙
法門、不立文字、教外別傳、付囑大迦葉。

Once at Vulture Peak, Śākyamuni held up a flower in front of the assembly.
Although a million gods and humans were present, no one responded
except Mahākāśyapa, the Golden Ascetic, who broke into a smile.

At this the Buddha said, "I possess the Treasury of the True Dharma
Eye, the ineffable mind of nirvana, the true form of the formless, the subtle
Dharma gate. It does not depend on words or letters and is a special trans-
mission outside the teachings. This I entrust to Mahākāśyapa."

1. Also *Wumen guan* 6, Main Case.

Case 136   迦葉剎竿   *Mahākāśyapa's Temple Flagpole* [1]

迦葉、因阿難問云、世尊傳金襴袈裟外、別傳何法。迦葉召云、阿
難。難應諾。迦葉云、倒却門前剎竿着。難於言下大悟。

Ānanda asked Mahākāśyapa, "Aside from passing on the brocade vestment,
was there any Dharma the Buddha transmitted to you?"

Mahākāśyapa called, "Ānanda!"

"Yes!" replied Ānanda.

Mahākāśyapa said, "Take down the flagpole at the temple gate."[2]

At these words Ānanda attained a great realization.

1. Also *Wumen guan* 22, Main Case.
2. The temple flagpole displayed the banner which signaled that a Dharma
lecture or debate was being held. The banner was taken down after the lecture.

Case 137   廣慧罪業   *Guanghui's "Evil Karma"*

廣慧璉、因楊大年問曰、承聞罪業皆因財寶所生。勸人疎於財利。況
南閻衆生以財爲命、邦國以財聚人。教中有財法二施、何得勸人疎
乎。璉曰、幡竿尖上鐵龍頭。大年曰、海壇馬子似驢大。璉云、楚鷄
不是丹山鳳。大年曰、佛滅二千年、比丘少慚愧。投機偈曰、八角
磨盤空裡走、金毛獅子變作狗。擬欲藏身北斗中、應須合掌南辰後。

Yang Danian asked Guanghui Yuanlian, "You say that all evil karma is born of wealth and that people should shun riches. Yet money is life to people in this world, and it is owing to prosperity that people gather in our country. Moreover, the teachings mention two types of offerings: Dharma offerings and material offerings. So why do you encourage people to forsake riches?"

Guanghui said, "The iron dragon-head on top of the flagpole."[1]

Danian replied, "The horses of Haidan are the size of donkeys."[2]

Guanghui responded, "A chicken from Chu is not the phoenix of Danshan."[3]

Danian said, "Two thousand years have passed since the death of the Buddha.[4] Monks today have no shame."[5]

A verse on Danian's insight said:

> An eight-sided millstone flies through the air; a golden-haired lion turns into a dog.
> If you wish to abide in the northern Big Dipper, you must bow to the Southern Cross.[6]

1. ZGJI: Iron dragon-heads were placed on top of temple flagpoles in order to attract people's attention. According to Dōmae, Danian is asking, "Why do you preach against wealth?" Guanghui replies, in effect, "It's like advertising for the temple."

2. Dōmae: Danian says, "So your true position and your public stance are a bit different?"

3. Dōmae: Guanghui replies, "There is a resemblance, but they are not the same."

4. It is believed that three ages have followed the time of the Buddha. The first age, that of the True Dharma, which lasted five hundred years (or a thousand years, depending on the source), was the era immediately after the lifetime of the Buddha, when the true Dharma was practiced and many people attained enlightenment. The second age, that of the Semblance Dharma, which also lasted five hundred years or a thousand years, was an era in which the Dharma became formalized and few people attained enlightenment. During the Latter Age of the Dharma, which is to last ten thousand years, the Buddhist doctrines still exist but there is no longer any practice or enlightenment.

5. Dōmae: The statement "monks no longer have a sense of shame" refers to the Buddhist belief that during the Latter Age of the Dharma monks no longer practice the Way.

6. Both verses of this poem indicate the marvelous functioning of no-mind or nonduality.

Case 138   乾峰一路   *Qianfeng's "Single Road"*[1]

乾峰和尚、僧因問、十方薄伽梵、一路涅槃門。未審、路頭在何麼
處。峰拈起拄杖、畫一畫曰、在這裡。後僧請益雲門。門拈起扇子
云、扇子趯跳、上三十三天、築著帝釋鼻孔。東海鯉魚打一棒、雨似
傾盆。會麼。

A monk asked Qianfeng, "'The Honored Ones of the ten directions have all
taken the single road to nirvana.'[2] Where is this road?"

Qianfeng took his staff and drew a line, saying, "It's here."

Later the monk asked Yunmen the same question. Yunmen held up his
fan and said, "This fan leaps into Trāyastrimśa Heaven and pokes Indra in
the nostrils;[3] it strikes the carp of the Eastern Sea a single blow and rain
pours down in buckets. Do you understand?"

1. Also *Wumen guan* 48, Main Case.

2. This line is from the *Śūraṅgama Sutra* 首楞嚴經 (T 19:124c). The stanza in
which it appears reads:

This Dharma may be called the wondrous lotus-flower,
The royal, indestructible, magnificent awakening.
This practice of samāpatti, though likened to illusion,
Can quickly bring you past the ones who need no further training.
This peerless Dharma is the road that all World-Honored Ones
Have walked to reach the gateway to nirvana.
(Buddhist Text Translation Society, 2009, p. 194)

3. Indra, one of the Vedic gods adopted into Buddhism as guardians, is the
chief deity of the Trāyastrimśa Heaven. See Case 133, note 1.

Case 139   南嶽磨塼   *Nanyue Polishes a Tile*

洪州 西馬祖大寂禪師、參侍南嶽密受心印。蓋拔同參、住傳法院、
常日坐禪。讓知是法器、往師處問曰、大德坐禪圖箇什麼。師云、圖
作佛。讓乃取一塼、於師庵前石上磨。師遂問、作什麼。讓曰、磨作
鏡。師云、磨塼豈得成鏡耶。讓云、坐禪豈得作佛耶。師曰、如何即
是。讓云、如人駕車、車若不行、打車即是、打牛即是。師無對。讓
又示曰、汝爲學坐禪、爲學坐佛。若學坐禪、禪非坐臥。若學坐佛、
佛非定相。於無住法、不應取捨。汝若坐佛、即是殺佛。若執坐相、
非達其理。師聞示誨、如飲醍醐。

Mazu Daji of Jiangxi in Hongzhou studied under Nanyue Huairang and from him secretly received the Mind Seal.[1]

During his training Mazu had surpassed the other monks and gone to live at the temple Chuanfa yuan, where he practiced seated meditation throughout the day. Recognizing him as a vessel of the Dharma, Huairang went and asked, "Worthy monk, why do you sit in meditation?"

Mazu replied, "I wish to become a buddha."

Thereupon Huairang picked up a tile and started to rub it against a stone in front of Mazu's hermitage. Finally Mazu asked him what he was doing. Huairang replied, "Polishing it to make it a mirror."

"How can you make a tile into a mirror by polishing it?" asked Mazu.

"How can you become a buddha by sitting in meditation?" responded Huairang.

Mazu asked, "Then what should I do?"

Huairang asked, "It's like riding in an ox cart. If the cart doesn't move do you hit the cart or do you hit the ox?"

Mazu had no reply.

Huairang continued, "Are you practicing seated meditation? Are you practicing to be a seated buddha? As for seated meditation, meditation isn't limited to sitting or lying down. As for being a seated buddha, "buddha" isn't limited to any fixed form. In the nonabiding Dharma, you should neither grasp nor reject. If you sit to be a buddha, this kills the buddha. If you cling to the sitting posture, you will never realize the essential principle."

When he heard this, Mazu felt as though he had just imbibed ghee.[2]

1. Mazu Daji 馬祖大寂 is another name for Mazu Daoyi (see Case 5). "Mind Seal" translates 心印, the seal of transmission of the Dharma.

2. Ghee 醍醐 (Skt. *maṇḍa*), the most highly refined form of butter, was said to be capable of curing all illnesses. In Buddhism it came to represent buddha nature and enlightenment.

Case 140 兜率荔支 *Doushuai's Lychees*

石霜素侍者、閩之古田毛巖乃生緣也。晚寓湘西鹿苑、以閒談自牧。
兜率悦公、時未出世、與之隣室。有客惠生荔枝。悦命素曰、此乃
老人鄉果、可同餉也。素慨然曰、自先師去世不見此矣。悦從而問
之、師爲誰耶。對以慈明。悦乃乘閒致密款其緒餘。素因問、子曾
見何人。悦以眞淨文和尚告之。素曰、文又見誰耶。悦曰、南禪師。
素曰、南區頭在石霜不久。其道盛如此。悦益駭異。尋袖香咨扣。素

曰、吾福鮮緣寡、豈可爲人師。但子之見解、試吐露看。悅即具陳。
素云、只可入佛、不可入魔。須知古德謂末後一句始到牢關。悅擬
對。又遽問、以無爲如何說。悅又擬對。而素忽高笑。悅恍然有得。
故嘗以語無盡居士張公。逮崇寧三禩、寂音尊者、謁無盡居士於峽
州善谿。無盡曰、昔見眞淨老師于歸宗、因語及兜率所謂末後句。語
尚未終、而眞淨忽怒罵曰、此吐血禿丁、脫空妄語不用信。既見其盛
怒、不敢更陳曲折。然惜眞淨不知此也。寂音曰、相公惟知兜率口授
末后句、至於眞淨老師眞藥現前、而不能辨何也。無盡駭曰、眞淨果
有此意那。寂音徐曰、疑則別參。無盡於言下、頓見眞淨用處。

Qingsu, the attendant of Shishuang Chuyuan, was a native of Gutian
Maoyan in Min Province. In his later years he stayed at the temple Luyuan
in Xiangxi, where he passed his days in leisurely retirement, enjoying quiet
conversation. Doushuai Congyue, not yet a teacher at the time, was staying in the room next to Qingsu's. A visitor presented him with some fresh
lychees. He called Qingsu, saying, "Old fellow, I have some fruit from your
homeland—let's eat it together."[1]

Qingsu said wistfully, "This is the first time I've seen lychees since my
teacher left this world."

"Oh? And who was your teacher?" asked Doushuai.

"Ciming [Shishuang Chuyuan]," answered Qingsu. Warming to him,
Doushuai offered him the rest of the fruit.[2] Qingsu then asked who Doushuai had studied under. "Zhenjing Kewen," answered Doushuai.

"Who did Kewen study under?" asked Qingsu.

"Huanglong Huinan," replied Doushuai.

"Old Flat-top Huinan[3] studied under Ciming, though not for long! Has
his line already flourished like this?"

Doushuai, ever more impressed, reached into his sleeve for incense to
offer.[4] Qingsu said, "I have little merit and no capacity to teach.[5] How could
I be anyone's guide? Still, you might as well present your understanding."
Doushuai proceeded to explain in some detail. Qingsu commented, "With
that you can enter the realm of the Buddha, but not the realm of Mara.[6]
Remember, the ancient masters said that it is only with the final word that
one reaches the impassable gate."[7] When Doushuai attempted to reply, Qingsu abruptly asked, "How do you explain nondoing?"

When Doushuai attempted once again to reply, Qingsu broke out in
hearty laughter. Doushuai suddenly understood. Later he spoke of this to
Layman Zhang Wujin.

In 1104, when Juefan Huihong[8] was visiting Layman Wujin at Shanxi
in Xiazhou, Wujin said, "Years ago I met Zhenjing at Guizong Temple

and, in the course of conversation, mentioned the 'final word' that [his student] Doushuai had spoken about. Before I finished, though, Zhenjing shouted out in sudden anger, 'That blood-puking shavepate, totally devoid of insight! Talking nonsense like "the final word"—he's utterly unworthy of trust!' Seeing his wrath, I refrained from further explanation. Still, I regret that Zhenjing never understood the matter of the final word."

Juefan said, "Sir, you were able to understand Doushuai's expression of the final word—why, then, when Zhenjing offered you true medicine, were you unable to recognize *that*?"

Surprised, Wujin asked, "Was that Zhenjing's true intention?"

Juefan answered calmly, "If you still don't understand, then take instruction with me."[9]

At these words Wujin suddenly perceived what Zhenjing had been doing.

1. The lychee is a fruit native to the tropical and subtropical regions of China, from which Qingsu, as well as his teacher Shishuang, had come.

2. The meaning is unclear, but commentators generally agree that Doushuai had until that moment regarded Qingsu as simply an ordinary retired monk, changing his view upon hearing that Qingsu was a student of Ciming, his own great-grandfather in the Dharma.

3. Huinan apparently had a flat-topped head. Qingsu's use of this nickname indicates that he had been on friendly terms with Doushuai's Dharma grandfather.

4. Offering incense constituted a formal request for instruction.

5. Qingsu was told by Ciming that he didn't have the makings of a teacher.

6. See Case 141.

7. "The final word" 末後句 is the word beyond all words.

8. Juefan Huihong was Doushuai's brother disciple under Zhenjing Kewen.

9. "Take instruction" translates 別參 (separate instruction), corresponding to 獨參 (individual instruction) in modern Japanese Rinzai Zen.

Case 141   佛境魔境   *Realm of the Buddha, Realm of Mara*

大慧曰、佛是衆生藥。衆生病除、藥亦無用。或病去藥存、入佛境界
而不能入魔境界。其病與衆生之未除之病等。病瘥藥除、佛魔俱拂、
始於此段大事因緣、有少分相應耳。張子韶、一日、問大慧曰、前輩
既得了、何故、理會臨濟四料揀、則甚議論問。大慧曰、公之所見、
只可入佛、不可入魔。豈可不從料揀中去耶。公遂舉、克符問臨濟、
至人境兩俱奪、不覺欣然。大慧曰、予則不然。公曰、師意如何。大
慧曰、打破蔡州城、殺却吳元濟。公於言下、得大自在。

Dahui said, "Buddha is medicine for sentient beings. When their disease is gone, the medicine is no longer needed. If the disease is gone but the medicine is still present, one enters the realm of the Buddha but cannot enter the realm of Mara. This is a disease as bad as the one the Buddha initially cured. Only when the disease is cured, the medicine gone, and both the Buddha and Mara swept away is one to some degree in accord with the Great Purpose of the Buddha."[1]

One day Zhang Zishao asked Dahui, "The masters before us had all attained realization. Why then did they offer various interpretations of Linji's four positions and vociferously argue over them?"[2]

Dahui commented, "With your views you can enter only the realm of the Buddha; you cannot enter the realm of Mara. You'll lose all contact with the four positions that way."

Zhang said, "When I understood Zhuozhou Kefu's asking Linji about 'taking away both the person and the surroundings,' I felt a sudden joy."[3]

Dahui replied, "That's not how it is with me."

"How do you see it?" asked Zhang.

"The walls of Caizhou are demolished, Wu Yuanji is killed."[4]

At these words Zhang attained great freedom.

1. The expression "Great Purpose of the Buddha" 大事因縁 comes from the following passage from the "Expedient Means" chapter (方便品) of the *Lotus Sutra*:

> The Buddhas, the World-Honored Ones, wish to open the door of Buddha wisdom to all living beings, to allow them to attain purity. That is why they appear in the world. They wish to show the Buddha wisdom to living beings, and therefore they appear in the world. They wish to cause living beings to awaken to the Buddha wisdom, and therefore they appear in the world. They wish to induce living beings to enter the path of Buddha wisdom, and therefore they appear in the world. Shariputra, this is the one great [purpose] for which the Buddhas appear in the world. (Watson 1993b, p. 31; T 9:1a)

2. For Linji's four positions 臨濟四料, see Case 208.

3. [Zhuozhou] asked, "What about 'to take away both person and surroundings'?" The master said, "No news from Bing and Fen, isolated and away from everywhere" (Sasaki 2009, p. 8).

During Linji's time Bing 并 and Fen 汾 corresponded to the northern part of present Shanxi, a region virtually independent of the central government owing to the power of the local military commissioners, who sometimes referred to themselves as kings.

4. Wu Yuanji 呉元済 (738–817) was an infamous rebel who fought against the Tang government. One story is that Wu was once garrisoned in the walled city of Caizhou 蔡州, which had a reputation for impregnability. In the winter of 817, however, a heavy snowfall left high drifts, allowing Li Su 李愬 (n.d.), commander

of the imperial army, to scale the walls, capture the city, and kill Wu (*Jiu Tang shu* 舊唐書 [Older chronicles of the Tang], 214).

Mujaku: "Demolishing the walls of Caizhou" refers to "taking away the surroundings"; "Wu Yuanji is killed" refers to "taking away the person."

Case 142   松源三轉   *Songyuan's Three Turning-Phrases*[1]

松源嶽和尚、三轉語云、大力量人、因甚擡脚不起。開口、爲甚不在舌頭上。明眼人、因甚脚跟下、紅絲線不斷。

Songyuan Chongyue, in three turning-phrases, asked:

How is it that those of great strength can't lift their legs?[2]
How is it that they speak without using their tongues?[3]
How is it that the clear-eyed can't sever the red threads under their feet?[4]

1. Also *Wumen guan* 20, Main Case.
2. Yamada: Why don't awakened people move when helping others? (1976, p. 162).
3. Yamada: Why, when teaching, don't enlightened people speak? (1976, p. 162).
4. ZGDJ: "The red threads under their feet" refers to the worldly passions and deluded thoughts, or to karmic ties.

Case 143   虛堂三問   *Xutang's Three Questions*

虛堂在靈隱鷲峰塔、杜絕世諦。衲子請益、遂立三問示之、各令著語。一己眼未明底、因甚將虛空作布袴著。二劃地爲牢底、因甚透者箇不過。三入海算沙底、因甚針鋒頭上翹足。

When Xutang was at Eagle Peak Tomb in Lingyin and had cut off worldly ties, monks came to him for instruction. He devised the following three questions and presented them to the monks, asking them to respond:

Why does one whose eye is not yet clear wear emptiness like a pair of trousers?
Why is one who marks [a circle on] the ground and calls it a prison unable to cross this [line]?
Why does one who enters the sea and counts the sand stand tiptoe on the point of a needle?

Case 144　大燈三轉　*Daitō's Three Turning-Phrases*

大燈國師示衆云、朝結眉夕交肩、我何似生。露柱終日往來、我因甚
麼不動。若透得這兩轉語、一生參學事畢矣。三段不同、收歸上科。

National Teacher Daitō addressed the assembly, saying:

> Morning and evening, we entangle eyebrows and rub shoulders. What
> is this "I"?
> All day long the pillar goes back and forth.[1] Why do I not move?
> If you can penetrate these two turning-phrases you have completed a
> lifetime's practice.

These three phrases[2] are not the same, but ultimately each returns to the
root of the first.

1. "Pillar" is a common metaphor in Zen for no-mind or the unconscious (see
Case 14, note 2).

2. The first edition of the *Kattōshū* (1689) has "two phrases," as the third is
simply a comment about the first two phrases.

Case 145　南泉住庵　*Nanquan Living in a Hermitage*

虛堂上堂、舉、南泉住庵時、一僧到。泉曰、我上山作務、齋時做飯
［喫］了、送一分來。其僧飯了、將家事一時打碎、就床上臥。泉伺久
不來。遂歸見僧臥、泉亦臥。僧便起去。泉住後曰、我往前住庵時、
有箇靈利道者、至今不見。師曰、王老師若不顧錐頭利、者僧要起去
不得。雖然石厭笋斜出、岸懸花倒生。頌曰、短袴長衫白苧巾、咿唖
月下急推輪。洛陽路上相逢着、盡是經商買賣人。

Xutang took the high seat and said:

> When Nanquan Puyuan was living in a hermitage,[1] a monk visited him. Nan-
> quan said, "I'm going to the mountain to work. At noon when you've finished
> with lunch, would you bring a portion to me?"
> The monk ate lunch, then broke the pots and dishes and lay down on the
> bed. Nanquan waited for a long time but the monk didn't come, so finally
> he went down to the hermitage and saw the monk lying there. Nanquan lay
> down too. Thereupon the monk got up and left.
> Later, after Nanquan became priest of a temple, he said, "When I was liv-
> ing in a hermitage, I met a very clever monk, the likes of whom I've never
> seen again."

Xutang commented, "If Nanquan had paid no attention to the monk and his awl-point wiles,[2] the monk could never have gotten up and left. But then, "When pushing out from under a stone, bamboo shoots grow sideways; when sprouting from under an overhang, flowers grow downward." Xutang added a verse:

> Wearing short breeches, long gowns, and white linen headbands,
> They busily push carts under the moon.[3]
> Later, seeing them [in the daylight] on the capital's streets,
> All turn out to be no more than peddlers and hawkers.

1. The master lived in a hermitage on Mount Nanquan for thirty years until taking a position as master of a large temple. See Biographical Notes.

2. "Awl-point wiles" indicates a superficial cleverness that, although sharp, is no larger than the point of an awl.

3. The *Kattōshū* version of this koan has "under the sun" 日下, a scribal error for the "under the moon" 月下 of the original in the *Record of Xutang*. The translation follows the *Record of Xutang* version.

Case 146   慈明榜字   *Ciming's Signpost*

慈明圓禪師、冬至日、榜僧堂前作此相。

○○○　　几　軿矴

題其右云、若人識得、不離四威儀中。首座一見謂眾云、和尚今日放參。虛堂別首座云、某甲代和尚、下延壽堂。東林顏拈云、鐵輪天子下閻浮、急急如律令、勅摄。

On the day of the winter solstice[1] Ciming Chuyuan set out in front of the monks' hall a signboard inscribed with the symbols:[2]

○○○　　几　軿矴

To the right of this was written: "If one understands *this*, it's present in everything you do."[3]

The head monk looked at the signboard and said to the assembly, "Today the master will hold no evening instruction!"[4]

Xutang added a comment to the head monk's: "I'll go down to the infirmary in place of the master."[5]

Wan'an Daoyan commented, "The Iron-Wheel Emperor is descending to this world![6] Demons, quickly, off with you![7] Apprehend them all!"[8]

1. The winter solstice marks the day when the yin forces (darkness, cold) reach their zenith and the yang forces (light, warmth) their nadir. It is simultaneously the day when yang starts once again to increase and yin to decrease. As such it represents in Zen the Great Death followed by rebirth.

2. The symbols, according to traditional commentaries, represent a Chinese-character puzzle that, when solved, reads 冬至凡東西自在, "It is the winter solstice—go east or west as you wish."

3. "Everything you do" translates 四威, the "four modes of conduct" (walking, standing, sitting, and lying down), i.e., the entire range of human activity.

4. Evening instruction 晚參 was, in Song times, an informal evening meeting between the master and the assembly held in the master's quarters.

5. In Chinese Zen, the expression "going down to the infirmary" generally indicated approaching death.

6. That is, "The end of the world is coming!" The Iron-Wheel Emperor 鐵輪天子, or Iron-Wheel King 鉄輪王, is one of the four cakravartins who govern the continents surrounding Mount Sumeru (see Case 4). The Gold-Wheel King rules the northern, eastern, western, and southern continents; the Silver-Wheel King the eastern, western, and southern continents; the Copper-Wheel King the eastern and southern continents; the Iron-Wheel King the southern continent.

7. The original Chinese, 急急如律令, can be translated as "Quickly, quickly! As prescribed by law!" Hori comments, "In the later Han period, public legal documents often ended with these words enjoining subjects to implement the law immediately. The phrase was then taken up by practicers of magic," who would chant the phrase while administering charms (2003, p. 186 [5.63]). The equivalent meaning in Zen would be, "No time to waste—throw off delusion!"

8. The *Kattōshū* has Ciming's cryptic symbols repeated after the characters 急急如律令, but in the traditional biographical material on Wan'an Daoyan the characters 勅摄 appear. This phrase was used by Taoist magicians after they recited charms; 勅 indicated an order made in place of the emperor, while 摄 meant to arrest or apprehend.

Case 147   慈明盆水   *Ciming's Bowl of Water*

慈明圓禪師、一日、於方丈內安一盆水、上橫一口劍、下着一雙草
鞋、橫按拄杖而坐。見僧入門便指。僧擬議、師即棒。

One day in his quarters Ciming Chuyuan put down a bowl of water, placed a sword on top and a pair of straw sandals underneath, and sat down beside it holding his staff. Seeing a monk enter the gate, he pointed. When the monk hesitated, the master struck him.[1]

1. For a similar koan, see Case 267.

Case 148   鐘声七條   *Putting on Your Vestment at the Sound of the Bell*[1]

雲門曰、世界恁麼廣闊、因甚向鐘聲裡披七條。

Yunmen said, "How vast the world is! So why do you put on your vestment at the sound of the bell?"[2]

1. Also *Wumen guan* 16, Main Case.
2. For "vestment," see Case 95, note 1.

Case 149   微細流注   *Subtle Flow*

潙山問仰山、寂子、心識微細流注、無來幾年。仰山不敢答。却云、
和尚無來幾年矣。潙山云、老僧無來已七年。潙山又問、寂子如何。
仰山云、慧寂正鬧。

Guishan Lingyou asked Yangshan Huiji, "How many years has it been since you ended the mind's subtle flow of defilements?"[1]

Yangshan didn't answer, but instead asked Guishan, "How many years has it been since the master ended it?"

Guishan said, "It has already been seven years since this old monk ended it." He then asked Yangshan, "And you?"

Yangshan replied, "Me, I'm quite active."

1. "The mind" translates 心識, short for 心意識, which combines: (1) 心 (*citta*, mind; i.e., the eighth consciousness, or ālaya-vijñāna, where the impressions resulting from an individual's karmic activities are stored and from which the other seven levels of consciousness arise); (2) 意 (*manas*, sentience; i.e., the seventh consciousness, or mano-vijñāna, where the consciousness of self forms); and (3) 識 (*vijñāna*, consciousness; i.e., the six consciousnesses of sight, hearing, smell, taste, touch, and conscious thought). The defilements (kleśa) are greed, anger, ignorance, and the various other factors that give rise to suffering and impede awakening.

Case 150   法雲示衆   *Fayun Addresses the Assembly*

法雲杲和尚、示衆云、老僧熙寧三年、文帳在鳳翔府供申。是年華山
崩、陷了八十里人家。汝輩後生茄子瓠子、那裡知得。

Fayun Gao said to the assembly, "In the third year of Xining (1070), I had to pay the Fengxiang authorities for an ordination certificate.[1] That year Mount Shaohua collapsed and buried houses for a distance of eighty *li*.[2] You worldly young slackers—how could you ever understand this?"

1. From the Tang or earlier, ordination certificates (文帳, 度牒)—documents certifying eligibility to enter the sangha—had to be purchased from the government. Originally this was to prevent the use of ordination as an escape from taxation and the corvée; later it was used to raise revenue. By the Song the certificates served as a form of tender, and honorary titles, such as the "purple robe," were available from the authorities for a price.

2. The Chinese *li* is a unit of measurement approximately one-quarter to one-third of a mile in length, depending on the era and location in which it was used. In modern China the *li* has been assigned a length of exactly five hundred meters. Mount Shaohua 少華 actually collapsed in 1072.

Case 151   仰山撲鏡   *Yangshan Smashes a Mirror*

仰山寂禪師、住東平時、溈山附書并鏡一面至。師陞座授書、乃提起
鏡示眾曰、大眾溈山將鏡來。而今且道、是溈山鏡東平鏡。若道是東
平鏡、又是溈山寄來。若道是溈山鏡、又在東平這裏。道得即存取、
道不得即打破去也。如是三舉。眾皆無對。師乃撲破。五祖戒代云、
更請和尚說道理看、驀奪打破。

When Yangshan Huiji was residing at Dongping, a letter and a mirror arrived from Guishan Lingyou. Yangshan ascended the high seat and received the letter. Then, holding up the mirror, he addressed the assembly.

"Monks, this mirror comes from Guishan. Tell me, is it Guishan's mirror or is it mine? If you say it's mine, still it was sent by Guishan. If you say it's Guishan's, still it's here in my hands. If you can say something, I'll spare the mirror; if you can't, I'll smash it." He repeated this three times, but no one in the assembly responded. The master then smashed the mirror.

Wuzu Shijie answered in place of the assembly: "[I would have said,] 'Master, please, try to explain your meaning a bit more clearly,' then grabbed the mirror and shattered it myself."[1]

1. Dōmae reads the line as: "Wuzu Shijie answered in place of the assembly: 'Master, please, try to explain your meaning a bit more clearly, then straightaway I'll grab the mirror and shatter it myself.'"

Case 152   雲門舉令   *Yunmen's Sermon*

雲門一日云、宗門作麼生舉令。代云、吽。

One day Yunmen asked, "In the Zen school, how do we promote the teachings?" In place of the assembly he answered, "*Hou!*"[1]

1. *Hou* 吽 is onomatopoeia for a cow mooing. Mujaku comments that in this case the character transliterates the Sanskrit syllable "huṁ" ("suchness," bhūtatathatā) and cautions against applying interpretive reasoning to any of Yunmen's statements.

Case 153   陳操登楼   *Chen Cao in a Tower*[1]

陳操、一日、與衆官登樓次、望見數僧來。一官人云、來者總是禪
僧。操云、不是。官人云、焉知不是。操云、待近來與汝勘過。僧到
樓前。操驀召云、上座。僧舉頭。操謂衆官云、不信道。

One day when Chen Cao was in a tower with some officials they saw several monks approaching. An official said, "Those monks who are coming are all Zen monks."
"That's not so," Chen Cao said.
"How do you know?" the official asked.
Chen Cao said, "Wait till they're closer and I'll check them out for you." When the monks reached the tower, Chen suddenly called out, "Venerable monks!"
The monks all looked up.
"Now do you believe me?" Chen Cao asked the officials.

1. Also *Blue Cliff Record* 33, Commentary on the Main Case.

Case 154   婆子燒庵   *An Old Woman Burns Down a Hermitage*

昔有婆子、供養一庵主經二十年。常令一二八女子送飯給侍。一日、
令女抱定曰、正與麼時如何。主曰、枯木倚寒巖、三冬無暖氣。女子
歸舉似婆。婆曰、我二十年祇供養得箇俗漢、遂遣出燒却庵。

There was an old woman who supported a hermit for twenty years. She always had a girl, sixteen or seventeen years old, take the hermit his food and wait on him. One day she told the girl to give the monk a close hug and ask, "What do you feel just now?" The hermit responded:

> A dead tree[1] on a cold cliff;
> Midwinter—no warmth.

The girl returned and told this to the old woman. The woman said, "For twenty years I've supported this vulgar good-for-nothing!" So saying, she threw the monk out and burned down the hermitage.

1. The "old tree" 古木 of the *Kattōshū* has been changed to the "dead tree" 枯木 of the original case in *Compendium of the Five Lamps* 6.

Case 155 別有生涯 *A Different Way of Doing Things*[1]

龍牙是曹洞下尊宿。若是德山臨濟門下、別有生涯。

Longya Judun was a priest of the Caodong school. If he had been a student of Linji or Deshan, he would have had a different way of doing things.[2]

1. Also *Blue Cliff Record* 20, Commentary on the Main Case.

2. Commentators situate this statement in the context of Longya's exchanges with his teacher, the Caodong master *Dongshan Liangjie*, and later with the masters Cuiwei Wuxue 翠微無學 (n.d.) and *Linji Yixuan*. The *Blue Cliff Record* comments:

> Longya once asked Liangjie, "What is the meaning of the Patriarch's coming from the West?" Liangjie replied, "I'll tell you when East River runs uphill." At this Longya was enlightened. Afterward, meeting Cuiwei, Longya asked, "What is the meaning of the Patriarch's coming from the West?" "Hand me the meditation-brace," said Cuiwei. When Longya gave him the brace, Cuiwei hit him with it. "Hit me if you wish," Longya said, "but still there's no meaning in the Patriarch's coming from the West." Later Longya met Linji and asked, "What is the meaning of the Patriarch's coming from the West?" "Hand me the cushion," replied Linji. Longya did so; Linji hit him with it. Longya said, "Hit me if you wish, but still there's no meaning in the Patriarch's coming from the West...."
>
> Later, when Longya was serving as abbot of a temple, a monk asked him, "Abbot, when you met those two masters, did you approve of them or not?" Longya answered, "I did approve of them, but still there's no meaning in the Patriarch's coming from the West." There are thorns in the soft mud [of Longya's kind words]. He approved of them, but in doing so he fell into secondary discrimination. Longya was firm in his understanding, but he was an adherent of the Dongshan line. If he had been in the line of Deshan or Linji he would have had a different way of doing things. If it was me [Yuanwu], I wouldn't have answered in that way. I would have said to the monk, "I didn't approve of them. The fact is there's no meaning in the Patriarch's coming from the West."

Case 156   一言駟馬   *One Word and a Four-Horse Team*

慈明因僧問、如何是本來面目。明云、一言已出、駟馬難追。

A monk asked Ciming Chuyuan, "What is the original face?"

Ciming replied, "If a single word gets out, not even a four-horse team can overtake it."[1]

1. This expression originally appears in the Confucian *Analects*, fascicle 12.

Case 157   法身喫飯   *The Dharmakāya Eats Food*[1]

法身喫飯話。師云、作麼生是汝喫飯底。師云、作麼生是汝全體。師
云、身與心相去多少。

Regarding the matter of the dharmakāya eating food,[2] the master asked, "What is it that eats when you eat food?"

Again he said, "What is your entire being?"

And again, "How far is it between body and mind?"

1. This koan cannot be found in any of the records. Dōmae suggests that it may have been created in Japan from statements by *Yunmen Wenyan*.

2. For "dharmakāya," see Case 17, note 1. "The matter of the dharmakāya eating food" refers to an exchange in the *Record of Yunmen*. A monk asked Yunmen, "What is it that transcends the dharmakāya?" Yunmen replied, "It wouldn't be hard to speak to you of transcendence, but what do you mean by 'dharmakāya'?" The monk said, "Master, please, consider my question!" "Let's set 'consideration' aside for the moment," answered Yunmen. "How does the dharmakāya talk?" The monk answered, "Like this! Like this!" Yunmen said, "That's something you can learn from sitting on the meditation platform. What I'm asking you now is, 'Does the dharmakāya eat food?'" The monk had nothing to say (T 47:573c).

Case 158   虛堂兩字   *Xutang's "Words"*

虛堂上堂、舉、玄沙問鏡清曰、不見一法、是大過患。汝道、不見甚
麼法。清指露柱曰、莫是不見者箇法麼。沙曰、浙中清水白米從汝
喫、佛法未在。虛堂曰、也好莫是兩字。會麼。寒雲抱幽石、霜月照
清池。

Xutang took the high seat and said:

Xuansha Shibei questioned Jingqing, "'Not to perceive a single dharma—this is a grave error.'[1] So tell me, what is this 'single dharma not perceived'?" Jingqing pointed at a pillar[2] and replied, "This is 'not to perceive a single dharma,' is it not?" Xuansha said, "You may enjoy the pure water and fine rice of Zhezhong, but as for the Buddhadharma, not yet!"[3]

Xutang commented, "How excellent, though, were Jingqing's words 'is it not?'[4] Do you understand?"

Cold clouds embrace the hidden rock,
The frosty moon illuminates the clear pool.

1. This is an out-of-context quote from *Avataṃsaka Sutra* 36 (T 10:257c). The original passage, 我不見一法為大過失如諸菩薩於他菩薩起瞋心者, translates as, "I do not see anything that is a bigger mistake than for enlightening beings to become angry at other enlightening beings" (Cleary 1993a, p. 952). However, since before the time of Xuansha Zen monks have taken just the characters 不見一法為大過失 and read them in the way that Xuansha does. This is a distinctly Zen interpretation.

2. "Pillar" is a common metaphor for the Zen concept of no-mind (see Case 14, note 2).

3. Zhezhong 浙中, Jingqing's home region, was a famous rice-producing area. One interpretation of his comment would be, "That view may be all right where you come from, but with me it won't pass!"

4. "Is it not?" translates 莫是, which indicates a rhetorical question.

Case 159   臨濟三句   *The Three Statements of Linji*[1]

臨濟上堂、僧問、如何是第一句。師云、三要印開朱點側、未容擬議
主賓分。問、如何是第二句。師云、妙解豈容無著問、漚和爭負截流
機。問、如何是第三句。師云、看取棚頭弄傀儡、抽牽都來裡有人。
師又曰、一句語須具三玄門。一玄門須具三要。有權有用、汝等諸
人、作麼生會。下座。

Linji took the high seat in the hall. A monk asked, "What is the First Statement?"

The master said, "When the seal of the Three Essentials[2] is lifted the vermilion stamp is sharp. There is no room for conjecture; host and guest are clearly defined."

"What is the Second Statement?"

The master said, "How could Mañjuśrī permit Wuzhuo's questioning?[3] How could expedient means oppose the activity that cuts through the flow?"[4]

"What is the Third Statement?"

The master said, "Look at the puppets performing on the stage! Their every movement is controlled by the one behind."[5]

The master further said, "Each statement must contain the three Mysterious Gates; each Mysterious Gate must contain the Three Essentials.[6] There are expedients, and there is functioning. How do all of you understand this?" The master then stepped down.

1. Also *Record of Linji*, Discourse 9.

2. The seal 印 is a sign or emblem signifying realization of the ultimate truth, which transcends all reasoning and yet clearly differentiates host and guest. For the Three Essentials, see note 6, below.

3. The Chinese term 妙解 (lit., "marvelous wisdom") is taken here to indicate Mañjuśrī, since Mañjuśrī is the Bodhisattva of Marvelous Wisdom. Wuzhuo 無著 was a monk said to have climbed Mount Wutai 五臺, the legendary home of Mañjuśrī in China, and there spoken to the bodhisattva.

4. Linji's response may be taken to mean that although Mañjuśrī's ultimate wisdom is beyond the reach of conceptual inquiry, it is nevertheless expressed in the world through teaching and expedient activities, which in no way obscure this wisdom.

5. Some commentators see this to mean that humans and other phenomena, like puppets on a stage, appear to be acting on their own yet are simply responding to the functioning of reality. Other commentators say that the puppet master represents the Zen teacher, using all manner of expedients to bring the students to enlightenment.

6. It is not certain what the Three Statements, the Three Essentials, and the Three Mysterious Gates represented for Linji. They have been equated with the Buddha, Dharma, and Way; with the dharmakāya, saṃbhogakāya, and nirmāṇakāya; and with the Chinese philosophical concepts of principle 理, wisdom 智, and function 行 (or 用). Commentators agree that they simply express the one reality in its manifestations as absolute, as wisdom, and as human activity.

Case 160   華嚴法界   *The* Avataṃsaka Sutra's *Dharma Realms*

華嚴之四法界、理法界、事法界、理事無礙法界、事事無礙法界。

The four dharma realms (*dharmadhātu*) of the *Avataṃsaka Sutra* are:

The realm of phenomena;

The realm of principle;

The realm of the unobstructed and mutual interpenetration of principle and phenomena;

The realm of the unobstructed and mutual interpenetration of phenomena and phenomena.[1]

1. The teaching of the four dharmadhātu is also mentioned in Case 89 of the *Blue Cliff Record*, Commentary on the Verse. This teaching is central to the Huayan school, which teaches the interrelationship of all phenomena:

> The teachings of Huayan have as their point of departure the theory of causation by the universal principle, or dharmadhātu. According to this, all dharmas [phenomena] of the universe are dependent on one another and condition each other, and none can subsist on its own. All dharmas are empty: both aspects of this emptiness, the static (理, absolute) and the active (事, phenomena), interpenetrate each other unobstructedly; every phenomenon is identical to every other. (REEPR, p. 145)

Case 161   洞山夏末   *Dongshan's "End of the Training Period"*[1]

洞山示衆云、初秋夏末、兄弟東去西去。直須向萬里無寸草處去。復
云、無寸草處、作麼生去。僧舉似石霜。霜曰、何不道出門便是草。
後洞山聞云、大唐國裡、能有幾箇人。

Dongshan Liangjie addressed the assembly, saying, "Autumn is starting and the training season has ended. Monks, go east or west as you wish,[2] but go where there's no blade of grass in ten thousand *li*."[3] He then asked, "How do you go to where there's no blade of grass in ten thousand *li*?"

A monk told Shishuang Qingzhu about this. Shishuang replied, "Why didn't you say, 'The moment you leave the gate there's grass'?"

Later Dongshan heard about this and said, "How many people like that are there in the great Tang Empire?"

1. Also *Record of Equanimity* 89.

2. The monastic year had two three-month training periods, known as 安居 (lit., "peaceful dwelling," since it was a time when the monks could remain in one place) or 夏 (lit., "summer," since the training periods occurred in India's summer rainy season), separated by two off-seasons when the monks were free to leave the monastery on pilgrimage.

3. Grass and weeds are metaphors for hindrances, delusions, and ordinary phenomena. See, for example, Case 7.

For *li*, see Case 150, note 2.

Case 162　曹山大海　*Caoshan's "Great Sea"*

曹山、僧問、承教有言、大海不宿死屍。如何是海。山云、包含萬
有。僧曰、爲什麼不宿死屍。山云、絕氣者不著。僧云、既是包含萬
有、爲什麼絕氣者不著。山云、萬有非其功、絕氣有其德。僧云、向
上還有事也無。山云、道有道無即得。爭奈龍王按劍何。

A monk asked Caoshan Benji, "I've heard that the teachings say, 'The Great
Sea doesn't harbor corpses.'[1] What is this sea?"

Caoshan answered, "That which includes all being."

The monk asked, "Then why doesn't it harbor corpses?"

"It doesn't accept those who have expired,"[2] replied Caoshan.

"If it contains all being," asked the monk, "why doesn't it accept those who
have expired?"

Caoshan answered, "'Being' is beyond merit, whereas those who have
expired still possess their virtue."[3]

The monk asked, "Can one go beyond even this?"

Caoshan answered, "You may say one can, you may say one can't, but the
Nāga King is drawing his sword."[4]

1. The monk refers to the *Avataṃsaka Sutra*, which says; "Bodhisattvas accept
no evil, just as the Great Sea doesn't harbor corpses" (T 10:442a). Similar statements are also found in earlier sutras, e.g., the *Dharma Sea Sutra* 法海經, which
states that those who break the precepts must leave the sangha, just as the sea
throws out corpses (T 1:818b).

2. In the traditional interpretation, "those who have expired" 絕氣者 ("those
whose breath has stopped") represents those who have died the Great Death.

3. This line, 萬有非其功、絕氣有其德, is enigmatic and the translation provisional. "'Being' is beyond merit" 萬有非其功 is similar to the notion that at the
highest level of service there is no "doer" (大功不宰) and thus no one to retain
merit. ("Merit" translates 功, which can indicate merit, spiritual practice, or
achievement resulting from practice.) "Those who have expired still have their
virtue" 絕氣有其德 indicates that "the expired" still linger in the realm of satori.

4. The sword of the Nāga King cuts off all duality.

Case 163　毘婆尸頌　*The Verse of Vipaśyin*

毘婆尸佛、傳法偈云、身從無相中受生、猶如幻出諸形像。幻人心識
本來無、罪福皆空無所住。

Vipaśyin,[1] in his transmission verse, said:

We receive life from out of the formless;
From which issue all phenomena, like phantoms.
A phantom-person's mind being void from the start,
Both fortune and misfortune are empty and without essence.

1. Vipaśyin was the first of the Seven Buddhas of the Past. See Case 34, note 2. The transmission verses of the Buddhas of the Past are first seen in the *Anthology of the Ancestral Hall* 祖堂集.

Case 164   雲門失通   *Yunmen Loses His Powers*[1]

靈樹生生不失通、雲門凡三生爲王。所以失通。

Lingshu Rumin, though reborn many times, never lost his supernatural powers. Yunmen was reborn three times as a king and thereby lost his powers.[2]

1. Also *Blue Cliff Record* 6, Commentary.
2. Yunmen served as head monk under Lingshu at Lingshu yuan 靈樹院 and succeeded him as abbot. Yamada: The legendary account is that Lingshu and Yunmen were in previous existences disciples of Śākyamuni Buddha. Lingshu bought some incense and presented it to Śākyamuni. Afterward he attained enlightenment and throughout his successive lives had the supernatural power of knowing the past and future. Yunmen was reborn three times as a king, losing his supernatural powers because he engaged in worldly affairs (1985, 1:312–13).

Case 165   殃崛産難   *Aṅgulimāla and the Difficult Delivery*

殃崛摩羅、因持鉢入城。到一長者家、値其婦産難。長者告云、沙門
是佛弟子、有何方便、救得我家産難。殃崛云、我乍入道、未知此
法。當去問佛却來相報。乃遽返白佛、具陳上事。佛告云、汝速去
說、我自從賢聖法來、未曾殺生。殃崛依佛所說、往告長者。者婦聞
之、當時分娩。母子平安。

Once Aṅgulimāla went into a city with his begging bowl and came to the home of a rich man. At the time the wealthy man's wife was going through a difficult delivery. The wealthy man asked Aṅgulimāla, "Śramaṇa, you are a disciple of the Buddha. Is there some way in which to spare my wife this difficult delivery?"

Aṅgulimāla replied, "I have only recently entered the Way and don't yet know such a method. I will immediately return to the Buddha, ask him, then come and tell you." He hurried back and related the above matter to the Buddha.

The Buddha told him, "Go quickly and tell him, 'Since coming to know the wise and holy Dharma, never once have I taken life.'"[1]

Following the Buddha's advice, Aṅgulimāla went back to the rich man and told him this. The moment the man's wife heard this, she gave birth to her child. The mother and child were safe.

1. Prior to joining the sangha and becoming a bhikku, Aṅgulimāla had been a notorious mass murderer. See *Aṅgulimāla* in the Biographical Notes.

Case 166   巖頭渡子   *Yantou the Ferryman*

巖頭值會昌沙汰而後、於鄂州湖邊作渡子。一日、因一婆子、抱一孩
兒來。乃問、呈橈舞棹即不問。且道、婆子手中兒、甚處得來。頭以
橈便打。婆曰、婆生七子、六箇不遇知音。只這一箇也不消得、便抛
向水中。

Yantou Quanhuo, following the Huichang persecution,[1] became a ferryman on a lake in Ezhou.[2] One day a woman with a baby in her arms came and asked, "Plying the oar and handling the pole are no concern of mine. But tell me, where did this baby in my arms come from?"

Yantou struck the woman with the oar.

The woman said, "I have borne seven children. Six of them never encountered a true friend,[3] nor will this one ever be any good." So saying, she threw the baby into the water.

1. The Huichang persecution 會昌沙汰 was a major suppression of Buddhism in 842–45 by Emperor Wuzong 武宗 (r. 841–46). According to contemporary accounts, over two hundred thousand monks and nuns were forcibly laicized and numberless temples and shrines were looted or destroyed. However, at the time it occurred Yantou Quanhuo was only seventeen years old and had not even begun his Zen training. Thus it had little relation to his becoming a ferryman, which occurred many years later, subsequent to his practice under *Deshan Xuanjian*.

2. Some texts follow this with: "He hung a board on both shores. People wishing to cross the lake would hit the board once. The master would say, 'Who is it? Which shore are you crossing to?' then pole his boat to get them."

3. A "true friend" 知音 is a "friend of the Way," someone who understands one's innermost mind.

Case 167   麻谷鋤草   *Magu Digs Up Weeds*

壽州良遂座主參麻谷。谷見來便攜鋤入菜園。鋤草略不相顧、便歸方
丈。次日復參。谷便閉却門。遂扣門。谷曰、誰。遂應聲未絶、豁然
大悟曰、和尚莫謾良遂好。若不來見和尚、幾被經論賺過一生。後來
告衆曰、良遂知處、諸人不知、諸人知處、良遂總知。

Lecture master Shouzhou Liangsui sought instruction from Magu Baotie.
Magu, seeing him come, took a spade, went to the garden, and started digging weeds without paying any attention to Liangsui. He then returned to
his quarters.

The next day, when Liangsui came for instruction again, Magu shut the
gate. Liangsui knocked on the door. Magu asked, "Who's there?"

As he was about to answer, Liangsui experienced a clear, deep realization.
He said, "Master, you shouldn't slight me. If I hadn't come here and met you,
I probably would have spent my life deceived by the sutras and sastras."

In later years Liangsui told the assembly, "That which I know, everyone
does not know; that which everyone knows, I know completely."

Case 168   皓月償債   *Haoyue's "Paying Debts"*

皓月供奉、問長沙岑和尚、古德云、了即業障本來空、未了應須償宿
債。只如師子尊者二祖大師、爲甚麼得償債去。沙云、大德不識本來
空。月曰、如何是本來空。沙云、業障是。如何是業障。沙云、本來
空是。月無語。沙以偈示之曰、假有元非有、假滅亦非無。涅槃償債
義、一性更無殊。

The court monk Haoyue[1] asked Changsha Jingcen, "An ancient worthy once
said,[2] 'With awakening, karmic obstructions are originally empty; without
awakening, past debts must be paid.' Why then did Venerable Āryasiṁha
and the Second Patriarch have to pay their debts?"[3]

Changsha answered, "Venerable monk, you don't understand what 'originally empty' means."

"What is original emptiness?" Haoyue asked.

"Karmic obstruction itself," replied Changsha.

"What is karmic obstruction?" asked Haoyue.

"Original emptiness itself," answered Changsha.

When Haoyue had nothing to say, Changsha instructed him with a verse:

Provisional existence is not existence;
Provisional extinction is not null.[4]
In their true sense, nirvana and repaying debts
Are of one nature and differ not at all.

1. The court monk 供奉 performed memorial services for the emperor.

2. The "ancient worthy" is *Yongjia Xuanjue*.

3. Both masters lost their lives in violent incidents that other masters ascribed to evil karma. See *Āryasiṁha* and *Huike* in the Biographical Notes.

4. An expression of the doctrine of śūnyatā, the teaching that all phenomena are empty and cannot be defined in terms of existence and nonexistence.

Case 169   大燈鐵話   Daitō's "Iron"

大燈之鐵話。

Daitō's talk about iron.[1]

1. Daitō is notable for the frequent mention of iron 鐵 in his work. The *Record of Daitō* contains such examples as: "Touch iron and make gold" 點鐵作金; "Chaos chews raw iron" 崑崙嚙生鐵; "An iron boat floats on the water" 鐵船水上浮; "An iron wheel crushes stone" 鐵輪砕石; "A silver mountain, an iron wall" 銀山鐵壁; "One slab of iron—ten thousand miles" 萬里一条鐵; "An iron ball has no seams" 鐵丸無縫罅; "Flowers blossom on an iron tree" 鐵樹開花.

Case 170   佛教祖意   Buddha's Teaching, Bodhidharma's Intention

古德曰、佛教說理致、祖意說機關。

An ancient worthy said, "Buddha's teaching is expressed through reason; Bodhidharma's intention is expressed through devices."[1]

1. "Reason" translates 理致, clear, logical explanation. "Bodhidharma's intention" is Bodhidharma's intention in coming from the West; "devices" translates 機關, the use of expedient means like the stick, the shout, questions-and-answers, and koans. The identity of the "ancient worthy" is uncertain. The Japanese Zen master *Musō Soseki* quotes a similar passage, also attributing it to an unidentified "man of old," and comments at some length in his *Dialogues in a Dream*:

> An ancient master said, "Prior to Mazu and Baizhang, many teachers utilized the 'teaching through principle' approach and few used the 'teaching through devices'

approach. Subsequent to Mazu and Baizhang, many teachers utilized the 'teaching through devices' approach and few used the 'teaching through principle' approach. In so doing, their policy was to 'watch the wind and set the sails accordingly.'"

Present-day students who prefer teaching through principle tend to demean teaching through devices, and those who prefer teaching through devices tend to demean teaching through principle. Neither type of student understands the methods of the founding masters. If you say that teaching through devices is the superior method, would you then say that all of the masters prior to Mazu and Baizhang lacked the Zen eye? If you say that teaching through principle is superior, would you say that Linji and Deshan did not know the true meaning of Zen?… A koan is simply an upāya; if one imposes interpretations upon the different expressions of this upāya, one obscures what the masters are truly attempting to convey. A completely liberated person can take gold and transform it to dirt, and can take dirt and transform it to gold. When such people hold something in their hands, how can you possibly know whether it is dirt or gold? It is no different with the teachings. When a clear-eyed master expresses a teaching, it is impossible to define it either as "teaching through principle" or "teaching through devices." (Chapter 81; translation from Kirchner 2010, pp. 169–70)

Case 171   末後評頌   *Comment and Verse on the Final Word*[1]

無門開禪師、舉德山托鉢話曰、若是末後句、巖頭德山倶未夢見在。
檢點將來、好似一棚傀儡。頌云、識得最初句、便會末後句。末後與
最初、不是者一句。

Wumen Huikai commented on the koan "Deshan Carries His Bowls":

As for the "final word," neither Yantou nor Deshan have so much as even dreamed of it. If you look closely, it is like a puppet show. The verse:

> If you understand the first word, you understand the final word.
> But, first or final, they are not the same word![2]

1. *Wumen guan* 13, Verse. For the koan "Deshan Carries His Bowls," see Cases 22-1, 22-2, and 54, above. For "final word," see also Case 140.

2. The Chinese of the final clause is ambiguous. Shibayama renders it as, "'It' is not a word" (1974, p. 100); Cleary has, "Are they not this one word?" (1993b, p. 63); Sekida has, "[They] are not one word" (1977, p. 56).

Yamamoto comments on the line by citing the koan that comprises Case 72 of the *Kattōshū*, in which the Buddha states, "For forty-nine years I have dwelt in the world, but I have yet to preach a single word" (1960, p. 173). In *Blue Cliff Record* 51, Yantou comments, "If you wish to know the final word, just this! just this!" (Main Case).

Case 172　慈明執爨　*Ciming Tends the Hearth*

慈明婆近寺而居、人莫之測。慈明乘閑必至彼。一日當參、粥罷久之
不聞摑鼓。楊岐爲監寺、問行者、今日當參、何不擊鼓。云、和尚
出未歸。徑往婆處。見明執爨婆煮粥。岐云、和尚今日當參、大衆久
待、何以不歸。明曰、你下得一轉語即歸。下不得各自東西去。楊岐
以笠子蓋頭上行數步。明大喜遂同歸。

Ciming's old woman[1] lived near the temple, and no one could fathom her.
Ciming would go there whenever he had free time. One morning on a
scheduled lecture-day the drum announcing the lecture failed to sound
even though breakfast had finished some time before. Yangqi Fanghui,
who was then the temple supervisor, asked a lay brother why the drum
hadn't sounded. "Because the abbot is away and hasn't returned," replied the
brother.

Yangqi immediately went to the woman's house and looked inside. Ciming was tending the hearth while the woman stirred some rice gruel. "Today
is a lecture day, and the assembly has been waiting a long time," said Yangqi.
"Why haven't you returned?"

"If you can give me a turning-phrase, I'll go back," replied Ciming. "If
not, then the whole lot of you can leave—to the east, west, or wherever."

Yangqi covered his head with his bamboo hat and walked several paces.
Very pleased, Ciming returned with him to the temple.[2]

1. "Old woman" translates 婆, a character indicating either an old woman or
a wife.

2. This case is an example of the qualities of Ciming mentioned in Case 106. See
also Case 189 (referring to note 2) for an incident relating to the present koan.

Case 173　慈明虎聲　*Ciming and the Tiger's Roar*

慈明圓禪師、因泉大道來參。明問曰、白雲橫谷口、道人何處來。泉
顧視左右云、夜來何處火、燒出古人墳。師呵云、未在更道。泉作虎
聲。師打一坐具。泉推倒慈明。明亦作虎聲。泉退身大嘆云、我參七
十餘員善知識、惟師可以繼得臨濟正宗。

Dadao Guquan called upon Ciming. Ciming asked him, "White clouds block
the mouth of the valley.[1] From where, then, does the wayfarer come?"

Dadao looked left and right, then said, "Last night a fire somewhere
burned out an old master's grave."[2]

Ciming scolded him, saying, "You're not yet there! Say more!"

Dadao made a tiger's roar. The master struck him with his sitting cloth,[3] whereupon Dadao pushed him over. Ciming then roared like a tiger.

Dadao withdrew and exclaimed in admiration, "I have visited over seventy enlightened teachers,[4] but only you succeed to the true teachings of Linji."

1. Mujaku: Ciming has closed the gate and allows neither sages nor fools to pass. The wayfarer may be taken to refer to Dadao.

2. Mujaku: Dadao compares himself to fire that has tested Ciming and revealed his eremitic nature.

3. For "sitting cloth," see Case 37, note 2.

4. For "enlightened teachers," see Case 13, note 1.

Case 174   慈明脱履   *Ciming Takes Off a Shoe*

慈明圓禪師、謁神鼎諲禪師。諲望尊一時。衲子非人類精奇、無敢登
其門者。師髮長不剪剃、弊衣楚音、通稱法姪。一衆大笑。神鼎遣童
子問、長老誰之嗣。師仰視屋曰、親見汾陽來。神鼎杖而出、顧見頎
然問曰、汾陽有西河獅子是不。師指其後絶叫曰、屋倒矣。童子返
走。神鼎囬顧相顜鑠。師地坐脱隻履而視之。諲老忘所問、又失師所
在。師徐起整衣、且行且語云、見面不如聞名。遂去。神鼎遣人追之
不可。乃嘆云、汾陽乃有此兒耶。

Ciming Chuyuan had an audience with master Shending Hongyin. At the time Hongyin was held in the highest repute, and it was only the finest of monks who dared enter his gate. Ciming stood there, his robe tattered and his hair long and unshaven, speaking in the dialect of Chu and calling himself a "Dharma nephew." The entire assembly had a good laugh.

Hongyin told an acolyte to ask Ciming, "Whose successor are you?"

Ciming gazed toward the roof and said, "Before coming here I had a heart-to-heart encounter with Fenyang Shanzhao."

At this Hongyin himself came out, staff in hand. Looking Ciming in the face, he asked politely, "Is it true that the Lion of West River was at Fenyang's place?"[1]

Ciming pointed behind Hongyin and roared, "The building is falling!"

At this the acolyte ran off, and Hongyin looked around in alarm. Ciming sat down on the ground, took off one of his shoes, and looked at Hongyin.

Hongyin not only forgot what he was going to say but didn't realize where Ciming was.

Ciming calmly stood up, straightened his robes, and said, "What I saw of him didn't measure up to what I heard of him." Then he quickly walked off.

Hongyin sent someone after him, but Ciming paid no heed. Hongyin said in admiration, "So, Fenyang had a child like this!"

1. "The Lion of West River" 西河獅子 was a nickname given to Ciming because of the intensity of his practice.

Case 175   關山本有   *Kanzan's "Inherently Perfect Buddha"*

圓覺經云、本有圓成佛、爲甚還作迷倒衆生。

The *Sutra of Complete Enlightenment* asks, "If we all are inherently perfect buddhas, why then have we become ignorant, deluded sentient beings?"[1]

1. T 17:915b. The *Kattōshū* mistakenly attributes the passage to the *Vimalakīrti Sutra*. No similar passage appears in this sutra, however. The closest equivalent is a passage in the *Sutra of Complete Enlightenment* that reads:

> World Honored One, if sentient beings have intrinsically accomplished Buddha-hood 本來成佛, how can there be so much ignorance? If all sentient beings originally have ignorance, why does the Tathagata say that they have intrinsically accomplished Buddhahood? If sentient beings in all ten directions intrinsically accomplished the Buddha Path and afterward gave rise to ignorance, then when will the Tathagata give rise to vexations again? (Sheng-yen 1997, p. 171)

It should be noted, however, that the precise term "inherently perfect buddha" 本有圓成佛 originated in Japan, and that use of the koan above began with the Japanese Zen master *Kanzan Egen*. The concept of the inherently perfect buddha formed a central tenet of Kanzan's teaching.

Case 176   臨濟赤肉   *Linji's "Hunk of Red Flesh"*[1]

臨濟上堂云、赤肉團上有一無位眞人、常從汝等諸人面門出入。未證據者看看。時有僧出問、如何是無位眞人。師下禪床把住云、道道。其僧擬議。師托開云、無位眞人是什麼乾屎橛、便歸方丈。

Linji took the high seat in the hall and said, "In this hunk of red flesh is a true person of no rank[2] who always goes in and out of the gates of your face.[3] Those of you who have not yet realized this person, look, look!"

A monk stepped forward and asked, "What is this true person of no rank?"

The master descended from his seat, grabbed the monk, and cried, "Speak, speak!" The monk hesitated.

The master shoved him away and said, "The true person of no rank—what a dried turd he is!" Then he returned to his quarters.

1. Also *Record of Linji*, Discourse 3; *Record of Equanimity* 38, Main Case.

2. The "hunk of red flesh" 赤肉團 can refer either to the physical body or to the heart. The "true person of no rank" 無位眞人 is an expression original to Linji but has its roots in the Taoist term "true person" 眞人, designating a realized practitioner. It was adopted into Buddhism prior to the time of Linji in order to indicate arhats and bodhisattvas.

3. "Gates of your face" 面門 refers to the facial sense organs.

Case 177   臨濟四境   *Linji's Four Realms*[1]

僧問臨濟、如何是四種無相境。師曰、你一念心疑、被地來礙。你一念心愛、被水來溺。你一念心瞋、被火來燒。你一念心喜、被風來飄。若能如是辨得、不被境轉、[處處用境]、東涌西沒、南涌北沒、中涌邊沒、邊涌中沒、履水如地、履地如水。緣何如此。爲達四大如夢如幻故。

Someone asked Linji, "What are the four realms of no-form?"

The master said, "A thought of doubt in your mind and you're obstructed by the element of earth; a thought of desire in your mind and you drown in the element water; a thought of anger in your mind and you're scorched by the element fire; a thought of joy in your mind and you're blown about by the element wind."[2]

Understand this, however, and you will no longer be tossed about by circumstances; instead you will utilize them wherever you go. You can appear in the east and vanish in the west, appear in the south and vanish in the north, appear in the center and vanish at the border, appear at the border and vanish in the center. You can walk on the water as though it is land and walk on the land as though it is water.[3]

Why can you do these things? Because you realize that the four elements are like dreams, like illusions.

1. Also *Record of Linji*, Discourse 15.

2. Earth, water, fire, and wind are the four basic elements according to ancient Indian thought.

3. The abilities described in this paragraph are the "six earth-shakings" that represent the free working of the awakened person. They are mentioned in a number of sutras, such as the *Mahā-prajñā-pāramitā Sutra*, which describes the six earth-shakings said to have occurred when the Buddha entered the Samadhi of the Joyful Play of the Lion (T 6:642c), and the *Avataṃsaka Sutra*, which describes the six earth-shakings and the eighteen movements caused by the Buddha's supernatural powers (T 10:278a).

Case 178　臨濟四喝　*Linji's Four Shouts*[1]

臨濟問僧、有時一喝、如金剛王寶劍、有時一喝、如踞地金毛獅子、有時一喝、如探竿影草、有時一喝、不作一喝用。汝作麼生會。僧擬議。師便喝。

Linji said to a monk, "Sometimes a shout is like the diamond sword of the Vajra King;[2] sometimes a shout is like a golden-haired lion crouching in wait;[3] sometimes a shout is like a pole for probing amid the shadowy weeds;[4] sometimes a shout doesn't function as a shout. How do you understand this?"

When the monk hesitated, the master gave a shout.

1. Also *Record of Linji*, Critical Examinations 20.
2. The diamond sword of the Vajra King is the diamond-hard sword of wisdom that cuts off delusion and ignorance.
3. A metaphor for focused strength and awareness.
4. The origin of the metaphor is unclear, but it appears to represent the methods a master uses to probe the student's understanding.

Case 179　一喝商量　*One Shout Remains*

臨濟錄馬防序曰、唯餘一喝、尚要商量。

Ma Fang's "Preface" to the *Record of Linji* says, "One shout still remains. This one requires further consideration."[1]

1. The full quote from Ma's "Preface" reads: "I have checked thoroughly and there's nothing omitted. Just one shout still remains, this one requires a question-and-answer investigation."

Case 180 臨濟主句 *Linji's "Host and Guest"* [1]

臨濟、因兩堂首座、相見同時下喝。僧問師、還有賓主也無。師云、
賓主歷然。師云、大衆要會臨濟賓主句、問取堂中二首座。即下座。

The head monks of the two halls at Linji's monastery met and simultaneously shouted.

A monk asked the master, "Was there a guest and a host there?"

"Guest and host were obvious," the master replied. He then said, "If you in the assembly want to understand what I mean by 'guest' and 'host,' go ask the head monks of the two halls." Then he stepped down.

1. Also *Record of Linji*, Discourse 4. The incident is also referred to in the *Blue Cliff Record* 38, Commentary to the Main Case.

Case 181 四賓主話 *The Four Guest-Host Relationships* [1]

臨濟禪師示衆云、[道流、如禪宗見解、死活循然]。參學之人、大須
子細。如主客相見、便有言論往來。或應物現形、或全體作用、或把
機權喜怒、或現半身、或乘獅子、或乘象王。如有眞正學人、便喝先
拈出一箇膠盆子。善知識不辨是境、便上他境上作模作樣。學人便
喝。前人不肯放。此是膏肓之病不堪醫。喚作客看主。或是善知識不
拈出物、隨學人問處即奪。學人被奪抵死不放。此是主看客。或有學
人、應一箇清淨境出善知識前。善知識辨得是境、把得抛向坑裏。學
人言、大好善知識。即云、咄哉不識好惡。學人便禮拜。此喚作主看
主。或有學人、披枷帶鎖出善知識前。善知識更與安一重枷鎖。學人
歡喜、彼此不辨。呼爲客看客。

Zen master Linji addressed the assembly, saying:

Followers of the Way, in the view of the Zen school death and life proceed in an orderly sequence. Students of Zen must examine [this] most carefully.

When host and guest meet they check each other out. At times, in response to something, they may manifest a certain form; they may act with their whole body; they may use tricks or devices to appear joyful or angry; they may reveal half of their body; they may ride a lion or a lordly elephant. [2]

A true student gives a shout and begins by holding out a tray of sticky glue. The teacher, not discerning where this comes from, seizes hold of it and performs all sorts of antics. The student shouts again, but the teacher is unwilling to abandon his views. This is a disease impossible to cure. It is called "the guest examines the host."

Sometimes a teacher offers nothing, but the moment the student asks a question, he takes it away. The student, deprived of his question, resists to the death and will not let go. This is called "the host examines the guest."

Sometimes a student comes before a teacher in a state of pure clarity. The teacher, discerning this realm, seizes it and flings it into a pit. "An excellent teacher!" exclaims the student, but the teacher replies, "Bah! Who are you to tell good from bad?!" The student then makes a deep bow. This is called "the host examines the host."

Or a student may appear before a teacher locked in a yoke and bound with chains.[3] To these the teacher adds still more yokes and chains, whereupon the student is so delighted that he doesn't know what's what. This is called "the guest examines the guest."

1. Also *Record of Linji*, Discourse 18.

2. "Riding a lion" and "riding a lordly elephant" are allusions to, respectively, the bodhisattvas Mañjuśrī (who is represented iconographically as mounted on a lion) and Samantabhadra (who is represented iconographically as mounted on a white elephant with six tusks).

3. Yokes and chains represent deluded ideas regarding Buddhism.

Case 182   百丈再参   *Baizhang Goes to See Mazu Again*[1]

百丈再參馬祖。[侍立次、祖以目視禪床角頭拂子]。 祖見來拈拂子堅
起。丈云、即此用離此用。祖掛拂子於舊處。侍立片時。祖曰、你已
後、鼓兩片皮、如何爲人。丈取拂子堅起。祖云、即此用離此用。丈
掛拂子於舊處。祖便振威一喝。丈大悟。後來、謂黃檗云、我當時被
馬祖一喝、直得三日耳聾。黃檗不覺悚然吐舌。

Baizhang called on Mazu again.[2] Seeing him come, Mazu picked up his whisk[3] and held it upright. Baizhang asked, "Are you one with this function, or separate from this function?"[4]

Mazu hung the whisk in its original place.[5] Baizhang remained standing in attendance for a while. Mazu asked him, "In the future, how will you preach so as to benefit people?"[6]

Baizhang took the whisk and held it upright.[7] Mazu said, "Are you one with that function, or separate from that function?"

Baizhang hung the whisk in its original place. Mazu thereupon gave a mighty shout, and Baizhang had a deep understanding.

In later years Baizhang said to Huangbo, "That great shout of Mazu left me deaf for three days." Huangbo, shuddering with fear and amazement, stood there open-mouthed with his tongue out.

1. Also *Blue Cliff Record* 11, Commentary on the Main Case. Dōmae: This exchange between Mazu and Baizhang followed the incident recorded as Case 53 of the *Blue Cliff Record*:

> Mazu and Baizhang were walking one day when they saw a wild duck fly by. Mazu asked, "What was that?" "A wild duck," answered Baizhang. "Where has it gone?" asked Mazu. "It's flown off," Baizhang replied. Mazu grabbed Baizhang's nose and twisted it. When Baizhang cried out in pain Mazu said, "And you said it had flown off!" At this Baizhang had an understanding.

Blue Cliff Record 53 and *Entangling Vines* 182 are concerned with the two fundamental aspects of Zen training: the element of wisdom or enlightenment and the element of compassion or function in the world. *Blue Cliff Record* 53, in which Baizhang experiences a profound awakening to the oneness of all things, relates to the first; *Entangling Vines* 182, in which Mazu presses Baizhang on how he intends to teach, relates to the second.

2. At this point the *Kattōshū* has the line, "As Baizhang stood in attendance, Mazu saw the whisk in the corner of the meditation seat" 侍立次祖以目視禪床角頭拂子. This line is an insertion from the *Compendium of the Five Lamps*; the rest of the koan follows the text as recorded in the *Transmission of the Lamp* anthologies. The line has been removed as it disrupts the narrative flow.

3. "Whisk" translates 拂子, the Chinese term for the Sanskrit "vyajana," meaning "fan," "brush," or "whisk." Whisks were used in the Indian sangha to shoo away annoying insects; those made with white hair, in particular, came to serve as signs of authority. In Chinese and Japanese Zen white-haired whisks symbolize the master's function as a teacher and guide.

4. The Chinese is ambiguous. Yamada regards the question as asking, "Is the very act of raising the whisk the Buddhadharma, or is Buddhadharma a separate something that raises the whisk?" (1985, 2:109). Mujaku reads it to mean, "Do you function in accord with the whisk, or apart from the whisk?" Katō comments that Baizhang could just as well have asked, "What is it? Wisdom or compassion? Reining in or letting go? Practicing or teaching?" (1939–40, 3:135).

Interestingly, Chinese translators read this as a statement, not a question, and render it in various ways: "This is the very functioning which one should keep from" (Luk 1974, p. 52); "It is that function, it leaves that function" (Chien 1992, p. 102); "In the very act of using it, you are detached from its use" (Wu 1996, p. 101).

5. That is, he returns "function" to its origin, "nondoing."

6. Literally, "Later, how will you move your two lips so as to benefit people?"

7. That is, he would take up the whisk and serve in Mazu's stead.

Case 183-1   慈明連喝   *Ciming's Consecutive Shouts*

楊岐問慈明、幽鳥語喃喃、辭雲入亂峰時如何。明云、我行荒草裡、
汝又入深村。岐云、官不容針、更借一問得麼。明便喝。岐云、好一
喝。明亦喝。岐又喝。明連喝兩喝。岐便禮拜。明云、這事是箇人正
能擔荷。岐拂袖出。

Yangqi Fanghui asked Ciming, "What about when 'an unseen bird, twitter-ing and chirping, leaves the clouds and enters the rugged peaks'?"[1]

Ciming replied, "I'll head for a wild, uncut meadow. You go to a secluded village."[2]

Yangqi said, "Officially even a needle is not permitted,[3] but would you allow me another question?"

At this Ciming gave a shout.

"A wonderful shout!" Yangqi said.

Ciming shouted again. Yangqi too shouted. Ciming then shouted twice in a row. Yangqi bowed.

Ciming said, "It's because you're such a man as this that the Great Matter can be entrusted to you." Yangqi shook his sleeves and left.

1. ZGJI: "To leave the exalted and enter the humble." Yangqi's training under Ciming was ending, and soon he would leave the monastery for Jiufeng 九峰, his native province. Ciming would leave for Mount Nanyue 南嶽.

2. "You can go where you want, I'll go where I want."

3. This is part of the expression, "Officially not even a needle is permitted; privately even a carriage can go through." Officially no objections are allowed, but unofficially much is permitted.

Case 183-2   虛堂幽谷   *Xutang's Dark Valley*

虛堂拈云、下喬木入幽谷、養子之緣。慈明爲甚麼連喝兩喝。

Xutang commented, "Descending from the lofty trees, he enters the dark valleys[1]—the compassion of a parent! But why did Ciming shout twice?"

1. Mencius, in the section on Duke Wen of Teng, has the passage, "I have heard of 'leaving dark valleys to live in high trees,' but I have never heard of 'leaving high trees to live in dark valleys,'" meaning that people may leave barbarism for civilization, but not the reverse. Zen turns this around, with "entering the dark valley" indicating descent from the lofty realm of enlightenment to work for the liberation of all beings in the "dark valleys" of the suffering world.

Case 184　興化兩遭　*Xinghua's Two Waves of the Hand*[1]

興化禪師、因同參來、纔上法堂。師便喝。僧亦喝。行三兩步。師又
喝。僧亦喝。須臾近前。師拈棒。僧又喝。師云、你看、這[瞎]漢猶
作主在。僧擬議。師便打直打下法堂。師則歸方丈。有僧問、適來僧
有甚言句、觸忤和尚。師云、是他適來、也有權、也有實、也有照、
也有用。我將手向伊面前橫兩遭、到這裡却用不得。似這瞎漢、不打
更待幾時。

A fellow student of Xinghua Cunjiang came and entered the Dharma Hall.
Xinghua gave a shout. The monk too gave a shout and advanced two or
three strides, whereupon Xinghua shouted again. The monk too shouted
again, and after a moment came forward. Xinghua held up his staff. The
monk again shouted.

"You see! This dolt is still trying to play the host!" remarked Xinghua.
The monk hesitated. Xinghua struck him and drove him out of the Dharma
Hall, then returned to his quarters.

Someone asked, "The monk who was just here—what did he say to
deserve the master's anger?"

Xinghua answered, "That monk had technique, he had essence, he had
illumination, he had function. But when I waved my hand[2] in front of him
two times he couldn't respond. If you don't hit a blind oaf like that he'll
never get anywhere."

1. This koan is mentioned in passing in Case 123, above: "The subtlety and
depth of Xinghua is seen in…the way he waved his hand two times in front of
the monk's face."

2. "Draw a line" 畫一畫, as found in the present *Kattōshū* text, has been replaced
with "waved my hand in front of him two times" 橫兩遭, to bring the koan into
line with the traditional biographical materials on Xinghua and with Case 123.

Case 185　南院啐啄　*Nanyuan's "Pecking and Tapping"*[1]

南院示眾云、諸方只具啐啄同時眼、不具啐啄同時用。有僧出問、如
何是啐啄同時用。南院云、作家不啐啄、啐啄同時失。僧云、猶是學
人疑處。院云、作麼生是你疑處。僧云、失。院便打。其僧不肯。院
便趕出。僧後到雲門會裡舉前話。有一僧云、南院棒折那。其僧豁
然有省。且道、意在什麼處。其僧却回見南院。院適已遷化。却見風

穴。纔禮拜。穴云、莫是當時問先師啐啄同時底僧麼。僧云、是。穴
云、你當時作麼生會。僧云、某甲當初時、如燈影裡行相似。穴云、
你會也。

Nanyuan, addressing the assembly, said, "You grasp the idea of simultaneous pecking and tapping,[2] but you lack the function of simultaneous pecking and tapping."

A monk came forward and asked, "What is the function of simultaneous
pecking and tapping?"

Nanyuan said, "A true adept has no need of pecking and tapping; the
moment there is pecking and tapping, the function is lost."

The monk said, "I'm still in doubt."

"What are you in doubt about?" Nanyuan asked.

"You lost it!"[3] the monk said. Nanyuan thereupon struck him with his
stick. The monk didn't concur, so Nanyuan drove him away. Later the monk
went to Yunmen's assembly, where he mentioned this conversation.

A monk asked, "And did Nanyuan break his stick?"[4] At this the first
monk had a clear, deep awakening. (Tell me, where is the meaning in this?)

The monk went back to see Nanyuan, but as Nanyuan had already passed
away, he called upon Nanyuan's successor, Fengxue Yanzhao, instead. As
soon as the monk had paid his respects, Fengxue asked, "Aren't you the
monk who, a while ago, was asking our late teacher about simultaneous
pecking and tapping?"

The monk said, "Yes."

Fengxue asked, "And what was your understanding then?"

The monk replied, "At that time it was as if I were walking in the dim light
of a lamp."

Fengxue said, "You have understood."[5]

1. Also *Blue Cliff Record* 16, Commentary.

2. When an egg is ready to hatch, the hen pecks on the outside of the shell just
as the chick begins to move and peck from the inside. Zen uses this as a metaphor
for the perfect accord between master and disciple, with the master acting at just
the right time to help the student break through his or her "shell."

3. The translation follows the comment in a lecture of Harada Shōdō Rōshi,
who interprets the monk's response as an indication that he saw Nanyuan himself as having just engaged in pecking and tapping, and thus as having lost the
function. The exchange can also be translated as: "'What are you in doubt about?'
Nanyuan asked. '[I don't understand] "lost,"' the monk said."

4. That is, "Did Nanyuan hit you hard enough (that is, with enough compassion) to break his stick?"

5. In commenting upon this koan, Hakuin recalled that when young he had

seen a cicada emerging from its chrysalis. In a well-meaning attempt to help the creature, he freed one of its wings. The wing never assumed a normal shape, however, and the cicada died. Hakuin always regretted his misdirected kindness (*Keisō dokuzui* 荊叢毒蘂 6).

Case 186   虚堂挂杖   *Xutang's Staff*

虚堂上堂、挂杖子尋常口吧吧地道、我能縱能奪、能殺能活。及問他
遠法師因甚不過虎溪、便道不得。且道病在那裡。

Xutang took the high seat and said, "This staff always talks big, saying 'I can bind and I can release; I can kill and I can give life.'[1] But ask it why Dharma Master Huiyuan never went beyond Tiger Creek,[2] and it cannot answer. Tell me, what is the root of this disease?"

1. The staff symbolizes the master. "I can bind, I can release; I can kill and I can give life" is a traditional expression of the master's complete freedom of function.
2. For background information, see *Huiyuan* in the Biographical Notes. Tiger Creek marked the boundary beyond which Huiyuan refused to go when seeing visitors off from his monastery on Mount Lu. Huiyuan's seclusion on the mountain was a particularly strong version of the rule against Zen monks leaving the monastery during the training season. Xutang asks why, when we are inherently free, it is forbidden to leave the monastic confines.

One anecdote, apparently apocryphal but customarily mentioned in Zen lectures on this koan, says that Huiyuan was once visited by two old friends, the Taoist Lu Xiujing 陸脩靜 and the Confucian Yao Yuanming 陶淵明. At the end of the day, as the three friends walked down the mountain, Huiyuan became so engrossed in conversation that he unwittingly crossed Tiger Creek. When the three of them saw what had happened, they all broke out in hearty laughter.

Case 187   臨濟築拳   *Linji Delivers a Blow*[1]

臨濟、初在黃檗會下、行業純一。首座乃歎曰、雖是後生、與眾有
異。遂問、上座在此多少時。師云、三年。首座云、曾參問也無。師
云、不曾參問、不知問箇什麼。首座云、汝何不去問堂頭和尚、如何
是佛法的的大意。師便去問、聲未絕、黃檗便打。師下來。首座云、
問話作麼生。師云、某甲問聲未絕、和尚便打。某甲不會。首座云、
但更去問。師又去問。黃檗又打。如是三度發問、三度被打。師來白

首座云、幸蒙慈悲、令某甲問訊和尚、三度發問、三度被打。自恨障
緣不領深旨。今且辭去。首座云、汝若去時、須辭和尚去。師禮拜
退。首座先到和尚處云、問話底後生、甚是如法。若來辭時、方便接
他。向後穿鑿、成一株大樹、與天下人、作蔭涼去在。師去辭。黃檗
云、不得往別處去。汝向高安灘頭大愚處去。必爲汝說。師到大愚。
大愚問、什麼處來。師云、黃檗處來。大愚云、黃檗有何言句。師
云、某甲三度問佛法的的大意、三度被打。不知某甲有過無過。大愚
云、黃檗與麼老婆、爲汝得徹困。更來這裡、問有過無過。師於言下
大悟云、元來黃檗佛法無多子。大愚搊住云、這尿床鬼子、適來道有
過無過、如今却道、黃檗佛法無多子。你見箇什麼道理、速道速道。
師於大愚脅下築三拳。大愚托開云、汝師黃檗、非干我事。師辭大
愚、却回黃檗。黃檗見來便問、這漢來來去去、有什麼了期。師云、
祇爲老婆心切。便人事了侍立。黃檗問、什麼處去來。師云、昨奉慈
旨、令參大愚去來。黃檗云、大愚有何言句。師遂舉前話。黃檗云、
作麼生得這漢來、待痛與一頓。師云、說什麼待來、即今便喫、隨後
便掌。黃檗云、這風顛漢、却來這裡捋虎鬚。師便喝。黃檗云、侍者
引這風顛漢參堂去。後潙山舉此話問仰山、臨濟當時、得大愚力、得
黃檗力。仰山云、非但騎虎頭、亦解把虎尾。

When Linji was in the assembly under Huangbo, he was pure and straight-forward in his practice. The head monk praised him, saying, "Though young, he's different from the other monks." So he asked, "Good monk, how long have you been here?"

Linji replied, "Three years."

"Have you ever asked for instruction?" inquired the head monk.

"No, never. I wouldn't know what to ask," answered Linji.

The head monk said, "Why don't you ask the head priest of the temple, 'What is the true meaning of the Buddhadharma?'"

Linji went to ask, but before he had finished Huangbo struck him. When Linji came back the head monk inquired, "How did your question go?"

"Before I had finished asking, the master hit me. I don't understand," said Linji.

"Just go back and ask again," said the head monk. Linji went again to ask and again was struck by Huangbo. In this way Linji asked his question three times and was hit three times.

Linji came and said to the head monk, "I had the good fortune to receive your compassion, and you directed me to question the master. Three times I questioned him, three times I was struck. To my regret I have some karmic obstruction and cannot grasp the profound meaning of this. I'll now be on my way."

The head monk said, "If you are going away, be sure to take your leave of the master." Linji made obeisances and withdrew. The head monk went to Huangbo's quarters ahead of Linji and said, "The young fellow who has been questioning you is in accord with the Dharma. If he comes to take his leave, please deal with him appropriately. With more training he is certain to become a great, fine tree, giving shade to people everywhere."

When Linji came to take his leave Huangbo said, "You mustn't go anywhere but to Dayu's place by the river in Gaoan. He will surely explain things for you."

Linji arrived at Dayu's place. Dayu asked, "Where have you come from?"

"From Huangbo," replied Linji.

"What did he have to say?" asked Dayu.

"Three times I asked him, 'What is the true meaning of the Buddhadharma?' and three times he hit me. I don't know if I was at fault or not."

"Such a kind old grandmother! Huangbo exhausted himself with your troubles, and now you come around asking if you were at fault or not!" said Dayu.

At these words Linji was greatly enlightened. "There isn't much to Huangbo's Buddhadharma after all!" he exclaimed.

Dayu grabbed Linji and said, "You bed-wetting little devil! You hardly finish asking if you were at fault, and then you say that there's not so much to Huangbo's Buddhadharma. What truth did you just see? Speak quickly, speak quickly!" Linji hit Dayu three times in the ribs. Shoving him away, Dayu exclaimed, "Huangbo is your teacher. This is no business of mine."

Linji left Dayu and returned to Huangbo. Seeing him arrive, Huangbo said, "This fellow! Coming and going, coming and going—when will it ever end!"

"It's all because of your grandmotherly kindness," Linji said. Having performed the proper courtesies, he stood waiting.

"Where have you been?" asked Huangbo.

"Recently you kindly directed me to see Dayu," said Linji. "Now I'm back."

"What did Dayu have to say?" asked Huangbo. Linji then told him of his conversation with Dayu. Huangbo said, "I'd like to get hold of that fellow and give him a good thrashing!"

"Why say you'd 'like to'? Have it right now!" Linji said, and gave Huangbo a slap.

"This lunatic, coming back here and pulling the tiger's whiskers!" cried Huangbo. Linji gave a shout. Huangbo said, "Attendant, take this lunatic back to the meditation hall."

Later Guishan brought up this story and asked Yangshan, "At that time was Linji helped through the ability of Dayu or through that of Huangbo?"

"He not only rode on the tiger's head but also grabbed its tail," answered Yangshan.

1. Also *Record of Linji*, Record of Pilgrimages 1; *Blue Cliff Record* 11, Commentary on the Main Case.

Case 188   洞山三頓   *Dongshan's "Three-Score Blows"*[1]

洞山初參雲門。門問云、近離甚處。山云、渣渡。門云、夏在甚麼
處。山云、湖南報慈。門云、幾時離彼中。山云、八月二十五。門
云、放你三頓棒、參堂去。師晚間入室、親近問云、某甲過在什麼
處。門云、飯袋子、江西湖南、便恁麼去。洞山於言下豁然大悟。遂
云、某甲他日、向無人烟處、卓箇庵子、不蓄一粒米、不種一莖菜、
常接待往來十方大善知識、盡與伊抽却釘、拔却楔、拈却膩脂帽子、
脫却鶻臭布衫、盡令洒洒落落地、作箇無事人去。門云、身如椰子
大、開得許大口。洞山便辭去。

When Dongshan Shouchu first met Yunmen, Yunmen asked, "Where did you just come from?"

Dongshan answered, "From Chadu."

"Where did you spend the training season?" Yunmen asked.

Dongshan said, "At Baoci in Hunan."

Yunmen asked, "And when did you leave there?"

"August twenty-fifth," Dongshan answered.

Yunmen said, "You're spared three-score blows of my stick. Go to the meditation hall."

After the evening lecture, Dongshan inquired privately of Yunmen, "Where was my error?"

Yunmen said, "You rice bag! Wandering about like that from Jiangxi to Hunan!"

At these words Dongshan attained a clear, deep awakening. He said, "Someday I'll go where there's no one around and build myself a hut; I'll store no rice and plant no vegetables but will receive worthy friends coming and going from all directions.[2] Pulling out their pegs and yanking out their wedges, snatching away their grubby hats and ripping off their smelly robes, I'll make them clean and free, I'll make them people with nothing to do."

Yunmen said, "You're no larger than a coconut, yet how big your mouth is!" Dongshan then departed.

1. In part, *Wumen guan* 15, Main Case; *Blue Cliff Record* 12, Commentary on the Verse.

2. For "worthy friends," see Case 13, note 1.

Case 189 慈明論棒 *Ciming Asks about the Three-Score Blows*

慈明謂黃龍云、書記學雲門禪、必善其旨。如曰放洞山三頓棒、洞山

于時、應打不應打。龍曰、應打。慈明色莊而言、聞三頓棒聲、便是

喫棒、則汝自旦及暮、聞鴉鳴鵲噪鐘魚鼓板之聲、亦應喫棒。喫棒何

時當已哉。龍瞠而却。慈明云、吾始疑不堪汝師、今可矣。即使拜。

Ciming Chuyuan said to Huanglong Huinan, "If the secretary [Huanglong] has studied Yunmen's Zen, surely you understand it. Tell me, when Dongshan Shouchu was spared three-score blows of Yunmen's staff, should he have been struck or should he not have been struck?"

"He should have been struck," answered Huanglong.

Ciming, his face stern, said, "If, after hearing that Yunmen spared Dongshan three-score blows, you feel that Dongshan should have been struck, then you should be struck from dawn to dusk, whether hearing the caw of a crow, the cry of a magpie, or the sounds of the bells, the wooden fish, and the gong.[1] When would you ever stop getting the stick?"

Huanglong, surprised, stepped back. Ciming said, "At first I thought I could not serve as your teacher, but now I see that I can." He allowed Huanglong to make obeisance.[2]

1. Bells 鐘 of various sizes are used at Zen monasteries to signal the time of day, the start of ceremonies, etc. The "wooden fish" 魚鼓 (lit., "fish drum") is a fish-shaped instrument hung outside the meditation hall or the refectory and struck to signal breakfast and lunch. (This wooden fish is different from the wooden fish 木魚—*mokugyo* in Japanese—presently used in Zen monasteries to set the beat during sutra chanting.) The gong 板 (short for "cloud-gong" 雲板) is a cloud-shaped metal plate that is sounded at the time of breakfast and lunch.

2. Huanglong as a young monk studied under a Yunmen-school master named Huaicheng 懷澄 (n.d.) and soon received transmission. However, after Yunfeng Wenyue 雲峯文悦 (998–1062) criticized his understanding and suggested that he train further under Ciming, Huanglong headed for Mount Shishuang, where Ciming was abbot at the time. However, disappointed upon hearing about Ciming's "old woman" (see Case 172), he decided not to go and instead to stay at Fuyan si 福嚴寺 on Mount Nanyue, where he was appointed secretary. As events would have it, when Fuyan si's abbot died Ciming was named to fill his

position. Traditional accounts suggest that at first Ciming regarded Huanglong as his equal in understanding and refused Huanglong's requests to train under him. The present case explains how he came to accept Huanglong as his disciple.

Case 190   州勘庵主   *Zhaozhou Checks Two Hermits*[1]

趙州、到一庵主處問、有麼有麼。主堅起拳頭。州曰、水淺不是泊船
處。便行。又到一庵主處問、有麼有麼。主又堅起拳頭。州云、能縱
能奪、能殺能活。便作禮。

Zhaozhou went to where a hermit was staying and asked, "Are you there? Are you there?" The hermit held up a fist. Zhaozhou said, "This water is too shallow for a ship to moor." Then he left.

Zhaozhou went to another hermit's place and asked, "Are you there? Are you there?" The hermit likewise raised his fist. Zhaozhou said, "You can give and you can take away; you can kill and you can bring to life."[2] He then bowed.

1 Also *Wumen guan* 11, Main Case.
2. For "to kill and to give life," see Case 186, note 1.

Case 191   瑯瑘先照   *Langye's "Perception First"*[1]

瑯瑘覺云、先照後用、露獅子之爪牙。先用後照、縱象王之威猛。照
用同時、如龍得水致雨騰雲。照用不同時、提獎嬌兒、撫怜愛子。此
古德建立法門。爲合如是、不合如是。若如是、似紀信乘九龍之輦。
若不合如是、若項羽失千里之騅。還有人爲瑯瑘出氣也無。如無、山
僧自道去也。卓拄杖、下座。

Langye Huijue said:

First perception, then function:[2] like a lion[3] exposing its claws and fangs.
First function, then perception: like the Elephant King[4] giving full expression to its great might.
Perception and function simultaneous: like a dragon taking to water, causing rain to fall and clouds to form.
Perception and function not simultaneous: like assisting a cute little girl or showing affection to a beloved child.

"This is the Dharma gate established by an ancient worthy.[5] Is this the way it should be, or is it not? If this is the way it should be, it's like Ji Xin riding in the Nine-Dragon Carriage.[6] If this is not the way it should be, it's like Xiang Yu losing Zhui, the horse that could run a thousand leagues in a day.[7]

"Is there anyone who can speak for Langye? If not, this mountain monk will speak for himself." So saying, he held his staff erect and descended from the seat.

1. Langye Huijue's comments on Linji's Four Perceptions and Functions 臨濟四照用 (see Case 210) are found in the version of the *Record of Linji* appearing in the *Rentian yanmu* 人天眼目, but not in other versions of the work.

2. "Perception" translates 照, which in this case means the master perceiving or investigating the capabilities of a student; "function" translates 用, which refers to the activity or function of guiding the student.

3. The lion is the transformation body of the bodhisattva Mañjuśrī, the symbol of wisdom.

4. The elephant is the transformation body of the bodhisattva Samantabhadra, the symbol of teaching and practice.

5. The ancient worthy is, of course, Linji.

6. "Ji Xin riding in the Nine-Dragon Carriage" is a classic Chinese image of fealty and self-sacrifice. For background information, see *Ji Xin* in the Biographical Notes.

7. The general Xiang Yu's loss of his horse Zhui helped to seal his defeat in battle. See *Xiang Yu* in the Biographical Notes.

Case 192   臨濟栽松   *Linji Plants Pines*[1]

臨濟禪師栽松次、黃檗問、深山裏栽許多作什麼。師云、一與山門作境致、二與後人作標榜。道了將钁頭打地三下。黃檗云、雖然如是、子已喫吾三十棒了也。師又以钁頭打地三下、作噓噓聲。黃檗云、吾宗到汝大興於世。後溈山舉此語問仰山、黃檗當時、祇囑臨濟一人、更有人在。仰山云、有。祇是年代深遠、不欲舉似和尚。溈山云、雖然如是、吾亦要知。汝但舉看。仰山云、一人指南吳越令行、遇大風即止。識風穴和尚也。

Once when Linji was planting pine trees, Huangbo asked, "Why plant so many trees in the deep mountains?"

Linji answered, "First, I want to create good surroundings for the temple. Second, I want to create a landmark for future generations." So saying, he took his mattock and hit the ground three times.

"Be that as it may, you've already tasted thirty blows of my stick," said Huangbo.

Again Linji hit the ground three times with his mattock, then let out a large breath, "*Haaaaa!*"

Huangbo said, "Under you, our school will flourish greatly throughout the world."

Later Guishan related this exchange to Yangshan Huiji. "At that time did Huangbo put his trust only in Linji, or is there someone else?" he asked.

"There is another," replied Yangshan, "but he'll come so far in the future that I don't wish to speak of him."

"Even so, I'd still like to know," said Guishan. "Tell me what you can."

Yangshan said, "A man points south; his law extends to Wu and Yue. When he encounters the great wind, he will settle." Yangshan thus prophesied the coming of Fengxue Yanzhao.[2]

1. Also *Record of Linji*, Record of Pilgrimages 2.

2. The identification of Yanzhao as the subject of Yangshan's prophecy is based on the fact that he studied under Nanyuan Huiyong ("Nanyuan" means "South Temple"), that Yanzhao himself came from the area of the ancient states of Wu and Yue near the coast of south-central China, and that he eventually resided on Dafeng 大風 (Great Wind) Mountain, at the temple called Fengxue 風穴 (Wind Cave).

Case 193   百丈說了   *Baizhang's "Already Explained"*

洪州百丈山惟政禪師、有一老宿、見日影透窓問曰、爲復窓就日、日
就窓。師曰、長老房内有客、歸去好。師問南泉曰、諸方善知識、還
有不說似人底法也無。南泉曰、有。師曰、作麼生。曰、不是心、不
是佛、[不是物]。師曰、恁麼即說似人了也。曰、某甲即恁麼、師伯作
麼生。[師]曰、我又不是善知識、爭知有說不說底法。曰、某甲不會、
請師伯說。[師]曰、我太煞爲汝說了也。

There was an old monk living at the temple of Baizhang Weizheng in Hongzhou. Seeing the sunlight streaming through a window, he asked, "Does the window go to the sunlight or does the sunlight go to the window?"

The master said, "Venerable elder, there's a guest in your room. You'd better return."[1]

Baizhang Weizheng asked Nanquan Puyuan, "Is there a Dharma that enlightened teachers everywhere have never expressed to people?"

Nanquan said, "There is."

Weizheng asked, "What is it?"

Nanquan answered, "Not-mind, not-buddha, [not-things]."[2]

Weizheng said, "You've just expressed it!"

Nanquan said, "That's the way I see it; how about you?"

Weizheng replied, "I'm not an 'enlightened teacher.' How should I know whether there's a Dharma that has or hasn't been expressed?"

Nanquan said, "I don't understand. Please, Dharma uncle, explain."

Weizheng responded, "I've already explained more than enough."

1. The passage to this point is sometimes treated as a separate koan. The remaining part of the passage, from "Baizhang Weizheng asked Nanquan Puyuan" to the end, appears as the Main Case of *Blue Cliff Record* 28 and the Main Case of *Wumen guan* 27.

2. "Not-things" is added from the versions of this koan found in the *Blue Cliff Record* and *Wumen guan*.

Case 194   德山行棒   *Deshan Uses His Stick*

德山小參云、老僧今夜不答話、有問話者三十棒。時有僧出禮拜。山
便打。僧云、某甲話也未問、爲什麼打。山云、你是何處人。僧云、
新羅人。山云、未跨船舷、好與三十棒。[僧於此有省]。法眼拈云、
大小德山、話作兩橛。圓明云、大小德山、龍頭蛇尾。雪竇云、二老
宿雖善裁長補短捨重從輕、要見德山亦未可在。何故。德山大似握闆
外威權、有當斷不斷不招其亂底劍。諸人要識新羅僧麼。只是撞着露
柱底、箇瞎漢。

At an informal lecture Deshan Xuanjian said, "Tonight I'll answer no questions. Anyone who asks will get thirty blows." At that moment a monk stepped forward and bowed. Deshan immediately struck him.

"There's something I wish to say, but I haven't even spoken yet," said the monk. "Why do you strike me?"

Deshan asked, "Where are you from?"

"From Silla,"[1] the monk answered.

Deshan said, "I should have given you thirty blows before you boarded the ship for here." [At this the monk was enlightened.]

Later Fayan Wenyi said, "Even the great Deshan said one thing and meant another." Yuanming said, "Even the great Deshan had the head of a dragon and the tail of a snake."[2]

Xuedou Chongxian commented, "The two venerable priests[3] skillfully pared the long and extended the short, reduced the heavy and augmented the light, but if they wish to know Deshan, that's still not enough. Why? Because Deshan is like a warlord holding power far from the walls of the imperial city who wields a sword that deters unrest even when the warlord is irresolute.[4] Do you want to know the monk from Silla? He's just a blind guy who ran into a pillar."[5]

1. Silla 新羅 was one of the three ancient kingdoms of the Korean Peninsula, along with Paekche and Koguryo.

2. This saying signifies a promising beginning but a disappointing end.

3. That is, Fayan and Yuanming.

4. The *Kattōshū*, unlike any of the original texts, has 還招 instead of 不招 in this sentence, which yields, "Because Deshan is like a warlord holding power far from the walls of the imperial city, who, if irresolute, would invite unrest." This scribal error probably resulted from the presence of a similar saying in the *Records of the Historian* 史記, "To lack resolution when resolution is called for invites unrest." The present text follows the original sources.

5. A pillar, or, more properly, an "exposed" pillar 露柱, is a common metaphor in Zen for no-mind or the unconscious (see Case 14, note 2), so that "run into a pillar" suggests an awakening. Xuedou is thus saying that even an eyeless monk will eventually "run into a pillar."

Case 195   臨濟瞎驢   *Linji's "Blind Ass"*[1]

臨濟臨遷化時、據坐云、吾滅後、不得滅却吾正法眼藏。三聖出云、
爭敢滅却和尚正法眼藏。師云、已後有人問你、向他道什麼。三聖
便喝。師云、誰知、吾正法眼藏、向這瞎驢邊滅却。言訖端然示寂。

When Linji was about to pass away, he seated himself and said, "After I'm gone, do not destroy the treasury of my True Dharma Eye!"

Sansheng Huiran came forward and said, "Why would anyone destroy the treasury of your True Dharma Eye?"

Linji asked him, "When I'm gone, if someone questions you, how will you respond?" To this Sansheng gave a shout.

"Who would have thought that the treasury of my True Dharma Eye would die out with this blind ass!" said Linji. So saying, he sat in formal posture and passed away.

1. Also *Record of Linji*, Record of Pilgrimages 21; *Blue Cliff Record* 49, Commentary on the Main Case; *Record of Equanimity* 13, Main Case.

Case 196　張拙看經　*Zhang Zhuo Sees the Sutra*[1]

昔有張拙秀才、看千佛名經、乃問長沙云、百千諸佛、但聞其名。未
審、居何國土、還化物也無。沙云、黃鶴樓崔顥題詩後、秀才曾題也
未。拙云、未曾題。沙云、得閑題取一篇也好。

Long ago there was a scholar-official named Zhang Zhuo. After reading the
Sutra of the Thousand Buddha-Names,[2] he asked Changsha, "All I saw was
the names of hundreds and thousands of buddhas. But what buddha lands
do they live in? Do they teach living beings?"

Changsha said, "Since Cui Hao composed his poem 'The Yellow Crane
Pavilion,'[3] have you written a poem on that subject?"

"No, I haven't," Zhang replied.

Changsha said, "If you have time, you should write one."

1. Also *Blue Cliff Record* 36, Commentary.

2. There are several sutras whose titles may correspond to the title *Sutra of the
Thousand Buddha-Names* 千佛名經, including 過去莊嚴劫千佛名經 (T 14:446); 現
在賢劫千佛名經 (T 14:447); and 未来星宿劫千佛名經 (T 14:448).

3. Cui Hao's poem celebrating the Yellow Crane Pavilion 黃鶴樓 at Wuchang-
cheng 武昌城 is considered one of the finest examples of Chinese poetry. Even
Li Bo 李白 (701–62), one of the greatest Tang poets, abandoned his plan to write a
poem about the pavilion after seeing Cui's piece, saying it could not be bettered.
Subsequently no poems about the pavilion were ever written. For further material on the poem, see *Cui Hao* in the Biographical Notes.

Case 197　南方一棒　*The Staff of the South*[1]

風穴、在南院會下作園頭。一日院到園裏問云、南方一棒、作麼生商
量。穴云、作奇特商量。穴却問、和尚此間、作麼生商量。院拈棒起
云、棒下無生忍、臨機不讓師。穴於是豁然大悟。

One day when Fengxue Yanzhao was working as gardener in the community under Nanyuan Huiyong, Nanyuan came and asked, "How is the staff
used in the south?"[2]

"With great skill,"[3] replied Fengxue. "And here—how does the master
use it?"

Nanyuan held up his staff and said, "Enlightened with a blow of the staff,[4]
depending on the circumstances, you defer not even to your teacher."

At this Fengxue was deeply enlightened.

1. Also *Blue Cliff Record* 38, Commentary.

2. Nanyuan asks how training is conducted south of Nanjing, at the monastery of *Jingqing Daofu* in the lineage of *Deshan Xuanjian*, where Fengxue had practiced earlier. Nanyuan himself was in the lineage of *Linji Yixuan*. The staff is a common metaphor in Zen for a master and his teaching methods.

3. The original Chinese, 作奇特商量, can be read as "they use skillful *mondō* (questions-and-answers)," since 商量 is sometimes used as a synonym for the Zen *mondō*. It may thus be seen as a more direct reply to Nanyuan's implied question, "How is training conducted in the south?"

4. "Enlightened" translates 無生忍, short for 無生法忍: recognition of the true nature of existence as unborn and unextinguishable.

Case 198   文殊來參   *Mañjuśrī Visits*[1]

僧問洞山、文殊普賢來參時如何。山云、趕向水牯牛群裡去。僧云、
和尚入地獄如箭。山云、全憑子力。

A monk asked Dongshan Shouchu, "What would you do if the bodhisattvas Mañjuśrī and Samantabhadra came to visit?"[2]

"I'd chase them off to the herd of water buffalo," answered Dongshan.

The monk said, "Master, you'll go to hell swift as an arrow!"

"It's all because of you," replied Dongshan.[3]

1. Also *Blue Cliff Record* 43, Commentary on the Main Case.

2. Mañjuśrī traditionally represents principle 理 (absolute, oneness, wisdom, essence, etc.); Samantabhadra traditionally represents phenomena 事 (relative, duality, compassion, function, etc.).

3. This reading follows that in the *Record of Dongshan Shouchu* 洞山守初錄, where the exchange originally appears. There, as in virtually all other sources, the final line reads 全憑子力, "It's entirely your fault," with the "you" 子 referring to the monk. The standard *Kattōshū* text follows the *Blue Cliff Record* 43, Commentary on the Main Case, which has 全得他力. The meaning of this line is unclear; Cleary translates it as "I've got all their strength" (1998, p. 217), with the "their" apparently referring to the buffaloes.

Case 199   一拳拳倒   *To Knock Down with One Blow*

眞淨、一日、謂老黃龍曰、白雲端頌臨濟三頓棒、與某甲見處一般。
南云、你如何會他底。淨便舉頌、一拳拳倒黃鶴樓、一趯趯翻鸚鵡

洲。有意氣時添意氣、不風流處也風流。龍喝云、白雲會、你不會。

師云、代眞淨如何道。

One day Zhenjing Kewen said to Huanglong Huinan, "Baiyun Shouduan's verse on 'Linji's three-score blows of the stick' expresses the same understanding as mine."[1]

"And how do you understand Baiyun's verse?" Huanglong asked.

Zhenjing thereupon repeated Baiyun's verse:

> Knock down the Yellow-Crane Pavilion[2] with a single blow;
> Send Parrot Island flying with a single kick.
> To an ardent spirit add yet more ardor still,
> No refinement—this, too, is refinement.

Huanglong said angrily, "Baiyun understood; you do not!"

The master commented, "What would you say in Zhenjing's place?"[3]

1. "Linji's three-score blows with a stick" refers to the episode described in Case 187 above, where Linji asks his teacher Huangbo three times, "What is the true meaning of the Buddhadharma?" and is struck by Huangbo each time. Several sources say that he received twenty blows on each occasion.

2. See Case 196 and *Cui Hao* in the Biographical Notes.

3. The present *Shūmon kattōshū* text has "Hakuin Ekaku" in place of "the master." Since the Japanese Zen master Hakuin Ekaku was born in 1686 and the *Kattōshū* was first published in 1689, this is obviously a later addition to the text (it first appears in the Ansei 安政 edition of 1858). The line has been restored to its original form in the Genroku edition (1689).

Case 200　雪峰打僧　*Xuefeng Strikes a Monk*

雪峰因僧辭。問甚處去。僧云、禮拜徑山和尚去。峰云、徑山忽問你此間佛法如何、你作麼生道。僧云、待問便道。峰便打。却囬問鏡清云、者僧過在甚處　便喫棒。清曰、問得徑山徹困也。峰云、徑山在浙中、因甚問得徹困。清云、不見道、遠問近對。峰休去。虛堂代云、魯般繩墨。

Xuefeng Yicun asked a monk who was leaving, "Where are you going?"

"To pay my respects to Jingshan Hongyin," answered the monk.

Xuefeng asked, "If Jingshan asks you what Xuefeng's Dharma is, how will you answer?"

"I'll answer when he asks me," said the monk. Xuefeng immediately struck him.

Xuefeng later turned to Jingqing and asked, "How did the monk err, that he deserved my stick?"

Jingqing answered, "The monk has already spoken with Jingshan and is on close terms with him."

Xuefeng said, "Jingshan is in Zhezhong. How could the monk have met him?"[1]

Jingqing replied, "Is it not said, 'Question afar, answer nearby'?"[2] Xuefeng agreed.

Xutang commented in his place, "[Jingqing's response is] like a chalk line by the master craftsman Bo of Lu!"[3]

1. Zhezhong 浙中 is about 800 kilometers from Xuefeng 雪峰 in Fujian.

2. Apparently the original saying meant that, when asked about distant, abstruse principles, one should answer with reference to nearby things.

3. Bo 般 was a legendary carpenter in the land of Lu 魯, said to have constructed a ladder to the sky. His measurements were always dead-on. A chalk line is a line made on a board or other surface by a string rubbed in chalk powder, used to indicate where a cut should be made.

Case 201 善財採藥 *Sudhana Gets Some Medicine*[1]

文殊一日、令善財去採藥。云、不是藥者採將來。善財徧採、無不是
藥。却來白云、無不是藥者。文殊云、是藥採將來。善財乃拈一枝草
度與文殊。文殊提起示衆云、此藥亦能殺人、亦能活人。

One day Mañjuśrī asked Sudhana to gather medicinal herbs and said, "Bring me anything that isn't medicine."

Sudhana searched everywhere, but there was nothing that wasn't medicine. He returned and said, "There is nothing that isn't medicine."

"Then bring me something that *is* medicine," Mañjuśrī said.

Sudhana picked a stalk of grass and gave it to Mañjuśrī. Mañjuśrī held up the stalk and said to the assembly, "This medicine can kill a person or give a person life."

1. Also found in the *Blue Cliff Record* 87, Commentary on the Main Case. Although presented in the form of an episode from the "Entry into the Realm of Reality" chapter of the *Avataṃsaka Sutra*, this case is not found in that sutra but has its origins in a similar exchange between Pingala and Jīvaka in the *Four-Part Vinaya* 四分律 (*Dharmagupta-vinaya*; T 22:851b).

Case 202   投子答佛   *Touzi Answers "Buddha"*[1]

僧問投子、如何是佛。子云、佛。如何是道。子云、道。如何是禪。
子云、禪。又問、月未圓時如何。子云、吞却三箇四箇。圓後如何。
子云、吐却七箇八箇。

A monk asked Touzi Datong, "What is buddha?"
Touzi answered, "Buddha."
"What is the Way?"
Touzi said, "The Way."
"What is Zen?"
Touzi said, "Zen."
The monk then asked, "What about when the moon isn't yet full?"
Touzi said, "I swallow three or four tenths."
"What about when the moon is full?"
Touzi replied, "I spit out seven or eight tenths."[2]

1. Also *Blue Cliff Record* 79, Commentary on the Verse.
2. Yamada reads the last four lines in the past tense: "The monk then asked, 'What about when the moon isn't yet full?' Touzi said, 'I've swallowed three or four tenths.' 'What about when the moon is full?' Touzi replied, 'I've spit out seven or eight tenths.'" (1985, 8:93)

Case 203   雲門喚遠   *Yunmen Calls Attendant Chengyuan*[1]

香林遠、居雲門左右十八年、雲門常只喚遠侍者。纔應諾、門云、是
什麼。香林當時、也下語呈見解、弄精魂終不相契。一日忽云、我會
也。門云、何不向上道將來。又住三年。

Xianglin Chengyuan served at Yunmen's side for eighteen years. Yunmen would always call, "Attendant Chengyuan!" The moment Xianglin responded Yunmen would ask, "What is *that*?"
Each time Xianglin offered comments, expressed views, and tried his best to respond, yet he never achieved accord with Yunmen.
One day, however, he suddenly said, "I understand."
Yunmen said, "Then say something further!"
Xianglin remained with him for another three years.[2]

1. Also *Blue Cliff Record* 17, Commentary. The *Blue Cliff Record* account continues, mentioning that much of the *Record of Yunmen* consists of Yunmen's words

and teachings to Xianglin as he attempted to bring his attendant to awakening during the latter's long years of service. Although Yunmen forbade his students from recording his words, Xianglin wore a robe made of paper onto which he would secretly copy Yunmen's words immediately after he heard them.

2. Yamada: Xianglin understood, but remained a further three years learning how to express his awakening in words. (1985, 2:357–58)

Case 204   楞嚴轉物   The Śūraṅgama Sutra's *"Turning Things Around"*

楞嚴經、佛謂阿難曰、若能轉物、即同如來。

In the *Śūraṅgama Sutra*, the Buddha said to Ānanda, "If you are skillful in turning things around, you are like the Tathāgata."[1]

1. *Śūraṅgama Sutra*, T 19:111c. The character 轉, translated "turning…around," means "redirect," "change," "transform," or "revolve." The concept is of skillfully using things as they come along, appropriately and without attachment. Two translations of the full passage in the *Śūraṅgama Sutra* are as follows:

All living beings, from time without beginning, have disregarded their own Selves by clinging to external objects, thereby missing their fundamental Minds. Thus they are being turned round by objects and perceive large and small sizes. If they can turn objects round, they will be like the Tathāgata, and their bodies and minds will be in the state of radiant perfection. (Luk 1966, p. 38)

From time without beginning, all beings have mistakenly identified themselves with what they are aware of. Controlled by their experience of perceived objects, they lose track of their fundamental minds. In this state they perceive visual awareness as large or small. But when they're in control of their experience of perceived objects, they are the same as the Thus-Come-Ones. Their bodies and minds, unmoving and replete with perfect understanding, become a place for awakening. (Buddhist Text Translation Society 2009, p. 65)

Case 205   守廓跛鱉   Shoukuo's *"Lame Nag"*[1]

鹿門守廓侍者、問德山曰、從上諸聖、向甚麼處去。山云、作麼作
麼。廓云、勅點飛龍馬、跛鱉出頭來。山休去。明日[山]浴出。廓度
茶與山。山撫廓背一下云、昨日公案作麼生。廓云、老漢今日方始瞥
地。山又休去。後虛堂拈云、盡謂德山兩處休去是養子緣。殊不知、
鬧市裡打靜槌、死水裡設羈絆。

Attendant Shoukuo of Lumen asked Deshan Xuanjian, "All the sages from times of old—where have they gone?"

"What? What?" Deshan asked back.

"I called for a swift steed," Shoukuo said, "but I got a lame nag." Deshan was silent.

The next day, after the bath, Shoukuo served tea to Deshan. Deshan patted Shoukuo on the back and asked, "What about yesterday's koan?"

Shoukuo said, "Today the old fellow has finally understood."

Deshan was again silent.

Later Xutang commented, "Everyone says that Deshan, in staying silent both times, acted with a parent's compassion. They don't realize that he had silenced the noisy market with his gavel and fastened tethers in the stagnant water."[2]

1. Also *Record of Equanimity* 14, Main Case.

2. The translation follows the reading of Mujaku. Mujaku, who interprets "stagnant water" 死水 as referring to Deshan's silences, comments, "In his silences Deshan bound Shoukuo to him. His was the heart of a bandit, not the compassion of a parent."

Case 206   長沙翫月   *Changsha Enjoys the Moon*[1]

長沙翫月次、仰山指月云、人人盡有這箇。只是用不得。沙云、恰是
便倩你用那。仰山云、你試用看。沙一蹋蹋倒。仰山起云、師叔一似
箇大蟲。

One evening Changsha Jingcen was enjoying the moon. Yangshan Huiji pointed to it and said, "Everyone without exception *has* it. They're just unable to *use* it."[2]

Changsha replied, "Precisely. So let's see you use it."

Yangshan said, "You try using it!"

Thereupon Changsha gave Yangshan a kick and knocked him down.

Getting up, Yangshan said, "Dharma Uncle,[3] you're just like a tiger!"[4]

1. Also *Blue Cliff Record* 36, Commentary on the Main Case.

2. The moon often serves as a metaphor for the enlightened mind.

3. Changsha was in the third generation from *Nanyue Huairang*; Yangshan was in the fourth generation from the same master.

4. The *Blue Cliff Record* account adds, "Hence Changsha was later called 'Cen the Tiger.'"

Case 207-1   臨濟洗腳   *Linji Washes His Feet*[1]

趙州行腳時、參臨濟禪師。遇師洗腳次、州便問、如何是祖師西來
意。師云、恰值老僧洗腳。州近前作聽勢。師云、更要第二杓惡水
潑在。州便下去。

During his pilgrimage Zhaozhou came to see Linji. He met him just as Linji
was washing his feet. Zhaozhou asked, "What is the meaning of Bodhidharma's coming from the West?"

"Right now I happen to be washing my feet," replied Linji.

Zhaozhou came closer and made a show of listening.[2]

Linji said, "Do I have to toss out a second ladleful of dirty water?!"

Zhaozhou departed.

1. Also *Record of Linji*, Critical Examinations 17. See Case 207-2 for the same
episode, but with the roles of Linji and Zhaozhou reversed.

2. This indicates a desire to hear more.

Case 207-2   松源上堂   *Songyuan Takes the High Seat*

松源上堂、舉、趙州訪臨濟。州纔洗腳。濟便下來問、如何是祖師西來
意。州云、正值老僧洗腳。濟近前作聽勢。州云、會則會㗛啄 [作] 麼。
濟拂袖便行。州云、三十年行腳、今日錯爲人下注腳。源云、半雨半
晴、桃紅李白。點著便行、不勞㗛啄。那箇是他錯下注腳處。試道看。

Songyuan Chongyue took the high seat and said:

Zhaozhou visited Linji. As he was washing his feet Linji came down and
asked, "What is the meaning of Bodhidharma's coming from the West?"

"Right now I'm washing my feet," replied Zhaozhou.

Linji came closer and made a show of listening.

Zhaozhou remarked, "If you understand, you understand. What's the use
of pecking at it?"[1] Linji shook his sleeves and left.

Zhaozhou said, "Thirty years I've been on pilgrimage, yet today I carelessly
offered advice."

Songyuan commented, "Half rain, half shine; peach blossoms are pink,
plum blossoms are white.[2] If you understand, then be on your way—no
need to peck at it. At what point did Zhaozhou carelessly offer advice? Try
to give an answer!"

1. The present *Kattōshū* version of this sentence, 會則會啗啄麼, has been changed in accordance with the original text, the *Record of Songyuan*, which reads 會則會啗啄作麼. The 作 before the final 麼 lends the question an ironic twist.

2. "Half rain, half shine" signifies a draw between the two. "Peach blossoms are pink, plum blossoms are white" implies that Zhaozhou and Linji each had his own way of doing things.

Case 208 臨濟四料 *Linji's Four Positions*[1]

臨濟、晩參示衆云、有時奪人不奪境。有時奪境不奪人。有時人境俱奪。有時人境俱不奪。

Linji said, "Sometimes I take away the person and not the surroundings; sometimes I take away the surroundings and not the person; sometimes I take away both the person and the surroundings; sometimes I take away neither the person nor the surroundings."

1. Also *Record of Linji*, Discourse 10.

Case 209 陸亙笑哭 *Lu Gen's Laughing and Crying*[1]

陸亙大夫參南泉。泉遷化。亙聞喪入寺下祭、却呵呵大笑。院主云、先師與大夫有師資之義、何不哭。大夫云、道得即哭。院主無語。亙大哭云、蒼天蒼天、先師去世遠矣。後來長慶聞云、大夫合笑不可哭。

The official Lu Gen studied under Nanquan Puyuan. When Nanquan passed away, he went to the memorial service at the temple, paid his respects, then gave a hearty laugh.

The temple supervisor said, "Our late master and you were teacher and student; why aren't you weeping?"

Lu said, "If you can say something, I'll weep." The supervisor was silent. Lu gave a loud wail. "Alas! Alas! Our late master is long gone from the world!"

Later Changqing Lan'an heard about this and commented, "Laugh, Lu Gen, don't cry!"[2]

1. Also *Blue Cliff Record* 12, Commentary on the Verse.

2. The commentary *Zen Forest Records* 林間錄 observes that, on the basis of other sources such as the *Jingde-Era Record of the Transmission of the Lamp* 景德傳燈錄, Changqing's comment ought to read, "Should Lu Gen have cried or should he not have cried?" 合哭不合哭 (T 51:279b).

Case 210   臨濟四用   *Linji's Four Functions*[1]

臨濟四照用、先照後用、先用後照、照用同時、照用不同時。

Sometimes perception precedes function;
Sometimes function precedes perception;
Sometimes perception and function are simultaneous;
Sometimes perception and function are not simultaneous.

1. For the Four Perceptions and Functions 四照用, see Case 191, note 1.

Case 211   乾峰舉一   *Qianfeng's "Take Up the One"*[1]

乾峰示衆云、舉一不得舉二。放過一著、落在第二。雲門出衆云、昨
日在一僧、從天台來却往南嶽去。峰云、典座今日不得普請。

Yuezhou Qianfeng said to the assembly, "Take up the One; do not take up
the Two. Neglect this first step, and you fall into that which is secondary."
    Yunmen stepped forward from the assembly and said, "Yesterday a monk
came from Tiantai, then went to Nanyue."[2]
    Qianfeng said, "Cook! There will be no work today!"[3]

1. Also *Blue Cliff Record* 24, Commentary on the Main Case.
2. Tiantai 天台 is located in Zhejiang 浙江 Province, and Nanyue 南嶽 is located
in Hunan 湖南 Province. Both are far from Qianfeng's place in Yuezhou 越州.
3. Generally, managing work was the province of the duty-monk 維那, not the
cook 典座. Work was sometimes canceled in a Chinese monastery as a reward
for an awakening or a particularly insightful act or statement.

Case 212   文殊起見   *Mañjuśrī Gives Rise to Views*[1]

南泉云、文殊普賢、昨夜三更、起佛見法見。各與三十棒、貶向二鐵
圍山去也。時趙州出衆云、和尚棒教誰喫。泉云、王老師有什麼過。
州禮拜。

Nanquan said, "Last night at midnight[2] Mañjuśrī and Samantabhadra were
formulating views on 'Buddha' and 'Dharma.' I gave each of them thirty
blows with my stick and expelled them to the Double Iron-Ring Mountains."[3]
    At that point Zhaozhou stepped forward from the assembly and said,
"Master, who, exactly, is the one who should have been struck?"
    "Was I at fault?" Nanquan asked. Zhaozhou bowed.

1. Also *Blue Cliff Record* 26, Commentary.

2. The term "midnight" is a common metaphor in Zen for the undifferentiated source.

3. In Buddhist cosmology, the Double Iron-Ring Mountains are the outermost pair of the nine mountain ranges that encircle Mount Sumeru. In the area between the two ranges there is no differentiation between yin and yang, absolute and relative, etc. The region is said to be the dwelling place of devils, demons, and preta (hungry ghosts).

Case 213   徹翁遺誡   *Tettō's Admonitions*

靈山徹翁和尚遺誡云、如來正法眼藏無付人。自荷擔至彌勒佛下生。
噫。

In his *Admonitions*, Tettō Gikō of Daitoku-ji said, "The Tathagata's Treasury of the True Dharma Eye I will entrust to no one. I will bear it myself until Maitreya descends to this world. *Ahh…!*"[1]

1. Tettō's statement is based on the legend, found in the *Transmission of the Lamp* and elsewhere, that, after transmitting the Dharma to Ānanda, Mahākāśyapa went to Cockfoot Mountain with the Buddha's robe to await the coming of Maitreya.

Case 214   無邊刹境   *The Infinite Realms*

無邊刹境、自他不隔於毫端。十世古今、始終不離於當念。

In the infinite realms, self and other are not separated by even a hairsbreadth. The ten periods of past, present, and future are never separate from this very instant.

Case 215   樂天問法   *Letian Asks about the Dharma*

白居易問鳥窠和尚、禪師坐處甚危險。窠曰、老僧有甚危險。侍郎危險尤甚。曰、弟子位鎮江山、何險之有。窠曰、薪火相交、識性不停。得非險乎。又問、如何是佛法大意。窠曰、諸惡莫作、衆善奉行。曰、三歲孩兒也解恁麼道。窠曰、三歲孩兒雖道得、八十老人行不得。白遂作禮而去。

Bai Juyi (Letian), the provincial governor, said to the priest Niaoke Daolin, "What a dangerous place you're sitting in."[1]

"What danger am I in?" said Niaoke. "The governor's danger is far greater."

"I govern this land," said Juyi. "What danger could I be in?"

Niaoke answered, "Passions burn, the intellect never rests. What could be more dangerous than that?"

The governor asked, "What is the central teaching of the Buddha-dharma?"

Niaoke replied, "Do no evil, practice all good."[2]

"Even a three-year-old child could have told me that," responded the governor.

"Even a three-year-old can say it, but even an eighty-year-old cannot practice it," said Niaoke.

Bai Juyi bowed and departed.

1. Niaoke Daolin was famous for doing zazen on the limb of a pine tree. See *Niaoke Daolin* in the Biographical Notes.

2. This saying appears in numerous texts; an early example is found in the *Dhammapada*: "Avoid all evil, perform all good, purify your own mind; this is the teaching of all buddhas" (T 4:567b).

Case 216   浮盃答婆   *Fubei Answers a Woman*

凌行婆問浮盃和尚、盡力道不得底一句、還分付阿誰。盃云、浮盃無
剩語。

A woman named Lingxing asked the priest Fubei, "The word that can't be said despite the greatest effort—to whom will you impart it?"

"I have no such idle talk," replied Fubei.

Case 217   色即是空   *Form Is Emptiness*

經云、色即是空、空即是色。

A sutra says, "Form itself is emptiness; emptiness itself is form."[1]

1. This passage is found in several of the *Prajñā-pāramitā* sutras, the best-known example being the *Heart Sutra* 摩訶般若波羅蜜多心經 (T 8:848c).

Case 218   臨濟教化   *Linji Asks for Alms*

> 運庵和尚上堂、舉、臨濟入京教化。至一家門首云、家常添鉢。婆
> 云、太無厭生。庵拈云、婆死而不弔。

Yun'an took the high seat and said:

> Linji entered the capital on his begging rounds.[1] He went to the door of a house and said, "Just put your usual fare into my bowl." The woman replied, "What a glutton!"

Yun'an commented, "When that old woman died, I wouldn't have given her a funeral!"

1. For "begging rounds" the original reads 教化, a term that literally means "to educate in the Dharma, to guide toward the truth" but which in Zen is also used to mean mendicancy. Alms-begging was regarded as a means to educate the laity in the virtue of *dāna*, giving.

Case 219   趙州爐話   *Zhaozhou's "Talk around the Fireside"*

> 趙州謂衆曰、我行脚到南方、向火爐頭、有箇無賓主話。直至如今、
> 無人舉著。

Zhaozhou said to the assembly, "When I was on pilgrimage in the south, once around the fireside there was talk of 'no guest or host.' Since then, no one has taken the matter up."[1]

1. In Zen there is a well-known saying, "By the fireside, there is no guest or host" 火爐頭無賓主. The ZGJI comments, "In the circle around the hearth there is no guest or host, there is no rank or ceremony."

Case 220   潙山舉米   *Guishan Picks Up a Grain of Rice*

> 潙山祐禪師、舉一粒米云、百千萬粒、從這一粒生、此一粒自何生。
> 自云、此一粒莫輕。

Guishan Lingyou picked up a grain of rice and said, "Millions upon millions of grains of rice issue from this single grain. Where does this grain issue from?"

Answering himself, he said, "You mustn't take this single grain lightly."[1]

1. The original exchange in the *Compendium of the Five Lamps*, chapter on Shishuang Qingzhu, is as follows:

> The master [Shishuang] went to Mount Gui and was placed in charge of rice supplies. One day as he was sifting rice, Guishan said to him, "You mustn't spill donated rice." "I haven't spilled any," replied the master. Guishan picked a single grain off the ground and said, "You claimed not to have spilled any. What's this?" The master had no reply. Guishan then said, "You mustn't take this single grain lightly. Millions upon millions of grains of rice issue from it." The master then said, "Millions upon millions of grains of rice issue from it. Where does *it* issue from?" Guishan gave a great laugh and returned to his quarters. That evening Guishan took the high seat and said, "There's a bug in the rice. Everyone, watch out for it!"
>
> Later Shishuang visited Daowu Yuanzhi and asked, "What is meant by, 'All that the eye perceives is bodhi'?" Daowu said, "Novice!" Shishuang replied, "Yes?" "Fill the water bottles," said Daowu. After a moment of silence Daowu said, "What did you ask a moment ago?" When Shishuang attempted to answer, Daowu stood up and left. With this Shishuang had an understanding." (x 80:118b)

Filling water bottles was one of the duties of novices; hence Daowu's comment has the same meaning as "Go sweep the garden" or "Go wash your bowls."

Case 221　常侍看毬　*Changshi Watches a Polo Game*

王常侍、參睦州蹤禪師。一日、蹤問、今日何故入院遲。王云、爲看馬打毬、所以來遲。蹤云、人打毬馬打毬。王云、人打毬。蹤云、人困麼。王云、困。蹤云、馬困麼。王云、困。蹤云、露柱困麼。王恤然無對。歸至私第中、夜間忽然省得。明日、見蹤云、某甲會得昨日事也。蹤云、露柱困麼。王云、困。蹤遂許之。佛眼遠禪師云、此是達磨大師宗旨。露柱不解打毬、如何却困。還有明得者麼。〔頌云〕、人困馬困、〔未是困〕、露柱之困始是困。好於言下證無生、莫向言中尋尺寸。百丈若無雙耳聾、臨濟爭解領三頓。盡將業識作流〔傳〕、此道今人棄如糞。

Governor Wang was practicing under Muzhou Daozong. One day Daozong asked, "Why were you late in coming to the temple today?"

"I arrived late because I was watching a game of polo,"[1] Wang answered. Daozong asked, "Does the person hit the ball, or does the horse hit it?" Wang replied, "The person hits the ball."

"Does the person tire?" asked Daozong.

"He tires," answered Wang.

"Does the horse tire?" asked Daozong.

"It tires," answered Wang.

"Does a pillar tire?"[2] asked Daozong.

Wang couldn't respond. He returned home, where, in the middle of the night, he had a sudden realization. The next day he saw Daozong and said, "I know what you meant yesterday."

"Does a pillar tire?" asked Daozong.

"It tires," replied Wang. Daozong accepted this response.

Foyan Qingyuan commented, "This indeed is the teaching of Bodhidharma. A pillar can't hit a ball; why then does it tire? Is there anyone who can clarify this?" [He commented further in verse:][3]

> "The person tires," "the horse tires"—this is not yet true tiring;
> "The pillar tires"—only then can one can speak of tiring.
> It is fine to realize the Unborn at a word,
> But do not seek for anything within words.
> If Baizhang had not been deafened by Mazu for three days,[4]
> How could Linji have understood the true meaning of Huangbo's three-score blows?[5]
> People today take karmic consciousness to be the true transmission of Bodhidharma,[6]
> And discard his Way as though it were dung.

1. 馬打毬, lit., "horse-hit-ball"; a game similar to polo, in which players mounted on horses attempt to hit a ball with curved sticks.

2. "Pillar" is a common metaphor in Zen for no-mind or the unconscious. See Case 14, note 2.

3. As originally recorded in the *Record of Foyan*, the following lines are a verse by Foyan; the present text has been emended accordingly.

4. See Case 182.

5. See Case 187.

6. Karmic consciousness 業識 is the unawakened, deluded consciousness that arises through the workings of fundamental ignorance.

Case 222   福田惡道   *No Merit, Evil Realms*

經云、其施汝者、不名福田、供養汝者、墮三惡道。

The sutra says, "Those who make offerings to you receive no merit; those who make donations to you fall into the three evil realms."[1]

1. From the *Vimalakīrti Sutra*, "Disciples" chapter. For the full passage see Case 70. For the three evil realms, see Case 70, note 1.

Case 223   清浄本然   *Pure Original Nature*[1]

長水問瑯瑘覺和尚、如何是清淨本然、云何忽生山河大地。覺勵聲
云、清淨本然、云何忽生山河大地。水言下領悟。

Changshui Zixuan asked Langye Huijue, "How is it that pure, original nature immediately gives rise to mountains, rivers, and the great earth?"[2]

Langye replied in a vigorous voice, "How is it that pure, original nature immediately gives rise to mountains, rivers, and the great earth?"

With these words, Changshui suddenly understood.

1. Also *Blue Cliff Record* 35, Commentary on the Verse; *Record of Equanimity* 100, Main Case.

2. The question is from a *Śūraṅgama Sutra* passage in which Pūrṇamaitrāyaṇīputra, the monk most skilled in preaching the Dharma, asks the Buddha:

If in fact the aggregates, the faculties, the various perceived objects, and the consciousness are all the Matrix of the Thus-Come-One, which is fundamentally pure, then how is it that suddenly there came into being the mountains, the rivers, and all else on this earth that exists subject to conditions? And why are all these subject to a succession of changes, ending and then beginning again? (Buddhist Text Translation Society 2009, p. 141)

Case 224   荒草不鋤   *An Uncut Weed Patch*[1]

臨濟禪師、因有座主問、三乘十二分教、豈不是明佛性。師云、荒草
不曾鋤。主云、佛豈賺人也。師云、佛在什麼處。主無語。

A lecture-master asked Linji, "The three vehicles' twelve divisions of teachings all reveal buddha nature, do they not?"[2]

"These wild weeds have never been cut," said Linji.

"Why would the Buddha have deceived people?" asked the lecture-master.

"Where is the Buddha?" asked Linji.

The lecture-master could not answer.

1. Also *Record of Linji*, Discourse 1.

2. "The three vehicles' twelve divisions of teachings" 三乘十二分教 refers to the totality of teachings by which the Buddha guided his students to enlightenment. The three vehicles 三乘 are the three traditional Buddhist paths via which liberation may be reached: śrāvaka, pratyekabuddha, and bodhisattva. The twelve divisions of the teachings 十二分教 are the various different expedients said to have been used by the Buddha.

Case 225   金翅鳥王   *The Garuḍa King*

關山國師、因會夢窓國師上堂、乃出問、金翅鳥王當宇宙、天龍向何
處回避。窓即披頭袈裟隱椅子下。山即禮拜。大燈聞云、我從來疑著
者漢。

Once when Musō Soseki was lecturing, Kanzan Egen stepped forward and said, "The Garuḍa King covers the universe.[1] Where will the Heavenly Dragon hide?"[2]

Musō immediately covered his head with his vestment and concealed himself under the lecture-seat. Kanzan bowed.[3]

Hearing of this, Daitō said, "I've always had my doubts about that guy."[4]

1. Garuḍas are mythological creatures, adopted by Buddhism from the Hindu pantheon. Half human and half eagle, they are said to feed on dragons. The Garuḍa King served as Vishnu's steed and is sometimes used to represent the Buddha.

2. The Heavenly Dragon refers to Musō Soseki, since Musō founded Tenryū-ji 天龍寺 ("Temple of the Heavenly Dragon"). The fact that Tenryū-ji was founded two years after Daitō's death indicates that this exchange is apocryphal.

3. Kanzan and Musō's exchange bears a strong resemblance to *Record of Equanimity* 44, "Xingyang's Garuḍa":

A monk asked Xingyang Pou, "The Dragon King emerges from the sea; heaven and earth are quiet. Facing it, how would you respond?" The master said, "The Garuḍa King covers the universe. Who can stick his head out here?" The monk said, "And what if someone does come forth?" Xingyang said, "It would be like an eagle catching a pigeon. If you still don't understand, check in front of the tower and you'll know what's real!"[a] The monk said, "If that's how it is, I'll fold my hands on my chest and retreat three steps." Xingyang said, "You black turtle under the Sumeru Seat! Don't wait for my stick to welt your forehead!"[b]

a. "Check in front of the tower and you'll know what's real": Zhao Sheng 平原君 (?–250) built a high tower with an excellent view. From this tower his concubine saw a hunchback on the street and broke out in laughter. The hunchback, furious, demanded her execution. Zhao promised to do so, but he executed a criminal in her place. The ruse was discovered, causing his retainers to lose trust in him and drift away. Finally Zhao executed the concubine and displayed her head in front of the tower. The hunchback was satisfied, and the retainers returned.

b. The black-turtle carving that supports the Sumeru Seat (the platform on which the Zen master delivers Dharma lectures) is a metaphor for an unawakened monk.

4. According to Mujaku, the comment by Daitō, the teacher of Kanzan, can be taken as an expression either of praise or censure. It is, however, commonly believed in Japanese Zen that Daitō did not hold Musō in the highest regard, since he, like Musō, had received Dharma transmission from the Japanese master Kōhō Kennichi 高峰顯日 (1241–1316), yet—unlike Musō—remained dissatisfied and therefore trained further under *Nanpo Jōmyō*.

Case 226   折半裂三   *Split in Two, Torn in Three*

雲門示眾云、折半裂三、針筒鼻孔、在甚麼處。爲我一一拈出來看。
自代云、上中下。

Yunmen addressed the assembly, saying, "When [the robe] is split in two, torn in three, where then is the eye of the needle?[1] Pick [the pieces] up one by one and bring them here to me."

On behalf of the audience he said, "Above, between, below."

1. "The eye of the needle" translates 針筒鼻. Since a needle is useless without an eye, the eye is regarded as the needle's essence, and the expression "eye of the needle" has become a synonym for "essence" or "most important part."

Case 227   斎僧功徳   *The Merit of Donating Food to the Sangha*

大慧普說、阿含經中有三卷、盡說斎僧功徳。宣律師問韋駄天、何等
功徳最大。答云、斎僧功徳最大。

In the *Discourses of Dahui* it is said:

Three fascicles of the *Āgama* sutras[1] describe the merit of donating food to the sangha. Precept master Daoxuan asked Skanda,[2] "What is the greatest of all meritorious deeds?" Skanda replied, "Donating food to the sangha."[3]

1. "*Āgama* sutras" is the Mahayana term for a series of four Sanskrit sutra collections that coincide roughly with the five Pali *Nikāya*s. The *Āgama* sutras are the *Dīrghāgama* (Long Collection, corresponding among the *Nikāya*s to the *Dīgha-nikāya*), *Madhyamāgama* (Medium Collection, corresponding to the *Majjhima-nikāya*), *Samyuktāgama* (Miscellaneous Collection, corresponding to the *Samyutta-nikāya*), and the *Ekottarikāgama* (Numerical Collection, corresponding to the *Anguttara-nikāya*).

2. Skanda is in Zen the principal guardian deity of the sangha, temple buildings, and temple supplies; his image is enshrined in the administrative section of Zen monasteries. There are various explanations of his origin. According to the ZGDJ, Skanda, a son of Śiva, was a Hindu god who served as one of the eight heavenly generals under Virūḍhaka (ruler of the southern continent of Jambudvīpa), and was subsequently adopted into the Buddhist pantheon. Known in China as Weituotian 韋駄天 and in Japan as Idaten, he is regarded as the fastest runner in the universe.

3. No such exchange between Daoxuan and Skanda can be found in the *Discourses of Dahui*.

Case 228   瑯琊洪鐘   *Langye's "Great Bell"*

松源上堂云、舉、瑯琊道、若論此事、如洪鐘待扣聲應長空、如寶鑑
當軒影臨萬像。又道、若論此事、說甚龍樹馬鳴提婆鶖子。辨似懸
河、智如流水、莫能知之。師云、瑯琊恁麼剖露、也是官路販私塩。

Songyuan Chongyue took the high seat and said:

Langye Huijue stated, "Were I to speak of this matter,[1] I'd say it's like a great bell that resounds throughout the universe the moment it's struck. It's like a bright mirror that reflects all things the moment it's set on its stand."[2] Langye also said, "Were I to speak of this matter, I would say that no one—be it Nāgārjuna, Aśvaghoṣa, Kāṇadeva, or Śāriputra—can express it, even if one possesses eloquence like a rushing stream and wisdom like flowing water."

Songyuan commented, "Langye divulged the matter in this way, but it's like selling salt privately on a public highway."[3]

1. "This matter" 此事 refers to buddha nature.

2. The passage of the *Record of Langye* continues, "It is not bounded by the sky above, nor by the earth below. It embraces both the wise and the foolish, and neither sages nor ordinary people can separate themselves from it" (x 68:316b).

3. The salt market was a government monopoly, and thus private sales were a crime. Songyuan thus suggests (seriously or not) that Langye was a rascal who offered the secrets of the Zen school on the public road. Another meaning of "selling salt privately on a public highway" relates to the secrecy of the transaction, which is known only to the buyer and seller. Zen uses this to refer to the fact that the perfect accord between the understanding of an awakened disciple and that of the master cannot be perceived by an unawakened outsider.

Case 229   法無二法   *In the Dharma There Is No Duality*

祖師云、法無二法、妄自愛著。將心用心、豈非大錯。趙州云、老僧
拈一枝草作丈六金身。有時將丈六金身作一枝草用。以至、臨濟三玄三
要、汾陽十智同眞、無非是這箇時節。如隔窓看馬騎、眨眼便蹉過。他
分明向你道、要識是非、面目見在。你若透得這金剛圈、吞得這栗棘
蓬、不妨是箇明眼衲僧。一任指東作西,指鹿爲馬。喚作世法也得、喚
作佛法也得、道有也得、道無也得、取不得捨不得、不可得中只麼得。
且道、是箇什麼物得恁麼奇特。良久云、面目見在。喝一喝下座。

[Dahui said,] "The Third Patriarch stated, 'In the Dharma there is no duality; deluded, we cling to what we desire. Using mind to grasp mind—is this not the greatest of errors?'[1]

"Zhaozhou said, 'At times I take a blade of grass and use it as the sixteen-foot body of buddha; at times I take the sixteen-foot body of buddha and use it as a blade of grass.'[2]

"Or again, all of the teachings, from Linji's Three Mysteries and Three Essentials[3] to Fenyang Shanzhao's Ten Realizations, Same Reality,[4] point to this very moment. It's like watching through a narrow window for a horse and rider to pass by—blink once and you miss them. Fenyang tells you quite clearly: 'You wish to know right and wrong? Your original face is right before you!'[5]

"If you can penetrate this diamond trap and swallow this chestnut burr, then you are a clear-eyed monk indeed, [free to] point to the east and call it the west, point to a deer and call it a horse. You may call it secular law or call it buddha law, call it being or call it nonbeing.[6] 'It can't be grasped, it can't be thrown away. Only in nonattaining can it be attained.'[7] So tell me, what is it that's so wonderful?"

He remained silent for a moment, then said, "Your original face is right before you!" He gave a shout and descended from his seat.

1. From *On Believing in Mind* (*Xinxinming* 信心銘).

2. Also *Blue Cliff Record* 8, Pointer.

3. For the Three Mysteries and Three Essentials, see Case 159, note 6. The Three Mysteries are the same as the Three Mysterious Gates 三玄門.

4. For Fenyang's "Ten Realizations, Same Reality," see Case 255.

5. A line from Fenyang's "Ten Realizations, Same Reality."

6. Metaphors for complete freedom of action. "Point to a deer and call it a horse" has its origins in an incident from Chinese history. The eunuch Zhao Gao (d. 207 BCE) of the Qin dynasty, in order to discover which officials would be likely to defy him, presented a deer at court and called it a horse. Those officials bold enough to say that it was actually a deer were later killed.

7. A line from Yongjia's *Song of Enlightenment*.

Case 230　菩提宿將　*A Veteran General of the Dharma Assembly*

菩提宿將坐重圍、劫外時聞木馬嘶。寸刃不施魔膽碎、望風先已堅降旗。

The veteran general of the Dharma assembly sits surrounded;[1]
In timeless time the neighs of wooden horses are heard.[2]

Though the general's sword is untouched, the demons' vitals are
  slashed;
Before the general's might they beat a hasty retreat.

1. This verse was written by Dahui on the occasion of a Dharma assembly (lit.,
"bodhi meeting" 菩提會) held at Yunfeng si 雲峰寺 on Mount Xuefeng 雪峰, in
the year 1134. "Veteran general" refers to the monastery's abbot at the time, a
Caodong priest named Zhenxie Qingliao 眞歇清了 (1088–1151).

2. "Timeless time" translates 劫外時, which literally refers to the transcendent
time separate from a kalpa, i.e., the period between the creation and re-creation
of a universe, containing the four kalpas of formation, existence, destruction,
and annihilation. The wooden horse 木馬 is a metaphor in Zen for no-mind;
the expression "neighs of wooden horses" alludes to the vitality of the Dharma
assembly.

Case 231   莊嚴三昧   *Flower Adornment Samadhi*

普賢菩薩、從佛華莊嚴三昧起。普慧菩薩、如雲興致二百問。普賢菩
薩、如缾瀉以二千酬。又何曾思量計較來。蓋得法自在、稱法性說。

When Samantabhadra Bodhisattva emerged from Buddha Flower Adornment Samadhi,[1] the Bodhisattva of Universal Wisdom posed two hundred
questions, like clouds appearing one after another. Samantabhadra responded
with two thousand replies,[2] like drawing water from a well. How could he
possibly have had time to think up these replies? This surely is "attainment of
Dharma freedom,"[3] or "preaching directly from Dharma nature."

1. One of the ten Flower Adornment samadhis described in the *Discourses of
Dahui* (T 47:863b).

2. According to the *Avataṃsaka Sutra*, Samantabhadra gave ten answers to
each of the two hundred questions posed by the Bodhisattva of Universal Wisdom. The questions of the Bodhisattva of Universal Wisdom begin at T 10:279b.

3. Dharma freedom 法自在, the ability to give expression to the infinite Dharma
gates, is one of ten powers attained by a bodhisattva.

Case 232   一切放下   *Let Go of Everything*

大慧普說、你要眞箇參、但一切放下。如大死人相似、百不知百不
會。驀地向不知不會處、得這一念子破、佛也不奈你何。

In the *Discourses of Dahui* it is said, "If you truly wish to practice, just let go of everything. Know nothing, understand nothing, like one who has died the Great Death. Proceeding straight ahead in this not-knowing and not-understanding, break through this single thought. Then even the Buddha can do nothing to you."

Case 233   擊動法鼓   *Sound the Dharma Drum*

擊動法鼓、諸天龍神齊集。道眼不明、諸天龍神、見你口 [吐] 黑煙。
寧不怖畏。

Sound the Dharma drum and the heavenly dragons and deities will gather.[1] If your Dharma eye is not clear, the dragons and deities will see black smoke issuing from your mouth. How can you not be afraid?

1. "Sound the Dharma drum" means to announce a Dharma lecture.

Case 234   心地含種   *The Mind-Ground Contains the Seeds*

南嶽大慧禪師偈曰、心地含諸種、遇澤悉皆萌。三昧花無相、何壞復
何成。

Nanyue Huairang said in a verse:

> The mind-ground contains all seeds;
> Upon receiving moisture, all will sprout.
> The flower of samadhi is formless;
> How can it cease or arise?[1]

1. The verse is the continuation of the exchange between Nanyue and Mazu related in Case 139. The full passage reads:

Mazu asked, "How should I apply my mind to accord with the samadhi of formlessness?" Nanyue replied, "Your practice of the teaching of the mind-ground is like the planting of seeds. My teaching of the Dharma essentials is like the rain from the sky that waters those seeds. Because you have a causal affinity with the Way, you will certainly perceive it." "If the Way is without form, how can it be perceived?" asked Mazu. Nanyue answered, "The Dharma eye of the mind-ground can perceive the Way, as well as the samadhi of formlessness." Mazu asked further, "Are these subject to arising and cessation?" Nanyue said, "If you perceive the Way in terms of formation and destruction, gathering and dispersing, then you are not truly perceiving the Way." [Nanyue then recited the verse above.] (x 68:3b)

Case 235　空空法界　*The Dharma Realm of the Emptiness of Emptiness*

古塔主曰、空空法界、本自無爲、隨緣應現、無所不爲。所以虛空世
界、萬象森羅、四時陰陽、否泰八節、草木枯榮、人天七趣、聖賢諸
佛、五教三乘、外道典籍、世出世間、皆從此出。故云、無不從此法
界流、究竟還歸此法界。經云、一切諸佛 [及諸佛] 阿耨多羅三藐三
菩提法、皆從此經出。楞嚴曰、於一毫端現寶王刹、坐微塵裡轉大法
輪。維摩曰、或爲日月天、梵王世界主、或時作地水、或時作火風。李
長者云、於法界海之智水、示作魚龍、處涅槃之大宅、現陰陽而化物。

Jianfu Chenggu said, "The Dharma realm of the emptiness of emptiness is free of striving from the very start,[1] yet as it manifests according to conditions nothing is left undone. The Great Void, the myriad things, the four seasons, yin and yang, stagnation and overflow,[2] the eight divisions of the year,[3] the life of plants, humans, and devas, the seven destinations,[4] the sages and the buddhas, the five periods,[5] the three vehicles,[6] the sacred writings of non-Buddhists, the mundane and the supramundane—all of these issue from this realm. Thus it is said[7] that nothing departs from this realm, and that it is to this that all ultimately returns.

"The *Diamond Sutra* says, 'From this scripture issue all buddhas as well as the Dharma of the supreme perfect enlightenment of all buddhas.'[8] The *Śūraṅgama Sutra* says, 'On the tip of a hair a buddha realm appears; seated in a mote of dust, I revolve the Dharma wheel.'[9] The *Vimalakīrti Sutra* says, 'At times become the sun or the moon; at times become a god or the Lord of the Brahma Heaven; at times become fire or water; at times become the earth or wind.'[10] Li Tongxuan says, 'In the wisdom-waters of the Dharma realm become the fish and dragons; in the great mansion of nirvana become yin and become yang and guide sentient beings.'"[11]

1. "The Dharma realm of the emptiness of emptiness" 空空法界 is the Dharma realm of that emptiness which is empty of even the concept of emptiness.

2. "Stagnation" 否 and "overflow" 泰 are two of the *I-ching* hexagrams. "Stagnation" refers to poverty, hard times, and other periods of weakness and decline; "overflow" refers to peace, prosperity, harmony, and good fortune.

3. The eight divisions of the old Chinese calendar comprise: (1) 立春 (start of spring), (2) 春分 (spring equinox), (3) 立夏 (start of summer), (4) 夏至 (summer solstice), (5) 立秋 (start of fall), (6) 秋分 (fall equinox), (7) 立冬 (start of winter), (8) 冬至 (winter solstice).

4. The seven destinations 七趣 are the six paths (hell-dweller 地獄, preta 餓鬼, animal 畜生, asura 阿修羅, human 人, and deity 天) plus sage 神仙.

5. The five periods 五時 are, according to the Tiantai system of classifying the Buddhist teachings, the five different periods in which the Buddha expounded

the Dharma: i) immediately after his enlightenment he expounded the abstruse teachings of the *Avataṃsaka Sutra*; ii) seeing that these were too profound for the times, he expounded the teachings of the Pāli Canon and *Āgama Sutras*, emphasizing detachment and the cessation of suffering; iii) to free his disciples of attachment to the limited teachings of the second period and introduce the Mahayana, the Buddha expounded the Pure Land and *Vimalakīrti Sutra* teachings; iv) to deepen understanding of the Mahayana he expounded the Wisdom teachings (e.g., the *Diamond* and *Prajñā-pāramitā* sutras); v) finally, he taught the full truth in the *Lotus Sutra* and *Nirvana Sutra*.

6. For "three vehicles," see Case 224, note 2.

7. "Thus it is said" translates 故云. In the standard text of the *Kattōshū* 放去 (let go) appears in place of 故云; this is a scribal error and has been emended to accord with the text as it originally appears in the *Biographies of Monks of the Chan School* 禪林僧寶傳 (X 79:517b).

8. T 8:749b.

9. T 19:121a. From a passage describing the tathāgata-garbha:

> The Matrix of the Thus-Come One is itself the wondrous, enlightened, luminous understanding, which illuminates the entire Dharma-realm. Within it, therefore, the one is infinitely many and the infinitely many are one. The great appears within the small, just as the small appears within the great. I sit unmoving in this still place for awakening, and my Dharma-body extends everywhere and encompasses the infinity of space in all ten directions. On the tip of a fine hair...." (Buddhist Text Translation Society 2009, p. 115)

10. T 14:550a.

11. From Li's *New Treatise on the Avataṃsaka Sutra* 新華嚴經論 (T 36:724c).

Case 236　一法若有　*If a Single Dharma Exists*

僧問[古德]、一法若有、毘盧墮在凡夫、萬法若無、普賢失其境界。
去此二途、請師速道。

A monk said [to an ancient worthy],[1] "If a single dharma exists, Vairocana Buddha becomes an ordinary deluded being. If the myriad dharmas do not exist, Samantabhadra Bodhisattva loses his domain.[2] Avoiding these two paths, quick, master, please say something!"

1. The "ancient worthy" was Lushan Huguo 廬山護國 (n.d.).

2. Vairocana Buddha is buddha-as-dharmakāya and thus transcends the world of phenomena (dharmas). Samantabhadra embodies the function of teaching and practice that is inherent to bodhisattvahood and thus operates in the phenomenal world of the dharmas.

Case 237   補陀巖上   *Atop Mount Putuo*

東林頌、南無觀世音菩薩、補陀巖上紅蓮舌。不知成佛是何時、打刀
須用并州鐵。

A verse by Donglin says:[1]

> Reverence to Bodhisattva Avalokiteśvara,
> Who preaches so eloquently atop Mount Putuo.[2]
> You wonder when you'll attain buddhahood?
> If you wish to forge a sword, use Bingzhou steel![3]

1. The *Kattōshū* attributes the verse to the poet *Dongpo*, but it is actually found among the poems of Donglin 東林, another name for *Gushan Shigui*.

2. Mount Putuo is the mountain upon which Avalokiteśvara is said to live. In Zen "Avalokiteśvara's eloquent preaching of the Dharma atop Mount Putuo" is seen as crows cawing and dogs barking in the everyday world.

3. Bingzhou 并州 was an area noted for the excellent quality of its steel.

Case 238   圓相因起   *The Origin of the Circle-Figures*

仰山圓相因起。圓相之作、始於南陽忠國師。以授侍者耽源。源承讖
記、傳于仰山。遂目爲潙仰宗風。明州五峰良和尚、嘗製四十則。明
教嵩禪師、爲之序稱道其美。良曰、總有六名。曰圓相。曰暗機。曰
義海。曰字海。曰意語。曰默論。耽源謂仰山曰、國師當時、傳得六
代祖師圓相共九十七箇、授與老僧。乃曰、吾滅後三十年、南方有一
沙彌到來、大興此教。次第傳授無令斷絕。我今附汝、汝當奉持。
遂將其本過與山。山接得一覽、便將火燒却。耽源、一日問、前來諸
相、甚宜祕惜。山曰、當時看了便燒却也。源曰、吾此法門、無人能
會。唯先師及諸祖師諸大聖人方可委悉。子何得焚之。山曰、慧寂一
覽、已知其意。但用得不可執本也。源曰、雖然如此、於子即得、後
人[信]之不及。山云、和尚若要、重錄不難。即重集一本呈上。更無遺
失。源曰、然。耽源上堂。山出眾作此[○]相、以手拓呈了、却叉手
立。源以兩手交作拳示之。山進前三步作女人拜。源點頭。山便禮拜。

This is how Yangshan Huiji's circle-figures originated.[1]

The making of circle-figures originated with National Teacher Nanyang Huizhong, who transmitted their use to his attendant Danyuan Yingzhen. Danyuan, following Nanyang's prophecy,[2] passed them on to Yangshan. In due course the circle-figures came to be associated with the teaching style of the Guiyang school.[3]

Venerable Liang of Wufeng in Ming Province compiled a forty-case koan collection, to which Fori Qisong added a preface praising its quality; in this work Liang commented, "Altogether, circle-figures have six names: circle-figure, hidden potential, ocean of meaning, ocean of writing, ideas and words, and silent discourse."[4]

Danyuan said to Yangshan, "The circle-figures that the National Teacher received from the Sixth Patriarch numbered ninety-seven in all, which the National Teacher passed on to me. At that time he said, 'Thirty years after my passing, a monk from the south will come and cause this teaching to flourish greatly; he will disseminate it and never let it die out.' I therefore now hand it to you—keep it safe."[5] He then entrusted the text to Yangshan.

Yangshan received it, looked it over, then immediately burned it.

One day Danyuan said to him, "That text I gave you earlier—you must keep it safely concealed."

Yangshan replied, "After you gave it to me, I burned it as soon as I'd looked it over."

Danyuan said, "That Dharma teaching of mine is not something that people usually understand. Only the ancient masters, ancestors, and great sages understood it in detail. How could you burn it?"

"I understood the meaning after reading it once," replied Yangshan. "What matters is the ability to use it; one mustn't cling to the text."

"Perhaps, but though that's fine as far as you're concerned it may not be so for those to come," said Danyuan.

Yangshan said, "If you wish, I can easily reproduce the text." Thus he recompiled it and presented it to Danyuan. Nothing was omitted, so Danyuan gave his approval.

Later Danyuan took the high seat. Yangshan came forward from the assembly, made a circle in the air, pushed it forward with both hands, then stood there with his hands held, one atop the other, against his chest. Danyuan clasped his hands together and presented them in the form of a fist, upon which Yangshan walked three steps closer and bowed in the manner of a woman.[6] Danyuan nodded, and Yangshan bowed.

1. The circle-figure 圓相 is the circle drawn by Zen masters to represent truth, suchness, Dharma nature, etc.

2. Nanyang's prophecy, mentioned later in this koan, was that "thirty years after my passing a monk from the south will come and cause this teaching to flourish greatly." The monk referred to was Yangshan.

3. Yangshan Huiji and his master Guishan Lingyou were the founders of the Guiyang school.

4. The usual order and definition of the six types of circle-figures is as follows:

   1) "Circle-figure" 圓相 expresses the absolute Buddhadharma.

   2) "Hidden potential" 暗機 expresses the function that precedes the opposition of host and guest.

   3) "Ocean of meaning" 義海 expresses the various types of samadhi.

   4) "Ocean of writing" 字海 expresses the words that transmit the Buddhadharma (the present text of the *Kattōshū* has "ocean of study" 學海, a scribal error that has been emended according to the original text as it is found in the *Eye of Humans and Gods* 人天眼目; T 48:321c).

   5) "Ideas and words" 意語 expresses the very meaning of the teachings.

   6) "Silent discourse" 默論 expresses the idea that the circle-figure itself is the meaning of the teachings.

5. Yangshan would fit the prophecy, as he was born in 807, thirty-two years after Nanyang's death in 775.

6. One interpretation of "bowing in the manner of a woman" is that it resembles a Western curtsy; another is that it involves crossing the hands across the breast and bending forward slightly; a third is that it entails bringing both knees to the floor and bowing the head.

Case 239   宏智四借   *Hongzhi's Four "Uses"*

宏智和尚四借、借功明位、借位明功。借借不借、全超不借借。

The four "uses" of Hongzhi Zhengjue:

> Using activity to reveal essence[1]
> Using essence to reveal activity
> Using neither activity nor essence[2]
> Fully transcending "neither activity nor essence"[3]

1. "Activity" and "awakening" translate, respectively, 功 and 位, both of which have various meanings in Zen. The basic meaning of 功 is "what one does or achieves"; in Zen it is used to indicate spiritual practice, the content of practice, or the result of practice. The ZGDJ defines it in this case as 作用, "activity" or "function."

The basic meaning of 位 is "where one is"; in Zen it indicates "rank," as in the Caodong doctrine of the Five Ranks 五位 or Linji's concept of the "true person of no rank" 無位眞人. Here, according to the ZGDJ, it indicates 正位, 證, or 本体, all of which signify "enlightenment" or "essence."

2. That is, going beyond activity and essence to śūnyatā.

3. Transcending even śūnyatā, so that not even the thought of enlightenment arises.

Case 240   生解未分   *After Birth and Before Discrimination*

香嚴云、生解未分時、如何是孩兒日用之三昧。

Xiangyan Zhixian said, "After birth and before the discriminatory faculties come into being, what is the everyday samadhi of the infant?"

Case 241   智不到處   *Where Wisdom Cannot Reach*

古德云、智不到處道一句。

An ancient worthy said,[1] "Speak a word from the place where wisdom cannot reach."

1. The ancient worthy is *Nanquan Puyuan*.

Case 242   古德大死   *An Ancient Worthy's "Great Death"*

古德云、如何是大死底。

An ancient worthy asked,[1] "What is it to die the Great Death?"

1. It is unknown who the "ancient worthy" was.

Case 243   慧覺無罪   *Huijue's "No Sin"*

有人問慧覺禪師、某甲平生愛殺牛、還有罪否。覺云、無罪。曰、爲
什麼無罪。覺曰、殺一箇、還一箇。

A man asked Guangxiao Huijue, "Every day I slaughter cattle. Is this a sin?"
"It is not a sin," answered Huijue.
"Why not?"
"You kill one, you return one," replied Huijue.

Case 244   宏智八句   *The Eight Phrases of Hongzhi*

宏智和尚八句。一段光明亙古今、有無照破脫情塵。當頭觸著彌天
過、退步承當特地新。紫極宮中鳥抱卵、銀河浪裏兔推輪。是須妙手
攜來用、百億分身處處眞。

The eight phrases of Hongzhi:

> A beam of wondrous light spans past and present,
> Shining through being and nonbeing, transcending all discrimination.[1]
> Grasp at it directly and you miss it completely;
> Step back and receive its light, and everything is fresh and new.
> In the vast Azure Palace a bird hatches an egg;[2]
> Among the waves of the Milky Way a rabbit pushes a cart.[3]
> Only the true adept can freely participate in this;
> Though divided into a billion, each and every piece is true.[4]

1. The term 情塵, translated here as "discrimination," can also mean the six senses and six sense-objects.

2. The Azure Palace is symbol for the daytime sky; the bird hatching an egg symbolizes the rising sun.

3. The Milky Way represents the night sky; the rabbit pushing the cart symbolizes the moon crossing the heavens.

Although this and the previous line are expressed in poetic language, the descriptive terms refer to the ordinary, everyday world. The two lines might therefore be reexpressed as: "The sun rises in the east, and the moon crosses the nighttime sky."

4. That is, the true adept can function in any form and perceives all places as true. ZGJI: Though the dharmakāya be divided into a billion, each and every piece is perfect and complete.

Case 245   踏著不嗔   *To Be Stepped On without Anger*

僧問慈明、如何是道。明曰、踏著不嗔[1]。

A monk asked Ciming Chuyuan, "What is the Way?"

"Though stepped upon, it doesn't anger,"[2] replied Ciming.

1. In the standard text of the *Kattōshū*, where the final four characters read 踏若不嗔, the character 若 is a scribal error for 著. The text has been emended according to the *Record of Ciming*.

2. This response plays on the word "Way" 道, the character for which indicates both "Tao" and "road." Both "ways" are walked on yet never complain. Another nuance is provided by the fact that 道 was an early Chinese translation for the Sanskrit "prajñā."

Case 246 月夜斷索 *A Piece of Rope on a Moonlit Night*[1]

京兆米和尚、因有老宿問、月中斷井索、時人喚作蛇。未審、七師見
佛、喚作什麼。米云、若有佛見、即同衆生。宿云、千年桃核。

An old monk asked Jingzhao Mihu, "On a moonlit night someone saw a
piece of well-bucket rope and thought it was a snake.[2] If you saw a buddha,
Qishi,[3] what would you think it was?"

Mihu replied, "Anyone holding the concept 'buddha' is the same as a
deluded being."

The old monk said, "This thousand-year peach pit!"[4]

1. Also *Blue Cliff Record* 48, Commentary on the Main Case.

2. The analogy of the rope and snake is used in the Yogācāra school to explain
the three modes of perceiving existence 三性. The first mode is that produced by
the deluded imagination, which sees as real that which does not actually exist
(e.g., the ātman); according to the analogy, this is the mode that mistakes the
rope for a snake. The second mode is that which sees existence in terms of causes
and conditions; this is the mode that realizes that the supposed snake is just a
rope. The third mode is that which sees existence in terms of its true nature; this
is the mode that sees the rope as constituted of hemp.

3. Qishi 七師 is another name for Jingzhao Mihu.

4. ZGJI: The expression "thousand-year peach pit" indicates a seed that won't
sprout even in a thousand years; thus, an abusive term for a monk who will
never awaken.

Case 247 憲宗問光 *Xianzong Asks about the Light*

唐憲宗帝、迎佛骨舍利、入内供養。夜放光明。早朝宣問、群臣皆
賀陛下聖德聖感。唯韓愈不賀。上宣問群臣。皆賀卿何獨不賀。愈
奏云、臣曾看佛書、佛光非青黄赤白等相、此是龍神衞護之光。帝
問、如何是佛光。愈無對。因此罪謫潮州。

Emperor Xianzong of the Tang dynasty received the Buddha's relics,
installed them in the palace, and made offerings to them. That night they
emitted light, so early the next morning the emperor asked his ministers
about this. All praised it as the result of the emperor's holy virtue and influence. Only Han Yu said nothing.[1]

The emperor said to Han, "All the other ministers have offered praise.
Why do you alone offer no praise?"

Han Yu answered, "According to what I have read in the Buddhist scriptures, the light of a buddha has no color such as blue, yellow, red, or white. It must have been the protective light of the dragon gods."

Thereupon the emperor asked, "Then what is the light of a buddha?" Han Yu had no response. For this he was punished by exile to Chaozhou.

1. Han Yu is well known in Chinese history as a strong exponent of Confucian thought and opponent of Buddhism. His opposition to Emperor Xianzong's enshrining of the Buddha's finger is particularly well known. Giles writes:

> In 819 [Han Yu] presented a memorial protesting against certain extravagant honors with which the Emperor Hsien Tsung proposed to receive a bone of Buddha. The monarch was furious; and but for the intercession of his friends P'ie Tu and others, it would have fared badly with the bold writer. As it was, he was banished to Ch'ao-chou Fu in Kuangtung, where he set himself to civilise the rude inhabitants of those wild parts. (1939, 255)

Case 248   大王來也   *The Great King Has Come*[1]

趙州一日坐次、侍者報云、大王來也。州云、大王萬福。侍者云、未
到和尚。州云、又道來也。

One day when Zhaozhou was sitting, his attendant announced, "The Great King has come."

Zhaozhou said, "Ten thousand blessings, Great King!"

The attendant said, "He hasn't arrived yet, Master."

Zhaozhou replied, "Again you say he has come!"[2]

1. Also *Blue Cliff Record* 9, Commentary on the Main Case.
2. Yamada interprets the line as, "Ah, the Great King again!" (1985, 2:41).

Case 249   路逢達道   *Responding to a Wayfarer on the Road*[1]

五祖演和尚云、路逢達道人、不將語默對。且道、將甚麼對。

Wuzu Fayan said, "If you meet an accomplished wayfarer on the road, don't respond with either speech or silence. So tell me, how do you respond?"

1. Also *Wumen guan* 36, Main Case, and *Blue Cliff Record* 82, Commentary on the Verse.

Case 250   黃檗禮佛   *Huangbo Bows to a Buddha Image*[1]

黃檗禮佛次、大中見而問曰、不著佛求、不著法求、不著衆求、禮拜
何所求。檗云、不著佛求、不著法求、不著衆求、常禮如是。大中
云、作禮何爲。檗便掌。大中云、太麁生。檗云、這裏什麼所在、說
麁說細、又掌。

One day when Huangbo was bowing before a buddha image, Xuanzong[2] saw him and asked, "If we should 'seek nothing from the Buddha, seek nothing from the Dharma, and seek nothing from the Sangha,'[3] then what do you seek with these prostrations?"

Huangbo replied, "Seeking nothing from the Buddha, seeking nothing from the Dharma, seeking nothing from the Sangha—that's how I always do prostrations."

Xuanzong said, "What's the use of doing prostrations?"

Immediately Huangbo slapped him.

"How coarse!" Xuanzong said.

"What sort of place is this to be talking of coarse or refined?" Huangbo replied, and slapped him again.

1. Also *Blue Cliff Record* 11, Commentary on the Verse.

2. Xuanzong was the younger brother of Emperor Muzong 穆宗 (795–824) and the future sixteenth emperor of the Tang dynasty. At the time of the incident related in this koan he was in hiding among the sangha to escape unfavorable political times. For further details see *Xuanzong* in the Biographical Notes.

3. "Seek nothing from the Buddha, seek nothing from the Dharma, and seek nothing from the Sangha" is a statement found in several sutras, most notably the *Vimalakīrti Sutra* (T 14:546a).

Case 251   那吒析肉   *Prince Nata Tears His Flesh*

那吒太子、析肉還母、析骨還父、然後現本身、運大神力、爲父母
說法。

Prince Nata tore off his flesh and returned it to his mother, broke his bones and returned them to his father. Then, revealing his original body, he employed his great supernatural powers to preach the Dharma to his parents.[1]

1. For background on this case, see *Nalakūvara* in the Biographical Notes.

Case 252   隱峰推車   *Yinfeng Pushes a Wheelbarrow*

鄧隱峰禪師、一日、推土車次、馬大師展脚在路上坐。師云、請師收
脚。大師云、已展不收。師云、進不退。乃推車碾過、大師脚損。祖
歸法堂執斧子曰、適來碾損老僧脚底出來。師便出於大師前引頸。大
師乃置斧。

One day as Deng Yinfeng was pushing a wheelbarrow he came across Mazu
Daoyi, who was sitting with his legs stretched across the path.

Yinfeng called out, "Master, please move your legs."

"What's already extended can't be pulled in," answered Mazu.

"What's already moving forward can't be drawn back," responded Yinfeng. He continued pushing the wheelbarrow, which rolled over the master's
legs and hurt them.

Later the master went to the Dharma Hall, hatchet in hand, and shouted,
"The one that just hurt my legs, come out!"

Yinfeng immediately went before the master and stretched out his neck.
Mazu put down the hatchet.

Case 253   關山罵僧   *Kanzan Scolds a Monk*

關山國師、見僧來參便罵。僧曰、某甲爲生死事大、特來參見和尚。
因甚罵詈。師曰、我這裡無生死。便打趁出。

Kanzan Egen saw a monk coming and scolded him. The monk said, "I came
all the way here to meet you concerning the Great Matter of birth-and-
death. Why do you scold me?"

"There's no birth-and-death at my place!" answered Kanzan, striking the
monk and driving him away.

Case 254   許老胡知   *I Accept That the Old Barbarian Knows*[1]

只許老胡知、不許老胡會。

I accept that the old barbarian knows, not that he understands.[2]

1. Also *Blue Cliff Record* 1, Commentary on the Verse; *Blue Cliff Record* 51,
Commentary on the Main Case, Capping Phrases on the Verse; *Wumen guan*
9, Commentary.

2. Commentators (e.g., Yamada 1976, p. 79) note that in this case the character 知 (translated as "knows," and which usually indicates intellectual knowledge) signifies prajna wisdom, while 會 (translated as "understands") represents conceptual knowledge. The "old barbarian" is identified as being either Śākyamuni or Bodhidharma. Aitken translates the line as: "I approve the Old Barbarian's realization, but I don't approve his understanding" (1990, p. 64).

Case 255 十智同眞 *Ten Realizations, Same Reality*

汾陽禪師示衆云、夫說法者、須具十智同眞。若不具十智同眞、邪正不辨、緇素不分、不能與人天爲眼目決斷是非。如鳥飛空而折翼、如箭射的而斷弦。弦斷故射不中的、翼折故空不能飛。弦壯翼牢空的俱徹。作麼生是十智同眞。與諸上座點出。一同一質、二同大事、三總同參、四同眞智、五同徧普、六同具足、七同得失、八同生殺、九同音吼、十同得入。又曰、與甚麼人同得入。與阿誰同音吼。作麼生是同生殺。甚麼物同得失。阿那箇同具足。是甚麼同徧普。何人同眞智。孰能總同參。那箇同大事。何物同一質。有點得出底麼。點得出者、不恡慈悲。點不出來、未有參學眼在。切須辨取。要識是非、面目現在。不可久立、珍重。

Fenyang Shanzhao said to the assembly:

Those who preach the Dharma must embody the ten realizations of the same reality.[1] If you do not possess them, you can't tell the false from the true, you can't distinguish black from white, you can't be the eyes of humans and gods to determine right and wrong. It's like a bird with a broken wing trying to fly in the sky, or like an archer with a severed bowstring trying to shoot a target. Because the bowstring is severed the arrow can't hit the target; because its wing is broken the bird can't fly in the sky. When the bowstring is whole and the wing is sound, then the target and the sky are both within reach.

What are these ten realizations? For the benefit of the assembly I will list them: (1) sameness of essence, (2) sameness of the Great Matter, (3) sameness of seeking, (4) sameness of wisdom, (5) sameness of universality, (6) sameness of endowment, (7) sameness of gain and loss, (8) sameness of giving of life and taking it away, (9) sameness of roaring, and (10) sameness of entering and attaining.[2]

Again he said:

Who is the same in attainment? Who has the same roar? Who is the same in giving life and taking it away? What is it to be the same in gain and loss? What is it to be the same in endowment? What is it to be the same in universality? Who is the same in true wisdom? Who is the same in seeking? What is it to be the same in the Great Matter? What is it to be the same in essence?

Is there anyone who can demonstrate these matters? If you can, do not withhold your compassion. If you cannot, you do not possess the true eye of practice. You must be able to explain them clearly. You wish to know right and wrong? Your original face is right before you!

You have been standing long.[3] Take good care of yourselves!

1. "Reality" translates 眞, which the Chinese also used to render concepts like "truth," "enlightenment," "tathā (suchness)," etc.
2. Dōmae comments on the ten "samenesses" as follows:
   1) Sameness of essence: master and disciple are equal in essence.
   2) Sameness of the Great Matter: all share the One Great Matter spoken of by the buddhas and the masters.
   3) Sameness of seeking: even Śākyamuni and Bodhidharma are still training.
   4) Sameness of wisdom: all share the wisdom of the masters.
   5) Sameness of universality: matter and mind are one, as seen from the aspect of matter (mountains, rivers, and the great earth, all are the fully revealed body of the Dharma King).
   6) Sameness of endowment: matter and mind are one, as seen from the aspect of mind (the infinite storehouse of the dharmadhatu).
   7) Sameness of gain and loss: gaining the inexhaustible dharmadhatu, losing the world of phenomena.
   8) Sameness of giving birth and killing: giving birth to the world of phenomena, killing the inexhaustible dharmadhatu.
   9) Sameness of roaring: master and disciple are equal in preaching the Dharma.
   10) Sameness of attainment: all will equally attain buddhahood.

3. In ancient Chinese Zen monasteries the custom was to stand during the master's lectures.

Case 256   天皇恁麼   *Tianhuang's "Like This"*

欽山與嚴頭雪峰到德山乃問、天皇也恁麼道、龍潭也恁麼道、未審德山
作麼生道。德山云、汝試舉天皇龍潭底看。欽山擬議。德山便打。欽山
歸延壽堂云、是則是、打我太煞。嚴頭云、汝與麼他後莫道見德山。

Qinshan Wensui went with Yantou Quanhuo and Xuefeng Yicun to visit Deshan Xuanjian.

Qinshan asked, "Tianhuang Daowu spoke of it this way, Longtan Chongxin, too, spoke of it this way.[1] So how do you speak of it?"

Deshan said to Qinshan, "Show me Tianhuang and Longtan's meaning." When Qinshan started to speak, Deshan hit him.

On the way to the infirmary[2] Qinshan said, "I know he was right, but he went too far in hitting me."

Yantou said, "If that's how you feel, don't ever claim to have met Deshan."

1. The implied topic is the Great Matter of Buddhism.

2. The *Transmission of the Lamp* version of this episode makes it clear that Qinshan was going to the infirmary because Deshan had hit him hard enough to injure him (T 51:340a).

Case 257　夾山法身　*Jiashan's "Dharmakāya"*

夾山初住京口寺。因僧問、如何是法身。山云、法身無相。又問、如
何是法眼。山云、法眼無瑕。時道吾在座[下]失笑。山請益。[後]散
衆參船子省發。後歸聚徒。道吾令僧往問、如何是法身。山云、法身
無相。又問、如何是法眼。山云、法眼無瑕。僧迴舉似道吾。吾云、
者漢此迴方徹。

When Jiashan Shanhui first lived in the temple at Jingkou, a monk asked him, "What is the dharmakāya?"

Jiashan answered, "The dharmakāya is without form."

The monk then asked, "What is the Dharma eye?"

Jiashan said, "The Dharma eye is without blemish."

At that time Daowu Yuanzhi, who was sitting nearby, couldn't help laughing. Later, after receiving Daowu's advice, Jiashan gave his followers their leave and went to study with Chuanzi, under whom he attained enlightenment.[1] He then returned and his followers assembled once again. Daowu sent a monk to ask him, "What is the dharmakāya?"

Jiashan answered, "The dharmakāya is without form."

The monk asked again, "What is the Dharma eye?"

Jiashan said, "The Dharma eye is without blemish."

The monk went back and reported this to Daowu. Daowu said, "This time the fellow thoroughly understands."

1. For background information on Jiashan's awakening under Chuanzi, see *Jiashan Shanhui* in the Biographical Notes.

Case 258　茶陵投機　*Chaling's Enlightenment Verse*

茶陵郁和尚、投機偈曰、我有明珠一顆、久被塵勞埋沒。今朝塵盡光
生、照破山河萬朵。

Chaling Yu said in his enlightenment verse:[1]

> I have a bright pearl,
> Long buried in the dusts of delusion.
> This morning the dust cleared and light shone forth,
> Illuminating the myriad mountains and rivers.

1. For "enlightenment verse," see Case 98, note 1.

Case 259　白雲未在　*Baiyun's "Still Lacking"*

白雲端禪師、語五祖演曰、有數禪客、自廬山來。皆有悟入處、教伊
說亦[說]得有來由。舉因緣問伊亦明得。教伊下語亦下得。祇是未在。

Once Baiyun Shouduan said to Wuzu Fayan:

> Several Zen monks visited from Mount Lu. All had had understandings
> and, when asked to expound the Dharma, did so clearly. When given
> koans, they responded lucidly; when asked for capping-phrases, they pro-
> duced them. But still they were lacking.

Case 260　太宗擎鉢　*Taizong Holds a Bowl*

宋太宗帝、一日擎鉢、問丞相王隨云、既是大庾嶺頭提不起、爲甚麼
却在寡人手裡。隨無對。

One day Emperor Taizong of the Song dynasty held up a bowl. He then
asked his prime minister, Wang Sui, "On top of Dayu Peak this bowl could
not be lifted.[1] How is it that it now rests in the hand of this man of little
merit?"[2]

Wang Sui had no reply.

1. The reference is to the inability of the senior monk Huiming to lift the robe
and bowl set upon a rock by the Sixth Patriarch. See Case 2, above.

2. The emperor's way of referring to himself.

Case 261   斷百思想   *Stop All Thoughts*[1]

臥輪禪師偈曰、臥輪有伎倆、能斷百思想。對境心不起、菩提日
日長。

Zen master Wolun said in a verse:

> Wolun has the ability
> To effectively stop all thoughts.
> No circumstances stir his mind;
> Day by day enlightenment grows.[2]

1. This verse is found the Ming edition of the *Platform Sutra of the Sixth Patriarch* (T 48:358a).

2. Wolun's approach to meditation, as expressed in this verse, was criticized in the "Encounters" 機緣 chapter of the *Platform Sutra of the Sixth Patriarch*. The Sixth Patriarch says, "This verse is not yet clear regarding the mind-ground. If one practices in accordance with it, one's bondage will only increase." Huineng then says:

> Huineng has no skill, he doesn't cut off all thoughts.
> In the face of circumstances,
> Mind arises again and again;
> How can enlightenment grow?

Case 262   趙州石橋   *Zhaozhou's Stone Bridge*[1]

趙州一日、同首座看石橋。乃問首座、是甚麼人造。座云、李膺。
師云、造時向甚麼處下手。座無對。師云、尋常說石橋、問著下手
處也不知。

One day Zhaozhou and the head monk were looking at the stone bridge.[2] Zhaozhou asked the monk, "Who built this?"

"Li Ying did," replied the head monk.

Zhaozhou said, "When he built it, where did he set to work?" The head monk had no reply.

Zhaozhou said, "Everyone talks of the stone bridge, but ask and they don't even know where [Li] set to work."

1. Also *Blue Cliff Record* 52, Commentary on the Main Case.

2. This stone bridge is a famous landmark not far from Zhaozhou's temple.

Case 263   佛早留心   *A Buddha Long Ago Set His Mind*[1]

毘婆尸佛、早留心、直到如今不得妙。

Vipaśyin Buddha long ago set his mind to practice but even now has yet to attain the Mystery.[2]

1. Also *Wumen guan* 22, Commentary on the Main Case.
2. Vipaśyin was the first of the Seven Buddhas of the Past (see Case 34, note 2).

Case 264   洞山果子   *Dongshan's Fruit*

洞山价禪師、因冬夜喫果子次、問泰首座云、有一物、上拄天下拄
地、黑似漆。常在動用中、動用中收不得。你道、過在甚麼處。泰
云、過在動用中。師乃喝令掇却果卓。

On the eve of the winter solstice[1] as they were eating some fruit, Dongshan Liangjie asked Head Monk Tai, "There is something that supports the heavens above and the earth below and is as black as lacquer. It's always totally active, yet can't be restricted to activity.[2] So tell me, what is its failing?"

"It's failing is in its activity," answered Tai.

Dongshan shouted and had the fruit taken away.

1. On the winter solstice the yin forces (darkness, cold) reach their zenith and the yang forces (light, warmth) their nadir, at which point yin starts to decrease and yang starts once again to increase. Dongshan's question alludes to the belief that at the moment of change the forces cancel each other out and there is for a moment only empty darkness, representing the Great Death.
2. "Activity" translates 動用, a difficult term to render into English. It combines the nuances of 動, which implies movement or action, and 用, which implies utilization or function.

Case 265   長慶拄杖   *Changqing's Staff*[1]

長慶稜禪師、拈拄杖示眾云、識得這箇、一生參學事畢。

Changqing, taking up his staff, said to the assembly, "Know *this*, and you have completed a lifetime's practice."[2]

1. Also *Blue Cliff Record* 18, Commentary on the Main Case.
2. The "this" 這箇 in the standard *Kattōshū* version is, in the *Blue Cliff Record* version, clearly identified as Changqing's staff.

Case 266 僧被蛇蹴 *A Monk Is Bitten by a Snake*

雲居悟禪師在龍門。一日、有僧被蛇傷足。佛眼問云、既是龍門、爲
甚麼却被蛇蹴。師即答、果然現大人相。後圓悟聞曰、龍門有此僧、
東山法道未寂寥。

One day while Yunju Shanwu was at Dragon Gate Mountain[1] a monk was bitten in the foot by a snake. Foyan Qingyuan[2] asked, "This is Dragon Gate Mountain. Why would someone be bitten by a snake?"[3]

Yunju answered, "Just as I thought, that monk shows the signs of a great man!"[4]

Later, when Yuanwu Keqin heard about this, he commented, "With such a monk [as Yunju] at the Dragon Gate, the lineage of Wuzu Fayan is in no danger of dying out."[5]

1. Dragon Gate Mountain 龍門山 is located in the Shuzhou 舒州 district of present-day Anhui 安徽.

2. Foyan Qingyuan was the master of the monastery on Dragon Gate Mountain; Yunju Shanwu was Foyan's student and eventually his Dharma successor.

3. Dragons are regarded in Asia as the rulers of the snake family. They are also looked upon as benevolent symbols of wisdom, and thus of enlightenment; as the protectors of Buddhism and Buddhist texts; and as the rulers of the waters, whether in the form of clouds, rivers, or oceans. Furthermore, as noted in Case 194, note 2, the saying "to have the head of a dragon and the tail of a snake" signifies a promising beginning but a disappointing end.

Perhaps playing on these concepts, Foyan asks, "Why would a monk on Dragon Gate Mountain get bitten by the dragons' subject, a snake?" Similarly, Mujaku comments, "Why was a monk, who should be swallowed by a dragon, bitten instead by a snake?"

4. The signs of a great man 大人相 are the thirty-two marks of a buddha. See Case 133, note 3. After this line, the *Categorized Anthology of the Zen Forest* 禪林類聚 adds, "With this comment, Yunju recognized him as a vessel of the Dharma."

5. Yuanwu Keqin and Foyan Qingyuan were fellow students and Dharma successors of Wuzu Fayan.

Case 267 國師水椀 *The National Teacher's Water Bowl*[1]

南陽忠國師、因紫璘供奉擬註思益經。師乃問、大德凡註經、須會佛
意始得。［云、］若不會爭解註得。師乃令侍者盛一椀水、著七粒米在

水中、椀面安一隻節。乃問、這箇是那義。璘無語。師云、老僧意尚
不會、豈況佛意。爭能註得經。

National Teacher Nanyang Huizhong, hearing that the court monk Zilin had lectured on the *Sutra Preached at the Request of Brahma-deva*,[2] said to the official, "It is only after truly understanding the Buddha's meaning that one is able to expound the scriptures."

"How would I be able to lecture if I didn't know the meaning?" replied the official.

Thereupon Huizhong had his attendant bring a bowl of water with seven grains of rice in it and a single chopstick lying across the top. He asked the official, "What does this mean?"

The official had no answer.

Huizhong said, "You don't even know my meaning! How can you understand the Buddha's meaning? How can you possibly expound the scriptures?"

1. Also *Blue Cliff Record* 48, Commentary on the Main Case.

2. 思益梵天所問經; T 15:586. The *Sutra Preached at the Request of Brahma-deva*, translated into Chinese by Kumārajiva, is an early Mahayana sutra similar to the *Vimalakīrti Sutra* in its teachings on nonduality, śūnyatā, and the equality of samsara and nirvana.

Case 268   三界輪廻   *Moving through the Three Realms*

寒山曰、咄哉咄哉、三界輪廻。

Hanshan said, "Hey! Hey! You're caught in the cycle of the Three Realms!"[1]

1. The Three Realms 三界 (Skt. *triloka*) are the "triple world" of samsara, within which sentient beings are reborn in the six realms of unenlightened existence (see Case 63, note 2). The Three Realms are: the kāmadhātu (欲界), the realm of form and sensual desire; the rūpadhātu (色界), the realm of pure form and desireless matter; and the arūpadhātu (無色界), the realm of formlessness or pure consciousness.

This line is found in the Preface of Lu Qiuyin 閭丘胤 to the *Collected Poems of Cold Mountain* 寒山子詩集, where Lu says of the poet Hanshan:

> Thus this man of accomplishment hid his true form, presenting himself as an ordinary man even as he guided others. At times he stood in the hallway singing, "Hey! Hey! You're caught in the cycle of the Three Realms!"

Case 269   明眼落井   *A Clear-Eyed Person Falls into a Well*[1]

巴陵鑒禪師、僧問、如何是道。師云、明眼人落井。

A monk asked Baling Haojian, "What is the Way?"
Baling said, "A clear-eyed person falls into a well."

> 1. Also *Blue Cliff Record* 13, Commentary on the Main Case.

Case 270-1   首山綱宗   *Shoushan's Principles of the Teaching*[1]

首山示衆云、咄哉巧女兒、擲梭不解織。看他鬪雞人、水牛也不識。

咄哉拙郎君、巧妙無人識。打破鳳林關、著靴水上立。

Shoushan Shengnian said to the assembly, "Hey, skillful weaver-woman!
Though your shuttle moves back and forth, you've never woven.[2] Those fel-
lows watching the cockfights, they know nothing of the water buffalo.[3]

"Hey, clumsy guy! No one knows your true skill. Breaking through the
Fenglin Barrier,[4] you put on shoes and stood on water."[5]

> 1. This case, both as a text and as a koan, is one of the most difficult in the
> *Kattōshū*. Several of the expressions, such as "skillful weaver-woman," are found
> nowhere else in the Zen literature. The present translation relies upon Dōmae
> and traditional Zen monastic interpretations.
> 2. The skillful weaver-woman can be equated with Śākyamuni, who capa-
> bly taught for forty-nine years and yet "never preached a word" (see Case 72,
> above).
> 3. "Those fellows watching the cockfights" are likened to those of Śākyamuni's
> disciples who are absorbed in their practice of the Dharma and concerned only
> with results. The buffalo is a common metaphor for self-nature; thus to know
> nothing of the water buffalo is to be unaware of one's own true nature.
> 4. The Fenglin Barrier 鳳林關 was an important checkpoint between Jingnan
> 荊南 and Henan 河南, guarding entrance into the central region of China.
> 5. Commentators identify the "clumsy guy" with Bodhidharma, whose "true
> skill"—his message of "seeing self-nature and attaining buddhahood"—was not
> understood by Emperor Wu (see Case 64, above) or by anyone else; who, after
> his unsatisfactory meeting with Emperor Wu, crossed the Yangzi (his "break-
> ing through the Fenglin Barrier"); and who thereafter meditated at Shaolin (his
> "putting on shoes and standing on water," with "putting on shoes and standing
> on water" being one of the supernatural powers traditionally ascribed to the
> buddhas and bodhisattvas, signifying their ability to be in the world and
> remain undefiled).

Case 270-2　拖泥帶水　*Filthy, Stagnant Water*

虛堂拈云、首山自謂得臨濟正傳。却作野干鳴、致令天下兒孫、箇箇
拖泥帶水。

Xutang commented, "Shoushan claimed to have received the true transmission of Linji's Dharma, but actually he was just uttering wild fox cries and causing students everywhere to be doused with filthy, stagnant water."

Case 271　撲落非他　*The Sound of the Wood Isn't Separate from Me*

興教壽禪師、在天台韶國師會中、普請次、聞墮薪有聲、豁然契悟。
乃云、撲落非他物、縱橫不是塵。山河并大地、全露法王身。虛堂拈
云、壽禪師、大似窮儒登群玉府、無不稱心滿意。只是中間、有一字
子未穩。

One day when Xingjiao Hongshou[1] was in the assembly under Tiantai Deshao he was working with the monks. Hearing some firewood fall to the ground, he had a clear awakening. He said:

> The sound of the wood isn't separate from me;[2]
> My surroundings aren't outside things.[3]
> Mountains, rivers, and the great earth
> All manifest the Dharma King's body.[4]

Xutang commented, "Like a penniless scholar given use of the Imperial Library, Xingjiao has all he desires and is utterly content.[5] But in his verse there's a word that still isn't quite right!"

1. Although the *Kattōshū* identifies the protagonist as *Yongming Yanshou*, this episode is in fact from the biography of *Xingjiao Hongshou*, a fellow disciple of Yongming under Tiantai Deshao.

2. "Not separate from me" translates 非他物, literally, "not something other."

3. "Outside objects" translates 塵 (dust), which means here the phenomena of the everyday world but which can also indicate defilements or kleśa.

4. Wu translates the verse with a more metaphysical flavor: "Plop, there it is! Nothing else than *That* which / Devoid of Matter, fills all corners of the universe! / Mountains, rivers, the entire world / One and all, they manifest the Body of the Dharma King" (1996, p. 243).

5. The Imperial Library was called the Storehouse of a Thousand Jewels 群玉府. An impoverished scholar lacked the means to purchase books, so access to the Imperial Library would be the greatest satisfaction.

Case 272 南泉遷化 *Nanquan's Death*

長沙岑禪師、因三聖令秀首座問云、南泉遷化向甚麼處去。師云、石頭
爲沙彌時、曾見六祖。秀云、不問爲沙彌時、南泉遷化向甚麼處去。師
云、教伊尋思去。秀云、和尚雖有千尺寒松、且無抽條石筍。師默然。
秀云、謝和尚答話。師亦默然。秀同舉似三聖。聖云、若實與麼、勝臨
濟七步。雖然如是、待我明日更驗過。至明日乃問、承聞、和尚昨日答
南泉遷化一則話。可謂、光前絕後、今古罕聞。師亦默然。

Sansheng Huiran had the head monk Xiu ask Changsha Jingcen, "When Nanquan Puyuan died, where did he go?"[1]

Changsha replied, "When Shitou Xiqian was a novice, he spoke with the Sixth Patriarch."

Xiu said, "I didn't ask about when someone was a novice. When Nanquan Puyuan died, where did he go?"

Changsha said, "The Sixth Patriarch told Shitou, 'Investigate.'"[2]

Xiu said, "You're a thousand-foot winter pine,[3] not a rock-moving bamboo."[4] Changsha was silent. Then Xiu said, "Thank you for your answer." Changsha remained silent.

Xiu went back and reported this to Sansheng, who responded, "If that's the way he responded, Changsha is seven steps beyond Linji. But tomorrow I'll go check for myself."[5]

The next day he went to Changsha and said, "I heard your answer concerning where Nanquan went when he died. There has been nothing to compare to it before this, and there will be nothing to equal it later. It is truly something rarely heard at any time."

Changsha was again silent.

1. Changsha Jingcen was a successor of Nanquan Puyuan. The question about Nanquan's death refers to Nanquan's response when asked where he would go after he died. "I'll be reborn as a water buffalo at the foot of the hill," he replied (see *Nanquan Puyuan* in the Biographical Notes). That an enlightened Zen master would be reborn in the realm of the animals was thought shocking at the time. According to the *Compendium of the Five Lamps*, Changsha, when asked about this on another occasion, answered, "In the household to the east he was reborn as a donkey; in the household to the west he was reborn as a horse…. If you want to ride, get on, if you want to dismount, get off" (x 80:95a).

2. Commentaries on this koan customarily mention the fact that the Sixth Patriarch's answer can be taken in two ways. According to the *Jingde-Era Record of the Transmission of the Lamp*, when Shitou was a novice at the Sixth Patriarch's temple he asked the Patriarch (then nearing the end of his life) how he should study later on. The Patriarch said, "Xunsiqu" 尋思去, which Shitou took

to mean, as it literally does, "examine" or "investigate." Thus Shitou meditated assiduously. When the head monk asked Shitou the reason for his sitting, Shitou repeated Huineng's advice, 尋思去. The head monk said, "You have an affinity with Master Qingyuan Xingsi 青原行思. You misunderstood the Patriarch when he said 'Xunsiqu' 尋思去. What he meant was, 'Go call upon 尋去 Master Si 思."

3. The image is of a great pine tree enduring the long winter, connoting rectitude and fortitude.

4. The image is of a bamboo shoot pushing out from under a rock, connoting vigor and adaptability.

5. "I'll go check for myself" translates 待我明日更驗過. The *Kattōshū* version has 待我明日更看過, "tomorrow I'll see through him myself." The text has been emended in accordance with the *Compendium of the Five Lamp* version (x 80:95c).

Reference Materials

Biographical Notes
Chart of Names in Pinyin
Chart of Names in Wade-Giles
Chart of Names in Japanese
Bibliography
Index

Biographical Notes

This section contains information from the traditional Zen biographies on the figures mentioned in the Kattōshū *koans. The material, intended primarily to provide context for the events related in the koans, is often legendary in nature. Cross-references are italicized.*

A

Ānanda (Anan 阿難, A-nan, Anan; Cases 45 n., 114 n., 136, 204, 213 n.), a cousin of the Buddha and the younger brother of *Devadatta*, was one of the ten major disciples of the Buddha. Remembered for his humility and gentle disposition, he served as Śākyamuni's personal attendant. Owing to his constant presence at the Buddha's side as well as to his phenomenal memory, he is said to have remembered more of the Dharma teachings than any other disciple. He was thus a central figure in the compilation of the Buddhist canon at the time of the First Buddhist Council, held just after the Buddha's passing. Zen legend has it that he failed to reach enlightenment during the Buddha's lifetime, but was finally awakened under *Mahākāśyapa*, the first Indian Zen ancestor; the circumstances of his awakening are related in Case 136.

Aṅgulimāla (Yangjue Moluo 殃掘摩羅, Yang-chüeh Mo-lo, Ōkutsu Mara; Case 165) was a mass murderer who later became one of Śākyamuni's greatest students. According to all accounts he was earnest, intelligent, and immensely strong as a young man. According to one version of his story he had nearly completed a course of studies under an eminent teacher when the teacher, jealous of Aṅgulimāla's abilities, demanded as a final task the little fingers from the right hands of a thousand victims. Aṅgulimāla went to a forest and started killing travelers to obtain the needed fingers, which he strung on a long necklace (the Skt. *aṅgulimāla* means "finger-garland"). He had accumulated 999 fingers when Śākyamuni happened to walk through the forest in which he dwelled. When he attempted to overtake the Buddha he found himself unable to catch up, even though Śākyamuni was walking at a normal pace. Śākyamuni then convinced him to abandon violence, and Aṅgulimāla, realizing the suffering he had caused, became a member of the sangha and eventually attained arhathood.

In another version of the story his teacher's wife, attracted to the handsome Aṅgulimāla but spurned by him, maligns him to her husband, who then tells Aṅgulimāla that if he cuts the fingers off one hundred travelers he will be reborn in the Brahma Heaven. The final person was not Śākyamuni but Aṅgulimāla's mother; Śākyamuni, seeing this with his supernatural powers, substitutes himself for the mother and is able to instruct Aṅgulimāla on the true Way.

Āryadeva (Tipo 提婆, Ti-p'o, Daiba; n.d.; Case 228), also known as Kānadeva (Jianatipo 迦那提婆, Chia-na Ti-p'o, Kanadaiba) because he had only one eye (*kāna* means "one-eye"). Honored as the fifteenth ancestor of the Indian Zen lineage, Āryadeva is said to have been exceptionally eloquent. When he met the great Buddhist philosopher *Nāgārjuna*, Nāgārjuna had a bowl of water filled to the brim placed in front of Āryadeva, who put a needle into the bowl without spilling a drop. Nāgārjuna was pleased and accepted Āryadeva as his student.

Under Nāgārjuna, Āryadeva went on to master the śūnyatā teachings of the Madhyamaka school. His understanding and skill in debate enabled him to defeat a number of non-Buddhist teachers; according to some accounts, he was murdered by one of the defeated teachers' disciples. Āryadeva is credited with several important treatises, including the *Catuḥśataka* (Four hundred verses; *Guangbai lun* 廣百論) and the *Śata-śāstra* (One hundred verses; *Bai lun* 百論). He is also honored as the founder of the Tipo school.

Āryasiṁha (Shizi Puti 師子菩提, Shih-tzu P'u-ti, Shishi Bodai; n.d.; Case 168), honored as the twenty-fourth ancestor of the Indian Zen lineage, was a Brahman scholar from central India who later became a disciple of Haklenayaśas (n.d.), the twenty-third ancestor. The story of his transmission is as follows:

> Āryasiṁha said, "I wish to pursue the Way. To what must I apply my mind?" Haklenayaśas replied, "In seeking the Way there is no striving with the mind." Āryasiṁha asked, "If there is no striving with the mind, what performs the work of the buddhas?" Haklenayaśas answered, "If there is striving, this is not virtue. Nondoing is the true work of the buddhas. A sutra says, 'The virtue I attain is free of self.'" At these words Āryasiṁha understood the wisdom of the buddhas.

Later in his life Āryasiṁha lived in Kashmir, where he united under Buddhism five groups of contemplatives: those who practiced samadhi, those who stressed intellectual speculation, those who held to form, those who rejected form, and those who maintained silence. Āryasiṁha's death is traditionally thought to have been a violent one. According to the *Jingde-Era Record of the Transmission of the Lamp* 景德傳燈錄, Āryasiṁha's teacher Haklenayaśas prophesied troubles for his student in the future. Fifty years later, when Āryasiṁha was teaching in Kashmir, he sensed the coming troubles and, realizing that they could not be avoided, transmitted his Dharma to his disciple Basiasita. There were two sorcerers, Mamokuta and Torakusha, who dressed in Buddhist robes and attempted to assassinate the king, thinking the Buddhists would be blamed. Although the assassination attempt failed, the Buddhists were indeed held responsible. The outraged king had the monasteries destroyed and the monks and nuns expelled, and he himself took a sword and confronted Āryasiṁha. "Have you grasped the fundamental emptiness of all forms?" he asked. "I have," answered Āryasiṁha. "Have you left behind birth-and-death?" the king asked. "I have," answered

Āryasimha. "If you have left behind birth-and-death," the king replied, "then give me your head!" "This body is not mine—how can I refuse you my head?" answered Āryasimha. At this the king decapitated him. Milk, not blood, flowed from the severed neck, while the king's arm fell off and the king himself died seven days later.

Aśvaghoṣa (Ashifujusha 阿濕縛寠沙, A-shih-feng-chüsha, Ashibakusha; 2nd c.; Case 228), a name often rendered in Chinese as Mama 馬鳴 (Ma-ming; J., Memyō) or Anapudi 阿那菩底 (A-na-p'u-ti; J., Anabotei). Aśvaghoṣa is regarded as the twelfth ancestor of the Indian Zen lineage. A second-century poet and scholar from Śrāvastī in central India, he is said to have been a Brahman critical of Buddhism before his conversion by Punyayaśas, the eleventh Indian Zen ancestor. His work *Buddhacharita* (The life of the Buddha) is considered one of the greatest masterpieces of Indian literature. Also attributed to him is the original text of the *Dacheng qixin lun* 大乘起信論 (On awakening faith in the Mahayana), although the true authorship is in question.

Avalokiteśvara (Guanyin 觀音, Kuan-yin, Kannon; Cases 12 n., 88, 237), the bodhisattva of great compassion, is regarded as the manifestation in bodhisattva form of the salvific function of Amitābha Buddha. The name "Avalokiteśvara" is generally interpreted to mean "the one who perceives the sounds (or cries) of the world." In order to better save sentient beings everywhere, Avalokiteśvara is said to appear in thirty-three different forms, including the wish-fulfilling Avalokiteśvara, the white-robed Avalokiteśvara, the horse-headed Avalokiteśvara, and the willow-branch-holding Avalokiteśvara. Among the most popular manifestations is the eleven-headed, thousand-armed Avalokiteśvara. A legend explains that, when he saw all the suffering in the world, Avalokiteśvara's head burst, after which Amitābha Buddha put the pieces back together in the form of eleven heads. The thousand arms symbolize Avalokiteśvara's vow to help all beings.

B

Bai Juyi 白居易 (Pai Chü-i, Haku Kyoi; 772–846; Case 215); also known as Bai Letian 白樂天 (Pai Lo-t'ien, Haku Rakuten). Giles writes:

> One of China's greatest poets. As a child he was most precocious, knowing a considerable number of the written characters at the early age of seven months, after having had each one pointed out only once by his nurse. He graduated as *chin shih* at the age of seventeen, and entered upon an official career. He became a member of the Han-lin College, and soon rose to high rank under the Emperor Hsien Tsung. However, one day he was suddenly banished to Chiang-chou as Magistrate, which somewhat disgusted him with public life. To console himself, he built a retreat at 香山 Hsiang-shan, by which name he is sometimes called; and there, together with eight congenial companions, he gave himself up to poetry and speculations upon a future life. To escape recognition and

annoyance, all names were dropped, and the party was generally known as 香山九老 the Nine Old Gentlemen of Hsiang-shan. This reaching the ears of the Emperor, he was transferred to be Governor of 忠州 Chung-chou; and on the accession of Mu Tsung in 821 he was sent as Governor to Hangchow. There he built one of the great embankments of the beautiful Western Lake, still known as Po's Embankment. He was subsequently Governor of Soochow, and finally rose in 841 to be President of the Board of War. His poems were collected by Imperial command and engraved upon tablets of stone, which were set up in a garden he had made for himself in imitation of his former beloved retreat at Hsiang-shan. In several of these he ridiculed in scathing language the preposterous claims of the *Tao Té Ching*. (1939, p. 630)

Baiyun Shouduan 白雲守端 (Pai-yün Shou-tuan, Hakuun Shutan; 1025–72; Cases 95, 199, 259) was born in Hengyang 衡陽 in Hunan 湖南; his family name was Zhou 周. After becoming a monk under *Chaling Yu* he studied with a number of masters during the course of a long pilgrimage. He finally joined the assembly under *Yangqi Fanghui*. After succeeding to Yangqi's Dharma he served as priest of a number of temples, including Haihui Chanyuan 海會禪院 on Mount Baiyun 白雲, from which his name derives. As the teacher of *Wuzu Fayan* he is an ancestor of all present-day Japanese Rinzai masters.

Baizhang Huaihai 百丈懷海 (Pai-chang Huai-hai, Hyakujō Ekai; 720–814; Cases 34, 78, 95 n., 117, 123, 170 n., 182, 221) was a native of Changle 長樂 in Fujian 福建. His family name was Wang 王. He received ordination at age twenty and studied the Tripitaka prior to entering the assembly under *Mazu Daoyi*, whose Dharma heir he became. After leaving Mazu he established a monastery on Mount Baizhang 百丈, a peak on Mount Daxiong 大雄. Huaihai is honored as the creator of the first distinctly Zen monastic code, the *Pure Rules for the Zen Community* 禪林清規. Although his original rule no longer exists, all subsequent Zen monasticism has been influenced by his concept of monastic practice and his overall architectural design for the monastery. Baizhang's vision of Zen monastic life institutionalized the acceptance of manual labor found in the earlier communities of the Fourth and Fifth Patriarchs; one of Baizhang's best-known sayings is his famous dictum, "A day of no work—a day of no eating" (Case 117). An equally well-known story tells of Baizhang's monks hiding his tools when they feared he was becoming too old and weak for his accustomed labor in the garden. Baizhang thereupon retired to his quarters and refused to eat until the monks returned the tools.

Baizhang's innovations in many ways marked the dividing point between Indian and Chinese Zen. In India, farm work had been forbidden, owing, among other things, to the inevitable loss of life it involved, whereas in Chinese Zen farming was viewed not only as a means of self-sufficiency but also as an excellent way of expressing the meditative mind in the activities of everyday life. Furthermore, Baizhang's establishment of a Zen monastic rule was instrumental in defining Zen as an independent Buddhist school (previously Zen monks had resided in temples of the Vinaya school). Baizhang is thus honored as one of the Zen school's founders in the Ancestors' Hall of major Zen monasteries.

The master's Dharma heirs include *Guishan Lingyou*, who, with *Yangshan Huiji*, was cofounder of the Guiyang lineage 潙仰宗, and *Huangbo Xiyun*, whose lineage, through *Linji Yixuan*, includes all present-day masters of Chinese and Korean Zen, and of Japanese Rinzai Zen.

Baizhang Weizheng 百丈惟政 (Pai-chang Wei-cheng, Hyakujō Isei; 8th–9th c.; Cases 93, 193) was also known as Baizhang Fazheng 百丈法正 (Pai-chang Fa-cheng, Hyakujō Hōshō) and Baizhang Niepan 百丈涅槃 (Pai-chang Nieh-p'an, Hyakujō Nehan). A Dharma heir of *Baizhang Huaihai* (sometimes identified as an heir of *Mazu Daoyi*, Baizhang's teacher), Weizheng succeeded Huaihai as abbot of the monastery on Mount Baizhang 百丈. His nickname "Niepan" 涅 槃 derived from his constant study of the *Niepan jing* 涅槃經 (*Nirvana Sutra*).

Bajiao Huiqing 芭蕉慧清 (Pa-chiao Hui-ch'ing, Bashō Esei; 10th c.; Case 71) was a native of Silla 新羅, one of the three main kingdoms of ancient Korea. A Dharma successor of Nanta Guangyong 南塔光涌 (Nan-ta Kuang-yung, Nantō Kōyū; 850–938) of the Guiyang school, Huiqing later moved to the province of Hubei 湖北 and lived on Mount Bajiao 芭蕉, from which he derived his name.

Baling Haojian 巴陵顥鑒 (Pa-ling Hao-chien, Haryō Kōkan; 10th c.; Case 269), a monk of the Five-Dynasty 五代 (907–60) era, was an eccentric known for always carrying around a tattered sitting-cloth. He studied under *Yunmen Wenyan* and eventually succeeded to his Dharma. It is said that at the time of his transmission he submitted, instead of the usual written exposition of his understanding, the exchange known as the Three Turning-Phrases of Baling: (1) "What is the Way?" The master said, "A clear-eyed person falls into a well" (Case 269); (2) "What is the Blown-hair Sword?"[1] The master said, "Branches of coral support the moon"; (3) "What is the Tipo school?"[2] The master said, "A silver bowl filled with snow."

Yunmen, extremely pleased, said, "On the anniversary of my death, simply recite these Three Turning-Phrases. That will suffice to repay my kindness." Later, as abbot of the temple Xinkai yuan 新開院 in Baling 巴陵, Hunan 湖南, Haojian is said to have marked his teacher's passing in that way.

1. The Blown-hair Sword 吹毛劍 is the name of a famous sword with a blade so sharp it could cut a hair blown against it. It symbolizes the keen functioning of the Zen master in cutting off the delusions of the student.

2. The Tipo school 提婆宗 is the teaching of the fifteenth Indian Zen ancestor, Āryadeva (also called Kānadeva; *tipo* 提婆 is the Chinese transliteration of Skt. *deva*, the abbreviation, in this case, of Kānadeva [C. Jianatipo 迦那提婆]). The school emphasized the śūnyatā teachings of the Madhyamaka school.

Baoshou Zhao 寶壽 沼 (Pao-shou Chao, Hōju Shō; 9th c.; Case 123) is remembered principally as the author of the "Memorial Tower Inscription of Chan Master Linji Yixuan," which provides a short biography of *Linji Yixuan*. Very little is known of his life, other than the fact that he was a Dharma heir of Linji and resided at Baoshou si 寶壽寺 in Zhenzhou 鎮州, present Hebei 河北.

Beijian Jujian 北礀居簡 (Pei-chien Chü-chien, Hokkan Kokan; 1164–1246; Case 95) was a native of Tongchuan 潼川, in present-day Sichuan 四川, with the family name Long 龍. He received ordination from the priest Yuancheng 圓澄 of the temple Guangfu yuan 廣福院 and studied under Biefeng 別峰 and Tudu 塗毒 of Mount Jin 徑. Upon attaining some degree of insight when reading the words of *Wan'an Daoyan* he went to Mount Yuwang 育王 in Zhejiang 浙江 to meet Fozhao Deguang 佛照德光 (Fo-chao Te-kuang, Busshō Tokkō; 1122–1203), who recognized his awakening. He remained with the assembly on Mount Yuwang for fifteen years. He later taught at the temple Bore Chanyuan 般若禪院 in Taizhou 臺州, Zhejiang, then moved to Bao'en Guangxiao Chansi 報恩光孝禪寺 in the same region. Prevented by illness from assuming the priesthood of the prestigious Donglin si 東林寺 on Mount Lu 廬, Jujian retired to Beijian 北礀 on Mount Feilai 飛來, where he built himself a hut and dwelt for ten years. He later served as abbot of a number of important temples.

Bhikku Meghaśri (Deyun Biqiu 德雲比丘, Te-yün Pi-ch'iu, Toku'un Biku; Case 89) was, after the bodhisattva Mañjuśrī, the first of the fifty-three "good friends" that the bodhisattva *Sudhana* met on his travels in search of the Way, as recorded in the "Entry into the Realm of Reality" chapter of the *Avataṁsaka Sutra*. Bhikku Meghaśri tells Sudhana that he has attained awareness of all the buddhas, and can perceive the buddhas of all the lands in the ten directions.

Bodhidharma (Putidamo 菩提達磨, P'u-t'i-ta-mo, Bodaidaruma; d. 528? 536? 543?; Cases 1, 9, 19-1, 34 n., 43, 46-2 n., 64, 109 n., 113, 170, 207-1, 207-2, 221, 254 n., 255 n., 270-1 n.). Bodhidharma is regarded as the twenty-eighth ancestor of the Indian Zen lineage and the first patriarch of the Chinese Zen lineage (he is often referred to simply as "the Patriarch" 祖師). According to the legendary accounts of his life, he was the third son of a king in southern India. After meeting Prajñātara, the twenty-seventh Indian ancestor of Zen, Bodhidharma left the palace to study Buddhism under his guidance. Prajñātara urged him to spread the Zen tradition to China, so some years after Prajñātara's death he made the long journey to that country and remained there the rest of his life. He first visited the land of Liang in southern China, where he had the famous exchange with Emperor Wu described in Case 64. He subsequently journeyed north and settled at Shaolin si 少林寺, where for nine years he sat in meditation in a cave. He transmitted the Dharma to his disciple *Huike*. His teaching appears to have aroused opposition—the chronicles report that on six occasions he miraculously escaped attempts by his enemies to poison him. Some accounts say that he finally returned to India; others that he died in China and was buried on Bear Ear Mountain 熊耳山; and still others that he crossed the sea to Japan.

C

Caoshan Benji 曹山本寂 (Ts'ao-shan Pen-chi, Sōzan Honjaku; 840–901; Cases 15, 111, 162), a native of Quanzhou 泉州 in present-day Fujian 福建 with the family name Huang 黃, studied Confucian thought before becoming a monk at the age of nineteen. After receiving the full precepts at Mount Lingshi 靈石 at age twenty-five, he joined the assembly under *Dongshan Liangjie* and eventually became Dongshan's Dharma heir; together with Dongshan he is regarded as the cofounder of the Caodong 曹洞 (J., Sōtō) school. His interpretation of Dongshan's Five Ranks represents, in the view of many Zen masters (including the great Japanese Rinzai master Hakuin Ekaku), the profoundest doctrine in Zen.

Chaling Yu 茶陵郁 (Ch'a-ling Yü, Charyō Iku; n.d.; Case 258). Chaling Yu is so called because he was born in the region of Chaling 茶陵 and later lived on Mount Yu 郁 in the same district. He is known primarily as the ordination master of *Baiyun Shouduan*. A devoted supporter of the sangha, Chaling received the following koan from a Zen monk: "A monk asked Fadeng 法燈, 'How can one step forward from the top of the hundred-foot pole?' Fadeng answered, 'Ah!'" ("Ah" 啞 is a "one-word barrier" signifying the ultimate inexpressibility of the Zen teachings.) Later a donkey Chaling was riding slipped after crossing a bridge over a ravine. Chaling fell, and at that moment he had a deep enlightenment. He immediately called upon *Yangqi Fanghui*, who confirmed his understanding. Chaling's enlightenment verse appears in Case 258.

Changqing Huileng 長慶慧稜 (Ch'ang-ch'ing Hui-leng, Chōkei Eryō; 854–932; Case 265) was a native of Hangzhou 杭州 in Zhejiang 浙江; his family name was Sun 孫. He became a monk at the age of thirteen in Suzhou 蘇州, modern Jiangsu 江蘇, and later journeyed south. He studied under *Lingyun Zhiqin* and *Xuansha Shibei*, and finally completed his training under *Xuefeng Yicun* in Fuzhou 福州, present-day Fujian 福建. Changqing was an earnest student; it is said that he wore out seven sitting cushions in his twenty years of monastic practice. According to the *Zutang ji* 祖堂集 (Annals of the ancestral hall), when he went to Xuefeng's monastery the master said to him, "I'll give you the medicine that horse doctors use to revive dead horses. Can you take it?" Changqing said he could, so Xuefeng advised him to "maintain body and mind as still as a burnt stump on a mountain. If you're slow you'll realize something in ten years; if you're average, then after seven; and if you're quick, then after three."

One night, after he had practiced in this way for two and a half years, Changqing rose from meditation to walk around the garden a bit, then lay down on the bare ground to sleep. Upon awaking he returned to the meditation hall. As he raised the bamboo screen at the entrance he suddenly saw the beam of the lantern inside and at that moment was enlightened. He went to the master's quarters and waited there for Xuefeng to finish his night's sleep. Suddenly he let out a laugh. Xuefeng came out and enquired what had happened. Changqing replied, "How strange! How strange! When the screen is rolled up, all under

Heaven is complete. Were someone to ask me what I've seen, I'd pick up my whisk and hit him on the mouth" (Miura and Sasaki 1966, p. 293).

Changqing subsequently traveled between Xuefeng's temple and other communities, and in 906 he finally settled in Quanzhou 泉州, where he taught a community of never less than fifteen hundred students at the temple Changqing yuan 長慶院, built for him by the prefect, Wang Yanbin 王延彬.

Changqing Lan'an 長慶懶安 (Ch'ang-ch'ing Lan-an, Chōkei Ran'an; 793–883; Cases 32, 209) was also known as Changqing Da'an 長慶大安 (Ch'ang-ch'ing Ta-an, Chōkei Daian), Guishan Lan'an 溈山懶安 (Kuei-shan Lan-an, Isan Ran'an), and Guishan Da'an 溈山大安 (Kuei-shan Ta-an, Isan Daian). A native of Fujian 福建 with the family name Chen 陳, he was ordained at a young age on Mount Huangbo 黃檗, then went to study under *Baizhang Huaihai*.

Lan'an is said to have asked Baizhang, "I seek to know buddha. What is it?" Baizhang answered, "You're like someone seeking an ox while riding an ox." Lan'an asked, "After realizing this, what then?" Baizhang replied, "Do as one who rides an ox, heading home." Lan'an said, "How should I guard it through to the end?" Baizhang said, "Like an oxherd who, with stick in hand, watches it and doesn't let it graze on other people's crops." Lan'an understood his meaning and never again ran about searching. (T 51:267b)

After receiving transmision from Baizhang, Lan'an went to Mount Gui 溈 to help *Guishan Lingyou*, his brother disciple under Baizhang, establish his new monastery there; when Lingyou passed away, Lan'an succeeded him as abbot. In his teaching Lan'an continued to use the metaphor of the ox:

> I have lived on Mount Gui for thirty years, eating Mount Gui's food and shitting Mount Gui's shit, but I did not study Mount Gui's Zen. I simply tended an ox. When the ox left the road and entered the grass I pulled it back with its nose ring; when it entered other people's fields I tamed it with the whip. For some time it has been gentle, amiably accepting my words. Now it has become "the white bull on the bare ground" [a Zen symbol for original nature] and is always before me, showing itself clearly throughout the day. Even if I try to chase it off it doesn't go away. (T 51:267c)

Later Lan'an went to Fuzhou 福州 in modern Fujian 福建 and taught at Changqing Chanyuan 長慶禪院. According to most accounts Lan'an returned to Mount Huangbo and died there at the age of ninety.

Changsha Jingcen 長沙景岑 (Ch'ang-sha Ching-ts'en, Chōsa Keishin; 9th c.; Cases 25 n., 79, 168, 196, 206, 272). Little is known of Jingcen's life except that he was an heir of *Nanquan Puyuan*; that, after leaving Nanquan, he founded the temple Luyuan yuan 鹿苑院 in present Hunan 湖南; and that he subsequently journeyed throughout the district of Changsha 長沙 in the same province spreading the Dharma teachings.

One of the best-known koans involving Changsha is that of the "hundred-foot pole," *Record of Equanimity* 79:

"The man sitting atop the hundred-foot pole: though he's gained entry, this is not yet the real. Atop the hundred-foot pole, he should step forward: the universe in all directions is the whole body." [A] monk said, "Atop the hundred-foot pole, how can you step forward?" Changsha said, "The mountains of Lang, the rivers of Li." The monk said, "I don't understand." Changsha said, "The whole land is under the imperial sway." (Cleary 1988, p. 335)

Similar to this is another of Jingcen's remaining teachings:

The entire universe is your eye; the entire universe is your complete body; the entire universe is your own luminance; the entire universe is within your own luminance. In the entire universe there is no one who is not your own self. I repeat what I am continually saying to you: All the Buddhas of the Three Worlds (past, present, and future) and all the sentient beings in the dharma-dhatu, these are the light of Great Intrinsic Wisdom (Mahāprajñā). (T 51:274a; Miura and Sasaki 1966, p. 275)

Changsheng Jiaoran 長生皎然 (Ch'ang-sheng Chiao-jan, Chōshō Kōnen; n.d.; Case 14). Little is known of this figure other than that he practiced under *Xuefeng Yicun* and resided on Mount Changsheng 長生 in Fuzhou 福州 in modern Fujian 福建.

Changshui Zixuan 長水子璿 (Ch'ang-shui Tzu-hsüan, Chōsui Shisen; d. 1038; Case 223) was a native of Jiaxing 嘉興 in Xiuzhou 秀州, present Zhejiang 浙江. He shaved his own head and took up the study of the *Śūraṅgama Sutra*, attaining a deep realization upon coming across a line on the nonarising of the two aspects of movement and stillness. Seeking to deepen his understanding, he subsequently studied under *Langye Huijue* and eventually succeeded to Langye's Dharma. He later resided at Changshui 長水 and wrote a ten-volume commentary on the *Śūraṅgama Sutra*; he was known for advocating the unity of Zen and scriptural study and worked for the revival of the philosophical Huayan 華嚴 school.

Chen Cao 陳操 (Ch'en Ts'ao, Chin Sō; 9th c.; Case 153), a government official and a Dharma heir of *Muzhou Daozong*, was one of the great lay Zen practitioners of the Tang dynasty; most of what is known of him comes from the information contained in *Blue Cliff Record* 33. It was at Chen Cao's residence that *Yunmen Wenyan* convalesced after his leg was broken in his encounter with Daozong.

Chouyan Liaoyun 稠巖了贇 (Ch'ou-yen Liao-yün, Chūgan Ryōhin; n.d.; Case 46-2). Dōmae identifies this figure as a Dharma successor of a certain Heshan Shouxun 何山守珣 (also known as Fodeng Shouxun 佛燈守珣). Chouyan served as priest of Chouyan si 稠巖寺 in the province of Zhejiang 浙江. Otherwise almost nothing is known of his life.

Chuanzi Decheng 船子德誠 (Ch'uan-tzü Te-ch'eng, Sensu Tokujō; 9th c.; Case 257). Chuanzi was a Dharma heir of Yaoshan Weiyen 藥山惟儼 (745/50–828/34), under whom he trained for thirty years. His Dharma brother was the great master Yunyan Tansheng 雲巖曇晟 (782–841), whose Dharma heir was *Dong-shan Liangjie*, one of the founders of the Caodong 曹洞 (Sōtō) school. Following the great persecution of Buddhism in 845, Decheng worked as a ferryman, from which his name derives ("Chuanzi" 船子 means "boatman"). His most famous Dharma heir was *Jiashan Shanhui*; after transmitting the Dharma to him he is said to have capsized his boat and vanished into the water.

Ciming 慈明 (Tz'u-ming, Jimyō). See *Shishuang Chuyuan*.

Cui Hao 崔顥 (Ts'ui Hao, Sai Kō; 704–54; Case 196) was a native of Bianzhou 荷州. He graduated as *jinshi* 進士 about 730, and was noted not only for his liter-ary talents, which impressed even the poetic genius Li Bo 李白, but also for his love of drinking and gambling. The most famous of his poems, "Yellow Crane Pavilion," has been translated under the title "Yellow Crane Tower" by Stephen Owen:

> That old man has already ridden [the yellow crane] away,
> And here in this land there remains only Yellow Crane Tower.
> The yellow crane, once it had gone, will never come again,
> But white clouds of a thousand years go aimlessly on and on,
> Clear and bright in the sunlit stream the trees of Hanyang,
> Springtime's grasses, lush and green, all over Parrot Isle.
> Sun's setting, the passes to home—where can they be?
> Beside this river of misty waves, it makes a man sad.
>
> (Minford and Lau 1994, p. 828)

The story of the Yellow Crane Pavilion is related as follows by Hori:

> The Yellow Crane Pavilion, overlooking the Yangtze River, is a famous land-mark in Hubei Province. Right across from it in the river lay the picturesque Isle of the Parrots. Long ago there used to be a drinking place here run by a man called Hsin. A strange old man used to come to Hsin's place to drink. Though he never had any money, Hsin never pressed him for payment. One day, after this had gone on for some time, the old man took the peel of an orange and with it drew a picture of a yellow crane on a blank wall. Later when customers would clap their hands and sing, the crane on the wall would flutter and dance. The bar became famous and Hsin became wealthy. Ten years went by and the strange old man appeared again. He blew a flute, a white cloud came down, the crane flew down from the wall. The old man climbed onto the back of the crane and then rode the white cloud off into the sky. Afterward Hsin built a large pavilion that he named the Yellow Crane Pavilion after the drawing of the yellow crane. (2003, p. 727)

Cui Langzhong 崔郎中 (Ts'ui Lang-chung, Sai Rōchū; 9th c.; Case 13). It is unknown who this figure was; the word 郎中 indicates an official who assisted the imperial secretary.

D

Dachuan Puji 大川普濟 (Ta-chuan Fu-chi, Daisen Fusai; 1179–1253; Case 8) was a native of the province of Zhejiang 浙江; his family name was Zhang 張. He became a monk at age nineteen and studied under various masters, succeeding to the Dharma of Zheweng Ruyan 浙翁如浣 (Che-weng Ju-yen, Setsuō Nyoen; 1151–1225) in the line of *Dahui Zonggao*. He later compiled the important Zen biographical work *Wudeng huiyuan* 五燈會元 (Compendium of the Five Lamps).

Dadao Guquan 大道谷泉 (Ta-tao Ku-ch'üan, Daidō Yokusen; 10th–11th c.; Case 173), also known as Bajiaoan Guquan 芭蕉菴谷泉 (Pa-chiao-an Ku-ch'üan, Bashōan Yokusen), was a native of Quanzhou 泉州, in present-day Fujian 福建. Soon after becoming a monk he began study under *Fenyang Shanzhao*, whose Dharma successor he became. He then embarked on an extended pilgrimage, meeting, among other masters, *Shishuang Chuyuan* (Ciming Chuyuan), as described in Case 173. The *Biographies of Monks of the Zen School* 禪林僧寶傳 (X 79:522b) describes him as one of Chinese Zen's notable eccentrics—intelligent but slovenly, boastful and disrespectful in manner, indifferent to worldly convention, and, after ordination, dismissive of the precepts. Acting as he pleased, he soon found himself unwelcome at most monasteries, a development that seemed of no concern to him. Later, however, he served as priest at several temples, among them Lingfeng si 靈峰寺 and Bajiao an 芭蕉菴, before dying at the age of ninety-two.

Dahui Zonggao 大慧宗杲 (Ta-hui Tsung-kao, Daie Sōkō; 1089–1163; Cases 19-2, 32, 46-4, 92, 134, 141, 227, 229, 230 n., 231 n., 232) was a native of Xuanzhou 宣州 in the province of Anhui 安徽; his family name was Xi 奚. After studying the Confucian teachings in his childhood he was ordained as a monk at the age of sixteen under a priest named Huiqi 慧齊 at the temple Huiyun si 慧雲寺. He took the full commandments the following year. Later he set out on an extended pilgrimage that took him to important Caodong masters of his time and to the Huanglong-line Linji master Zhantang Wenzhun 湛堂文準 (1061–1115). After Wenzhun's death he went to the temple Tianning Wanshou si 天寧萬壽寺 and studied under *Yuanwu Keqin*; the story of his awakening under Yuanwu is related in Case 92. At Wanshou si, Dahui was a brother disciple of Huqiu Shaolong 虎丘紹隆 (Hu-ch'iu Shao-lung, Kukyū Jōryū; 1077–1136), one of the ancestors of all present-day Japanese Rinzai masters. After receiving Dharma transmission from Yuanwu, Dahui succeeded him as master of Wanshou si. His renown grew, and in 1126 he received a purple robe and the honorary name Great Master Fori 佛日大師 from Lü Shun 呂舜, Minister of the Right.

Zonggao went south following the fall of the Northern Song dynasty to the Jurchen invaders in 1127 and resided with his teacher Yuanwu, who was then living at the temple Zhenru yuan 眞如院 on Mount Yunju 雲居. After Yuanwu's return to Sichuan in 1130, Zonggao stayed for a time in a hermitage on the site of an old Yunmen-school temple, then moved to Yunmen an 雲門庵 in Jiangxi 江西 and, later, Yangyu an 洋嶼庵 in Fujian 福建. It was from this period that Zonggao became known for his criticism of "silent illumination Zen" and support of "koan-introspecting Zen."

From 1137 Zonggao lived at Nengren Chanyuan 能仁禪院 on Mount Jing 徑 in Zhejiang 浙江, where he had been invited to serve by Zhang Jun 張浚, the prime minister and a former student of Yuanwu. Defrocked in 1141 for supporting armed resistance against the Jurchen, Zonggao went to Hengyang 衡陽 in Hunan 湖南 and, about ten years later, to Meiyang 梅陽 in Guangdong 廣東. There he helped the populace, which was suffering from a plague. He was officially pardoned in 1155 but remained in Meiyang until 1158, when, on imperial command, he returned to Mount Jing and taught an assembly of nearly 1,700 monks until his death in 1163.

Daitō 大燈 (or, more generally, National Teacher Daitō 大燈國師). The posthumous title of the Japanese monk *Shūhō Myōchō*.

Damei Fachang 大梅法常 (Ta-mei Fa-ch'ang; Daibai Hōjō; 752–839; Cases 5, 66) was a native of Xiangyang 襄陽 in present-day Hubei 湖北; his family name was Zheng 鄭. He studied doctrine for thirty years before entering the assembly under *Mazu Daoyi*, where he was awakened by Mazu's statement, "This very mind is buddha" (see Case 5). After receiving transmission from Mazu he practiced in seclusion for forty years on Mount Damei 大梅 (Great Plum Mountain), in modern Zhejiang 浙江. One day a monk sent by Mazu to check on Damei asked, "What did Mazu say that caused you to live on this mountain?" Damei replied, "Mazu said, 'This very mind is buddha.'" "Nowadays Mazu teaches differently," said the monk. "Now he says, 'Not mind, not buddha.'" Damei responded, "That old monk is always confusing people! He may say, 'Not mind, not buddha,' but I'll stay with, 'This very mind is buddha!'" When the monk reported this to Mazu, Mazu said, "Monks, the plum is ripe" ("Damei" means "Great Plum"). An increasing number of seekers gathered around Damei, and finally the community founded the monastery Husheng si 護聖寺, where Damei taught an assembly of six to seven hundred monks. One day Damei said:

> Monks, strive to reach the root; do not chase after the branches. Reach the root, and the rest will naturally follow. If you wish to perceive the root, just see into your own mind. This mind is the source of all, both mundane and supramundane. When mind arises the various dharmas arise; when mind is extinguished, the various dharmas disappear. When the mind is unattached to good and evil, all things are in their true state. (T 51:254c)

Danxia Tianran 丹霞天然 (Tan-hsia T'ien-jan, Tanka Tennen; 738/39–824; Case 44). Danxia's place of origin and family name are unknown. As a young man he and his friend *Pang Yun* (later known as the Zen poet Layman Pang 龐居士) were on their way to the capital to take the government examinations when they encountered a Zen monk, who asked, "How can becoming an official compare with becoming a buddha?" and suggested that they meet *Mazu Daoyi*. Mazu accepted Pang as a student but told Danxia to go instead to *Shitou Xiqian*. The young man went to Shitou's monastery on Mount Nanyue, where he worked for several years as a manual laborer before finally becoming ordained.

According to one account, Danxia received the name Tianran when Shitou, shaving Danxia's head for the first time, noticed the crown of Danxia's head suddenly rise up of itself. "*Tianran* 天然 (spontaneously)!" Shitou said in surprise. Another account, in *Blue Cliff Record* 76, has Danxia returning to Mazu's monastery after three years of training under Shitou. As soon as he arrived he straddled the Mañjuśrī image. When the monks complained of this to Mazu, Mazu replied, "My son is just being natural 天然." After similar behavior at Shitou's monastery, Shitou commented, "This young student will end up smashing shrines and images"; his words were borne out in Danxia's burning of the buddha image at Huilin si 慧林寺, described in Case 44.

After receiving transmission from Shitou, Danxia went on pilgrimage for a number of years; his exchanges during this time with his old friend Pang are particularly well known. He finally settled on Mount Danxia 丹霞 in Hunan 湖南, where an assembly of over three hundred monks gathered around him. One day he announced that he was leaving on pilgrimage again. Putting on his hat and straw sandals and taking up his staff, he died before his foot touched the ground. Danxia is known for his excellent poetry, and his verses are often quoted in Zen literature like the *Record of Linji*.

Danyuan Yingzhen 耽源應眞 (Tan-yüan Ying-chen, Tangen Ōshin; 8–9th c.; Cases 65, 238). Little is known of Yingzhen except that he served as the attendant of *Nanyang Huizhong*, one of the Sixth Patriarch's most important successors. As described in Case 238, he received from Nanyang the teaching on the ninety-seven circle-figures (圓相), which he passed on to his student *Yangshan Huiji*.

Daowu Yuanzhi 道吾圓智 (Tao-wu Yüan-chih, Dōgo Enchi; 768/69–835; Cases 220 n., 257), also known as Daowu Zongzhi 道吾宗智, was a native of Jiangxi 江西, with the lay name Zhang 張. While still a child he received ordination from *Baizhang Weizheng*, then studied under Yaoshan Weiyan 藥山惟儼 (744/45/51–827/28/34), whose Dharma heir he eventually became. He later settled and taught on Mount Daowu 道吾 in Tanzhou 潭州, in the province of Hunan 湖南. Yuanzhi's Dharma-brother (and actual brother) was Yunyan Tansheng 雲巖曇晟 (782–841), a forebear of the Caodong school; the brothers appear together in a number of koans, usually with Daowu in the role of the compassionate and more deeply awakened older brother (e.g., x 80:113b–c). Daowu received the title Great Master Xiuyi 修一大師.

Daoxuan 道宣 (Tao-hsüan, Dōsen; 596–667; Case 227) was an early Chinese Buddhist historian and the founder of the Nanshan Vinaya school 南山律宗. He become a monk in 611 and later received the full precepts under the priest Zhishou 智首 (567–635), then in 624 began training on Mount Zhongnan 終南.

There he founded the Nanshan Vinaya school, based on the *Four-part Vinaya* 四分律 (*Dharmaguptavinaya*). From 645 he assisted the great translator monk Xuanzang 玄奘 (600?–664). He was also a prolific writer, producing a number of volumes on the Vinaya and also such historical works as the *Xu gaoseng zhuan* 續高僧傳 (Supplementary "Biographies of Eminent Monks"; T 50:2060). His Nanshan school is the only Vinaya school to have survived in China and is thus the tradition under which all Chinese monks receive the precepts.

*Dayu*大愚 (Ta-yü, Daigu; 8–9th c.; Case 187). Very little is known of this figure; the *Jingde-Era Record of the Transmission of the Lamp* says of Dayu that he was a disciple of the master *Guizong Zhichang*, a Dharma successor of *Mazu Daoyi* who resided at the temple Guizong si 歸宗寺 on Mount Lu 廬 (T 51:273c).

Dazhu Huihai 大珠慧海 (Ta-chu Hui-hai, Daiju Ekai; n.d.; Case 70) was a native of Fujian 福建, with the family name Zhu 朱. He was ordained at the temple Dayun. si 大雲寺 under the priest Daozhi 道智, then went to study with *Mazu Daoyi*. The *Jingde-Era Record of the Transmission of the Lamp* records that when Mazu asked Dazhu why he came, Dazhu replied, "I seek the Buddhadharma." Mazu asked, "Without examining the treasure in your very own home, why do you leave the house and run about searching? There is nothing here. What Buddhadharma do you seek?" Dazhu bowed and asked, "What is the treasure of my very own home?" Mazu answered, "That which is right now questioning me is your very own treasure. It contains everything, with nothing lacking. You are free to use it as you wish. Why do you seek outside?"

Huihai later returned to his hometown to care for his aging ordination teacher. There he wrote his great treatise, the *Essentials of Instantaneous Awakening* 頓悟入道要門論. When Mazu read this he reported to the assembly, "In Yuezhou 越州 there is a great pearl. Its perfect, bright light penetrates everywhere without hindrance." From then on Huihai was known as Dazhu 大珠, "The Great Pearl." At the beginning of the *Essentials of Instantaneous Awakening* is the following exchange:

"How should one practice in order to attain liberation?"
"The only way to attain liberation is through sudden awakening."
"What is sudden awakening?"
"'Sudden' means immediately dropping deluded thought. 'Awakening' means realizing that there is nothing to be attained."
"From where should one practice?"
"From the root."
"What is the root?"
"Mind is the root." (X 63:18a)

Deng Yinfeng 鄧隱峰 (Teng Yin-feng, Tō Inpō; n.d.; Case 252) was a native of Shaowu 邵武 in present-day Fujian; Deng was his family name. He trained under *Shitou Xiqian* and *Mazu Daoyi*, and eventually succeeded to the latter's Dharma. Later he spent his winters at Mount Nanyue 南嶽 in present-day Hunan 湖南 and his summers at Mount Wutai 五臺 in Shanxi 山西. Legend has it that one day he set out to climb the peak of Mount Wutai but in the course of the climb encountered the battling forces of the imperial army and the rebel Wu Yuanji 吳元濟 (783/93–817). He threw his staff into the air and flew through the sky over the soldiers, who ceased fighting when they saw the monk's feat. Deng is said to have died standing up in front of the Diamond Cave 金剛窟 on Mount Wutai.

Deshan Xuanjian 德山宣鑑 (Te-shan Hsüan-chien, Tokusan Senkan; 782–865; Cases 22-1, 22-2, 54, 123, 128, 155, 166 n., 170 n., 171, 194, 197 n., 205, 256) was a native of Jiannan 劍南 in Sichuan 四川, with the family name of Zhou 周. He was deeply interested in doctrine and the sutras as a young monk, devoting so much attention to the *Diamond Sutra* (*Jingang jing* 金剛經) that he earned the nickname "*Diamond Sutra* Zhou" (Zhou Jingang). Hearing of the "mind is buddha" teachings of the Southern school of Zen, he packed his commentaries and set off south intending to prove the Zen people wrong. As he approached his destination he stopped at a teahouse for some refreshments (點心, lit., "to refresh the mind"). The old woman at the teahouse, seeing his commentaries on the *Diamond Sutra*, said, "The *Diamond Sutra* says, 'Past mind is unobtainable, present mind is unobtainable, and future mind is unobtainable.' What mind is the learned monk seeking to refresh?" Unable to answer, Deshan went to the master *Longtan Chongxin*, whose name he heard from the old woman. The story of his enlightenment is related in Case 128.

After leaving Longtan he visited the master *Guishan Lingyou*, then lived in solitude for thirty years in Liyang 澧陽, Hunan 湖南. During the Buddhist persecution under Emperor Wuzong 武宗 (r. 814–46) Deshan took refuge in a cave on Mount Dufu 獨浮. Following Wuzong's death he was called by the provincial governor to serve as abbot of the monastery Gude Chanyuan 古德禪院 on Mount De 德, where he soon attracted a large following. He often used the stick in his teaching (as *Linji Yixuan* often used the shout); one of his well-known statements was, "If you can speak, thirty blows! If you can't speak, thirty blows!" Deshan received the honorary title Great Master Jianxing 見性大師.

Devadatta (Tipodaduo 提婆達多, Ti-p'o-ta-to, Daibadatta; Case 113). Devadatta, a cousin of *Śākyamuni* and a brother of *Ānanda*, is said to have had a dislike for Śākyamuni since childhood, to the extent of killing a white elephant that Śākyamuni presented to him. Later he became a disciple after hearing one of the Buddha's sermons. He grew jealous of his cousin, however, and tried to take over leadership of the sangha. He convinced the prince Ajātaśatru, son of the Buddha's patron King Bimbisāra, to murder his father and usurp the throne, then, with Ajātaśatru's support, made several attempts on Śākyamuni's life. In the first attempt, hired assassins were so impressed by the Buddha that they became his disciples. In the second, Devadatta attempted to roll a boulder over Śākyamuni, but the stone stopped short. In the third, Devadatta released a mad elephant in Śākyamuni's path, but the elephant was rendered gentle by the

Buddha's compassion. Devadatta then attempted to divide the sangha by advocating rigorous asceticism and accusing Śākyamuni of soft living. Initially five hundred newly converted monks from the sangha in Vaishālī followed him but were later brought back to Śākyamuni's fold by *Śariputra* and *Maudgalyāyana*. Devadatta is said to have finally fallen into hell alive. In the "Devadatta" chapter of the *Lotus Sutra*, however, Śākyamuni says that Devadatta was his teacher in a previous existence and will be reborn in the future as a buddha named Heavenly Emperor.

Dongpo 東坡 (Tung-p'o, Tōba; 1037–1101; Case 237 n.), also known as Su Dongpo 蘇東坡 (Su Tung-p'o, So Tōba) or Su Shi 蘇軾 (Su Shih, Soshoku), was a government official and literary figure with a particular interest in Zen. He is honored as one of the Eight Great Poets of the Tang and Song dynasties. In 1057, when he was just nineteen years old, he passed the highest-level government examination, and in 1060 entered the civil service. Criticism of certain government policies that he regarded as oppressive led to his dismissal to Huangzhou 黄州. There he built himself a hut on the east slope of a hill and took Dongpo 東坡, "East Slope," as his "fancy name" 號. He appears to have enjoyed the rural life of Huangzhou, and it was there that he began Zen meditation. He was later recalled to the palace and rose to the position of president of the Board of Rites, but he again ran afoul of the authorities and was sent to the remote island of Hainan 海南 south of China. In 1101 he was recalled and restored to honor, but he died soon afterward.

Dongshan Huikong 東山慧空 (Tung-shan Hui-kong, Tōzan Ekū; 1096–1158; Case 19-2), also known as Xuefeng Huikong 雪峰慧空 (Hsüeh-feng Hui-kong, Seppō Ekū), was a native of Fuzhou 福州 in modern Fujian 福建, with the lay name Chen 陳. Ordained at the age of fourteen, he studied under the master Letan Shanqing 泐潭善清 (1057–1142) in the Huanglong line of the Linji school. After succeeding to Shanqing's Dharma he taught at the monastery on Mount Xuefeng 雪峰 in Fujian.

Dongshan Liangjie 洞山良价 (Tung-shan Liang-chieh, Tōzan Ryōkai; 807–69; Cases 109 n., 129, 155 n., 161, 264) was a native of Yuezhou 越州, in present-day Zhejiang 浙江, with the family name Yu 俞. Placed in a local temple as a boy, his ability was recognized (see Case 109 n.) and he was sent to study under Wuxie Lingmo 五洩靈默 (747–818), an heir of *Mazu Daoyi*. Liangjie later practiced under *Nanquan Puyuan* and *Guishan Lingyou*. Unable to penetrate the meaning of *Nanyang Huizhong*'s phrase "the preaching of Dharma by the sentientless" 無情說法, Liangjie was advised by Guishan to meet Yunyan Tansheng 雲巖曇晟 (782–841). When Liangjie arrived at Yunyan's monastery he asked, "Who can hear the insentient when they expound the Dharma?" Yunyan answered, "The insentient can." Liangjie then asked, "Can the reverend priest hear it?" Yunyan replied, "If I did hear it, you wouldn't hear my preaching of the Dharma." "Why wouldn't I hear it?" asked Liangjie. Yunyan held up his whisk and said, "Do you hear this?" "No, I don't," replied Liangjie. "If you can't hear even my sermon, how can you hear the sermon of the insentient?" Liangjie then asked, "What sutra does the preaching of the insentient correspond to?" Yunyan answered, "Haven't you seen the passage in the *Amitābha Sutra*, 'The rivers, the birds, the trees, and the forests all chant the name of buddha, all chant the name of Dharma'?" At this Liangjie gained some insight, and recited the verse:

How wonderful, how wonderful!
The preaching of the sentientless is inconceivable!
Listening with the ear, it is difficult to understand.
Hearing with the eye, then you know it. (Miura and Sasaki 1966, p. 293)

When Liangjie was taking his leave of Yunyan, he asked, "If someone asks me to describe you a hundred years from now, how should I respond?" Yunyan replied, "Say only, 'Just this! This!' In taking on this matter you must examine most closely." Later, while crossing a stream, Liangjie saw his reflection in the water and suddenly understood Yunyan's full meaning. He commented:

Seeking it from others is forbidden, for thus it becomes farther and farther estranged. Now that I go my way entirely alone, there is nowhere I cannot meet it. Now it is just what I am, now I am not what it is. Thus must one understand, then one accords with the Truly So. (Miura and Sasaki 1966, p. 293)

Liangjie traveled for several years visiting other masters, then took up residence on Mount Xinfeng 新豐 for a time following the end of the Buddhist persecution under Emperor Wuzong 武宗 (r. 814–46). Later he settled on Mount Dong 洞 in present-day Jiangxi 江西 and there instructed his many disciples. At the end of his life he was asked by a monk, "When the reverend priest is unwell, is there still someone who suffers no illness?" "There is," answered Liangjie. The monk asked, "Does the one who suffers no illness look after the reverend priest?" Liangjie replied, "It is for me to look after him." When asked how he did so, Liangjie said, "When I look, I see no illness." Just before his death, it is said, he commented to his monks, "The hearts of the homeless should not rely on material things. This is true practice. Why grieve when death brings rest to this life of sorrow?" After serving a "fools' feast" to chide his grieving followers for their attachment to him, he passed away in the sitting posture. His most famous teaching is that of the Five Ranks 五位, later developed and systematized by his heir *Caoshan Benji*, together with whom Liangjie is considered cofounder of the Caodong 曹洞 school.

Dongshan Shouchu 洞山守初 (Tung-shan Shou-ch'u, Tōzan Shusho; 910–90; Cases 62, 188, 189, 198) was a native of Shanxi 陝西 with the family name Fu 傅. He received ordination at sixteen and studied the vinaya before studying under *Yunmen Wenyan*. The story of his enlightenment is related in Case 188. He is known for his distinction between "dead words" (those that rely on discursive thinking) and "living words" (those not limited by reason). He resided on

Mount Dong 洞 in present-day Hubei 湖北 (a different Mount Dong 洞 from that of *Dongshan Liangjie*, which is located in present Jiangxi 江西).

Doushuai Congyue 兜率從悦 (Tou-shuai Ts'ung-yüeh, Tosotsu Jūetsu; 1044–91; Cases 7, 140) was a native of Qianzhou 虔州 in modern Jiangxi 江西; his family name was Yu 熊. He became a monk at the age of fifteen and studied under several masters, but despite (or because of) his unusual intelligence he found it difficult to accept guidance. After sharp criticism from Yungai Shouzhi 雲蓋 守智 (1025–1115) he reconsidered his attitude and went to study under *Zhenjing Kewen*. He received transmission from Kewen and went to Mount Luyuan 鹿 苑 in present-day Hunan 湖南. After several years of teaching there he had the encounter with the old monk *Qingsu*, described in Case 140; following this he practiced under Qingsu until he received the master's sanction. At the invitation of the governor of Hongzhou 洪州 he lectured at Mount Doushuai 兜率 from 1089 until his death two years later.

F

Fan Yanzhi 藩延之 (Fan Yen-chih, Han Enshi; n.d.; Case 10) was a reclusive successor of *Huanglong Huinan*. He was also known as Layman Qingyi 清逸.

Fayan Wenyi 法眼文益 (Fa-yen Wen-i, Hōgen Mon'eki; 885–958; Cases 9, 36, 58 n., 67, 99, 194) was a native of Yuhang 餘杭 in Zhejiang 浙江; his family name was Lu 魯. He entered the temple at the age of seven and spent his early years mastering the teachings of the Confucian classics and Buddhist sutras, devoting particular attention to the *Avataṁsaka Sutra*. After taking the full precepts he studied Zen under *Changqing Huileng*. Later, while on pilgrimage, Fayan took shelter during a storm in the monastery of Luohan Guichen 羅漢桂琛 (869–928), who asked him why he was on pilgrimage. "I don't know," answered Wenyi, to which Luohan responded, "Not-knowing is closest!" When Fayan was about to leave after the snowstorm, he and the abbot had the following exchange:

> "You say that the three realms are nothing but Mind, and all dharmas nothing but Consciousness. Now tell me, is that stone out there in the courtyard within your mind or outside your mind?" "Within my mind," [Fayan] replied. At this the abbot said, "Oh you wanderer, what makes it so necessary for you to travel with a stone on your mind?" (x 83:643b; Wu 1996, p. 233)

Fayan remained at Luohan's monastery, subjecting himself to Luohan's strict rejection of conceptual interpretations. After succeeding to Luohan's Dharma Fayan served as abbot of several temples, including Bao'en Chansi 報恩禪寺, and produced sixty-three Dharma heirs. Fayan used his great learning to emphasize not only transcendent enlightenment but also its practical expression in the religious life. When a monk asked what the ancient buddhas are, Fayan replied, "Right *now* there's nothing to reject!" When asked about the mind of the ancient buddhas he answered, "From it flow compassion and true equanimity." Fayan is recognized as the founder of the Fayan school of Zen, which flourished for several generations before being absorbed by the school of Linji.

Fayun Gao 法雲杲 (Fa-yun Kao, Hōun Kō; n.d.; Case 150) was a successor of *Zhenjing Kewen* and resided at the temple Fayun si 法雲寺 in Dongjing 東京.

Fengxue Yanzhao 風穴延沼 (Feng-hsüeh Yen-chao, Fuketsu Enshō; 896–973; Cases 81, 124, 185, 192, 197) was a native of Yuhang 餘杭 in Zhejiang 浙江; his family name was Liu 劉. Upon failing to pass the civil-service examinations he became a monk, first studying the doctrines of the *Lotus Sutra* and practicing Tiantai śamatha-vipaśyanā 止觀 meditation. He first studied Zen under *Jingqing Daofu* in Zhejiang, then under *Shoukuo* at Huayan yuan 華嚴院 in Xiangzhou 襄州 (present Hubei 湖北), and finally under *Nanyuan Huiyong* in the province of Henan 河南. Under Nanyuan's strict guidance Yanzhao, initially quite proud of his understanding, attained a deeper awakening. After succeeding to Nanyuan's Dharma he set out on pilgrimage again, eventually taking up residence at Fengxue si 風穴寺, an abandoned temple on Mount Fengxue 風穴 in Ruzhou 汝州, present Henan. Zen tradition holds that he thereby fulfilled the prophecy about the Linji school's future made by *Yangshan Huiji* to *Guishan Lingyou* (see Case 192, note 2). Yanzhao lived alone at Fengxue si for nearly ten years, after which a number of students gathered around him. In this remote area they avoided the social disturbances that marked the end of the Tang dynasty. In 951 he moved to Guanghui si 廣慧寺, a new temple built for him by the local prefect of Yingzhou 郢州, and taught there for twenty years. Yanzhao is of central importance in the history of the Linji school, as it was through him that the teachings of the lineage were transmitted to later generations. The most important of Yanzhao's heirs was *Shoushan Shengnian*.

Fenyang Shanzhao 汾陽善昭 (Fen-yang Shan-chao, Fun'yō Zenshō; 947–1024; Cases 174, 229, 255) was a native of Taiyuan 太原, in present Shanxi 山西; his lay name was Yu 俞. Shanzhao traveled extensively and visited many teachers (seventy-one, according to Zen tradition) before joining the assembly under *Shoushan Shengnian*. After succeeding to Shoushan's Dharma he became priest of the temple Taizi yuan 太子院 on Mount Fenyang 汾陽, in Fenzhou 汾州 in present Shanxi. There he remained for the rest of his life teaching and engaging in the literary work that was to make him a central figure in the development of the koan as a method of Zen instruction. Shanzhao added his own verses to koans to help create a genre that was to find its highest expression in the *Blue Cliff Record* and other great works of Zen literature in the Song dynasty. Perhaps because many of the masters under whom he trained during his long pilgrimage were of the Caodong school, he became the first Linji master to employ the Caodong school's Five Ranks system. Through his heir *Shishuang Chuyuan* (Ciming) the Linji teachings were transmitted to later generations.

Fenzhou Wuye 汾州無業 (Fen-chou Wu-yeh, Funshū Mugō; 760–821; Case 74) was a native of Shangluo 上洛 in Shangzhou 商州, in present-day Shanxi 陝西; his family name was Du 杜. From the age of nine he studied the Mahayana sutras at Kaiyuan si 開元寺; it was said that he could memorize the texts, five lines at a time, at a single reading. He received ordination at the age of twelve and the full precepts at the age of twenty. He was well-versed in the vinaya and often lectured on the *Mahāparinirvāṇa Sutra.*

Hearing of *Mazu Daoyi*, Wuye went to visit him. The master, noting Wuye's imposing appearance and voice, remarked, "An impressive buddha hall, but no buddha inside." Wuye knelt down and said, "I have studied and understood the teachings of the Three Vehicles, but I have not yet understood the Zen teaching that mind, just as it is, is buddha." Mazu replied, "It is the very mind that has not yet understood—there is nothing else." Wuye questioned further, "What is the secretly transmitted mind-seal that the Patriarch brought from the West?" Mazu replied, "Virtuous monk, you're becoming annoying; go now and come again some other time." As Wuye stepped out Mazu called, "Virtuous monk!" When Wuye looked around Mazu said, "What is *that!*" Wuye understood and bowed to Mazu. Mazu said, "This stupid oaf! What's all this bowing about?"

Later Wuye traveled to Mount Tiantai 天台, the memorial tower of the Sixth Patriarch, and other sacred places. At Jinge si 金閣寺 in Qingliang 清涼 he studied the Tripitaka. He finally settled at Kaiyuan si 開元寺 in Xihe 西河, where he taught the Dharma for twenty years. He was repeatedly invited to the imperial court, but he always declined on grounds of ill health. Finally agreeing to go, he bathed, shaved his head, and called his disciples, saying:

> This nature of yours that sees, hears, perceives, and knows is the same age as empty space, and is neither born nor annihilated. All states are originally void, and there is not a single thing to be obtained. The deluded do not understand this and are deceived by phenomena, thus undergoing rebirth endlessly. Know that mind-nature *is* from the very beginning; it is not produced, and, like a diamond, it cannot be destroyed. All phenomena are like shadows and echoes, lacking in essence. Thus the [*Avataṁsaka*] *Sutra* says, "Only this one is true; the other two are not." If you are always aware that everything is void, then there is nothing to engage. This is the way the buddhas use their minds. Strive always to practice this. (T 51:257b)

The master then died in the sitting position. He was given the honorary title National Teacher Dada 大達國師.

Foguo 佛果. See *Yuanwu Keqin.*

Fojian Huiqin 佛鑑慧懃 (Fo-chien Hui-ch'in, Bukkan Egon; 1059–1117; Case 77) was a native of Shuzhou 舒州, in present-day Anhui 安徽; his family name was Wang 汪. After succeeding to the Dharma of *Wuzu Fayan* he resided at the temple Xingguo si 興國寺, on Mount Taiping 太平 in Shuzhou. Along with *Foyan Qingyuan* and *Yuanwu Keqin*, he is regarded as one of the "Three Buddhas" of Wuzu Fayan, as all three had the character 佛, "buddha," in their name or title.

In 1111, at the command of the imperial court, he became abbot of Zhihai si 智海寺, in the city of Dongdu 東都. Later he moved to Mount Jiang 蔣.

Fori Qisong 佛日契嵩 (Fo-jih Ch'i-sung, Butsunichi Kaisū; 1007–72; Case 238) was a native of Tengzhou 藤州, in present-day Guangxi 廣西; his family name was Li 李. He entered the temple at the age of seven and received ordination at thirteen. Embarking on pilgrimage at nineteen, he studied under *Shending Hongyin* before entering the assembly under Dongshan Xiaocong 洞山曉聰 (10–11th c.), whose successor he eventually became. He later served as abbot of Lingyin si 靈隱寺. He argued against Confucian critics of Buddhism, stressing the commonality of the respective traditions' teachings. In response to Tiantai-school attacks on the authenticity of the Zen tradition he wrote the *Record of the Transmission of the Dharma in the True School* 傳法正宗記 (T 51:2078), an account of the transmission from Śākyamuni through the twenty-eight Indian ancestors, the first six Chinese ancestors, and the masters of the Five Schools. Two other works written for the same purpose were the *Definitive Chart of the Ancestry for the Transmission of the Dharma in the True School* 傳法正宗定祖圖 (T 51:2079) and the *Treatise on the Transmission of the Dharma in the True School* 傳法正宗論 (T 51:2080).

Foyan Qingyuan 佛眼清遠 (Fo-yen Ch'ing-yüan, Butsugen Seion; 1067–1120; Cases 77, 221, 266) was a native of Shu 蜀, present-day Sichuan 四川; his family name was Li 李. After receiving the precepts at the age of fourteen, Qingyuan devoted himself to the study of the vinaya and the *Lotus Sutra*. One day he encountered a passage in the *Lotus Sutra* that his teacher could not explain: "This Law is not something that can be understood through pondering or analysis" (Watson 1993b, p. 31; T 9:7a). Realizing the limits of doctrinal study, he turned to the practice of Zen. After visiting several masters he joined the assembly under *Wuzu Fayan*, whose Dharma heir he eventually became. He later lectured at Tianning Wanshou si 天寧萬壽寺 in Shuzhou 舒州, present-day Anhui, and resided at Longmen si 龍門寺, also in Shuzhou, and at Baoshan si 褒山寺 in Hezhou 和州. He received a purple robe and the honorary name Zen Master Foyan 佛眼禪師 from Deng Xunwu 鄧洵武.

Fu Dashi 傅大士 (Fu Ta-shih, Fu Daishi; 497–569; Case 80) is the title of Fu Xi 傅翕, a Buddhist layman who lived in the Yiwu 義烏 district of present-day Zhejiang 浙江. He married at the age of sixteen and had two sons. He was a fisherman until, in his early twenties, he heard a mendicant foreign monk (who some say was *Bodhidharma*) preach the Buddhist teachings. Deeply moved, Fu gave up fishing and became a farmer. Living with his family in a small hut under two sala trees on nearby Mount Song 松, he cultivated his fields during the day and at night engaged in meditative practices. He described his lifestyle as follows: "With empty hands I hold a hoe, while walking I ride a water buffalo; a man walks over a bridge—the bridge flows, the water does not."

Fu took the name Shanhui Dashi 善慧大士 ("Good Wisdom Bodhisattva") and devoted his life to practice, teaching, and compassionate works. During the Datong 大通 era (527–29) the area in which he lived was stricken by famine; to obtain money for food Fu sold all his fields, and he even convinced his wife and sons to sell themselves into slavery (they were released several months later).

In 534 he sent a letter to Emperor Wu 武帝 of Liang (r. 502–49) and in 534 was summoned to Nanking by the emperor for an audience. In Nanking he lectured on the sutras, much impressing the emperor. In 539 Fu returned to his old home and established the temple Shuanglin si 雙林寺 on Mount Song. In 548 he again sold his property, went without food, and vowed to immolate himself in order to end the suffering of the people during the disorders accompanying the fall of the Liang 梁 dynasty. He was dissuaded by his many followers from self-immolation, but several years later, during another famine, he labored in the fields and gathered wild foods to feed the hungry. All the time he continued his own ascetic practices and held large religious gatherings for his followers.

Fu is credited with the invention of the revolving sutra library, one turn of which is said to generate merit equal to reading the sutras themselves. Since his death at the age of seventy-three he has been regarded as an incarnation of *Maitreya*, the buddha of the future; he is also known as the *Vimalakīrti* of China. Some of the teachings ascribed to Fu are given in a work attributed to him, the *Mind King* 心王銘. One passage reads:

> When you realize original mind, the mind sees Buddha. The mind is Buddha; this Buddha is mind. Every thought is Buddha mind; Buddha mind dwells on Buddha. If you wish to accomplish this soon, be vigilant and disciplined. Pure precepts purify the mind; the mind then is Buddha. Apart from this Mind King, there is no other Buddha. (Sheng-yen 1987, p. 18)

Fubei 浮盃 (Fu-pei, Fuhai; 8th c.; Case 216). Little is known of this figure except that he was a Dharma heir of *Mazu Daoyi*.

G

Guanghui Yuanlian 廣慧元璉 (Kuang-hui Yüan-lien, Kōe Ganren; 951–1036; Case 137) was a native of Quanzhou 泉州, present-day Fujian 福建, with the family name Chen 陳. Ordained at the age of fifteen, he studied under more than fifty masters before finally attaining enlightenment under *Shoushan Shengnian*. He became priest of Guanghui yuan 廣慧院 in 1004. His honorary title is Zen Master Zhenhui 眞慧禪師.

Guangxiao Huijue 光孝慧覺 (Kuang-hsiao Hui-chüeh, Kōkō Ekaku; 9–10th c.; Cases 9, 243), also known as Jue Tiezui 覺鐵觜 (Chüeh T'ieh-tsui, Kaku Tetsushi), was a successor of *Zhaozhou Congshen*. Little is known of him except that he resided at Guangxiao yuan 光孝院, from which he took his name.

Guishan Lingyou 溈山靈祐 (Kuei-shan Ling-yu, Isan Reiyū; 771–853; Cases 8, 60, 63 n., 65, 76, 116, 149, 151, 187, 192, 220, 238 n.) was a native of Changxi 長溪 in

Fuzhou 福州; his family name was Zhao 趙. He became a monk at the age of fifteen, and at twenty-two, after studying the vinaya, joined the assembly under *Baizhang Huaihai*, whose Dharma heir he became. His enlightenment, according to the *Pointing at the Moon Record* 指月錄, occurred when Baizhang asked him to see if any fire remained in the stove. After searching, Guishan reported that none was there. Baizhang, poking around himself and finding a small ember, remarked, "You said there was none. How about *this!*"

For many years Guishan served as the head cook for Baizhang's community. Baizhang, seeking a suitable leader for a new monastery on Mount Gui 溈, put a jug on the floor and asked, "If you can't call this a jug, then what do you call it?" The head monk answered, "You can't call it a wooden sandal!" Guishan, however, simply kicked the jug over and walked away. Baizhang thereupon named Guishan head of the new monastery. On Mount Gui, located in Tanzhou 潭州, Guishan built himself a hut and continued his practice. After about eight years students began to gather around him, and their number eventually reached fifteen hundred. Guishan, notable for his calmness, patience, and skill at teaching, produced forty-one successors, the most important of whom were *Yangshan Huiji, Lingyun Zhiqin*, and *Xiangyan Zhixian*. Together with Yangshan, Guishan is regarded as the cofounder of the Guiyang lineage 溈仰宗; many koans consist of exchanges between these two figures, as in *Kattōshū* Cases 60, 65, 116, 149, 187, and 192. One important characteristic of this lineage was its use of the "circle-figures" 圓相 (see Case 238). Among Guishan's teachings is one that clarifies the relation between instantaneous enlightenment and gradual cultivation. It reads, in part:

> If a man is truly enlightened and has realized the fundamental, and he is aware of it himself, in such a case he is actually no longer tied to the poles of cultivation and non-cultivation. But ordinarily, even though the original mind has been awakened by an intervening cause 緣, so that the man is instantaneously enlightened in his reason and spirit, yet there remains the inertia of habit, formed since the beginning of time, which cannot be totally eliminated at a stroke. He must be taught to cut off completely the stream of his habitual ideas and views caused by the still operative karmas. This (process of purification) is cultivation. I don't say that he must follow a hard-and-fast special method. He need only be taught the general direction that his cultivation must take. (Wu 1996, pp. 162–63; X 83:532b–c)

Guizong Zhichang 歸宗智常 (Kuei-tsung Chih-ch'ang, Kisu Chijō; 8th–9th c.; Case 123), also known as Lushan Zhichang 廬山智常 (Lu-shan Chih-ch'ang, Rozan Chijō), was a Dharma heir of *Mazu Daoyi*; nothing is known of his early life. After finishing his study under Mazu he went to Mount Lu 廬, where he resided at the temple Guizong si 歸宗寺. He was active as a teacher of both monks and lay students, and he left many exchanges that display his distinctive approach as a teacher. *Huangbo Xiyun* praised him as the one among Mazu's many Dharma heirs who went beyond all the others. Zhichang's eyes, like those of China's ancient sage rulers, are said to have had double pupils. He attempted to render this rather surprising feature less noticeable by rubbing his eyes with a medicine that turned them red, earning for himself the nickname Chiyan Guizong 赤眼歸宗 (Red-eyed Guizong). The *Jingde-Era Record of the Transmission of the Lamp* records the following words of Guizong:

> Everyone, do not apply your minds mistakenly. No one else can do it for you, and there is nowhere to apply your mind. Seek not from others; it is because you have always relied on the understanding of others that whatever is said hinders you and the light cannot get through, as though something were in front of your eyes. (T 51:255c)

Gulin Qingmao 古林清茂 (Ku-lin Ch'ing-mao, Kurin Seimo; 1262–1329; Case 113) was a native of Wenzhou 温州, present Zhejiang 浙江; his family name was Lin 林. He became a monk at the monastery Guoqing si 國清寺 on Mount Tiantai 天台 at the age of thirteen. Later he left on pilgrimage, studying under several masters before entering the assembly under Hengchuan Rugong 横川如珙 (1222–89). After succeeding to Hengchuan's Dharma he resided for nine years at Baiyun si 白雲寺 on Mount Tianping 天平, then served as abbot at the temples Kaiyuan si 開元寺 in Pingjiangfu 平江府, Yongfu si 永福寺 in Raozhou 饒州, and Baoning si 保寧寺 in Jiankangfu 建康府. He received the honorary title Foxing Chanshi 佛性禪師.

Gushan Shigui 鼓山士珪 (Ku-shan Shih-kuei, Kuzan Shikei; 1083–1146; Cases 56, 237), also known as Zhuan Shigui 竹庵士珪 (Chu-an Shih-kuei, Chikuan Shikei), was a native of Chengdu 成都, in modern Sichuan 四川; his family name was Shi 史. While still young he entered the temple Daci si 大慈寺, where he studied the *Śūraṅgama Sutra*. He then embarked on a long pilgrimage that eventually took him to *Foyan Qingyuan* at Mount Longmen 龍門, where he stayed until he succeeded to Foyan's Dharma. Subsequently he resided at Tianning si 天寧寺 in Hezhou 和州, Donglin si 東林寺 (also in Hezhou), and a succession of other temples.

H

Hakuin Ekaku 白隱慧鶴 (1686–1769; Cases 14 n., 16 n., 24 n., 185 n., 199 n.), the great reviver of the Japanese Rinzai school, was a native of Hara 原 in the province of Suruga 駿河, present Shizuoka 静岡 Prefecture. As a young boy he displayed a remarkable memory and strong character, but he is said to have been terrified by images of hell. At fifteen he became a monk at the nearby temple Shōin-ji 松蔭寺. At nineteen he had a crisis that caused him to leave meditation training for several years and devote himself to the study of literature, but later, upon reading how *Shishuang Chuyuan* kept himself awake during his meditation at night by sticking his thigh with an awl, he returned to his zazen practice with renewed determination. At twenty-four he had an awakening upon hearing the sound of a temple bell, an experience he deepened through training under Dōkyō Etan 道鏡慧端 (1642–1721) of Shōju-an 正受庵, in present Nagano 長野 Prefecture. Further training and experiences followed, even after he returned to Suruga as abbot of Shōin-ji. His decisive spiritual breakthrough occurred when he was forty-two years old.

Hakuin was tirelessly active in teaching the Dharma. He traveled widely, lectured on many of the basic Zen texts, and produced a large body of writings, both in vernacular Japanese and classical Chinese. He started systematization of the Rinzai koan curriculum and attacked what he regarded as distortions of Zen training, such as "silent illumination" zazen and the practice of *nenbutsu* by Zen monks. He stressed the importance of bodhicitta, in both its aspects of personal enlightenment (*kenshō* 見性) and the saving of all sentient beings.

Han Yu 韓愈 (Han Yü, Kan Yu; 768–824; Case 247) was one of the greatest of Tang dynasty poets and a strong proponent of Confucianism.

> Han was a staunch Confucianist in an era when most of his intellectual peers were concerned with Buddhism or Taoism. In 819 he wrote a memorial to the throne protesting the reception given a Buddhist relic (said to be a finger bone of the historical Buddha) by the emperor T'ang Hsien-tsung. In it he referred to Buddhism as a barbarian practice brought in from foreign countries. (O'Neill 1987, p. 122)

Giles writes:

> Han Yü [was] a native of Teng-chou in Honan.... He devoted himself assiduously to study; and it was recorded as something unusual that he burnt grease and oil in order to prolong his hours of work. On graduating he was appointed to a subordinate official post, and after a highly chequered career, rose to be president of the Board of Rites. In 803, in consequence of an offensive memorial on the subject of tax-collection in Chih-li, he was degraded and sent to 陽 山 Yang-shan in Kuangtung.... It was not long ere he was recalled to the capital and reinstated in office; but he had been delicate all his life and had grown prematurely old, thus being unable to resist a severe illness which came upon him. As a writer he occupies a foremost place in Chinese literature. He is considered to be the first of the great literary trio of the T'ang dynasty, the other two being Li Po and Tu Fu. (1939, pp. 254–55)

Hanshan 寒山 (Han-shan, Kanzan; 8–9th c.; Case 268) was an eccentric Tang-period Buddhist poet of whom very little is known. He appears to have lived in the eighth to ninth centuries and is said to have resided as a hermit in a large cave on Mount Han 寒 (Cold Mountain), a peak on Mount Tiantai 天台, in present Zhejiang 浙江. It is uncertain whether he was lay or ordained. He kept company with another eccentric, Shide 拾得, an orphan who worked as a kitchen helper in the monastery Guoqing si 國清寺. Hanshan wrote poems on rocks and trees; these were collected to form the work known as the *Hanshanshi* 寒山詩, the "Poems of Cold Mountain." A typical example is as follows:

> Among a thousand clouds and ten thousand streams,
> Here lives an idle man,
> In the daytime wandering over green mountains,
> At night coming home to sleep by the cliff.
> Swiftly the springs and autumns pass,
> But my mind is at peace, free from dust or delusion.
> How pleasant, to know I need nothing to lean on,
> To be still as the waters of the autumn river!
> (Watson 1970, p. 79)

Haoyue 皓月 (Hao-yüeh, Kōgetsu; 9th c.; Case 168). Little is known of this figure other than that he studied under *Changsha Jingcen*. He is said to have been fourth in the line of court monks 供奉 to serve the Tang government.

Hongren 弘忍 (Hung-jen, Gunin; 600–674; Case 2), usually referred to by his traditional title, the Fifth Patriarch, was born in Huangmei 黄梅 in Qizhou 蕲州, in modern Hubei 湖北; his family name was Zhou 周. Hongren entered the monkhood as a young boy after the Fourth Patriarch, Daoxin 道信 (580–651), noticed him while passing near the Zhou family's home and immediately recognized the child's unusual ability. Hongren studied under Daoxin on Mount Shuangfeng 双峰 in the Huangmei region and eventually succeeded to his Dharma. He moved from Mount Shuangfeng eastward to Mount Pingmao 憑茂, also in Huangmei, where he spent the rest of his life at the temple Dongshan si 東山寺 teaching a following that numbered over seven hundred. Among the most famous of his students were *Huineng*, ancestor of the Southern school of Zen, and Shenxiu 神秀 (Shen-hsiu, Jinshū; 606–706), ancestor of the Northern school.

Hongzhi Zhengjue 宏智正覺 (Hung-chih Cheng-chüeh, Wanshi Shōgaku; 1091–1157; Cases 239, 244), also called Tiantong Hongzhi 天童宏智 (T'ien-t'ung Hung-chih, Tendō Wanshi) after Tiantong monastery, was a native of Xizhou 隰州, in modern Shanxi 山西; his family name was Li 李. He is said to have been extraordinarily intelligent as a child, memorizing several thousand characters by the age of seven. He became a novice monk at eleven and received the full precepts at fourteen. At eighteen he left on pilgrimage, determined to visit the greatest masters of his day. He went first to Kumu Facheng 枯木法成 (n.d.), a Caodong master residing in Ruzhou 汝州, modern Henan 河南. Kumu was famous as an exponent of sitting meditation—the word *kumu* 枯木 means "dead tree," from the term applied to the students of *Shishuang Qingzhu*, who were said to sit so long in zazen as to appear like rows of dead trees. Several years later Hongzhi was sent by Kumu to the Caodong master Danxia Zichun 丹霞子淳 (d. 1119), also in Henan. After Hongzhi succeeded to Danxia's Dharma he resided at several temples, including Taiping si 太平寺 in Shuzhou 舒州,

present-day Anhui 安徽, and the monastery on Mount Yunju 雲居, in modern Jiangxi 江西. He finally settled at Mount Tiantong 天童, in present Zhejiang 浙江, where he stayed nearly thirty years, teaching the large assembly of students who gathered under him. He built what had been a small temple into a great monastic complex able to accommodate twelve hundred students. Hongzhi was also a skilled writer who authored several influential works on Zen, including the one-hundred-case koan collection *Record of Equanimity* 従容録. He and his approach to meditation, known as "silent illumination Zen" 黙照禅, became well-known in China, and he was referred to as one of the two great Ambrosia Gates of the Zen school, along with *Dahui Zonggao*.

Hongzhi is known in Zen history for his long-continued debate with Dahui over the matter of the "silent illumination Zen" of the Caodong school versus the "koan-introspecting Zen" 看話禅 of the Linji school. However, the relationship between Hongzhi and Dahui may not have been as acrimonious as it might seem. When Hongzhi sensed the approach of death, for example, he wrote to Dahui entrusting him with the completion of the *Record of Equanimity*.

Hu Dingjiao 胡釘鉸 (Hu Ting-chiao, Ko Teikō; 9th c.; Case 123). Prior to starting his Zen training Hu was a tinker (his name, Dingjiao 釘鉸, literally means "nail" 釘 and "shears" 鉸) and was well known as a poet. Otherwise almost nothing is known of this figure.

Huangbo Weisheng 黄檗惟勝 (Huang-po Wei-sheng, Ōbaku Ishō; 11th c.; Case 52) was a native of Tongchuan 潼川, in present-day Sichuan 四川, with the family name Luo 羅. He first engaged in doctrinal studies, then studied Zen under *Huanglong Huinan*, whose successor he became.

Huangbo Xiyun 黄檗希運 (Huang-po Hsi-yün, Ōbaku Kiun; d. 850?; Cases 34, 42, 95 n., 121, 122, 123 n., 182, 187, 192, 199 n., 221, 250) was a native of Min 閩 in Fuzhou 福州, in present Fujian 福建. He entered the temple Jianfu si 建福寺 on Mount Huangbo 黄檗 in Fuzhou while still very young. He later set out on a pilgrimage that took him to Mount Tiantai 天台 and the capital, Chang'an 長安. He then traveled to the province of Jiangxi 江西 in order to study with *Mazu Daoyi*, but, finding that Mazu was no longer alive, continued on to the monastery of *Baizhang Huaihai*, one of the great disciples of Mazu and, according to traditional Zen accounts, the organizer of Zen monastic life. Huangbo eventually succeeded to Baizhang's Dharma and, from about the year 833, resided at Da'an si 大安寺 in the city of Hongzhou 洪州. There he became acquainted with the governor, *Pei Xiu*, who was to become an influential supporter and eventually one of his Dharma heirs. Several years later Pei constructed a large temple for him in the mountains west of Hongzhou. Huangbo named this temple Hongzhou Huangboshan 洪州黄檗山, in memory of the temple in Fuzhou where he had resided in his youth. He taught many disciples, the most important of whom for later Zen history was *Linji Yixuan*, founder of the Linji school. Huangbo was awarded the posthumous title Zen Master Duanji 斷際禅師.

Huanglong Huinan 黃龍慧南 (Huang-lung Hui-nan, Ōryō Enan; 1002–69; Cases 10, 52, 140, 189, 199) was a native of Xinzhou Yushan 信州玉山 in present Jiangxi 江西. His lay name was Zhang 章. Huinan received ordination at the age of eleven, and later studied under several masters, including Zibao 自寶 of the temple Guizong si 歸宗寺, Chengshi 澄諟 of the temple Qixian si 棲賢寺, and the Yunmen master Huaicheng 懷澄 of Sanjue shan 三角山. After receiving transmission from Huaicheng, Huinan departed on a pilgrimage during which he encountered a monk named Yunfeng Wenyue 雲峯文悦 (998–1062), who criticized Huaicheng's understanding and suggested that he see *Shishuang Chuyuan*. On his way to Shishuang's monastery Huinan stayed at the temple Fuyan si 福嚴寺, where he was appointed secretary. When Fuyan si's priest died, Shishuang Chuyuan was named to fill his position. After some initial uncertainty, Shishuang accepted Huinan as his disciple (see Case 189). Huinan later experienced a deep enlightenment with the koan "Zhaozhou Sees Through an Old Woman" (Case 12).

After leaving Shishuang, Huinan returned to Guizong si but was imprisoned following a fire at the temple. Upon receiving a pardon he retired for a time to Mount Huangbo 黃檗, then took up residence on Mount Huanglong 黃龍 in present Jiangxi 江西. He was the founder of the Huanglong line, which, along with the Yangqi 楊岐 line, was one of the two principal teaching lineages of the Linji school. This line was later brought to Japan by Myōan Eisai (Yōsai) 明庵 栄西 (1141–1215), to become the first Zen lineage formally transmitted to Japan.

Huike 慧可 (Hui-k'o, Eka; 487–593; Cases 1, 43, 113, 168), the Second Patriarch of the Chinese Zen lineage, studied the Confucian and Taoist classics in his youth, then became a monk under a certain Zen Master Baojing 寶靜禪師 and studied the Hinayana and Mahayana teachings. He is said to have then spent eight years in meditation, culminating in a vision that guided him to seek the instruction of *Bodhidharma*. He arrived at Bodhidharma's temple, Shaolin si 少 林寺, on a winter day. Bodhidharma, meditating in his cave, did not acknowledge Huike's presence, so Huike stood waiting all night. Finally Bodhidharma asked him, "You have been standing long in the snow. What are you seeking?" Huike replied, "I request the master, in his mercy, to open the Gate of Ambrosia and liberate all sentient beings." The great teacher said, "The supreme, marvelous Way of all buddhas can be attained only by long continued effort practicing what is difficult to practice and enduring what is difficult to endure. Why should one with a shallow heart and arrogant mind like yourself seek the true vehicle and suffer such hardships in vain?" Huike thereupon took out a knife and cut off his left arm to demonstrate his detachment from his body and his desire to study the Way. Bodhidharma then accepted him as his disciple; later, the exchange recorded in Case 1 took place.

Huike studied under Bodhidharma for about five or six years and received transmission of the Dharma. Later he designated his student *Sengcan* as his successor and left to preach in the world, claiming he had karmic debts from a former life to repay. He is said to have spent thirty years teaching among the common people in the city of Ye 鄴, entering the taverns and working with the laborers. When asked why he, a man of the Way, was behaving in this way, he answered, "I am cultivating my mind in my own manner—what concern is it of yours?" Huike's preaching activities became so popular that they finally aroused the envy of an important Dharma master named Bianhe 辨和. Bianhe's denunciations led to Huike's execution for preaching false doctrines, a sentence that the master accepted calmly (see Case 168).

Huiming 慧明 (Hui-ming, Emyō; 7th c.; Cases 2, 260 n.) was born in the area of Poyang 鄱陽, in present Jiangxi 江西; his family name was Chen 陳. Since he was of royal descent he was awarded the title "General" when his country fell and he lost his position. He became a monk at an early age at the temple Yongchang si 永昌寺, then studied Zen under the Fifth Patriarch, *Hongren*. Following his exchange with the Sixth Patriarch, *Huineng*, described in Case 2, he is said to have dwelt for three years on Mount Lu 廬, after which he made his way to Mount Meng 蒙 in Yuanzhou 袁州. As the first character of his name, 慧, was the same as that of Huineng 慧能, he changed it to 道 and thereafter called himself Mengshan Daoming 蒙山道明.

Huineng 慧能 (Hui-neng, Enō; 638–713; also Dajian Huineng 大鑑慧能, Ta-chien Hui-neng, Daikan Enō; Cases 2, 83, 96, 118, 238, 260 n., 261 n., 272) is honored as the Sixth Patriarch of Chinese Zen and founder of the Southern school; with him Zen is regarded as having taken on a truly Chinese character.

According to the traditional accounts of his life, Huineng was a native of Xinzhou 新州 in present Guangdong 廣東; his lay name was Lu 盧. His family was originally from Fanyang 范陽 in modern Hebei 河北, but his father, demoted from a government post, had moved south to the Guangdong region, where he died when Huineng was only three years old. The boy was raised by his widowed mother, and as he grew older he helped support her by selling firewood. One day in town he was deeply moved when he heard the line "Give rise to the mind that does not abide in anything" from the *Diamond Sutra*. Learning that the reciter had received the sutra from the Fifth Patriarch, *Hongren*, Huineng set off in search of the Dharma. He first went to nearby Shaozhou 韶州, where the people, impressed with him, restored the temple Baolin si 寶林寺 in neighboring Caoxi 曹溪 and asked him to be the priest. Huineng was not yet satisfied with his understanding, however, and thus traveled north to Hongren's monastery on Mount Huangmei 黄梅. According to the *Platform Sutra of the Sixth Patriarch*, Hongren, hearing that Huineng came from Guangdong, remarked that "a barbarian from the south cannot become a Buddha." Huineng responded, "In buddha nature there is no north and south." Hongren was impressed and put him to work as a rice huller.

One day Hongren, wishing to name a successor, asked the monks to write a verse expressing their understanding. The first verse was that of the senior monk, Shenxiu 神秀 (605–706): "The body is the bodhi tree, the mind is like the stand of a bright mirror. At all times strive to polish it, and let no dust collect." Later the illiterate Huineng heard a monk reciting Shenxiu's verse and, recognizing its shortcomings, had the following verse posted: "Originally there is no tree of enlightenment, nor a stand with a bright mirror. Fundamentally not one thing exists—where is there for dust to collect?" Although Hongren realized the superiority of Huineng's verse, he withheld praise so that Shenxiu's supporters would not harm the layman. That night, however, he presented Huineng with the Patriarch's robe and bowl, and told him to flee south for his own safety. This set the stage for the events described in *Kattōshū* Case 2.

Huineng subsequently spent sixteen years in seclusion; in 676, still a layman, he appeared at Faxing si 法性寺 (see Case 83). The priest, Yinzong 印宗 (627–713), recognizing his deep understanding, shaved his head and gave him the full commandments. The following year Huineng returned to his former temple, Baolin si, where he taught until his death in 713. With him the patriarchate ended in accordance with the wishes of Hongren, who felt that it was merely a cause of contention. Huineng left behind numerous important disciples, among them Heze Shenhui 荷澤神會 (670–762), the main proponent of the Southern school; Qingyuan Xingsi 青原行思 (d. 740), whose descendants founded what is now the Sōtō school; and *Nanyue Huairang*, whose descendants founded what is now the Rinzai school.

Huitang Zuxin 晦堂祖心 (Hui-t'ang Tsu-hsin, Maidō Soshin; 1025–1100; Case 18), also known as Huanglong Zuxin 黄龍祖心, was a native of Nanxiong 南雄 in Guangdong 廣東. He entered temple life at the age of ten, and later studied under Yunfeng Wenyue 雲峰文悦 (998–1062) and *Huanglong Huinan*, eventually succeeding Huanglong as abbot of the monastery on Mount Huanglong 黄龍. He received the title Zen Master Baojue 寶覺禪師.

Huiyuan 慧遠 (Hui-yüan, Eon; 334–416; Case 186), one of the leading figures of early Chinese Buddhist history, was a native of Yanmen 雁門, in present Shanxi 山西; his family name was Jia 賈. He studied the Confucian and Taoist teachings before becoming, at twenty-one, a disciple of the great Buddhist scholar and meditator Daoan 道安 (312–85). Under Daoan he studied the *Prajñā-pāramitā* sutras, using Taoist concepts as an aid to understanding. In 381 Huiyuan moved from Xiangyang 襄陽, in present-day Hubei 湖北, southward to Mount Lu 盧, where he spent the remainder of his years at Donglin si 東林寺, the monastery built for him and his many followers. His biography states, "His shadow never left the mountain, his footprints never entered the secular world. When he bade farewell to his guests, he went only as far as the Tiger Creek" (Chen 1964, p. 105; see also Case 186).

Under Huiyuan, Mount Lu became a major Buddhist center noted for its monastic discipline, doctrinal study, and meditative practice. Huiyuan supported the efforts of the Kashmirian monk Sanghadeva to translate into Chinese the works of the Sarvāstivāda school of Buddhism, and he was otherwise active in disseminating the Buddhist teachings. In an extensive correspondence with the great translator-monk Kumārajiva (344–413) he posed numerous questions in an attempt to clarify such basic Buddhist concepts as "dharma-kāya," "arhat," and "bodhisattva." With a group of his disciples Huiyuan formed the White Lotus Society 白蓮社, dedicated to rebirth in the Pure Land of Amitābha Buddha, and for this reason he is honored as the founder of the Pure Land tradition. When the government under Huan Xuan 桓玄 attempted to assert control over the sangha, Huiyuan wrote a tract entitled *Priests Do Not Bow before Kings* 沙門不敬王者論, arguing that those in sacred orders need not subordinate themselves to secular authority, and that, with their understanding of karma, they would always be responsible citizens.

Huo'an Shiti 或庵師體 (Huo-an Shih-t'i, Wakuan Shitai; 1108–79; Case 109 n.) was a native of Danqiu Huangyan 丹丘黄巖 in present-day Zhejiang 浙江; his family name was Luo 羅. He entered the temple Miaozhi yuan 妙智院 at the age of fifteen and became a novice at twenty. After receiving the full precepts he studied under the master Cian Jingyuan 此庵景元 (1094–46), a successor of *Yuanwu Keqin*. After receiving transmission from the master, Huo'an retired to a hut on Mount Baishifeng 白石峰 with the intention of remaining there the rest of his days. However, hearing that Fohai Huiyuan 佛海慧遠 (1103–76) was moving to the monastery Guoqing si 國清寺 on Mount Tiantai 天台, he traveled there to help him establish the community. He later resided on Mount Jiao 焦 in Zhenjiangfu 鎮江府, in present Jiangsu 江蘇. He was known for always keeping in his *sanzen* room a broom handle, which he used as an expedient in teaching the Dharma.

Hutou 虎頭 (Hu-t'ou, Kotō; n.d.; Case 19-1). Nothing is known of this figure.

J

Ji Xin 紀信 (Chi Hsin, Ki Shin; n.d.; Case 191) was a prominent retainer of Liu Bang 劉邦 (247–195 BCE), one of the two great generals in the wars that led to the fall of the Qin 秦 dynasty (221–206 BCE). Giles writes:

> [Chi Hsin (Jixin) was] a captain in Liu Pang's 劉邦 army. When the latter was besieged by Hsiang Chi 項籍 [see *Xiang Yu*] at Jung-yang 滎陽, with little hope of escape, Chi disguised himself as Liu Pang and proceeded to the enemy's lines [riding in Liu Pang's Nine-Dragon Carriage] to tender his submission. In the excitement that ensued, Liu Pang succeeded in getting clear away; but when the ruse was discovered, Hsiang Chi ordered Chi Hsin to be burnt alive. A shrine was erected to his memory in Shun-ch'ing 順慶 in modern Ssu-ch'uan, as a patriot whose loyalty saved the country, and as one who reckoned his own life of no account compared with that of his sovereign. (1939, p. 118)

Jianfu Chenggu 薦福承古 (Chien-fu Ch'eng-ku, Senpuku Shōko; d. 1045; Case 235), also known as Gutazhu 古塔主, was a native of Xizhou 西州 in Shanxi 陝西. He became a monk under a certain Daguang Jingxuan 大光敬玄 at Mount Liao 了 in Tanzhou 潭州, and later studied with Nanyue Liangya 南嶽良雅, a Dharma heir of the Yunmen master *Dongshan Shouchu*. While under Nanyue he had an awakening upon hearing some words of *Yunmen Wenyan*. He later went to the monasteries on Mount Lu 廬 and Mount Oufeng 歐峰 before taking up residence at Hongjue tayuan 弘覺塔院 on Mount Yunju 雲居. He first lectured at Mount Zhi 芝, claiming to be a Dharma successor of Yunmen. Later he was invited to be abbot of the temple Jianfu si 薦福寺, where he was active in teaching. There were widespread repercussions when it was subsequently learned that he had never actually met Yunmen.

Jiashan Shanhui 夾山善會 (Chia-shan Shan-hui, Kassan Zenne; 805–81; Cases 99, 101, 105, 257) was a native of Hanguang 漢廣, in modern Henan 河南; his lay name was Liao 廖. He entered temple life at age nine, becoming an acolyte at Mount Longya 龍牙 in Tanzhou 潭州, present Hunan 湖南. He took the full commandments in Jiangling 江陵, present-day Hubei 湖北, and devoted himself to the study of Buddhist doctrine and the practice of meditation. He later moved to the city of Jingkou 京口 in Runzhou 潤州, present Jiangsu 江蘇. As described in Case 257, one night during a lecture Jiashan gave some answers to a questioning monk that dissatisfied *Daowu Yuanzhi*, who advised Jiashan to visit the "Boatman Monk" *Chuanzi Decheng*. Daowu described Chuanzi as a teacher that "above, hasn't a tile to cover his head, and below, hasn't a gimlet point of ground to stand on."

Jiashan went to the river Wujiang 吳江 in modern Jiangsu 江蘇, where Chuanzi had his boat. It is said that he and Chuanzi had an immediate meeting of minds, and that Chuanzi, after sanctioning his understanding, advised him to dwell in the mountains and devote himself to finding even just a single true student to maintain the Dharma. Chuanzi then capsized his boat and was never seen again. Jiashan followed Chuanzi's advice, secluding himself in the mountains for over thirty years. In 870 he settled on Mount Jia 夾, in present Hunan, and began to teach the students who came to him. Finally the temple Lingquan yuan 靈泉院 was built for them. In Case 99 Jiashan poetically describes his "state" or "surroundings" there. It was at Lingquan yuan that, two hundred years later, the great master *Yuanwu Keqin* delivered the lectures that were compiled into the *Blue Cliff Record*.

Jingqing Daofu 鏡清道怤 (Ching-ch'ing Tao-fu, Kyōsei Dōfu; 868–937; Cases 158, 197 n., 200) was a native of Yongjia 永嘉 in Wenzhou 溫州, present Zhejiang 浙江; his family name was Chen 陳. While still young he entered the temple Kaiyuan si 開元寺. Later he joined the assembly under *Xuefeng Yicun* on Mount Xianggu 象骨 in present Fujian 福建. At their first meeting Xuefeng, hearing that Daofu came from Yongjia, commented that he was from the same region as *Yongjia Xuanjue*. "Where, though, did Yongjia come from?" responded Daofu. After succeeding to Xuefeng's Dharma, Jingqing went to Yuezhou 越州, in present-day Zhejiang, and there resided at the temple Jingqing si 鏡清寺. Later, at the invitation of the imperial court, he became abbot of Tianlong si 天龍寺 and Hangzhou Longce si 杭州龍册寺.

Jingshan Hongyin 徑山洪諲 (Ching-shan Hung-yin, Kinzan Kōin; d. 901; Case 200) was a native of Wuxing 吳興 in present Zhejiang 浙江; his family name was Wu 吳. At the age of nineteen he became a monk at the temple Kaiyuan si 開元寺 under a priest named Wushang 無上 and at the age of twenty-two took the full precepts at Mount Song 嵩 in Henan 河南. He first studied under Yunyan Tansheng 雲巖曇晟 (Yün-yen T'an-sheng, Ungan Donjō; 782–841), but, failing to accord with Yunyan's teaching style, later joined the assembly under *Guishan Lingyou* on Mount Jing 徑. Following Guishan's death in 866, Hongyin, at the request of the other monks, took his place to become the third abbot of the monastery on Mount Jing.

Jingzhao Mihu 京兆米胡 (Ching-chao Mi-hu, Keichō Beiko; n.d.; Case 246), also known as Qishi 七師, Mi Qishi 米七師, and Mihu 米胡, was a successor of *Guishan Lingyou*. Little else is known of him other than the stories that remain in koans, most of which feature his exchanges with *Yangshan Huiji* and *Dongshan Liangjie*.

Jue Tiezui 覺鐵觜. Another name for *Guangxiao Huijue*.

Juefan Huihong 覺範慧洪 (Chüeh-fan Hui-hung, Kakuhan Ekō; 1071–1128; Case 140), also known as Jiyin Zunzhe 寂音尊者 (Chi-yin Tsun-che, Jakuon Sonja), was a native of Ruizhou 瑞州, in modern Jiangxi 江西; his lay name was Peng 彭. He became a monk at the age of fourteen and began doctrinal studies; a brilliant student, he was reportedly able to memorize an entire book at a single reading. He took the full precepts at nineteen at the temple Tianwang si 天王寺 in Loyang 洛陽, then studied the Madhyamaka and Yogācāra teachings under a Dharma master named Xuanmi 宣密. Later he began his formal Zen training under *Zhenjing Kewen*. After succeeding to Zhenjing's Dharma he entered the temple Qingliang si 清涼寺 in Ruizhou. During the Chongning 崇寧 era (1102–6) he was imprisoned a total of four times owing to false charges brought against him by a priest who disagreed with his teachings. He was aided at this time by *Zhang Wujin* and Guo Tianmin 郭天民, both of them prominent government officials and lay Zen practitioners. Later he went to Xiangxi 湘西 in present Xiangnan 湘南, and there he resided at the hermitage Mingbai an 明白庵, devoting himself to scholarship. He produced several important commentaries and biographies, including the *Zen Forest Records* 林間錄, *Biographies of Monks of the Zen School* 禪林僧寶傳, and *Biographies of Eminent Monks* 高僧傳.

Juzhou Baotan 橘洲寶曇 (Chü-chou Pao-t'an, Kisshū Hōdon; 1129–97; Case 123) was a native of Longyou 龍游 in Jiadingfu 嘉定府, modern Sichuan 四川; his family name was Xu 許. He was a successor of *Dahui Zonggao*, and resided at Yanshou Chanyuan 延壽禪院 on Mount Zhangxi 仗錫 in Zhejiang 浙江. He is best known as the compiler of the biographical collection *Treasury of Great Light* 大光明藏.

K

Kānadeva. See *Āryadeva*.

Kanzan Egen 關山慧玄 (1277–1360; Cases 35, 175 n., 225, 253) was a Japanese monk, born as the second son of the aristocratic Takanashi 高梨 family in Shinano 信濃 (present-day Nagano 長野 Prefecture). He received ordination at Kenchō-ji 建長寺 under the priest Tōden Shikei 東傳士啓 (d. 1374); in 1307 he met *Nanpo Jōmyō*, from whom he received the name Egen 慧玄, but there is no evidence that he studied under him. In 1309 Egen returned to Shinano and remained there until 1327, when he met *Shūhō Myōchō* at Kenchō-ji and became his student. In 1330 he experienced a deep enlightenment with the koan "Yunmen's 'Barrier,'" Case 8 of the *Blue Cliff Record*:

> At the end of the training period Cuiyan Lingcan said to the assembly, "Monks, I have preached to you throughout the retreat. Look and tell me if I have any eyebrows left."
> Paofu said, "One who steals is uneasy at heart."
> Changqing Huileng said, "They've grown!"
> Yunmen said, "*Kan!*" [which literally means "Barrier!" but which is untranslatable in the context of the koan].

After receiving transmission from Myōchō, Kanzan is said to have gone to the mountain village of Ibuka 伊深, in Mino 美濃, present-day Gifu 岐阜 Prefecture, where he worked as a laborer to integrate his realization into his daily life. In 1337 he was called back to the capital and installed as the founding priest of the temple Myōshin-ji 妙心寺. He is said to have died in his traveling clothes, in the standing posture. Although he had only one Dharma successor—Juō Sōhitsu 授翁宗弼 (1296–1380)—his lineage, known as the Ōtōkan 應燈關 lineage (see p. 10, above) has continued through the present day, and, through *Hakuin Ekaku*, includes every Rinzai Zen master in Japan.

Kanzan is remembered for his austere lifestyle. A famous (and undoubtedly apocryphal) story relates how one day his contemporary *Musō Soseki* came to Myōshin-ji on an unannounced visit. Kanzan had nothing to offer his guest, so he sent a monk to a neighborhood shop for some bean cakes. These he served to Soseki on the cover of his inkstone box, as he had no proper tray for the purpose. Soseki is said to have been much impressed by the simplicity of Kanzan's life and to have later predicted that Kanzan's lineage would prevail over his own.

Kāśyapa Buddha (Jiashe Fo 迦葉佛, Chia-she Fo, Kashō Butsu; Cases 34, 70 n.)

was the sixth and last of the nonhistorical buddhas (the buddhas said to have preceded Śākyamuni). According to legend he lived in an age when the human lifespan was twenty thousand years, and he liberated twenty thousand people at one gathering. The *Jingde-Era Record of the Transmission of the Lamp* gives his verse as: "All sentient beings are naturally pure; originally they have no birth, no death. Bodies and minds are born of delusion; there is no weal or woe in illusory life" (Ogata 1990, p. 3).

L

Langye Huijue 瑯琊慧覺 (Lang-yeh Hui-chüeh, Rōya Ekaku; 11th c.; Cases 27 n., 114, 191, 223, 228) was a native of the capital city Luoyang 洛陽. After the death of his father Langye went to Hangyang 衡陽, where his father had served as governor, to help with the funeral proceedings. On his return he stopped at the ancient monastery located on Mount Yao 藥 in Liyang 澧陽. While there he experienced such a deep feeling of affinity for the place that he decided to renounce lay life and enter the monkhood. After ordination he went on pilgrimage and visited many masters, finally entering the assembly under *Fenyang Shanzhao*, whose Dharma successor he became. He then went to Chuzhou 滁州 in present Anhui 安徽, where he settled on Mount Langye 瑯琊. He and his contemporary *Xuedou Chongxian* were known as the "Two Amṛta Gates" of their era for their skill in teaching Linji Zen. Langye was given the honorary title Zen Master Guangzhao 廣照禪師. Among his important students was *Changshui Zixuan*.

Li Tongxuan 李通玄 (Li T'ung-hsüan, Ri Tsūgen; 635–730 [646–740]; Case 235) was a native of Cangzhou 滄州 in modern Hebei 河北; some accounts say he was related to the imperial family. In later life he became interested in *Avataṁsaka* philosophy and authored a number of works, including the *New Treatise on the Avataṁsaka Sutra* 新華嚴經論 and the *Comprehensive Treatise on the Avataṁsaka Sutra* 華嚴經合論. He also stressed the importance of meditation, and the ultimate unity of delusion and enlightenment. His writings were a major influence on later East Asian Buddhist thought.

Li Ying 李膺 (Li Ying, Ri Yō; d. 169; Case 262) was a Han-dynasty official of exceptional ability and force of character. Giles writes:

> [Li Ying was] a native of Ying-ch'uan in Anhui... In AD 156 he was appointed by the Emperor Huan Ti to operate against the Kitan Tartars who were raiding the frontier, and his appearance on the scene created such consternation in the Tartar ranks that they sent back all the men and women who had been carried away as captives. For these services he was advanced to high office, and for a long time exercised great influence. When appointed in 159 to be Governor of Honan, 張朔 Chang Shuo, brother to the eunuch Chang Jang, then magistrate at 野王 Yeh-wang, was so alarmed that he fled to the capital and hid himself in a pillar

in his brother's house. But Li Ying, who had discovered his iniquities, tracked him to his hiding-place, dragged him forth, and after due trial caused him to be executed. This bold act frightened the eunuchs into good behaviour for a long time. At the death of the Emperor in 167, Ch'en Fan and Topu Wu took the lead in the administration; and when they fell victim to eunuch intrigues, Li Ying fell with them. He was thrown into prison and beaten to death. Personally he was a man of very abrupt character. He had in consequence few friends; and those who sought him out were said to "go to the dragon's door." (1939, pp. 474–75)

Liang, Venerable 良和尚 (Liang, Ryō; n.d.; Case 238). It is uncertain who Venerable Liang is. Dōmae suggests that the name may refer to Wufeng Puliang 五峰普良 (n.d.), a successor of Changlu Yingfu 長蘆應夫 (n.d.) of the Yunmen school.

Lingshu Rumin 靈樹如敏 (Ling-shu Ju-min, Reiju Nyobin; d. 920; Case 164) was a native of Minchuan 閩川, present Fujian 福建. After receiving ordination he studied under *Changqing Lan'an.* He became Changqing's Dharma heir and went to Shaozhou 韶州, in present Guangdong 廣東, where he resided at the temple Lingshu yuan 靈樹院. Lingshu was credited with the supernatural ability to know the past and future. He didn't appoint a head monk at Lingshu yuan for the first twenty years he was there. Then one day he told his monks to prepare for the arrival of the head monk. When *Yunmen Wenyan* arrived at the monastery later the same day he was immediately appointed to that position. Yunmen later became Rumin's successor as abbot.

Lingyun Zhiqin 靈雲志勤 (Ling-yün Chih-ch'in, Reiun Shigon; 9th c.; Cases 8, 14) was a native of Changxi 長溪 in Fuzhou 福州, present-day Fujian 福建. Little is known of his life, other than the fact that he studied under *Guishan Lingyou,* was designated one of that master's forty-one Dharma heirs, and later resided at the monasteries on Mount Lingyun 靈雲 in Fuzhou and Mount Dagui 大潙 in Tanzhou 潭州, present Hunan 湖南. Lingyun is perhaps best known in Zen circles for the story of his enlightenment at the sight of peach blossoms and his subsequent enlightenment verse (see Case 8).

Linji Yixuan 臨濟義玄 (Lin-chi I-hsüan, Rinzai Gigen; d. 866; Cases 32, 80, 84, 95 n., 122, 123, 141, 155, 159, 170 n., 173, 176, 177, 178, 180, 181, 187, 191 n., 192, 195, 197 n., 199, 207-1, 207-2, 208, 210, 218, 221, 224, 229, 239 n., 270-2, 272), founder of the Linji school of Chinese Zen, was a native of Nanhua 南華 in Cao 曹, modern Shandong 山東; his family name was Ching 邢. Little is known of his early life. After becoming a monk he devoted himself to studying the Tripitaka and became well versed in the sutras and commentaries. Seeking deeper understanding, he journeyed south to the monastery of *Huangbo Xiyun* in Jiangxi 江西. The story of his early training there and his subsequent enlightenment is related in detail in Case 187. Linji stayed with Huangbo for another ten years after his enlightenment (for an incident that occurred during this time, see Case 192), then left on a long pilgrimage. He finally settled in Zhenzhou 鎮州, present Hebei 河北, at a small temple called Linji yuan 臨濟院. There he remained for ten years, teaching the relatively small number of students who gathered around him. Around 861 he left Zhenzhou and moved to the temple Guanyin si 觀音寺 in Weifu 魏府, Hebei, where he lived in retirement until his death in 866.

Linji was known for his forceful teaching methods employing the stick and the shout (see Case 178); many of his creative Zen doctrines became koans (see, for example, Cases 80, 141 n., 159, 176, 177, 181, 208, and 210). Through his student *Xinghua Cunjiang*, Linji founded the school that bears his name.

Longqing Qingxian 隆慶慶閑 (Lung-ch'ing Ch'ing-hsien, Ryūkei Keikan; d. 1081; Case 10) was a native of Fuzhou 福州; his family name was Zhuo 卓. He became a monk at the age of eleven and at twenty set out on a long pilgrimage. He eventually became a Dharma successor of *Huanglong Huinan*. He later resided at Longqing yuan 隆慶院 on Mount Ren 仁 in Jizhou 吉州.

Longtan Chongxin 龍潭崇信 (Lung-t'an Ch'ung-hsin, Ryūtan Sōshin; 9th c.; Cases 128, 256) became a monk under *Tianhuang Daowu* and succeeded to his Dharma. He later went to Longtan 龍潭 in Lizhou 澧州, present-day Hunan 湖南, where he built himself a hermitage. Among his students was the great master *Deshan Xuanjian*, a contemporary of *Linji Yixuan*. Otherwise little is known of his life.

Longya Judun 龍牙居遁 (Lung-ya Chü-tun, Ryūge Kodon; 835–923; Case 155) was a native of Nancheng 南城 in Fuzhou 撫州, present-day Jiangxi 江西; his lay name was Guo 郭. He entered the temple Mantian si 滿田寺 at the age of fourteen. After receiving the full precepts on Mount Song 嵩 he set off on pilgrimage, visiting many of the leading masters of the time and eventually choosing as his teacher the Caodong master *Dongshan Liangjie*. Judun set off again on pilgrimage after succeeding to Liangjie's Dharma, meeting, among others, *Linji Yixuan* and Cuiwei Wuxue 翠微無學 (9th c.), with whom he had the exchanges related in Case 155 n. Judun eventually became abbot at Miaoji Chanyuan 妙濟禪院 on Mount Longya 龍牙 in Hunan 湖南, where there were always at least five hundred monks under him.

Judun was noted for his poems, many of which survive in works like the *Poems of Venerable Longya Judun* 龍牙和尚居遁頌 and the *Jingde-Era Record of the Transmission of the Lamp*. His title is Zen Master Zhengkong 證空禪師.

Lu Gen 陸亘 (Lu Ken, Riku Kō; c. 765–c. 835; Case 209), from the district of Wu 吳 in modern Jiangsu 江蘇, went by the style of Jingshan 景山. Although already in his mid-forties when he passed the government examinations in 808, he held a number of provincial posts, including, in his later years, the governorship of Xuanzhou 宣州 and Xizhou 歙州 in the province of Anhui 安徽, while simultaneously serving as head of the Bureau of Censors. In 828, during his tenure as governor of Xuanzhou, he met *Nanquan Puyuan* and asked him to teach in the city; he became Puyuan's student and eventually his Dharma successor.

A number of exchanges between Lu and his teacher remain in the Zen records. One example is:

> Lu asked the master, "Once a man raised a goose in a bottle. The goose grew larger and it became impossible to get it out. The man wished to free the goose without breaking the bottle nor hurting the bird. Reverend Sir, how would you do so?" Nanquan called, "Your Honor!" "Yes," replied Lu. "It's out!' said Nanquan. At this the governor gained some degree of insight. (T 51:279b)

Luopu Yuan'an 洛浦元安 (Lo-p'u Yüan-an, Rakuho Gen'an; 834–98; Case 119) was a native of Linyou 麟遊, present Shanxi 陝西; his family name was Dan 淡. At the age of twenty he became a monk at the local temple Huai'en si 懷恩寺, then left on pilgrimage. He studied under the masters Cuiwei Wuxue 翠微無學 (9th c.), *Linji Yixuan* (whom he served as attendant), and *Jiashan Shanhui*. After succeeding to Jiashan's Dharma he resided on Mount Luopu 樂普 (also written 洛浦) in Lizhou 澧州, Hunan 湖南, then at Suxi 蘇谿 in Langzhou 朗州. He was highly regarded as a teacher, attracting students from all over China. Several well-known incidents in the *Record of Linji* involve Luopu's exchanges with Linji and other masters. The following example is typical:

> The master heard that Deshan of the second generation said, "Thirty blows if you can speak; thirty blows if you can't." The master told Luopu to go and ask Deshan, "'Why thirty blows to one who can speak?' Wait until he hits at you, then grab his stick and give him a jab. See what he does then." When Luopu reached Deshan's place he questioned him as instructed. Deshan hit at him. Luopu seized the stick and gave Deshan a jab with it. Deshan went back to his quarters. Luopu returned and told Linji what had taken place. "I've always held wonder for that fellow," the master said. "Be that as it may, did you understand Deshan?" Luopu hesitated. The master hit him. (Sasaki 2009, pp. 300–301)

Luoshan Daoxian 羅山道閑 (Lo-shan T'ao-hsien, Razan Dōkan; 9th c.; Case 132) was a native of Changxi 長溪 in Puzhou 普州, present-day Fujian 福建; his family name was Chen 陳. He entered the monkhood at the temple on Mount Gui 龜 and, after receiving the full precepts, set out on an extended pilgrimage during which he visited various masters, among them *Shishuang Qingzhu*. He finally attained peace of mind under *Yantou Quanhuo* in Ezhou 鄂州, present Hunan 湖南. After succeeding to Yantou's Dharma, Daoxian went to Mount Wutai 五臺 in Shanxi 山西, where he stayed for several years. Later he was invited to live at the temple on Mount Luo 羅 by the prince of Min 閩 in Fuzhou. There he taught until his death. He was awarded the title Great Master Fabao 法寶大師.

M

Ma Fang 馬防 (Ma Fang, Ba Hō; n.d.; Case 179) was a government official (Administrator of Chengde Military Prefecture) and author of the Preface to the *Record of Linji*. Nothing else is known of his life.

Magu Baotie 麻谷寶鐵 (Ma-ku Pao-t'ieh, Mayoku Hōtetsu; 8th c.; Cases 131, 167). Magu was a Dharma heir of *Mazu Daoyi*, and resided on Mount Magu 麻谷 in Puzhou 蒲州, modern Shanxi 山西. Little else is known of him beyond the incidents recorded in koan collections.

Mahākāśyapa (Mohe Jiashe 摩訶迦葉, Mo-ho Chia-she, Makakashō; Cases 95, 135, 136, 213 n.) was one of the Ten Great Disciples of Śākyamuni and was renowned for his ascetic practices. He is said to have been the son of a Brahman family and to have married despite a strong desire to become a renunciant. This desire was shared by his wife, and, after several years of celibate married life, the two left home to become seekers. Soon afterward Mahākāśyapa met the Buddha and asked to become his disciple. It is said that a mere eight days after joining the sangha he attained arhatship. The Buddha had great confidence in Mahākāśyapa's accomplishments, to the point of occasionally asking Mahākāśyapa to preach in his stead. Following the demise of the Buddha he assumed leadership of the sangha and convened the First Council to collect and systematize the Buddha's teachings. He is honored as the first ancestor of Indian Zen (see Case 135 for the incident in which the Buddha transmitted his Dharma to Mahākāśyapa) and is said to have named *Ānanda* as his successor.

Maitreya (Mile 彌勒, Mi-le, Miroku; Cases 3, 82, 213) is the buddha of the next world age. He is to be born, according to various traditions, anywhere from 30,000 years to 5,670,000,000 years from the time of Śākyamuni's death. At present he is said to reside in Tushita Heaven, the fourth of the six heavens in the realm of desire, practicing samadhi and teaching the Dharma to the heavenly beings until his rebirth in the world as the next buddha.

Mañjuśrī (Wenshu 文殊, Wen-shu, Monju; Cases 12 n., 17 n., 24, 48, 72, 87, 133, 159, 181 n., 191 n., 198, 201, 212) is the Mahayana bodhisattva representative of prajñā wisdom. His name is translated into Chinese as Miaode 妙德, "Marvelous Virtue." He often appears as one of the two bodhisattva attendants of Śākyamuni Buddha, together with *Samantabhadra*, and is usually shown holding a scroll (symbolizing wisdom) or a sword (symbolizing the cutting off of delusion). In China, Mañjuśrī is said to dwell on Mount Wutai in Shanxi.

Manora, or Manorhita, Manorata (Monaluo 摩拏羅, Mo-na-la, Manura; Case 27) is traditionally regarded as the twenty-second ancestor of Indian Zen. Manora was the crown prince of the land of Nadī, but he renounced the kingdom to become a monk when he encountered the great Buddhist philosopher Vasubandhu (the twenty-first ancestor of Indian Zen). After succeeding to Vasubandhu's Dharma he was active in western India, promoting the Mahayana and refuting Hinayana teachings. Later he went to the land of Tokhāra, where he transmitted the Dharma to Haklenayaśas, the twenty-third ancestor.

Maudgalyāyana (Mulian 目連, Mu-lien, Mokuren; Cases 97, 133) was one of the Ten Great Disciples of Śākyamuni and was renowned as the greatest in supernatural powers. The son of a Brahman family in the village of Kolita, he and his childhood friend Śariputra became disciples of the non-Buddhist philosopher Sanjaya Belaṭṭhiputta. One day Śariputra encountered a disciple of the Buddha and was so impressed by his demeanor and words that he and Maudgalyāyana decided to join the Buddhist sangha. This they did together with 250 of Sanjaya's disciples. Maudgalyāyana was murdered by enemies of the Buddha shortly before the death of the Buddha himself.

Mazu Daoyi 馬祖道一 (Ma-tsu Tao-i, Baso Dōitsu; 709–88; Cases 5, 23, 53, 78, 103 n., 123, 139, 170 n., 182, 221, 234 n., 252) was a native of Hanzhou 漢州 in Sichuan 四川; his family name was Ma 馬. He is said to have had eyes like a tiger, a tongue long enough to cover his nose, feet with wheel-shaped marks on their soles, and a gait like that of a bull. After mastering the standard educational studies by the age of nine he entered the temple Luohan si 羅漢寺 in Hanzhou. After receiving ordination and the precepts he practiced meditation on Mount Changsong 長松 in Yizhou 益州, present Sichuan, and Mount Mingyue 明月 in Jingzhou 荊州, modern Hubei 湖北. He was sought out there by the master *Nanyue Huairang*; the story of their encounter is related in Case 139. Nanyue's sole Dharma heir, Mazu went on to become one of the greatest teachers in Tang-dynasty Zen, developing many of the training methods—such as use of the shout and the stick—subsequently employed by masters to shake monks out of their ordinary consciousness. For a typical example of Mazu's teaching style, see Case 182.

The Zen records list 139 Dharma heirs for Mazu, the most historically important of whom was *Baizhang Huaihai*, the founder of the Zen monastic system and teacher of *Huangbo Xiyun*. Other eminent disciples included *Nanquan Puyuan* and *Damei Fachang*.

Mian Xianjie 密庵咸傑 (Mi-an Hsien-chieh, Mittan Kanketsu; 1118–86; Cases 22-2, 30, 113 n.) was a native of Fuqing 福清 in Fuzhou 福州, present-day Fujian 福建; his family name was Zheng 鄭. He traveled widely visiting teachers, finally receiving transmission from the Linji Yangqi-line master *Ying'an Tanhua*. He subsequently served as priest at a number of temples, including the great monasteries at Mount Jing 徑, Mount Lingyin 靈隱, and Mount Tiantong 天童. As the successor of Ying'an and the teacher of *Songyuan Chongyue*, he is in the line from which all present-day Japanese Rinzai Zen masters descend.

Mingzhao Deqian 明招德謙 (Ming-chao Te-ch'ien, Myōshō Tokken; ca. 9–10th c.; Case 32). Nothing is known of Deqian's life until he joined the assembly under *Luoshan Daoxian*, whose Dharma successor he became. He served as head monk at Zhizhe si 智者寺 in Wuzhou 婺州, present-day Zhejiang 浙江, and later resided at Mount Mingzhao 明招, where he taught monks, nuns, and laypeople for over forty years. He was also known as Duganlong 獨眼龍, "One-eyed Dragon," because he was blind in one eye.

Musō Soseki 夢窓疎石 (1275–1351; Cases 170 n., 225), an early Japanese Zen priest best known by his title National Teacher Musō 夢窓國師, was a native of Ise 伊

勢, in present Mie 三重 Prefecture. When Musō was three his family moved to Kai 甲斐 (present Yamanashi 山梨 Prefecture). Soseki first studied the esoteric teachings of the Tendai 天台 school at the temple Heien-ji 平塩寺, not far from his home. Despairing of resolving the question of birth-and-death through rituals and doctrinal studies, he turned to Zen, training under Muin Enban 無隠圓範 (1230–1307), Yishan Yining 一山一寧 (J., Issan Ichinei; 1247–1317), and others before meeting Kōhō Kennichi 高峯顯日 (1241–1316). After a decisive awakening experience during a solitary retreat in eastern Japan he was recognized as a Dharma successor by Kōhō. He refined his understanding for twenty more years, practicing in remote mountain hermitages, until summoned to the capital in 1325 by Emperor Go-Daigo 後醍醐 (r. 1318–39) to serve as abbot of Nanzen-ji 南禪寺. After a year he returned to eastern Japan for further practice. In 1333 he was again summoned to Kyoto to assume the abbacy of Rinsen-ji 臨川寺 and to serve another year as abbot of Nanzen-ji. He was sought out as an advisor and meditation teacher by emperors, military leaders, and hundreds of ordained and lay followers for the remainder of his life. He also founded a number of temples in Kyoto and elsewhere, prominent among them being Zuisen-ji 瑞泉寺, Tōji-in 等持院, and Tenryū-ji 天龍寺. Musō was important in the development of Japanese Buddhist culture, particularly literature and garden design. He was a dedicated meditation master as well; the monastic rule that he established at Rinsen-ji was one of the earliest such codes in Japan.

Muzhou Daozong 睦州道蹤 (Mu-chou Tao-tsung, Bokujū Dōshō; 8–9th c.; Case 221), also known as Daoming 道明 (Tao-ming, Dōmyō), was a native of Jiangnan 江南; his family name was Chen 陳. After studying the vinaya he entered the assembly under *Huangbo Xiyun*, whose Dharma heir he became. He then lived at Longxing si 龍興寺 in Muzhou 睦州, in present-day Zhejiang 浙江, teaching an assembly of a hundred monks. He later left the monastery and lived in a house with his mother, supporting himself by weaving sandals and thus acquiring the nickname Chen Puxie 陳蒲鞋, "Rush-sandal Chen." He became something of an eccentric recluse, refusing to meet the monks who came for instruction and treating those who persisted with great severity. Among those who knocked on his gate was the great *Yunmen Wenyan*; for the encounter between the two that occasioned Yunmen's enlightenment, see the entry for Yunmen.

N

Nāgārjuna (Longshu 龍樹; Lung-shu, Ryūju; 150–250?; Case 228), one of the greatest Buddhist philosophers, is honored as the fourteenth ancestor of Indian Zen. According to certain of the traditional accounts, he was a South Indian Brahman who became a sage teaching dragons in the mountains (the word *nāgā* means "serpent" or "dragon"; *arjuna* refers to a type of tree). One day he met Kapimala, the thirteenth Indian Zen ancestor, and wondered about the depth of the master's understanding. Kapimala said:

"I know what you are wondering.… Your duty is to renounce the world, not to bother yourself about how much knowledge someone else has." Hearing this, Nāgārjuna confessed his error. Then the Master liberated him and all of his 500 dragon congregation. (Ogata 1990, pp. 25–26)

Later Nāgārjuna traveled about India collecting Mahayana texts; legend has it that he obtained the most profound teachings in caves near the palace of the Dragon King under the sea. His commentaries systematized the śūnyatā philosophy of the *prajñāpāramitā* texts and laid the foundation for the Middle Way doctrine of the Madhyamaka school. He is honored as an ancestor not only of the Zen school but of all the Mahayana schools. Chief among his works is the *Mūla-madhyamaka-kārikā* (*Fundamental Verses on the Middle Way* 中論), which presents the essentials of his thought in twenty-seven chapters.

Nalakūvara (Nazha 那吒, Na-cha, Nata; Cases 46-2, 261) is a legendary figure said to have been the eldest of the five children of the Indian god Vaiśravaṇa. He has five heads and eight arms, is immensely strong, and serves as a tutelary deity of Buddhism. Zen legend has it that he returned his flesh and bones to his parents, then, manifesting his true body, preached the Dharma to them.

Nanpo Jōmyō 南浦紹明 (1235–1309; Cases 61, 225 n.) was a native of Abe 安倍 in Suruga 駿河, present Shizuoka 静岡 Prefecture, Japan; his family name was Fujiwara 藤原. He entered the monkhood at age fifteen and began Zen training at eighteen at Kenchō-ji 建長寺 in Kamakura 鎌倉, present Kanagawa 神奈川 Prefecture. In 1259, after a number of years of practice under the Chinese master Lanxi Daolong 蘭溪道隆 (J., Rankei Dōryū; 1213–78), the founder of Kenchō-ji, he sailed for China to study under *Xutang Zhiyu*. He received Xutang's seal of transmission in 1265 and returned to Kamakura in 1267. In 1270, after several more years of practice with his former teacher Lanxi, he assumed the abbacy of Kōtoku-ji 興徳寺 in the city of Chikuzen 筑前, on the island of Kyūshū 九州. Three years later he became priest of Sōfuku-ji 崇福寺 in nearby Dazaifu 大宰府, and he taught there for thirty-three years. In 1304 he was summoned to Kyoto and, one year later, appointed abbot of Manjū-ji 萬壽寺. In 1308 he moved once again to Kamakura at the request of the shogun to become abbot of Kenchō-ji, where he taught until his death on 8 February 1309. He received the imperial title National Teacher Enzū Daiō 圓通大應國師. Daiō Kokushi, as he is now generally called, was the first of the three masters—Daiō, *Daitō*, and *Kanzan Egen*—who established the Ōtōkan 應燈關 lineage. This lineage, through *Hakuin Ekaku*, presently includes every Rinzai Zen master in Japan.

Nanquan Puyuan 南泉普願 (Nan-ch'üan Pu-yuan, Nansen Fugan; 748–835; Cases 33, 63 n., 68, 78, 79, 90, 103, 104, 110, 115, 123, 133, 145, 193, 209, 212, 241, 272) was a native of Xinzheng 新鄭 in present-day Henan 河南, with the family name Wang 王. He became a novice at the age of nine at Mount Dawei 大隗 in his native province and took full commandments on Mount Song 嵩 at age thirty. He first devoted himself to the study of the vinaya, then investigated the teachings of the *Laṅkāvatara Sutra* and *Avataṁsaka Sutra*. Following this he turned to the Sanlun 三論 school, a doctrinal school based on the Madhyamaka thought of *Nāgārjuna* and his followers. He then began his Zen studies under *Mazu Daoyi*.

In 795, after succeeding to Mazu's Dharma, Puyuan built himself a hermitage on Mount Nanquan 南泉 in Chizhou 池州 and remained on the mountain for the next thirty years. In 828 *Lu Gen*, the governor of Xuancheng 宣城 in the same province, asked the master to teach in the city; Lu maintained his relationship with Puyuan and later become a Dharma successor. A large assembly gathered under Puyuan at his temple, Nanquan yuan 南泉院; among his important successors were *Changsha Jingcen, Zhaozhou Congshen*, and *Zihu Lizong* 子湖 利蹤 (c. 800–880).

In one story Puyuan is said to have visited the home of a nearby aristocrat. The evening before the master arrived the local earth deity informed the lord of Puyuan's imminent visit, so the lord made preparations. When Nanquan learned how the lord had found out about his coming, he lamented, "Because I lack power in my practice, the gods and demons spy on me."

The *Jingde-Era Record of the Transmission of the Lamp* describes the time of Puyuan's death as follows:

> When the Master was about to die, the head monk asked him, "Your Reverence, a hundred years from now where will you be?" "I shall be a water buffalo at the foot of the hill," said the Master. "Will it be all right for me to follow you?" asked the head monk. "If you follow me, you must hold a stalk of grass in your mouth," was [Puyuan's] reply.
>
> At daybreak on the morning of the 27th of January, 835, the Master said to his disciples, "The star has been fading and the lamp growing dim for a long time. Do not say that I came or went." His words ceased, and he passed away. He was in his eighty-seventh year. (Miura and Sasaki 1966, pp. 273–74; T 51:259a–b)

Nantang Yuanjing 南堂元靜 (Nan-t'ang Yüan-ching, Nandō Genjō; 1065–1135; Cases 40, 63) was a native of Yushan 玉山 in Langzhou 閬州, modern Sichuan 四川. At the age of ten he became seriously ill, which awoke in him the desire to become a monk. He entered the temple Baosheng yuan 寶生院 in Chengdu 成都, Sichuan, and in 1088 received full ordination. He then traveled south on pilgrimage. He trained for a time under a Zen master named Yong'an En 永安恩, then joined the assembly under *Wuzu Fayan*. After receiving transmission from Fayan he went to Mount Dasui 大隨 in Pengzhou 彭州, also in the province of Sichuan, and there established the temple Nantang 南堂. He later served as priest at such important temples as Zhaojue si 照覺寺 and Nengren si 能仁寺 in Chengdu.

Nanyang Huizhong 南陽慧忠 (Nan-yang Hui-chung, Nan'yō Echū; 675–775; Cases 31, 238, 267) was a native of Yuezhou 越州, in present-day Zhejiang 浙江; his family name was Ran 冉. When he was sixteen he joined the community at

Caoxi 曹溪 under *Huineng*, the Sixth Patriarch, and eventually succeeded to Huineng's Dharma. Following Huineng's death he left on an extended pilgrimage to various Buddhist sites that eventually took him to Mount Baiya 白崖 in Nanyang 南陽, in present-day Henan 河南. There he practiced for over forty years in the Dangzi Valley 党子谷, never descending the mountain until summoned to the imperial court in Chang'an by Emperor Suzong 肅宗 in 761. In the capital, Nanyang resided at the subtemple Xichan yuan 西禪院 of Qianfu si 千福寺. Later Emperor Daizong 代宗 established the temple Guangzhai si 光宅寺 for his use and conferred upon him the honorary title National Teacher Liangdi 兩帝國師, "National Teacher of Two Emperors." He is considered one of the five great disciples of Huineng, together with *Nanyue Huairang, Yongjia Xuanjue*, Heze Shenhui 荷澤神會 (670–762), and Qingyuan Xingsi 青原行思 (d. 740). One of the best-known stories relating to Nanyang, related in *Blue Cliff Record* 18 and the *Jingde-Era Record of the Transmission of the Lamp,* concerns his request to Emperor Daizong to build him a "seamless tower" following his death:

> When he felt his death approaching National Teacher Huizhong paid a visit to Emperor Daizong. The emperor asked, "After your nirvana, how can I, your disciple, honor your memory?" The teacher said, "Build me a seamless tower." The emperor said, "Tell me, how should such a monument look?"
>
> Nanyang said nothing. After a time he asked, "Do you understand?" The emperor said, "I don't understand." Nanyang said, "After I have gone please ask my attendant, Danyuan. He understands this matter well."… [After the National Teacher's death on the ninth day of the twelfth month of 775,] Emperor Daizong called Danyuan to the court and asked him about Nanyang's comment. Danyuan was silent for a time, then asked, "Do you understand?" The emperor said, "I don't understand." Danyuan recited a verse:

> South of Xiang, north of Tan;
> In between, gold fills the entire land.
> Beneath a shadowless tree, ferry boats;
> In the crystal palace there is no knowing. (T 51:245a)

Nanyuan Huiyong 南院慧顒 (Nan-yüan Hui-yung, Nan'in Egyō; ca. 860–930; Cases 185, 192 n., 197), also known as Baoying 寶應, was a native of Hebei 河北. He was a successor of *Xinghua Cunjiang*, one of the few Dharma heirs of *Linji Yixuan*. His name derives from the fact that he taught at the Nanyuan 南院 ("South Hall") temple in Ruzhou 汝州. Otherwise little is known of his life. The teachings of the Linji lineage were transmitted through him and his only successor, *Fengxue Yanzhao*.

Nanyue Huairang 南嶽懷讓 (Nan-yüeh Huai-jang, Nangaku Ejō; 677–744; Cases 53, 118, 139, 206 n., 234) was a native of Jinzhou 金州, present Shandong 山東; his lay name was Du 杜. He left home at the age of fifteen to join the assembly under Honjing 弘景, a vinaya master at the temple Yuquan si 玉泉寺 in Jingzhou 荊州, modern Hubei 湖北. Later he went to Mount Song 嵩, also in Jingzhou, to study under *Songshan Hui'an*, one of the great disciples of the Fifth Patriarch, *Hongren*. On Hui'an's advice he went to the Sixth Patriarch, *Huineng*, and had the exchange related in Case 118. As the teacher of *Mazu Daoyi* and the ancestor of the lineage that gave rise to the Linji school, he is regarded as one of Huineng's two most historically important successors, together with Qingyuan Xingsi 青原行思 (d. 740), whose lineage gave rise to the Caodong school. From 713 he resided at the temple Bore si 般若寺 on Mount Nanyue 南嶽. A famous example of his teaching style is seen in Case 139.

Niaoke Daolin 鳥窠道林 (Niao-k'o Tao-lin, Chōka Dōrin; 741–824; Case 215) was a native of Fuyangxian 富陽縣 in Hangzhou 杭州, present Zhejiang 浙江; his family name was Pan 潘. He became a novice at age nine, and at twenty-one received the full precepts at the temple Guoyuan si 果願寺 in Jingzhou 荊州, modern Hubei 湖北. Subsequently he went to Chang'an, where he studied the *Avataṃsaka Sutra* and the *Treatise on Awakening Faith in the Mahayana* 大乘 起信論. He then practiced Zen under the Niutou (Oxhead) 牛頭 school master Jingshan Faqin 徑山法欽 (714–92). After succeeding to Faqin's Dharma he went to the temple Zouwang si 奏望寺, north of West Lake 西湖 in Hangzhou, where he lived in a large pine tree with spreading branches, thus acquiring the nickname Niaoke 鳥窠 ("Bird-nest"). The exchange recorded in Case 215 is the most famous episode involving Daolin.

P

Pang Yun 龐蘊 (P'ang Yün, Hō On; d. 808; Cases 23, 66, 85, 86), generally known as Pang Jushi 龐居士 (P'ang Chü-shih; Hō Koji), meaning "Layman Pang." His style was Daoxuan 道玄. Pang was born in Hengyang 衡陽, Hunan 湖南, to a family famed for its Confucian scholarship. He married and had children but soon realized the futility of worldly ambitions. Loading his possessions on a boat, he sank it and left home with his daughter to follow a religious life. He remained a layman, supporting himself as a maker of bambooware that his daughter sold in nearby villages. He first trained in Zen under *Shitou Xiqian*, to whom he expressed his understanding in one of the most famous poems in Zen:

> My daily activities are not unusual, I'm just naturally in harmony with them. Grasping nothing, discarding nothing, in every place there's no hindrance, no conflict…. My supernatural power and marvelous activity—drawing water and carrying firewood. (Sasaki, Iriya, and Fraser 1971, p. 46)

He later set out with his friend *Danxia Tianran* to visit *Mazu Daoyi*, who accepted him as a disciple while telling Danxia to see Shitou Xiqian. Pang practiced at Mazu's monastery for two years; his deep awakening under Mazu is described in *Kattōshū* Case 23. Pang later visited various masters; many of his exchanges with them form famous koans. After Pang moved north with his daughter to Xiangyang 襄陽 in present-day Hubei 湖北 he became friends with the prefect *Yu Di*. Pang was an accomplished Zen poet, and many of his verses have been preserved.

Pei Xiu 裴休 (P'ei Hsiu, Hi Kyū; 797–870; Case 32), a government official and famous Buddhist lay devotee, was born, according to some accounts, in the province of Shanxi 山西; others have his native place as Henan 河南. His style was Gongmei 公美. He served in a number of government posts, including that of governor of several districts. His first Zen teacher was Guifeng Zongmi 圭峰宗密 (780–841), fifth ancestor of the Heze 荷澤 school of Zen. After Pei was appointed governor of Zhongling 鍾陵 he met *Huangbo Xiyun*; in 842 he became the master's disciple and, eventually, his Dharma successor. He constructed for Xiyun a temple in the mountains of Gao'an 高安 in Hongzhou 洪州, and he later compiled the *Essentials of Transmitting the Mind* 傳心法要, a record of Huangbo's teachings. Pei was active in helping his Buddhist friends, including Huangbo, *Gui-shan Lingyou*, and Huangbo's disciple Qianqing Chu'nan 千頃楚南 (813–88), during the great persecution of Buddhism in 845 under Emperor Wuzong 武宗 (r. 814–46). It is said that in his devotion to Buddhism he took no meat or wine, wore a Buddhist robe instead of the usual official dress, and went out on mendicancy rounds among the taverns and houses of the singing girls.

Piyun 披雲 (P'i-yün, Hiun; 8th c.; Case 131). Nothing is known of this figure other than what is mentioned in koans. His actions indicate that he was senior to *Magu Baotie*, or a master of equal standing.

Q

Qianfeng. See *Yuezhou Qianfeng*.

Qingliang Taiqin 清涼泰欽 (Ch'ing-liang Tai-ch'in, Shōryō Taikin; d. 974; Case 67) was a native of Weifu 魏府, present Hebei 河北. He studied Zen under *Fayan Wenyi*; after succeeding to his Dharma he resided at Shuanglin yuan 雙林院 in Hongzhou 洪州, then at Qingliang si 清涼寺 in Jinling 金陵. His posthumous title was Zen Master Fadeng 法燈禪師.

Qingshui 清稅 (Ch'ing-shui, Seizei; ca. 9–10th c.; Case 111). Nothing is known of this figure.

Qingsu 清素 (Ch'ing-su, Seiso; 11th c.; Case 140). Little is known of Qingsu other than the fact that he served as *Shishuang Chuyuan*'s attendant for thirteen years, receiving Dharma transmission but never becoming a teacher.

Qinshan Wensui 欽山文邃 (Ch'in-shan Wen-sui, Kinzan Bunsui; 9th c.; Case 256) was a native of Fuzhou 福州 in modern Fujian 福建. While still young he entered the temple on Mount Daci 大慈 in present-day Zhejiang 浙江 to study under Daci Huanzhong 大慈寰中 (780–862), a disciple of *Baizhang Huaihai*. At the temple he met *Yantou Quanhuo* and *Xuefeng Yicun*, still monks in training at the time, who recognized Qinshan as a vessel of the Dharma and included him on their subsequent pilgrimages. Many of the stories that remain of their travels have become koans (e.g., Case 256). The three eventually entered the assembly under *Deshan Xuanjian* on Mount De 德 in Hunan 湖南. Although Yantou and Xuefeng flourished under Deshan's strict training, Qinshan could not break through and subsequently entered the community of *Dongshan Liangjie*, whose Dharma successor he became. From the age of twenty-seven Qinshan taught on Mount Qin 欽 in Nongzhou 濃州.

R

Ruiyan Shiyan 瑞巖師彥 (Jui-yen Shih-yen, Zuigan Shigen; ca. 9th c.; Case 11) was a native of Minyue 閩越 in Fujian 福建; his family name was Xu 許. He received ordination at a very young age and was known as a strict follower of the precepts. Little is known of him other than the fact that he was a Dharma heir of *Yantou Quanhuo*. After finishing his training under Yantou he resided at Ruiyan yuan 瑞巖院 in Taizhou 臺州.

S

Śākyamuni (Shijiamouni 釋迦牟尼, Shih-chia-mou-ni, Shakamuni; ca. 5th c. BCE; Cases [including references to "the Buddha"] 3, 17 n., 28-2 n., 34 n., 38, 47, 48, 62 n., 70, 72, 79 n., 87 n., 95, 108, 112, 113 n., 114, 124, 133, 135, 136, 137, 140, 141, 164 n., 165, 170, 171 n., 177 n., 204, 213 n., 223 n., 224, 225 n., 232, 235 n., 247, 250, 254 n., 255 n., 267, 270-1 n.). Śākyamuni, a name meaning "the sage of the Śakya clan," was the historical Buddha. According to the traditional Zen histories, he was born to King Suddhodana of Kapilavastu, a city in what is now southern Nepal, and given the name Siddhārtha Gautama. He grew up in sheltered circumstances, married at sixteen, and had a son, but at the age of twenty-nine he left the palace to live as a homeless seeker after awakening to the suffering of worldly existence. He practiced under the meditation teachers Arada Kalama and Udraka Ramaputra without attaining his goal of liberation, then turned to extreme asceticism. Finally, at the age of thirty-five, after years of ascetic practices had left him too weak to walk, he restored his strength with milk received from a milkmaid, sat under the Bodhi-tree, and vowed to meditate until he attained liberation. Finally, on the morning of the eighth day (some accounts say on the forty-ninth day), he saw the morning star and realized full enlightenment. From that time on he lived a peripatetic lifestyle, teaching the truth he had realized and guiding the growing number of followers who constituted the sangha. He died at the age of eighty after eating tainted food.

Samantabhadra (Puxian 普賢, P'u-hsien, Fugen; Cases 12 n., 17 n., 181 n., 191 n., 198, 212, 231, 236), "The One of All-Pervading Beneficence." One of the most important of the legendary Mahayana bodhisattvas, Samantabhadra is the guardian of the Dharma and symbolizes the function—the teaching and practice—of the buddha. He is often depicted riding on an elephant and shown together with Mañjuśrī, the Bodhisattva of Marvelous Wisdom.

Sansheng Huiran 三聖慧然 (San-sheng Hui-jan, Sanshō Enen; 9th c.; Cases 123, 195, 272) was a Dharma heir of *Linji Yixuan*; after Linji's death he visited *Yangshan Huiji, Deshan Xuanjian*, and *Xuefeng Yicun*. Little else is known of him. He is traditionally regarded as the compiler of the *Record of Linji*, and in his later life he resided at Sansheng yuan 三聖院 in Zhenzhou 鎮州, in present Hebei 河北.

Śariputra (Shelifu 舍利弗, She-li-fu, Sharihotsu; Case 228) was one of the Ten Great Disciples of *Śākyamuni* and was renowned as the greatest in wisdom. He is said to have been the son of a brāhman family in the village of Nālaka, north of Rājagriha, and was friends from childhood with *Maudgalyāyana*. He and Maudgalyāyana joined the followers of the sceptic philosopher Sanjaya Belatthiputta, but they became Śākyamuni's disciples (together with 250 of Sanjaya's disciples) after Śariputra met the Buddha's student Aśvajit and heard the doctrine of causation. Śariputra and Maudgalyāyana were regarded as the greatest among the sangha; Śariputra in particular was skilled in understanding and explaining the Dharma teachings. Śariputra died of illness shortly before the death of the Buddha himself.

Sengcan 僧璨 (Seng-ts'an; Sōsan; d. 606?; Case 229) is traditionally honored as the Third Patriarch of Chinese Zen, but little reliable information exists on his life. The traditional biographies say that he was a layman already in midlife when he first met the Second Patriarch *Huike* and that after receiving ordination and Dharma transmission he resided on Mount Sikong 司空 in Shuzhou 舒州, in present-day Anhui 安徽. As a result of the Buddhist suppression by Emperor Wu in 574 he went to Mount Wangong 皖公 in the same province and secluded himself there for more than ten years. After transmitting the Dharma to Daoxin 道信 (580–651), who became the Fourth Patriarch, he retired to Mount Luofu 羅浮 in present Guangdong 廣東 for the final three years of his life. Zen legend has it that he died standing up, grasping the branch of a tree. Sengcan is traditionally regarded as the author of the Zen poem *On Believing in Mind* 信心銘, although modern scholarship regards this as unlikely.

Sengzhao 僧肇 (Seng-chao, Sōjō; 374/78–414; Case 81 n.), one of the greatest Chinese monks of the period when Buddhism was taking root in China, was a native of the capital city of Chang'an. His family being poor, he worked as a scribe from the time he was young, bringing him into contact with the Chinese literary tradition. Although he greatly admired the Confucian and Taoist writings, he immediately recognized the superiority of Buddhism when he read the *Vimalakīrti Sutra*. He therefore became a Buddhist monk and devoted himself to the study of the scriptures, taking a deep interest in Buddhist philosophy.

He later journeyed to the central Asian kingdom of Liang 涼 to study under the great Kuchan translator-scholar monk Kumārajīva (Jiumoluoshi 鳩摩羅什; 359–409), under whom he studied the Madhyamaka philosophy of *Nāgārjuna*.

He accompanied Kumārajīva when the latter was brought to Chang'an in 402 by Yao Xing 姚興 (366–416), ruler of the Later Qin 後秦 dynasty (384–417), and became a leading member of the large group that helped Kumārajīva in his translation work. After a time Sengzhao started producing original treatises of his own, including a collection known as the *Zhao's Treatises* 肇論, the most important treatise in which is *Prajñā Is Not Knowledge* 般若無知論. This treatise, highly praised by Kumārajīva and such Chinese Buddhist thinkers as *Huiyuan*, interpreted, in Chinese intellectual terms, the Mahayana concept of *prajñā* and the Middle Way of Nāgārjuna. There is a Zen tradition that Sengzhao had to kill himself on the order of the ruler Yao Xing but begged a week of grace in order to write a work called the *Baozang lun* 寶藏論; the tradition appears to be spurious and the treatise apocryphal.

Although Sengzhao was not a member of the Zen school, in several of his treatises he speaks of the importance of an intuitive awakening to the ineffable truth, and his affinity for the standpoint of Zen is obvious. His work has always been deeply admired by Zen masters, and his words appear in several koans.

Shangu 山谷 (Shan-ku, Sankoku; 1050–1110; Case 18) is the style of the poet Huang Tingjian 黄庭堅 (Huang T'ing-chien, Kō Teiken). Giles says:

> A native of…Kiangsi, who graduated as *chin shih* and entered the public service, rising to high office in the Imperial Academy and Grand Secretariat. When his mother was seized with illness, he watched her for a whole year without leaving her bedside or even taking off his clothes; and at her death he mourned so bitterly that he himself fell ill and nearly lost his life. For this he has been placed among the twenty-four examples of filial piety. In consequence of his fearless tongue his official career was somewhat chequered; but he was greatly distinguished as a poet and calligraphist, and was ranked as one of the Four Great Scholars of the empire… He was fond of Buddhist speculations, and gave himself the sobriquet of 山谷道人 [Shangu Daoren]. (1939, pp. 338–39)

Shending Hongyin 神鼎洪諲 (Shen-ting Hong-yin, Shintei Kōin; 10–11th c.; Case 174) was a native of Xiangzhou 襄州, modern Hubei 湖北; his family name was Hu 扈. After receiving ordination he entered the assembly under *Shoushan Shengnian* and eventually succeeded to his Dharma. He later resided on Mount Shending 神鼎 in Tanzhou 潭州, in present Hunan 湖南.

Shexian Guixing 葉縣歸省 (She-hsien Kuei-hsing, Sekken Kisei; 10–11th c.; Case 134) was a native of Jizhou 冀州 in present Hebei 河北; his family name was Jia 賈. He became a monk and took the full precepts at the temple Baoshou yuan 保壽院 in Yizhou 易州. Later he embarked on a long pilgrimage south, eventually joining the assembly under the Linji master *Shoushan Shengnian* in Ruzhou 汝州, part of modern Hebei 河北. After receiving transmission from Shoushan he resided at the temple Guangjiao yuan 廣教院 on Mount Bao'an 寶安, also in Ruzhou.

Shishuang Chuyuan 石霜楚圓 (Shih-shuang Ch'u-yüan, Sekisō Soen; 986–1039; Cases 25, 106, 140, 146, 147, 156, 172, 173, 174, 183-1, 183-2, 189, 245), commonly referred to in Zen texts by his posthumous title Ciming 慈明 (Tz'u-ming, Jimyō), was a native of Quanzhou 全州 in what is presently Guangxi 廣西; his family name was Li 李. At the age of twenty-two he became a monk at the temple Yinjing si 隱靜寺 on Mount Xiang 湘, and he later joined the assembly under *Fenyang Shanzhao*. For two years Fenyang refused to let Shishuang into his room for instruction and constantly berated him. When finally Shishuang complained, Fenyang berated him even more severely; when Shishuang tried to respond, the master put his hand over Shishuang's mouth. With this Shishuang had a deep awakening. He stayed with Fenyang for another seven years. Although Shishuang was somewhat eccentric in his behavior he is said to have been an exceptionally serious practitioner. According to the *Encouraging Study of the Zen Barriers* 禪關策進, Shishuang trained day and night, jabbing himself in the leg with an awl whenever he felt sleepy during evening meditation. His devotion earned him the nickname "Lion of West River."

After receiving Dharma transmission, Shishuang served as abbot of a number of temples, including Guangli yuan 廣利院 on Mount Nanyuan 南源, Chongsheng si 崇勝寺 on Mount Shishuang 石霜, Fuyan yuan 福巖院 on Mount Nanyue 南嶽, and Xinghua yuan 興化院 in Tanzhou 潭州. Although Shishuang died at the relatively young age of fifty-three, he was an extremely influential teacher who left over fifty Dharma heirs. Of special importance for Zen history are *Yangqi Fanghui* and *Huanglong Huinan*, who started the Yangqi and Huanglong teaching lines, the two main traditions of Linji Zen.

Shishuang Qingzhu 石霜慶諸 (Shih-shuang Ch'ing-chu, Sekisō Keisho; 807–88; Cases 25 n., 69, 161, 220 n.) was a native of Xinkan 新嫌 in Jizhou 吉州, present Jiangxi 江西; his family name was Chen 陳. At age thirteen he became a monk under Xishan Shaojian 西山紹鑑 in Hongzhou 洪州, present Jiangxi, and at twenty-three he took the full precepts at Mount Song 嵩嶽. After studying the vinaya he went to the monasteries of *Guishan Lingyou* on Mount Gui 潙 and *Daowu Yuanzhi* on Mount Daowu 道吾. After succeeding to Daowu's Dharma he lived unknown among the ordinary people. Finally he was sought out by *Dongshan Liangjie* and persuaded to serve as the second abbot of the temple Chongsheng si 崇勝寺 on Mount Shishuang 石霜, following Daci Huanzhong 大慈寰中 (780–862). Shishuang taught the Dharma there for over twenty years, with a special stress on the approach to practice that came to be known as "silent illumination Zen" 默照禪. Shishuang's monks, instructed never to lie down, sat for so long every day that, it is said, they resembled rows of dead tree stumps. "Cease and stop," he taught. "One thought—ten-thousand years. Be like a cold incense burner in an abandoned temple." The austerity of Shishuang's style of Zen reflected the simplicity of his life. When the Tang emperor Xizong

僖宗 (r. 874–89), hearing of the master, attempted to confer upon him a purple robe, Shishuang declined the honor.

Shishuang Xingkong 石霜性空 (Shih-shuang Hsing-k'ung, Sekisō Shōkū; n.d.; Case 65). Little is known of the life of this figure, other than that he was a Dharma successor of *Baizhang Huaihai* and that he resided on Mount Shishuang 石霜 in Tanzhou 潭州, present Hunan 湖南.

Shitou Xiqian 石頭希遷 (Shih-t'ou Hsi-ch'ien, Sekitō Kisen; 700–791; Cases 125 n., 272), one of the central figures in the development of Chinese Zen, was a native of Gaoyao 高要 in Duanzhou 端州, present Guangdong 廣東; his family name was Chen 陳. He is described in the traditional literature as an unusually self-assured child who would destroy shrines to the malevolent deities worshipped in his region and release the oxen offered for sacrifice. At the age of twelve he went to nearby Caoxi 曹溪 and met the Sixth Patriarch, *Huineng*, under whom he became a monk and practiced meditation until the great master's death the following year (713). In 728 he took the full commandments on Mount Luofu 羅浮 in present Guangdong, and soon afterward went to Mount Qingyuan 青原 in Jizhou 吉州, present Jiangxi 江西, to join the assembly under Huineng's Dharma heir Qingyuan Xingsi 青原行思 (d. 740). Upon Shitou's appearance, Qingyuan commented, "Though horned creatures in my assembly are many, one unicorn is enough" (the unicorn in China is an auspicious creature whose appearance foretells an extraordinary event). In 742, after receiving Qingyuan's sanction, Shitou went to reside at the temple Nan si 南寺, on Mount Heng 衡, part of Mount Nanyue 南嶽 in Hunan 湖南. On top of a large flat rock to the east of the temple he built a hermitage where he sat in meditation, thus acquiring his name Shitou, meaning "on top of the rock." Shitou taught there until 764, when he went to Liangduan 梁端 in Tanzhou 潭州, in present Hunan. Some sources indicate that he later returned to Mount Heng. Shitou left a number of important heirs, foremost among whom were Yaoshan Weiyen 藥山惟儼 (745/50–828/34) and *Tianhuang Daowu*. From his line arose three of the Five Houses of Chinese Zen: the Caodong 曹洞, Yunmen 雲門, and Fayan 法眼. The nature of Shitou's teachings can be seen in the following passage:

> This very Mind, just this is Buddha. Mind, Buddha and sentient beings, perfect wisdom and the defiling passions—these are but different names for one and the same substance. All of you must know your own Mind-essence, know that its substance is apart from extinction and permanence, and that its nature is neither stained nor pure; know that it is absolutely still and completely whole, and that [in it] secular and sacred are exactly the same; know that its responding to circumstances is limitless, and that it is apart from mind and consciousness. The Three Worlds and the Six Ways [of Transmigration] are only appearances [produced by] your own mind, like reflections of the moon in water, or images seen in a mirror. How can [this Mind] be subject to birth and death? If you know this well, you will lack for nothing. (Miura and Sasaki 1966, p. 301)

Shoukuo 守廓 (Shou-k'uo, Shukaku; ca. 9–10th c.; Case 205) was the personal attendant of *Xinghua Cunjiang* and succeeded to his Dharma. He appears in several koans; otherwise little is known of him.

Shoushan Shengnian 首山省念 (Shou-shan Sheng-nien, Shuzan Shōnen; 926–93; Cases 58, 124, 133 n., 134, 270-1, 270-2) was a native of Laizhou 萊州 in what is presently Shandong 山東; his family name was Di 狄. After becoming a monk at a local temple named Nanchan yuan 南禪院 he entered the assembly under *Fengxue Yanzhao* at the temple Guanghui si 廣慧寺 in Yingzhou 郢州. At the time Fengxue was convinced that with him (Fengxue) the Dharma lineage of Linji was destined to come to an end. When he expressed this conviction to Shoushan one day, the latter asked if he had no disciples worthy of succeeding him. Fengxue replied that, despite the great capabilities of some of his students, none had yet seen self-nature. Shoushan suggested that he pursue the matter further. The ensuing incident, in which Fengxue recognized Shoushan's understanding, is recorded in Case 124.

Shoushan subsequently went to the district of Ruzhou 汝州 and lived on Mount Shou 首, from which he derived his name. Later he served as abbot at the temple Guangjiao yuan 廣教院 on Mount Bao'an 寶安, in modern Hebei 河北. Although Shoushan does not stand out like the giants of Tang-dynasty Zen, it was in large part through him that the Linji-school lineage survived the turbulent period that followed the end of the Tang period.

Shouzhou Liangsui 壽州良遂 (Shou-chou Liang-sui, Jushū Ryōsui; n.d.; Case 167). Little is known of Shouzhou other than the fact that he was a successor of *Magu Baotie* and was active as a Zen master in the Shouzhou 壽州 region of present-day Anhui 安徽.

Shuangshan Yuan 雙杉元 (Shuang-shan Yüan, Sōsan Gen; n.d.; Case 30) was from Fuzhou 福州 in present-day Fujian 福建; his family name was Zheng 鄭. He succeeded to the Dharma of a certain Yinjing Zhirou 隱靜致柔 in the lineage of *Mian Xianjie*.

Shūhō Myōchō 宗峰妙超 (1282–1338; Cases 107, 144, 169, 225), best known by his title Daitō Kokushi 大燈國師, was a Japanese monk born in Harima 播磨 (present-day Osaka 大阪); his family name was Urakami 浦上. He was ordained at Enkyō-ji 圓鏡寺 on Mount Shosha 書寫 at age eleven and studied Tendai doctrine. In 1301 he became a student of Kōhō Kennichi 高峰顯日 (1241–1316) at Manju-ji 萬壽寺 in Kamakura, then in 1304 began practice under *Nanpo Jōmyō* in Kyoto. He accompanied Nanpo to Kamakura when the master was appointed abbot of Kenchō-ji 建長寺 in 1308. Just ten days after arriving there Myōchō had a breakthrough with "Yunmen's 'Barrier,'" Case 8 of the *Blue Cliff Record*.

After Nanpo died several months later Shūhō returned to Kyoto and commenced the "twenty years of practice" that Nanpo had enjoined upon him after his enlightenment. Zen legend has it that he spent this time living with the beggars under the Gojō 五条 Bridge near the center of the city and that Emperor

Hanazono 花園 (r. 1308–18), deciding to find him, went to the area and started handing out melons. When he saw an unusual looking beggar he said, "Take this melon without using your hands." "Give it to me without using your hands," the beggar replied, and the emperor knew this was Shūhō. The historical facts are rather less romantic. Although Shūhō's "twenty years of practice" would have lasted until 1328 after his departure from Kamakura in 1308, it is known that already in 1316 he was lecturing before Emperor Hanazono. Shūhō's years of seclusion were spent primarily at the small temples Ungo-ji 雲居寺 and Daitoku-ji 大德寺 in Kyoto.

In 1325 a great debate, known as the Shōchū 正中 Debate, was held between representatives of the older established sects and the Zen school. Shūhō's performance on this occasion is said to have been so compelling that his chief opponent, a Tendai monk named Gen'e 幻惠 (d. 1350), converted to Zen and became Shūhō's student.

Daitoku-ji was enlarged for Shūhō with the support of both Emperor Go-Daigo 後醍醐 (r. 1318–39) and the Cloistered Emperor Hanazono (now Shūhō's disciple). Shūhō resided at Daitoku-ji and taught there for the rest of his life, lecturing also at the imperial court. Shūhō had never been able to sit in the full lotus position because of a crippled leg, but at the end of his life he forced himself into the position, breaking his leg and staining his robe with blood. He died in the sitting posture after writing the following poem:

The Blown Hair [Sword] is always burnished.
When the wheel of free activity turns,
The empty void gnashes its teeth.
                (Miura and Sasaki 1966, p. 234)

Shūhō was second in the Ōtōkan 應燈關 lineage, after his teacher Nanpo Jōmyō (Daiō Kokushi 大應國師) and prior to his disciple Kanzan Egen 關山慧玄 (see p. 10, above). This lineage includes every Rinzai Zen master in Japan today.

Shui'an Shiyi 水庵師一 (Shui-an Shih-i, Sui'an Shi'ichi; 1107–76; Case 109) was a native of Dongyang 東陽 in Wuzhou 婺州, in modern Zhejiang 浙江; his lay name was Ma 馬. After receiving ordination as a monk at age sixteen he trained in Zen under the Caodong master Huizhao Qingyu 慧照慶預 (1078–1140) and the Yangqi-line Linji master Shanguo Yue'an 善果月庵 (1079–1152) before joining the assembly under Fozhi Duanyu 佛智端裕 (1085–1150) at Xichan si 西禪寺. After succeeding to Fozhi's Dharma he taught at Ciyun si 慈雲寺 and a succession of other temples.

Shushan Guangren 疎山光仁 (Shu-shan Kuang-jen, Sozan Kōnin; 837–909; Cases 32, 132), also known as Shushan Kuangren 疎山匡仁 (Su-shan K'uang-jen, Sozan Kyōnin), was a native of Ganyang 淦陽 in Luling 廬陵, in present-day Jiangxi 江西; his lay name was Li 李. He studied doctrine at Donglin si 東林寺 on Mount Lu 廬 but became dissatisfied and set out on a pilgrimage that took him to *Xianglin Chengyuan* before he finally joined the assembly under *Dongshan Liangjie*.

After Dongshan's death Shushan visited a number of famous Zen masters, including *Guishan Lingyou*, *Yunmen Wenyan*, and *Jiashan Shanhui*, then went to Mount Su 疎 in Fuzhou 撫州, in present Jiangxi, where he spent the rest of his life.

Shushan was short, earning him the disparaging nickname "Uncle Dwarf" 矮師叔, but he is said to have had a keen mind, eloquent tongue, and perceptive eye. Several of the stories about him display a cunning side to his personality, such as the following one, related in the entry on Caoshan Benji in the *Biographies of Monks of the Zen School* 禪林僧寶傳:

> Knowing that Dongshan was about to transmit his Dharma to Benji, Uncle Dwarf secretly crawled under the Master's rope-bottomed chair…. Dongshan was unaware of this. At midnight the Master handed to Benji the Jeweled-mirror Samadhi, the Secret of the Five Ranks, and the Three Kinds of Leakage, previously given him by his master Yunyan Tansheng. When the transmission was completed, Benji bowed twice and hurried out. Uncle Dwarf now stuck out his head and bawled, "Dongshan's Zen is in the palm of my hand!" Dongshan was greatly astonished, and said, "Stealing the Dharma by using the dirtiest of means will avail you nothing." (Miura and Sasaki 1966, pp. 286–87; adapted. x 79:492b)

Shushan nevertheless became a genuine heir of Dongshan, listed in all of the lineage charts. As a teacher himself he produced four Dharma heirs.

Sixin Wuxin 死心悟新 (Ssu-hsin Wu-hsin, Shishin Goshin; 1043–1114; Case 18) was a native of Qujiang 曲江 in present Guangdong 廣東; his family name was Huang 黃. He entered the temple Fotuo yuan 佛陀院 as a youth and studied under a priest named Dexiu 德修 (n.d.). Later he went on pilgrimage, and in 1075 he joined the assembly at Huanglong si 黃龍寺 under *Huitang Zuxin*, in the Huanglong 黃龍 line of Linji Zen. While on pilgrimage he heard a clap of thunder and was enlightened; returning to Huitang, he said, "Everyone in the world has attained Zen, they just haven't realized it." After succeeding to Huitang's Dharma, Wuxin remained at Huanglong si for some time, then left again on pilgrimage. He lectured at Yunyan si 雲巖寺 in 1092, then moved to Cuiyan si 翠巖寺 in 1097. In 1111 he returned to Huanglong si, where he died three years later.

Songshan Hui'an 嵩山慧安 (Sung-shan Hui-an, Sūzan Ean; 582–709; Case 118), also known as Lao'an 老安, Dao'an 道安, or Da'an 大安, was one of the sixteen great disciples of the Fifth Patriarch, *Hongren*. A native of Zhijiang 支江 in Jingzhou 荊州, modern Hubei 湖北, his lay name was Wei 衛. It is said that during a large irrigation project in the early seventh century Huian managed to save many workers on the verge of starvation by begging food for them. Emperor Yang 煬 (r. 605–18) summoned him to the court, but Hui'an avoided the honor by moving to Mount Taihe 太和. During the Zhenguan 貞觀 era (627–49) he studied under Hongren and eventually succeeded to his Dharma. He was summoned by Emperor Gaozong 高宗 (r. 650–83), but he went instead to Mount Song 嵩 in

Jingzhou. There he remained, teaching the many students who gathered around him, including *Nanyue Huairang*. In 706 Emperor Zhongzong 中宗 (r. 705–10) honored him with a purple robe. He died in 709 at the age of 127.

Songyuan Chongyue 松源崇嶽 (Sung-yüan Ch'ung-yüeh, Shōgen Sūgaku; 1132–1202; Cases 95, 142, 207-2, 228) was a native of Longquan 龍泉 in Chuzhou 處州, modern Zhejiang 浙江; his family name was Wu 吳. Although he wished to become a monk from the time he was a child, it was only at the age of twenty-three that he entered the temple Daming si 大明寺 and took the five novice precepts. At first he studied under a certain Lingshi Miao 靈石妙, then sought instruction from *Dahui Zonggao* and *Ying'an Tanhua*. In 1163 he was ordained at Bailian Jingshe 白蓮精舍, then visited various teachers in the region. Following further study under the Dahui-line master Muan Anyong 木庵安永 (?–1173) in Min 閩, he entered the monastery of *Mian Xianjie* at Mount Xi 西 in Zhejiang, and eventually succeeded to that master's Dharma. He first lectured at Chengzhao Chanyuan 澄照禪院 in Pingjiangfu 平江府, modern Jiangsu 江蘇. He subsequently resided in a number of important temples and was the founder of Xianqin Baoci si 顯親報慈寺.

Sudhana (Shancai Tongzi 善財童子, Shan-ts'ai T'ung-tzu, Zenzai Dōshi; Cases 88 n., 89, 201) is the legendary hero of the "Chapter on Entering the Dharma Realm" 入法界品 and "Chapter on the Activities of Samantabhadra" 普賢菩薩行品 of the *Avataṁsaka Sutra*, which are among the most popular Buddhist writings in East Asia. They describe the epic search for enlightenment by Sudhana, who, under the guidance of the bodhisattva Mañjuśrī, visits fifty-three teachers. His pilgrimage finally takes him to the bodhisattva Maitreya, who is to be the buddha of the future. Maitreya finds him worthy to enter the tower of Vairocana Buddha (buddha as a manifestation of the dharmakāya), where Sudhana experiences all of the various Dharma realms (dharmadhatu). Sudhana is finally brought to the full realization of bodhisattvahood through the teaching of Samantabhadra Bodhisattva.

T

Taihang Kebin 太行克賓 (T'ai-hang K'o-pin, Taikō Kokuhin; ca. 9th c.; Case 130) was a Dharma heir of *Xinghua Cunjiang*. While under Xinghua he served as *weina* 維那, the monk in charge of supervising the personnel and work of the monastery. After training under Xinghua he resided on Mount Taihang 太行 for a time, then returned to Xinghua's temple to serve as his successor.

Taizong 太宗 (T'ai-tsung, Taisō; 939–97; Case 260), also known as Zhao Kuangyi 趙匡儀 (Chao K'uang-i, Jō Kyōgi), was the second emperor of the Song dynasty. Giles writes:

> Brother of Chao K'uang-yin [Zhao Kuangyin 趙匡胤, 927–76; founder of the Sung dynasty], whom he succeeded in 976 as second Emperor of the Sung

dynasty. He showed some indecent haste to change the year-title, and exhibited a harshness—foreign to his general character—toward his younger brother and nephew, which drove them to commit suicide. But altogether he was mild, forbearing, and economical, and an ardent student, especially of history. He paid great attention to education and to revenue. In 982 the *chih shih* were first ranked in the existing three classes. In 987 the empire, which since the suppression of the Northern Han State in 979 had almost equalled in extent the China of the T'ang dynasty, was divided into fifteen provinces, each under a Governor; and thus the power of the former great provincial Governors finally ceased.... Occasional droughts and famines were recorded, but on the whole the reign was a time of peace and prosperity. (1939, pp. 64–65)

Tettō Gikō 徹翁義亨 (1295–1369; Case 213), also known as Reizan Tettō 靈山徹翁, was a Japanese monk born in the Izumo 出雲 area of present Shimane 島根 Prefecture. He became a monk at the age of six and studied under the Chinese master Jingtang Jueyuan 鏡堂覺圓 (J., Kyōdō Kakuen; 1244–1306) at Kennin-ji 建仁寺 in Kyoto. He received the full precepts at the age of nineteen. Following Jingtang's death he studied under *Shūhō Myōchō* and became not only his Dharma successor but also, in 1337, his successor as abbot of Daitoku-ji. He later retired to the Daitoku-ji subtemple Tokuzen-ji 德禪寺.

Tianhuang Daowu 天皇道悟 (T'ien-huang Tao-wu, Tennō Dōgo; 748–807; Case 256) was a native of Dongyang 東陽, Jinhua 金華, in modern Zhejiang 浙江; his family name was Zhang 張. He became a monk at the age of fourteen, and at twenty-five he received the full precepts at the temple Zhulin si 竹林寺 in Hangzhou 杭州, also in Zhejiang. For some time after this he engaged in ascetic practices. While traveling in Yuhang 餘杭 he met Jingshan Faqin 徑山法欽 (714–92), the founder of the great monastery on Mount Jing 徑, and spent five years studying with him. He subsequently trained under *Mazu Daoyi* in Zhongling 鍾陵 in modern Jiangxi 江西, then, two years later, joined the assembly under *Shitou Xiqian*. After succeeding to Shitou's Dharma he lived on Mount Chaizi 柴紫 near the city of Dangyang 当陽 in present Hubei 湖北, where many students gathered around him. Later he served as abbot of the temple Tianhuang si 天皇寺 near Dangyang, teaching Shitou's style of Zen to his followers, ordained and lay alike, until his death at the age of fifty-nine.

Tiantai Deshao 天台德韶 (T'ien-t'ai Te-shao, Tendai Tokushō; 891–972; Case 271) was a native of Longquan 龍泉 in Chuzhou 處州, modern Zhejiang 浙江; his family name was Chen 陳. At the age of seventeen he became a monk at the temple Longgui si 龍歸寺 in Chuzhou, and soon afterward left on a pilgrimage that took him to a number of teachers, including *Touzi Datong* and *Longya Judun*, before he entered the monastery of *Fayan Wenyi*. There he remained and eventually succeeded to Fayan's Dharma. Later he went to Mount Tiantai 天台, where he restored the monastery of Zhiyi 智沮 (538–97), the great priest who founded the Tiantai school. In a poem greatly admired by Fayan, he wrote: "The top of Penetrating-the-Mystery Mountain / Is not the human world / Outside the mind there are no things / Green mountains fill the eyes."

Touzi Datong 投子大同 (T'ou-tzu Ta-t'ung, Tōsu Daidō; 819–914; Case 202) was a native of Shuzhou 舒州 in present-day Anhui 安徽; his family name was Liu 劉. He became a monk while still a child and devoted himself to the study of the *Avataṁsaka Sutra*. Later he practiced under the Zen master Cuiwei Wuxue 翠微無學 (9th c.). After succeeding to Cuiwei's Dharma he returned to his native land and lived on Mount Touzi 投子, where he taught actively for over thirty years. Like his friend *Zhaozhou Congshen*, he was renowned for his skillful use of words. He lived to the age of ninety-six and was honored with the posthumous title Great Master Ciji 慈濟大師.

Touzi Fazong 投子法宗 (T'ou-tzu Fa-tsung, Tōsu Hōshū; n.d.; Case 100) was a Dharma successor of *Xuedou Chongxian*; otherwise little of his biography is known. In *Blue Cliff Record* 58, Commentary on the Main Case, Fazong is described as having been monastery scribe under Xuedou. Xuedou gave him the first phrase of the Third Patriarch's poem *On Believing in Mind* 信心銘, "The supreme path is not difficult; just avoid picking and choosing," and it was with this that he attained enlightenment. He is said to have been rather eccentric in behavior. In the later part of his life he lived as a hermit on Mount Touzi 投子 in Anhui 安徽.

U

Udayana (Youtianwang 優塡王, Yu-t'ien-wang, Uten'ō; Case 133) was a legendary figure said to have been king of the land of Kauśāmbī at the time of Śākyamuni. At the urging of his wife he converted to Buddhism and became one of Śākyamuni's followers. The story of his image of the Buddha has its origins in *Āgama* 28 (T 2:706a). Buddhist legend has it that this image was the first buddha image ever made, and that it made its way east to Japan and is now enshrined in Kyoto at Seiryō-ji 清涼寺.

V

Vimalakīrti (Weimojie 維摩詰, Wei-mo-chieh, Yuimakitsu; Cases 80, 108, 112, 133, 175), the legendary protagonist of the *Vimalakīrti Sutra*, was a wealthy householder living in the city of Vaiśālī who was the most deeply enlightened of the Buddha's disciples. In China particularly he is regarded as the ideal lay Buddhist, one who dwells in the ordinary world and yet lives the śūnyatā-based life of the bodhisattva. The *Vimalakīrti Sutra* describes Vimalakīrti lying in bed with an illness that the layman himself has created as a teaching device to help his many well-wishers understand the Dharma more deeply. The Buddha, with a similar goal in mind, asks his main disciples to call upon the bedridden Vimalakīrti. One after another they excuse themselves as unworthy, explaining that Vimalakīrti has in the past exposed the narrowness of their views and indicated the higher path of the Mahayana bodhisattva. When *Mañjuśrī*, the bodhisattva of wisdom, finally agrees to make the call he is accompanied by tens of thousands of the Buddha's followers to Vimalakīrti's ten-foot-square room, which miraculously accommodates each and every one of them.

> Mañjuśrī now inquires about the householder's illness, and Vimalakīrti answers this and other questions in such a way as to describe fully the bodhisattva practices as they are carried out in the life of the devout householder. The climax of the interview is reached when Vimalakīrti, having asked various bodhisattvas present about how a bodhisattva can enter the gate of non-duality, at Mañjuśrī's request answers the question himself by his "Great Silence." (Miura and Sasaki 1966, p. 422)

Vipaśyin (Piposhi 毘婆尸, P'i-p'o-shih, Bibashi; Cases 34 n., 163, 263). The first of the six nonhistorical Buddhas said to have preceded *Śākyamuni*.

W

Wan'an Daoyan 卍庵道顏 (Wan-an Tao-yan, Man'an Dōgan; 1094–1164; Cases 19-2 n., 146), also known as Donglin Daoyan 東林道顏, was a native of Feiwu 飛烏, in Tongchuan 潼川, present-day Sichuan 四川. His family, surnamed Xianyu 鮮于, was known for its Confucian scholarship. Daoyan became a monk while still young; after studying the precepts he visited various masters, finally joining the assembly under *Dahui Zonggao*. After receiving Dharma transmission from Dahui he resided at the temples Jianfu si 薦福寺, Bao'en si 報恩寺, and Baiyang si 白揚寺. In his later years he resided at Donglin si 東林寺 in Jiangzhou 江州, in present-day Jiangxi 江西.

Wang Changshi 王常侍 (Wang Ch'ang-shih; Ō Jōji; 9th c.; Case 221), better known as Wang Jingchu 王敬初, was a native of Xiangzhou 襄州, modern Hubei 湖北. He was a government official during the mid-Tang dynasty (the title *changshi* 常侍 appended to his surname Wang is an official rank). As indicated in Case 221, he studied under *Muzhou Daoming* and attained enlightenment. Later he became the disciple, and eventually the Dharma heir, of *Guishan Lingyou*. Wang was the author of a stone inscription in the Founders Hall of Yanqing si 延慶寺 in Hubei.

Wang Sui 王隨 (Wang Sui; Ō Zui; 10th–11th c.; Case 260) was prime minister and a lay disciple of *Shoushan Shengnian*. He compiled the *Chuandeng yuying ji* 傳燈玉英集 (Precious flowers of the lamp transmission).

Wolun 臥輪 (Wo-lun, Garin; n.d.; Case 261) was a monk of the early Tang dynasty, identified in the Zen biographies as a quietistic meditation master not of Bodhidharma's lineage but of the Pure Land tradition. According to the *Jingde-Era Record of the Transmission of the Lamp*, "Wolun" was a place-name, not a personal name.

Wumen Huikai 無門慧開 (Wu-men Hui-k'ai, Mumon Ekai; 1183–1260; Case 171), compiler of the important koan collection *Wumen guan* 無門關, was a native of Jiantang 錢塘 in Hangzhou 杭州, present Zhejiang 浙江; his family name was Liang 梁. He received ordination under a certain Tianlong Gong 天龍肱, then visited various masters until he finally entered the assembly under the Yangqi-line master Yuelun Shiguan 月輪師觀 (1143–1217) at Wanshou si 萬壽寺 in Suzhou 蘇州, modern Jiangsu 江蘇. Huikai struggled with the koan "Zhaozhou's 'Wu'" for six years, until finally experiencing a profound awakening when he heard the sound of the temple drum. From the age of thirty-six, after receiving Yuelun's seal of transmission, he resided at a succession of great monasteries, including Tianning si 天寧寺, Huanglong si 黃龍寺, and Kaiyuan si 開元寺. In 1245 he was asked by Emperor Lizong 理宗 (r. 1224–64) to serve as the founding priest of the important temple Huguo Renwang si 護國仁王寺 near Hangzhou. Throughout his life Huikai was a man of simple habits, wearing plain robes and engaging in manual labor; his approach to Zen practice was direct and severe. Among his successors was the important Japanese Zen monk Shinchi Kakushin 心地覺心 (1207–98), who brought the *Wumen guan* to Japan.

Wuzu Fayan 五祖法演 (Wu-tsu Fa-yen, Goso Hōen; 1024?–1104; Cases 3, 8, 16, 28-1, 32, 37, 40, 77, 84, 98 n., 249, 259, 266) was a native of Mianzhou 綿州 in Sichuan 四川; his family name was Deng 鄧. After becoming a monk at the age of thirty-five he first studied the teachings of the Yogācāra school. Dissatisfied, he set off in search of a master of the buddha-mind school. He studied under Fakong Zongben 法空宗本 (1020–99) before joining the assembly under Yuanjian Fayuan 圓鑑法遠 (991–1067); on Yuanjian's advice he went to *Yangqi Fanghui*'s successor *Baiyun Shouduan*, whose heir he eventually became. He later settled on Mount Huangmei 黃梅, also known as Mount Wuzu 五祖 (Fifth Patriarch Mountain) because the Fifth Patriarch, *Hongren*, had lived there. Fayan, an unassuming man known for his plain-spoken lectures, trained a number of important heirs; the most important for later Zen history was *Yuanwu Keqin*, from whom all modern Japanese Rinzai masters descend. Fayan was the teacher of the so-called Three Buddhas, *Fojian Huiqin*, *Foyan Qingyuan*, and *Foguo Keqin* (*Yuanwu Keqin*), all three of whom had the character *fo* 佛, "buddha," in their name or title.

Wuzu Shijie 五祖師戒 (Wu-tsu Shih-chieh, Goso Shikai; 10th c.; Case 151) was a Yunmen-school monk and Dharma heir of Shuangquan Shikuan 双泉師寛 (n.d.). He later lived on Mount Wuzu 五祖 in Qizhou 蘄州, present Hubei 湖北. In his old age he retired to Mount Dayu 大愚 in Hongzhou 洪州.

X

Xiang Yu 項羽 (Hsiang Yü; Kō U; 232–202 BCE; Case 191), also known by his given name, Xiang Ji 項籍 (Hsiang Chi, Kō Seki), was, with his rival Liu Bang 劉邦 (247–195 BCE), one of the two great generals in the wars that led to the fall of the

Qin 秦 dynasty (221–206 BCE). He is said to have been seven feet tall and possessed of enormous strength, with a horse, Zhui 騅, that could run a thousand leagues in a day. Though a strong and skillful leader, Xiang Yu earned himself a reputation for treachery and cruelty. After achieving a string of victories and attaining the position of King of Chu 楚, he was defeated by Liu Bang at the battle of Gaixia 垓下.

Xianglin Chengyuan 香林澄遠 (Hsiang-lin Ch'eng-yüan, Kyōrin Chōon; 908–87; Cases 41, 203) was a native of Mianzhu 綿竹 in Hanzhou 漢州, modern Sichuan 四川. He became a monk at the age of sixteen; later he went on a long pilgrimage that finally took him to the monastery of *Yunmen Wenyan*. After succeeding to Yunmen's Dharma he resided at the temple Xianglin yuan 香林院 on Mount Qingcheng 青城 in Yizhou 益州, present Sichuan, where he taught Yunmen's style of Zen to students both lay and ordained for over forty years.

Xiangyan Zhixian 香嚴智閑 (Hsiang-yen Chih-hsien, Kyōgen Chikan; d. 898; Cases 19-1, 19-2, 26, 123, 240) was a native of Qingzhou 青州, in modern Shandong 山東. He studied under *Baizhang Huaihai* and later went to *Guishan Lingyou*. One day Guishan said to him, "I do not ask what you have recorded from the scriptures and commentaries. I ask for a word from your original nature, before you left the womb and before you knew east from west." Zhixian's initial answers were rejected, and when he asked Guishan to explain the master merely said, "If I explained it would be no more than my own point of view. Of what benefit would that be in clarifying your mind's eye?" After searching fruitlessly through his sutras and commentaries, he said, "A picture of a rice cake doesn't satisfy hunger." He threw away his books and vowed to live out his life as a wandering monk. When he came to the tomb of *Nanyang Huizhong* at the temple Xiangyan si 香嚴寺 on Mount Baiya 白崖 he took up residence there and devoted himself to caring for the grave; his enlightenment, described in Case 26, took place at this temple. Later Guishan's disciple *Yangshan Huiji*, hearing Zhixian's verse, visited him and asked for another verse, saying that if Zhixian's enlightenment were genuine he would have no trouble expressing it in a different way. Zhixian responded with the verse: "Last year's poverty was not [true] poverty / This year's poverty is, for the first time, [true] poverty. / Last year's poverty still had a place to stick an awl / This year's poverty lacks even an awl." "You have attained Tathāgata Zen," Yangshan commented, "but even in your dreams you haven't seen Ancestor Zen." Zhixian then produced another verse: "I have the ability / To see *it* in the twinkle of an eye / If you do not understand / You cannot call yourself a monk." With this Yangshan recognized his understanding and praised him to Guishan. Zhixian later received the honorary title Zen Master Xideng 襲燈禪師.

Xianzong 憲宗 (Hsien-tsung, Kensō; 778–820; Case 247) was the title of the eleventh Tang emperor, Li Chun 李純. He came to the throne in 805 and in 809 initiated important government reforms that banned slavery, regulated revenue, and limited taxes. He was a strong ruler who reestablished central government control over the provincial governors in a war lasting from 814 to 819. Toward the end of his life he became a devout follower of Buddhism and attempted to find the secrets of immortality.

Xinghua Cunjiang 興化存獎 (Hsing-hua Ts'un-chiang, Kōke Zonshō; 830–88; Cases 59, 123, 130, 184) was born in Queli 闕里 in the province of Shandong 山東; his family name was Kong 孔. In 861 he journeyed to Zhenzhou 鎮州 to practice under *Linji Yixuan*. After a stay of about one year he departed on an extended pilgrimage, but he later rejoined the assembly and remained with Linji until the master's death several years later. He was one of Linji's few Dharma successors and is honored as the second ancestor of the Linji lineage. As related in Case 123, note 9, Xinghua deepened his understanding following Linji's death with further training under his fellow students *Sansheng Huiran* and Dajue 大覺 (9th c.). Xinghua later resided at the temple Xinghua si 興化寺 in the province of Wei 魏. He is traditionally regarded as the editor of the *Record of Linji*, as well as the compiler of the "Xinglu" 行錄 (Record of pilgrimages) section of the work.

Xingjiao Hongshou 興教洪壽 (Hsing-chiao Hung-shou, Kōkyō Kōju; 944–1022; Case 271) was a native of Jiantang 錢塘 in Hangzhou 杭州, present Zhejiang 浙江; his family name was Cao 曹. While a child he became a monk at the temple Tianlong si 天龍寺 near his home. After taking the full precepts he went on pilgrimage and studied the vinaya. He eventually joined the assembly under *Tiantai Deshao*. After succeeding to Deshao's Dharma he retired to Mount Daci 大慈 near his place of birth and lived in a hermitage he built for himself. In 1016 he was invited to become abbot of the temple Xingjiao si 興教寺 in Hangzhou; after five years he retired to the temple Shangfang si 上方寺.

Xitang Zhizang 西堂智藏 (Hsi-t'ang Chih-tsang, Seidō Chizō; 735–814; Case 78) was a native of Qianhua 虔化 in Nankangjun 南康郡, present Jiangxi 江西; his family name was Liao 廖. He became a novice at the age of eight and received the full bhikku precepts at twenty-five. He studied under *Mazu Daoyi* and is considered, along with *Baizhang Huaihai*, *Nanquan Puyuan*, and Xingchan Weikuan 興禪惟寬 (755–817), to have been one of Mazu's greatest Dharma heirs. Following Mazu's death he was asked to succeed Mazu as abbot. He received two honorary titles: Zen Master Daxuanjiao 大宣教禪師 and Zen Master Dajue 大覺禪師. A typical episode involving Xitang is as follows:

> One day Master Daoyi had Xitang take a letter to *Nanyang Huizhong* in the capital, Chang'an. Nanyang asked, "What is the teaching of your master?" Xitang walked from east to west and stood there. Nanyang said, "Is that all? Is there anything else?" Thereupon Xitang walked back to the east and stood there. The National Teacher said, "This is what Master Mazu is teaching. What about you?" Xitang said, "Teacher, I have already given it to you" (T 51:252a).

Xiu 秀 (Hsiu, Shū; n.d.; Case 272). Nothing is known of this figure.

Xuansha Shibei 玄沙師備 (Hsüan-sha Shih-pei, Gensha Shibi; 835–908; Cases 8, 43, 113, 158) was a native of Minxian 閩縣 in the province of Fujian 福建; his family name was Xie 謝. He was an illiterate fisherman until the age of thirty but, desiring to leave the world, became a monk under the priest Lingxun 靈訓 (9th c.) of Mount Furong 芙蓉. Five years later he received the full precepts under the vinaya master Daoyuan 道玄 of Kaiyuan si 開元寺. He later joined the assembly under *Xuefeng Yicun*, whose Dharma heir he became. Among Xuefeng's other disciples Shibei was known as "Ascetic Bei" for his strict maintenance of the precepts, his satisfaction with coarse robes and straw sandals, and his dedication to the practice of zazen. His enlightenment occurred when he stubbed his toe just as he was crossing the mountain pass out of his native Fujian at the start of a pilgrimage (see Case 43, note 3). It is said that the relationship between Xuefeng and Xuansha, who were not far separated in age, was quite close and that they understood each other so well that they needed no words. As the teacher of *Fayan Wenyi*, Xuansha was one of the forebears of the Fayan school 法眼宗.

Xuanzong 宣宗 (Hsüan-tsung, Sensō; 810–59; Case 250) was the title of Li Shen 李忱, the sixteenth Tang emperor; he is also known by the title Dazhong 大中. Xuanzong, the younger brother of Emperor Muzong 穆宗 (795–824), was intensely disliked by the fifteenth emperor Wuzong 武宗 (814–46), the fifth son of Muzong, and was forced to seek refuge among the Buddhist sangha until Wuzong's death. Ascending to the throne in 846, Xuanzong halted the latter's severe persecution of Buddhism, during which thousands of temples and monasteries were destroyed and countless monks and nuns were laicized. He executed the Taoist advisors who had incited Wuzong's Buddhist persecution, encouraged temple reconstruction, and permitted laicized clergy over the age of fifty to return to their vocations. Of Xuanzong, Giles writes:

> Clever and just, open to reproof and economical, an industrious ruler and fond of his people, he earned for himself the flattering title 小太宗 Little T'ai Tsung, i.e., another Li Shih-min [597–649; the brilliant and revered second Tang emperor]. (1939, p. 458)

Xuedou Chongxian 雪竇重顯 (Hsüeh-tou Ch'ung-hsien, Setchō Jūken; 980–1052; Cases 19-1, 194) was a native of Suizhou 遂州, in present Sichuan 四川; his family name was Li 李. While still young he became a monk at the temple Puan yuan 普安院 under a priest named Renxian 仁銑. After taking the full precepts he visited a number of Zen masters, finally entering the assembly under Zhimen Guangzuo 智門光祚 (d. 1031), a Yunmen-line master living in Suizhou 隋州, in modern Hubei 湖北. After succeeding to Zhimen's Dharma Chongxian resided at Mount Cuifeng 翠峰 in Suzhou 蘇州, modern Jiangsu 江蘇, and then at Zisheng si 資聖寺 on Mount Xuedou 雪竇 in Zhejiang 浙江, where he lived for thirty years until his death at the age of seventy-two. He was very active in teaching

and writing, earning a reputation as the reviver of the Yunmen school and producing more than seventy heirs. He was also a talented poet, and his writings
are considered among the best in the literature of Zen. Particularly well known
is his work *Xuedou baize songgu* 雪竇百則頌古, a compendium of one hundred
koans with Xuedou's own verses on each case; this became the basis of the later
koan collection *Biyan lu* (*Blue Cliff Record*). After his death Emperor Renzong
仁宗 (r. 1022–62) conferred upon him the posthumous title Great Master Miao-
jue 明覺大師.

Xuefeng Yicun 雪峰義存 (Hsüeh-feng I-ts'un, Seppō Gison; 822–908; Cases 22-1,
43, 200, 256) was a native of Nan'an 南安 in Quanzhou 泉州, present Fujian 福
建, with the family name Zeng 曾. Xuefeng is said to have been deeply interested in things related to Buddhism from the time he was a young child. At the
age of twelve he became a novice at the temple Yujian si 玉澗寺 in Putian 莆
田, and at seventeen he received full ordination. During the great persecution
of Buddhism in 845 under Emperor Wuzong 武宗 (814–46) Xuefeng disguised
himself in lay clothing but nevertheless continued his practice at Mount Furong
芙蓉 under the Zen master Lingxun 靈訓 (9th c.), the first teacher of *Xuansha
Shibei*.

   In 853 he joined the assembly under Daci Huanzhong 大慈寰中 (780–862), a
disciple of *Baizhang Huaihai*. *Yantou Quanhuo* and *Qinshan Wensui* were also
there as monks in training at the time; the three became Dharma friends and
subsequently set off on an extended pilgrimage to the Jiangnan 江南 region to
study under various masters, notably *Yangshan Huiji*, *Touzi Datong*, and *Dongshan Liangjie*. Under Dongshan, Xuefeng served as cook for the community. At
the age of thirty-nine, on Dongshan's advice, Xuefeng left to study with *Deshan
Xuanjian*, accompanied by Yantou and Qinshan.

   Under Deshan he attained a degree of insight, but it was several years later,
while he was on pilgrimage with Yantou, that he finally attained full awakening.
At the inn where they were lodging during a long snowstorm Xuefeng devoted
himself to meditation while Yantou slept and relaxed. When Xuefeng reproved
his brother disciple, Yantou compared him to a clay idol in a village shrine.
Xuefeng thereupon admitted his inability to attain true peace of mind. In
response to Yantou's offer to check his understanding, he spoke of the insights
he had had while listening to the words of his various teachers. Finally Yantou
said, "Haven't you heard that that which enters through the front gate is not the
family treasure?… If you wish to spread the great teaching, it must pour forth
from your own heart, and cover heaven and earth." With these words Xuefeng
was thoroughly enlightened.

   In 866, several years after Deshan's death, Xuefeng, Yantou, and Qinshan set
off to meet *Linji Yixuan*, but parted company after meeting Linji's disciple Elder
Ding on the way and hearing that the great master had died. Xuefeng went
to Min 閩 and built a hermitage in Jian'an 建安. In 875 he founded the temple

Chongsheng si 崇聖寺 (Xuefeng si 雪峰寺) on Mount Xianggu 象骨 in Fujian. The assembly under him numbered fifteen hundred; his fifty-six Dharma successors included such important figures as *Xuansha Shibei* and *Yunmen Wenyan*, from whom two of the most important lines of Zen teaching developed.

Xutang Zhiyu 虛堂智愚 (Hsü t'ang Chih-yü, Kidō Chigu; 1185–1269; Cases 28-2, 61, 71, 87, 104, 105, 133 n., 143, 145, 146, 158, 183-2, 186, 200, 205, 270-2, 271) was a native of Siming 四明, in present-day Zhejiang 浙江; his family name was Chen 陳. He entered a local temple named Puming si 普明寺 at the age of sixteen and studied under a priest named Shiyun 師蘊. After an extended pilgrimage he arrived at Mount Jing 徑 in Hangzhou 杭州, where he joined the assembly under *Yun'an Puyan* and eventually became the master's Dharma heir. He visited a number of other masters after leaving Yun'an and eventually served as priest of several important temples. After a temporary retirement occasioned by political difficulties he was imperially appointed to head the temple Jingci si 淨慈寺 and Yun'an's monastery on Mount Jing.

Among Xutang's students was the Japanese monk *Nanpo Jōmyō*, the founder of the Japanese Rinzai lineage that includes all present-day Rinzai masters in Japan. The koans included in the "Alternate Answers" 代別 section of the *Recorded Sayings of Xutang* 虛堂錄 are still used in advanced Japanese Rinzai-school koan training.

Y

Yang Danian 楊大年 (Yang Ta-nien, Yō Dainen; n.d.; Case 137), also known as Yang Yi 楊億 (Yang I, Yō Oku), was a native of Puchengxian 浦城縣 in present Fujian 福建. His brilliance was recognized from childhood; at the age of eleven, at the request of Emperor *Taizong*, he wrote five scrolls of poetry in the imperial presence. He later held a succession of official posts, including prefect of Henan 河南 and Ruzhou 汝州. A serious Zen practitioner, he became a Dharma successor of *Guanghui Yuanlian*; he was one of the compilers of the *Jingde-Era Record of the Transmission of the Lamp* and the author of the preface.

Yangqi Fanghui 楊岐方會 (Yang-ch'i Fang-hui, Yōgi Hōe; 992–1049; Cases 172, 183-1), founder of the Yangqi branch of Linji-school Zen, was a native of Yi-chunxian 宜春縣 in Yuanzhou 袁州, present-day Jiangxi 江西; his family name was Leng 冷. It is said that he took a trip to the monastery on Mount Jiufeng 九峰 in Ruizhou 瑞州, present Jiangxi, and, unable to bear the thought of leaving, shaved his head and became a monk. He later traveled widely in search of a teacher, finally entering the assembly under *Shishuang Chuyuan* on Mount Nanyuan 南源. He followed Shishuang when the latter moved to Mount Shishuang 石霜. After succeeding to Shishuang's Dharma he taught at Putong Chanyuan 普通禪院 on Mount Yangqi 楊岐 in Yuanzhou, then, in 1046, moved to the temple Haihui si 海會寺 on Mount Yungai 雲蓋 in Tanzhou 潭州, in present Hunan 湖南. The teaching line he founded remains alive today in Japanese

Rinzai Zen, making Yangqi an ancestor of all present-day Japanese Rinzai masters.

Yangshan Huiji 仰山慧寂 (Yang-shan Hui-chi, Kyōzan Ejaku; 807–83; Cases 60, 65, 76, 82, 116, 123, 149, 151, 187, 192, 206, 238) was a native of of Shaozhou 韶州 in present Guangdong 廣東. His family name was She 葉. He sought to become a monk from the age of fifteen but met with his parents' opposition; at the age of seventeen he finally gained their permission after cutting off two of his fingers to demonstrate his determination.

After studying the vinaya at Nanhua si 南華寺 he visited several of the greatest masters of his time, finally joining the assembly under *Danyuan Yingzhen.* Upon attaining a measure of awakening he left again on pilgrimage and entered the temple of *Guishan Lingyou,* then living in Tanzhou 潭州. One day he asked Guishan, "Where does the true buddha abide?" Guishan answered, "Through the marvelous functioning of awareness without thought, turn the mind inward to contemplate the infinity of the spirit's light. With thinking exhausted the mind returns to its source, where nature and form are eternal and phenomena and principal are nondual. There is the true buddha suchness!" With these words Yangshan attained complete enlightenment. After fifteen years Yangshan succeeded to Guishan's Dharma; he and Guishan are honored as the cofounders of the Guiyang 潙仰 school. Later he lived on Mount Yang 仰 in Yuanzhou 遠州, in present-day Jiangxi 江西; at Guanyin yuan 觀音院, also in Jiangxi; and on Mount Dongping 東平 in Shaozhou. To Guishan's style of Zen he added use of the circle-figures 圓相 that he had received from Danyuan (see Case 238), and that became one of the characteristic teachings of the Guiyang lineage. His posthumous title is Great Master Zhitong 智通大師; his nickname was "Little Śākyamuni."

Yantou Quanhuo 巖頭全奯 (Yen-t'ou Ch'uan-huo, Gantō Zenkatsu; 828–87; Cases 22-1, 61, 166, 171, 256) was a native of Nan'an 南安 in Quanzhou 泉州, part of the present-day province of Fujian 福建; his family name was Ke 柯. He became a novice under a certain Master Yi 義公 of the temple Lingquan si 靈泉寺 and received the full precepts at the temple Ximing si 西明寺 in Chang'an. At first he devoted himself to the study of the scriptures, particularly the *Nirvana Sutra,* but later he became interested in the practice of Zen. At the temple of Daci Huanzhong 大慈寰中 (780–862) he met *Xuefeng Yicun* and *Qinshan Wensui,* monks in training at that time. The three set off on a pilgrimage that took them to *Yangshan Huiji, Touzi Datong, Dongshan Liangjie,* and *Deshan Xuanjian.* Yantou was one of Deshan's most brilliant students; many koans consist of exchanges between him, Deshan, and Deshan's other students, with Yantou generally having the last word.

According to the Zen legend that forms the background of Case 166, sometime after succeeding to Deshan's Dharma Yantou worked as a ferryman on a lake in Ezhou 鄂州, in the southeastern part of present-day Hubei. Subsequently he lived on Mount Yantou 巖頭 in the same province. When public order broke down near the final years of the Tang dynasty the assembly dispersed, but Yantou remained. One day bandits came to the monastery when Yantou was sitting in meditation. Angry at finding nothing worth taking, they stabbed the master. Yantou remained calm, it is said, but gave a great shout that resounded for a distance of ten *li*.

Yanyang Shanxin 嚴陽善信 (Yen-yang Shan-hsin, Gen'yō Zenshin; n.d.; Case 6) was a Dharma heir of the great Zen master *Zhaozhou Congshen*; otherwise little is known of him. After finishing his training he resided at the temple Xinxing yuan 新興院 on Mount Yanyang 嚴陽. He is said to have kept a tiger and a snake that would eat from his hand.

Ying'an Tanhua 應庵曇華 (Ying-an T'an-hua, Ōan Donge; 1103–63; Cases 30, 59, 75) was a native of Huangmei 黃梅 in present Hubei 湖北; his surname was Jiang 江. At age seventeen he became a monk at the temple Dongchan si 東禪寺 in the same province, then traveled to Suizhou 隋州, present Hubei, to begin his Zen training under a Caodong master named Shuinan Shousui 水南守遂 (1072–1147). From there he visited *Yuanwu Keqin*, who advised him to study with Yuanwu's disciple Huqiu Shaolong 虎丘紹隆 (1077–1136). After succeeding to Huqiu's Dharma he served as priest of a number of temples, finally settling at the great monastery on Mount Tiantong 天童, in present-day Zhejiang 浙江. He and his contemporary *Dahui Zonggao* were known as the Linji school's "Two Amṛta Gates" for their era owing to their skill and vigor as masters. Ying'an, the teacher of *Mian Xianjie*, is an ancestor of all Rinzai Zen masters in Japan today.

Yongjia Xuanjue 永嘉玄覺 (Yung-chia Hsüan-chüeh, Yōka Genkaku; 675–713; Cases 168 n., 229 n.), one of the greatest disciples of the Sixth Patriarch *Huineng*, was a native of Yongjia 永嘉 in Wenzhou 温州, present Zhejiang 浙江. His lay name was Dai 戴. He became a monk while still quite young and studied the Tripitaka; he also practiced the śamatha-vipaśyanā 止觀 meditation of the Tiantai 天台 school and is said to have mastered the practice of maintaining the meditative mind within all the activities of life.

At the urging of another priest he went to visit Huineng. Upon meeting him Yongjia showed none of the usual signs of respect, but instead he circled Huineng three times, then stood calmly. When Huineng asked about this behavior, Yongjia replied, "The matter of birth-and-death is urgent, and impermanence is terribly swift." "Why don't you experience no-birth and awaken to the not-swift?" asked Huineng. "To experience it is itself no-birth, to awaken is itself the not-swift [i.e., that which is unmoving]," answered Yongjia. "That's right!" said the Sixth Patriarch, upon which Yongjia bowed and paid his respects.

Though he stayed at Huineng's monastery only a single night, he was recognized as one of the Patriarch's successors. He returned to Wenzhou and taught the multitude of students who gathered around him. Among his works is the

The Song of Enlightenment 證道歌. His detailed instructions on praxis in the Zen tradition were set out in the *Anthology of Yongjia of the Chan School* 禪宗永嘉集 (T 48:2013), from which the following passage comes:

> He who aspires to seek the great Way must first of all make pure the three acts [of body, word, and thought] through pure practice. Then, in the four forms of demeanor—sitting, standing, walking, and lying—he will enter the Way by degrees. When he has reached the state where the objects of the six roots have been thoroughly penetrated while conforming with conditions, and the objective world and the subjective mind 境智 both have been stilled, he will mysteriously meet with the marvelous principle. (T 48:388b; from Sasaki 2009, p. 222)

Yongming Yanshou 永明延壽 (Yung-ming Yen-shou, Yōmei Enju; 904–75; Case 271 n.) was a native of Yuhang 餘杭 in Zhejiang 浙江; his family name was Wang 王. Although he wished to enter the monkhood from the time he was a child, it was only after serving as an official until the age of twenty-eight that he could receive ordination under Cuiyan Lingcan 翠巖令參 (n.d.). He eventually became the Dharma heir of *Tiantai Deshao*, and thus the third ancestor of the Fayan 法眼 school. He later lived at the temples Zisheng si 資聖寺 on Mount Xuedou 雪竇; Xueyin si 雪隱寺 in Wuyue 吳越; and Yongming si 永明寺 in Hangzhou 杭州. He wrote the *Record of the Source Mirror* 宗鏡錄, highly regarded in Korea; thirty-six Korean monks were sent to study with him, with the result that the Fayan school flourished in Korea even as it ultimately disappeared in China. In Zen circles Yongming is especially known for his use of the *nenbutsu* 念佛 practice, the invoking of Amitābha Buddha's name, believing that the combined practice of meditation and the *nenbutsu* was the surest path to enlightenment. This approach came to characterize Chinese Zen training.

Yu Di 于頔 (Yü Ti, U Teki; d. 818; Cases 39, 86) was a native of the Henan 河南 region. Following a distinguished military career he served as governor of the districts of Huzhou 湖州 (791–93), Suzhou 蘇州 (793–98), and Xiangzhou 襄州 (798–808). He was an able administrator, though arrogant and dictatorial. During his tenure in Xiangzhou he launched a persecution of Buddhism that ended only with his conversion by *Ziyu Daotong*, in an exchange described, in part, in Case 39. The full story is that Yu Di ordered all mendicant monks in his jurisdiction brought to the central court in the district capital, Xiangyang 襄陽, where they were condemned to death. Hearing of this, Daotong journeyed to Xiangzhou, where he was arrested at the border and brought to the central court. There he faced Yu:

> The Prefect, seated grandly on a chair, put a hand on the hilt of his sword and asked, "Bah! You teacher. Don't you know that the Prefect of Xiangyang has the freedom to put you to the sword?" The Master said, "Don't you know a King of Dharma doesn't fear birth-and-death?" The Prefect said, "Priest, have you ears in your head?" The Master responded, "My eyebrows and eyes are unhindered. When I, a poor monk, meet with the Prefect in an interview, what kind of

hindrance could there be?" At this the Prefect threw away his sword, donned his official uniform, bowed low, and asked, "I have heard there is a statement in the teaching that says that the black wind blows the ships, and wafts them to the land of the Rakṣasas. What does this mean?" "Yu Di!" the Master called. The Prefect's face changed color. The Master remarked, "The land of the Rakṣasas is not far!" The Prefect again asked, "What about Buddha?" "Yu Di!" the Master called again. The Prefect answered, "Yes?" The Master said: "Don't seek anywhere else." At these words the Prefect attained great enlightenment, bowed low, and became his disciple. (Sasaki, Iriya, and Fraser 1971, pp. 22–23; adapted)

In 808 Yu Di's son married the eldest daughter of Emperor Xianzong 憲宗 (r. 805–20). He went to live in Chang'an and was given a ministerial post, but in 813 fell from favor and was demoted. He died soon afterward.

Yu Di was, along with *Pei Xiu*, *Yang Danian*, and Li Zunxu 李遵勗 (d. 1038), one of the Four Worthies 四賢—Chinese government officials who were accomplished Zen practitioners. Yu was a good friend of the great layman *Pang Yun* (see Case 86), and the compiler of Pang's recorded sayings.

Yuanming 圓明 (Yüan-ming, Enmyō; n.d.; Case 194) was the imperially bestowed title of Deshan Yuanmi 德山緣密, a monk of the early Song period. He was a successor of *Yunmen Wenyan* and lived on Mount De 德 in Langzhou 朗州.

Yuanwu Keqin 圓悟克勤 (Yüan-wu K'o-ch'in; Engo Kokugon; 1063–1135; Cases 32, 73, 77, 89, 92, 96, 98, 99 n., 112, 155 n., 266) was a native of Songning 嵩寧, in Pengzhou 彭州, modern Sichuan 四川; his surname was Luo 駱. His family had a long tradition of Confucian scholarship, and Yuanwu, able to memorize a text of a thousand characters in a single day, showed promise in this direction. However, Yuanwu felt a strong connection with Buddhism after visiting a temple and reading several Buddhist texts. He became a monk and devoted himself to the study of Buddhist thought until a serious illness made him despair of resolving the problem of samsara through the mastery of doctrine.

Taking up the practice of meditation, he embarked on a long pilgrimage that took him to a number of teachers. Most sanctioned his understanding, but *Wuzu Fayan* would not. As Keqin left in anger, Fayan called out, "Remember me when you are ill." Soon afterward, at Mount Jin 金, Keqin fell sick and, taking this as a sign, returned to Fayan and remained with the master until he succeeded to his Dharma. In 1102 Keqin returned to Sichuan to care for his ill mother, and, at the request of the local prefect, lectured at Liuzu si 六祖寺 and Zhaojue si 招覺寺. In the Zhenghe 政和 era (1111–17) Keqin went south and met the official *Zhang Wujin*, who became a follower and invited him to reside at Lingquan yuan 靈泉院 on Mount Jia 夾, in present Hunan 湖南.

By now Keqin was well known and had many students, including important government officials. He served as the priest of a succession of notable temples, including Daolin si 道林寺 in Tanzhou 潭州, Tianning si 天寧寺 in Dongjing 東

京, and Zhenru yuan 真如院 on Mount Yunju 雲居. It was while at the temples Zhaojue si, Lingquan yuan, and Daolin si that Yuanwu delivered the lectures that later formed the great Zen literary work *Blue Cliff Record*. A purple robe and the title Zen Master Foguo 佛果禪師 were conferred on him by Emperor Huizong 徽宗 (r. 1100–25). The name by which he is best known, Zen Master Yuanwu 圜悟禪師, was bestowed on him by Emperor Gaozong 高宗 (r. 1127–62). Keqin had sixteen Dharma heirs; of these the two most important were *Dahui Zonggao* and Huqiu Shaolong 虎丘紹隆 (1077–1136). Through Huqiu, Yuanwu is an ancestor of all present-day Rinzai Zen masters.

Yuezhou Qianfeng 越州乾峰 (Yüeh-chou Ch'ien-feng; Esshū Kenpō; n.d.; Cases 17, 138, 211) was a Caodong master of the late Tang period and a Dharma heir of *Dongshan Liangjie*. He lived in Yuezhou 越州, in present-day Zhejiang 浙江; otherwise nothing is known of him.

Yun'an Puyan 運庵普巖 (Yün-an P'u-yen, Un'an Fugan; 1156–1226; Cases 95, 218) was a native of Siming 四明 in modern Zhejiang 浙江; his family name was Du 杜. After receiving ordination he studied under several masters, including Wuyong Jingquan 無用淨全 (1137–1207). In 1184 he joined the assembly under *Songyuan Chongyue* at the temple Chengzhao Chanyuan 澄照禪院 in Pingjiangfu 平江府, in present-day Jiangsu 江蘇. When Songyuan later went to the temple Guangxiao si 光孝寺, also in Jiangsu, and Shiji Chanyuan 實際禪院 in Anhui 安徽, Yun'an accompanied him, spending altogether eighteen years under his guidance and receiving transmission as his Dharma heir. Following Songyuan's death in 1202 he returned to his hometown of Siming and resided at the hermitage Yun'an 運庵, built for him by his older brother. In 1206 he was invited to serve as abbot of the temples Dasheng Puzhao si 大聖普照寺 in Jiangsu, Guangxiao si in Jiangsu, and Husheng Wanshou si 護聖萬壽寺 in Zhejiang. His most historically important disciple was *Xutang Zhiyu*, teacher of the Japanese monk *Nanpo Jōmyō*.

Yunju Daojian 雲居道簡 (Yün-chü Tao-chien, Ungo Dōkan; n.d.; Cases 105 n., 108) was a native of Fanyang 范陽, in present-day Hebei 河北. He served as an administrator on Mount Yunju 雲居 and practiced under the Caodong master Yunju Daoying 雲居道膺 (d. 902), an heir of *Dongshan Liangjie*. Daojian succeeded Daoying to become the second abbot of the monastery on Mount Yunju.

Yunju Shanwu 雲居善悟 (Yün-chü Shan-wu, Ungo Zengo; 1074–1132; Case 266) was a native of Xingdao 興道 in Yangzhou 洋州, present Shanxi 陝西; his family name was Li 李. He entered the temple at the age of eleven, and, after studying for a time with a certain master Chong 沖, entered the assembly at Mount Longmen 龍門 under *Foyan Qingyuan*, whose Dharma heir he eventually became. He later resided at Tianning si 天寧寺 in Jizhou 吉州, present Jiangxi 江西, then at the monastery on Mount Yunju 雲居 in Jiangxi. He received an imperial summons to serve as abbot of the great monastery on Mount Jin 金 in Jiangsu 江蘇 but deferred on account of illness.

Yunmen Wenyan 雲門文偃 (Yün-men Wen-yen, Unmon Bun'en; 864–949; Cases 4, 8 n., 17, 20, 21, 29, 49, 55 n., 84, 88, 91, 92, 114, 120, 138, 148, 152, 157 n., 164, 185, 188, 189, 203, 211, 226), founder of the Yunmen school and the last of the Tang-period Zen giants, was a native of Suzhou 蘇州, in modern Jiangsu 江蘇. His family name was Zhang 張. He first studied Zen under *Muzhou Daozong*, on whose gate he had to knock three times before Daoming finally opened it. When Yunmen thrust his leg into the opening Daoming grabbed him and shouted, "Speak! Speak!" Yunmen hesitated, whereupon Daoming slammed the gate on Yunmen's leg, breaking it. Yunmen yelled in pain, but at that moment he was enlightened (though his leg was crippled for the rest of his life). On the advice of the aged Daoming, Yunmen went to *Xuefeng Yicun* and eventually became his Dharma heir. He then joined the assembly of *Lingshu Rumin* at Lingshu yuan 靈樹院, where he was immediately appointed head monk, and later named Lingshu's successor as abbot. Subsequently Yunmen went to the region of present-day Guangdong and founded Guangtai Chanyuan 光泰禪院 on Mount Yunmen 雲門. In his eighty-fifth year Yunmen, despite his crippled leg, seated himself in the full lotus posture and passed away. Yunmen was a powerful speaker and was also known for his terse answers, many of which were of one word only and came to be known as "Yunmen's one-word barriers."

Z

Zhang Wujin 張無盡 (Chang Wu-chin, Chō Mujin; 1043–1121; Case 140), better known as Zhang Shangying 張商英 (Chang Shang-ying, Chō Shōei), was a native of Xinjin 新津 in Shu 蜀, in present-day Sichuan 四川. He passed the higher civil-service exam at the age of nineteen and was later appointed magistrate of Nan-chuanxian 南川縣 in recognition of his services in pacifying disturbances in the Sichuan area. After rising to the position of prime minister he was demoted for a time to governor of Hengzhou 衡州 because of policy failures, but he was subsequently reinstated as prime minister. He practiced Zen under *Doushuai Congyue* and succeeded to his Dharma; he also had a close relationship with *Yuanwu Keqin*. He compiled several texts, among them the *Supplementary Biographies of [Mount] Qingliang* 續清涼傳 (T 51:2100), describing Mount Wutai 五臺 and the cult of *Mañjuśrī* there, and the *Sushu* 素書, characterized by Giles as "a short and shallow ethico-political treatise" (1939, p. 39). His Buddhist name was Layman Wujin 無盡居士.

Zhang Zhuo 張拙 (Chang Cho, Chō Setsu; n.d.; Case 196) was a layman of the Five Dynasties and early Song period. He studied under Deyin Guanxiu 德隱貫休 (832–912) and *Shishuang Qingzhu*, whose Dharma heir he became.

Zhang Zishao 張子韶 (Chang Tzu-shao, Chō Shishō; 1092–1159; Case 141), better known as Zhang Jiucheng 張九成 (Chang Chiu-chêng, Chō Kujō), was a native of Kaifeng 開封, in present-day Henan 河南. Zhang, an important disciple of *Dahui Zonggao*, was also known by the Buddhist names Wugou 無垢 and Hengpu 橫浦. Giles writes:

> Chang… came out first of a number of *chin shih*, examined according to instructions from the Emperor on various topics, and received a post. His sympathies with the people caused him to be unpopular with his superiors, and he was compelled to resign. He was then recommended by Chao Ting, and was appointed to the Court of Sacrificial Worship; but ere long he incurred the odium of Ch'in Kuei, whose peace policy with the Tartars he strenuously opposed. He had been on terms of intimacy with a Buddhist priest, named [Dahui Zonggao]; and he was accused of forming an illegal association and slandering the Court. "This man," said the Emperor, "fears nothing and nobody," and sent him into banishment; from which he returned, upon Ch'in Kuei's death, to be Magistrate at Wenchow. Canonized as 文忠. (1939, p. 16)

Zhao Biaozhi 趙表之 (Chao Piao-chih, Jō Hyōshi; n.d.; Case 32). Nothing is known of this figure.

Zhaozhou Congshen 趙州從諗 (Chao-chou Ts'ung-shen, Jōshū Jūshin; 778–897; Cases 6, 9, 12, 13, 35, 46-1, 46-2, 46-3, 46-4, 46-5, 46-6 n., 54, 90, 103, 104, 121, 123 n., 190, 207-1, 207-2, 212, 219, 229, 248, 262), one of the greatest of all Chinese Zen masters, was born in Caozhou 曹州 in present Shandong 山東; his family name was He 郝. He became a student of *Nanquan Puyuan* at the age of eighteen; although enlightened the same year, he stayed under Nanquan until the latter's death nearly forty years later. At the age of sixty, after tending his teacher's grave for several years, Zhaozhou set out on a twenty-year pilgrimage that took him to many of the greatest Zen masters of that time; he is said to have vowed, "I will seek instruction from even a seven-year-old whose understanding is greater than mine, and I will teach even a one-hundred-year-old whose understanding is less than mine." At age eighty he was invited to become abbot of the temple Guanyin yuan 觀音院 in the city of Zhaozhou 趙州 (Guanyin yuan is now known as Bailin si 柏林寺 [Juniper Grove Temple] after Zhaozhou's famous "Juniper Tree in the Garden" 柏樹子 koan). There he instructed the numerous disciples who gathered under him until his death at the age of 119. His lifestyle was simple in the extreme, and he refused funds even for the repair of the temple buildings. Zhaozhou's lips were said to "flash light," as he employed neither the staff nor the shout in his teaching, but relied instead on his penetrating utterances. Many of his exchanges with students and other masters became famous koans, including Zhaozhou's "*Wu.*"

Zhenjing Kewen 眞淨克文 (Chen-ching K'o-wen, Shinjō Kokubun; 1025–1102; Cases 27, 71, 140, 199), also known as Letan Kewen 泐潭克文 (Le-t'an K'o-wen, Rokutan Kokubun) and Baofeng Kewen 寶峰克文 (Pao-feng K'o-wen, Hōhō Kokubun), was a native of Shanfu 陝府, present Henan 河南; his family name was Zheng 鄭. Extremely bright as a child, he was sent away to study by his father, who had remarried and was concerned about how his son was getting along with his new wife. Later the boy went to Fuzhou 復州, modern Hubei 湖北, and began study under a priest named Siguang 思廣, whose sermons had impressed him; it was from Siguang that he received the name Kewen 克文. At twenty-five Kewen was ordained and received the precepts. At first he studied the sutras and treatises, but, learning of Zen, he traveled south and in 1065 spent a training period at the monastery on Mount Dagui 大潙. While there he heard the story of the official who said to *Yunmen Wenyan*, "The Buddhadharma is like the moon in the water, isn't it." The master replied, "No traces remain in clear water." At this Kewen had a deep insight. He later went to *Huanglong Huinan* and eventually succeeded to his Dharma.

Subsequently he resided at a number of temples. In 1072 he went to Gao'an 高安 in Hongzhou 洪州 and there, at the invitation of the prefect, served for twelve years as abbot of the temple on Mount Dong 洞. Later he went to Jinling 金陵, where the local sovereign became a follower and built for him the temple Baoning si 報寧寺 and also bestowed upon him the honorary title Great Master Zhenjing 眞淨大師. Subsequently he returned to Gao'an and lived in retirement in Toulao an 投老庵, a hermitage he built for himself at the foot of Mount Jiufeng 九峰. Six years later he went to Mount Lu 廬, where he resided at the temple Guizong si 歸宗寺. Following this he was invited by *Zhang Wujin* to become abbot at Baofeng si 寶峰寺 in Letan 泐潭; he finally passed away in retirement at the Yun an 雲庵, the "Cloud Hermitage." He is said to have left thirty-eight Dharma successors.

Zhongfeng Mingben 中峰明本 (Chung-feng Ming-pen, Chūhō Myōhon; 1263–1323; Case 46-3) was a native of Jiantang 錢塘 in Hangzhou 杭州, present Zhejiang 浙江; his family name was Sun 孫. While still quite young he went to Mount Tianmu 天目 in Zhejiang to study under the Yangqi-line Linji priest Gaofeng Yuanmiao 高峰原妙 (1238–95), from whom he received ordination at the age of twenty-four. He was deeply moved by a passage in the *Diamond Sutra*, and later he had a deep awakening as he watched the flow of water from a spring. After receiving transmission from Yuanmiao he had no fixed residence, living sometimes in hermitages and sometimes on boats; he referred to himself as Huanzhu 幻住, "Phantom Resident." Respected by the clergy and laypeople alike, he was known as the Old Buddha of Jiangnan. Emperor Renzong 仁宗 (r. 1312–20) called him to the court, but Mingben refused to go; even so the emperor conferred upon him a robe and an honorary title. The master was also held in great respect by Renzong's successor, Emperor Yingzong 英宗 (r. 1321–23). Despite his lack of a fixed abode Mingben had many students, including royalty, commoners, and monks from China and elsewhere. He was well known and highly respected in Japan, and many Japanese monks went to the continent to practice under him; the Japanese master *Musō Soseki*, though he never actually met Mingben, carried on a correspondence with him. Among

Mingben's Dharma heirs were the Japanese Zen monks Kosen Ingen 古先印元 (1295–1374), Myōsō Saitetsu 明叟濟哲 (d. 1347), Fukuan Sōki 復庵宗己 (1280–1358), and Enkei Soyū 遠溪祖雄 (1288–1344). The lineage founded by these Japanese disciples came to be known as the Genjū Line 幻住派, characterized by its adherence to the reclusiveness and combined Zen-Pure Land thought favored by Mingben. The lineage flourished through to Edo-period times.

Zhuozhou Kefu 涿州克符 (Cho-chou K'o-fu, Takujū Kokufu; n.d.; Case 141), also known as Zhiyi Daozhe 紙衣道者 (Chih-i Tao-che, Shi'i Dōsha, a name that means "Paper-robed Wayfarer"), was a man of Zhuozhou 涿州, modern Hebei 河北. He practiced under *Linji Yixuan* and became one of his Dharma heirs. He received his nickname from the fact that he always wore a robe made of paper.

Zilin 紫璘 (Tsu-lin, Shirin; n.d.; Case 267). Zilin's name was originally written 子璘; this was changed to 紫璘 (lit., "Purple Lin") after a purple robe was bestowed upon him by Emperor Suzong 蕭宗 (711–62). Otherwise nothing is known of this figure, except that, as his title 供奉 indicates, he was a monk who served at the imperial court.

Ziyu Daotong 紫玉道通 (Tsu-yü Tao-t'ung, Shigyoku Dōtsū; 727–813; Case 39) was a native of Lujiang 廬江; his family name was He 何. As a young man he succeeded his father as the magistrate of Nan'an 南安 in Quanzhou 泉州, in present-day Fujian 福建, but he left home to become a monk. He joined the assembly under *Mazu Daoyi*, who, at the time of his death, told him, "Where the jade shines on a beautiful mountain your work will prosper. When you find this place, remain there." Though Daotong did not understand these words at the time, later, when visiting Luoyang 洛陽, he saw in the distance a distinctive mountain of great beauty, whose name turned out to be Mount Ziyu 紫玉, "Purple Jade." He went there, built a hermitage for himself, and taught the many students who later gathered around him. In one of his recorded exchanges a monk asks,

> "What is the way to escape from the three worlds?…" The Master replied, "How long have you been in them?" The monk persisted, asking, "How can one get out of them?" The Master answered, "Green mountains do not obstruct the passing through of white clouds." (Ogata 1990, p. 205)

Chart of Names in Pinyin

Pinyin	Characters	Wade-Giles	Japanese
Anan	阿難	A-nan	Anan
Ashifujusha	阿濕縛寠沙	A-shih-feng-chü-sha	Ashibakusha
Bai Juyi	白居易	Po Chü-i	Haku Kyoi
Bai Letian	白樂天	Pai Lo-t'ien	Haku Rakuten
Baiyun Shouduan	白雲守端	Pai-yün Shou-tuan	Hakuun Shutan
Baizhang Huaihai	百丈懷海	Pai-chang Huai-hai	Hyakujō Ekai
Baizhang Weizheng	百丈惟政	Pai-chang Wei-cheng	Hyakujō Isei
Bajiao Huiqing	芭蕉慧清	Pa-chiao Hui-ch'ing	Bashō Esei
Baling Haojian	巴陵顥鑒	Pa-ling Hao-chien	Haryō Kōkan
Baofeng Kewen	寶峰克文	Pao-feng K'o-wen	Hōhō Kokubun
Baoshou Zhao	寶壽沼	Pao-shou Chao	Hōju Shō
Beijian Jujian	北礀居簡	Pei-chien Chü-chien	Hokkan Kokan
Caoshan Benji	曹山本寂	Ts'ao-shan Pen-chi	Sōzan Honjaku
Chaling Yu	茶陵郁	Ch'a-ling Yü	Charyō Iku
Changqing Da'an	長慶大安	Ch'ang-ch'ing Ta-an	Chōkei Daian
Changqing Huileng	長慶慧稜	Ch'ang-ch'ing Hui-leng	Chōkei Eryō
Changqing Lan'an	長慶懶安	Ch'ang-ch'ing Lan-an	Chōkei Ran'an
Changsha Jingcen	長沙景岑	Ch'ang-sha Ching-ts'en	Chōsa Keishin
Changsheng Jiaoran	長生皎然	Ch'ang-sheng Chiao-jan	Chōshō Kōnen
Changshui Zixuan	長水子璿	Ch'ang-shui Tzu-hsüan	Chōsui Shisen
Chen Cao	陳操	Ch'en Ts'ao	Chin Sō
Chouyan Liaoyun	稠巖了贇	Ch'ou-yen Liao-yün	Chūgan Ryōhin
Chuanzi Decheng	船子德誠	Ch'uan-tzü Te-ch'eng	Sensu Tokujō
Cui Hao	崔顥	Ts'ui Hao	Sai Kō
Cui Langzhong	崔郎中	Ts'ui Lang-chung	Sai Rōchū
Dachuan Puji	大川普濟	Ta-chuan Fu-chi	Daisen Fusai
Dadao Guquan	大道谷泉	Ta-tao Ku-ch'üan	Daidō Yokusen
Dahui Zonggao	大慧宗杲	Ta-hui Tsung-kao	Daie Sōkō
Dajian Huineng	大鑑慧能	Ta-chien Hui-neng	Daikan Enō
Damei Fachang	大梅法常	Ta-mei Fa-ch'ang	Daibai Hōjō
Danxia Tianran	丹霞天然	Tan-hsia T'ien-jan	Tanka Tennen
Danyuan Yingzhen	耽源應眞	Tan-yüan Ying-chen	Tangen Ōshin
Daowu Yuanzhi	道吾圓智	Tao-wu Yüan-chih	Dōgo Enchi
Daoxuan	道宣	Tao-hsüan	Dōsen

Dayu	大愚	Ta-yü	Daigu
Dazhu Huihai	大珠慧海	Ta-chu Hui-hai	Daiju Ekai
Deng Yinfeng	鄧隱峰	Teng Yin-feng	Tō Inpō
Deshan Xuanjian	德山宣鑑	Te-shan Hsüan-chien	Tokusan Senkan
Deyun Biqiu	德雲比丘	Te-yün Pi-ch'iu	Toku'un Biku
Dongpo	東坡	Tung-p'o	Tōba
Dongshan Huikong	東山慧空	Tung-shan Hui-kong	Tōzan Ekū
Dongshan Liangjie	洞山良价	Tung-shan Liang-chieh	Tōzan Ryōkai
Dongshan Shouchu	洞山守初	Tung-shan Shou-ch'u	Tōzan Shusho
Doushuai Congyue	兜率從悅	Tou-shuai Ts'ung-yüeh	Tosotsu Jūetsu
Fan Yanzhi	藩延之	Fan Yen-chih	Han Enshi
Fayan Wenyi	法眼文益	Fa-yen Wen-i	Hōgen Mon'eki
Fayun Gao	法雲杲	Fa-yun Kao	Hōun Kō
Fengxue Yanzhao	風穴延沼	Feng-hsüeh Yen-chao	Fuketsu Enshō
Fenyang Shanzhao	汾陽善昭	Fen-yang Shan-chao	Fun'yō Zenshō
Fenzhou Wuye	汾州無業	Fen-chou Wu-yeh	Funshū Mugō
Fojian Huiqin	佛鑑慧懃	Fo-chien Hui-ch'in	Bukkan Egon
Fori Qisong	佛日契嵩	Fo-jih Ch'i-sung	Butsunichi Kaisū
Foyan Qingyuan	佛眼清遠	Fo-yen Ch'ing-yüan	Butsugen Seion
Fu Dashi	傅大士	Fu Ta-shih	Fu Daishi
Fubei	浮盃	Fu-pei	Fuhai
Guanghui Yuanlian	廣慧元璉	Kuang-hui Yüan-lien	Kōe Ganren
Guangxiao Huijue	光孝慧覺	Kuang-hsiao Hui-chüeh	Kōkō Ekaku
Guanyin	觀音	Kuan-yin	Kannon
Guishan Lan'an	溈山懶安	Kuei-shan Lan-an	Isan Ran'an
Guishan Lingyou	溈山靈祐	Kuei-shan Ling-yu	Isan Reiyū
Guishan Da'an	溈山大安	Kuei-shan Ta-an	Isan Daian
Guizong Zhichang	歸宗智常	Kuei-tsung Chih-ch'ang	Kisu Chijō
Gulin Qingmao	古林清茂	Ku-lin Ch'ing-mao	Kurin Seimo
Gushan Shigui	鼓山士珪	Ku-shan Shih-kuei	Kuzan Shikei
Han Yu	韓愈	Han Yü	Kan Yu
Hanshan	寒山	Han-shan	Kanzan
Haoyue	皓月	Hao-yüeh	Kōgetsu
Hongren	弘忍	Hung-jen	Gunin
Hongzhi Zhengjue	宏智正覺	Hung-chih Cheng-chüeh	Wanshi Shōgaku
Hu Dingjiao	胡釘鉸	Hu Ting-chiao	Ko Teikō
Huang Tingjian	黃庭堅	Huang T'ing-chien	Kō Teiken
Huangbo Weisheng	黃檗惟勝	Huang-po Wei-sheng	Ōbaku Ishō
Huangbo Xiyun	黃檗希運	Huang-po Hsi-yün	Ōbaku Kiun
Huanglong Huinan	黃龍慧南	Huang-lung Hui-nan	Ōryō Enan
Huike	慧可	Hui-k'o	Eka
Huiming	慧明	Hui-ming	Emyō
Huineng	慧能	Hui-neng	Enō

Huitang Zuxin	晦堂祖心	Hui-t'ang Tsu-hsin	Maidō Soshin
Huiyuan	慧遠	Hui-yüan	Eon
Huo'an Shiti	或庵師體	Huo-an Shih-t'i	Wakuan Shitai
Hutou	虎頭	Hu-t'ou	Kotō
Ji Xin	紀信	Chi Hsin	Ki Shin
Jianatipo	迦那提婆	Chia-na-ti-p'o	Kanadaiba
Jianfu Chenggu	薦福承古	Chien-fu Ch'eng-ku	Senpuku Shōko
Jiashan Shanhui	夾山善會	Chia-shan Shan-hui	Kassan Zenne
Jiashe Fo	迦葉佛	Chia-she Fo	Kashō Butsu
Jingqing Daofu	鏡清道怤	Ching-ch'ing Tao-fu	Kyōsei Dōfu
Jingshan Hongyin	徑山洪諲	Ching-shan Hung-yin	Kinzan Kōin
Jingzhao Mihu	京兆米胡	Ching-chao Mi-hu	Keichō Beiko
Jiyin Zunzhe	寂音尊者	Chi-yin Tsun-che	Jakuon Sonja
Jue Tiezui	覺鐵觜	Chüeh T'ieh-tsui	Kaku Tetsushi
Juefan Huihong	覺範慧洪	Chüeh-fan Hui-hung	Kakuhan Ekō
Juzhou Baotan	橘洲寶曇	Chü-chou Pao-t'an	Kisshū Hōdon
Langye Huijue	瑯瑘慧覺	Lang-yeh Hui-chüeh	Rōya Ekaku
Letan Kewen	泐潭克文	Le-t'an K'o-wen	Rokutan Kokubun
Li Tongxuan	李通玄	Li T'ung-hsüan	Ri Tsūgen
Li Ying	李膺	Li Ying	Ri Yō
Liang	良	Liang	Ryō
Lingshu Rumin	靈樹如敏	Ling-shu Ju-min	Reiju Nyobin
Lingyun Zhiqin	靈雲志勤	Ling-yün Chih-ch'in	Reiun Shigon
Linji Yixuan	臨濟義玄	Lin-chi I-hsüan	Rinzai Gigen
Longqing Qingxian	隆慶慶閑	Lung-ch'ing Ch'ing-hsien	Ryūkei Keikan
Longshu	龍樹	Lung-shu	Ryūju
Longtan Chongxin	龍潭崇信	Lung-t'an Ch'ung-hsin	Ryūtan Sōshin
Longya Judun	龍牙居遁	Lung-ya Chü-tun	Ryūge Kodon
Lu Gen	陸亙	Lu Ken	Riku Kō
Luopu Yuan'an	洛浦元安	Lo-p'u Yüan-an	Rakuho Gen'an
Luoshan Daoxian	羅山道閑	Lo-shan T'ao-hsien	Razan Dōkan
Magu Baotie	麻谷寶鐵	Ma-ku Pao-t'ieh	Mayoku Hōtetsu
Mazu Daoyi	馬祖道一	Ma-tsu Tao-i	Baso Dōitsu
Mian Xianjie	密庵咸傑	Mi-an Hsien-chieh	Mittan Kanketsu
Mile	彌勒	Mi-le	Miroku
Mingzhao Deqian	明招德謙	Ming-chao Te-ch'ien	Myōshō Tokken
Mohe Jiashe	摩訶迦葉	Mo-ho Chia-she	Makakashō
Monaluo	摩拏羅	Mo-na-la	Manura
Mulian	目連	Mu-lien	Mokuren
Muzhou Daoming	睦州道明	Mu-chou Tao-ming	Bokujū Dōmyō
Nazha	那吒	Na-cha	Nata
Nanquan Puyuan	南泉普願	Nan-ch'üan Pu-yuan	Nansen Fugan
Nantang Yuanjing	南堂元靜	Nan-t'ang Yüan-ching	Nandō Genjō

Nanyuan Huiyong	南院慧顒	Nan-yüan Hui-yung	Nan'in Egyō
Nanyang Huizhong	南陽慧忠	Nan-yang Hui-chung	Nan'yō Echū
Nanyue Huairang	南嶽懷讓	Nan-yüeh Huai-jang	Nangaku Ejō
Niaoke Daolin	鳥窠道林	Niao-k'o Tao-lin	Chōka Dōrin
Pang Jushi	龐居士	P'ang Chü-shih	Hō Koji
Pang Yun	龐蘊	P'ang Yün	Hō On
Pei Xiu	裴休	P'ei Hsiu	Hi Kyū
Piposhi	毘婆尸	P'i-p'o-shih	Bibashi
Piyun	披雲	P'i-yün	Hiun
Putidamo	菩提達磨	P'u-t'i-ta-mo	Bodaidaruma
Puxian	普賢	P'u-hsien	Fugen
Qingliang Taiqin	清涼泰欽	Ch'ing-liang Tai-ch'in	Shōryō Taikin
Qingshui	清稅	Ch'ing-shui	Seizei
Qingsu	清素	Ch'ing-su	Seiso
Qinshan Wensui	欽山文邃	Ch'in-shan Wen-sui	Kinzan Bunsui
Ruiyan Shiyan	瑞巖師彥	Jui-yen Shih-yen	Zuigan Shigen
Sansheng Huiran	三聖慧然	San-sheng Hui-jan	Sanshō Enen
Sengcan	僧璨	Seng-ts'an	Sōsan
Sengzhao	僧肇	Seng-chao	Sōjō
Shancai Tongzi	善財童子	Shan-ts'ai T'ung-tzu	Zenzai Dōshi
Shangu	山谷	Shan-ku	Sankoku
Shelifu	舍利弗	She-li-fu	Sharihotsu
Shending Hongyin	神鼎洪諲	Shen-ting Hong-yin	Shintei Kōin
Shexian Guixing	葉縣歸省	She-hsien Kuei-hsing	Sekken Kisei
Shijiamouni	釋迦牟尼	Shih-chia-mou-ni	Shakamuni
Shishuang Chuyuan	石霜楚圓	Shih-shuang Ch'u-yüan	Sekisō Soen
Shishuang Qingzhu	石霜慶諸	Shih-shuang Ch'ing-chu	Sekisō Keisho
Shishuang Xingkong	石霜性空	Shih-shuang Hsing-k'ung	Sekisō Shōkū
Shitou Xiqian	石頭希遷	Shih-t'ou Hsi-ch'ien	Sekitō Kisen
Shizi Puti	師子菩提	Shih-tzu P'u-ti	Shishi Bodai
Shoukuo	守廓	Shou-k'uo	Shukaku
Shoushan Shengnian	首山省念	Shou-shan Sheng-nien	Shuzan Shōnen
Shouzhou Liangsui	壽州良遂	Shou-chou Liang-sui	Jushū Ryōsui
Shuangshan Yuan	雙杉元	Shuang-shan Yüan	Sōsan Gen
Shui'an Shiyi	水庵師一	Shui-an Shih-i	Sui'an Shi'ichi
Shushan Guangren	疎山光仁	Shu-shan Kuang-jen	Sozan Kōnin
Sixin Wuxin	死心悟新	Ssu-hsin Wu-hsin	Shishin Goshin
Songshan Huian	嵩山慧安	Sung-shan Hui-an	Sūzan Ean
Songyuan Chongyue	松源崇嶽	Sung-yüan Ch'ung-yüeh	Shōgen Sūgaku
Taihang Kebin	太行克賓	T'ai-hang K'o-pin	Taikō Kokuhin
Taizong	太宗	T'ai-tsung	Taisō
Tianhuang Daowu	天皇道悟	T'ien-huang Tao-wu	Tennō Dōgo
Tiantai Deshao	天台德韶	T'ien-t'ai Te-shao	Tendai Tokushō

Tiantong Hongzhi	天童宏智	T'ien-t'ung Hung-chih	Tendō Wanshi
Tipo	提婆	Ti-p'o	Daiba
Tipodaduo	提婆達多	Ti-p'o-ta-to	Daibadatta
Touzi Datong	投子大同	T'ou-tzu Ta-t'ung	Tōsu Daidō
Touzi Fazong	投子法宗	T'ou-tzu Fa-tsung	Tōsu Hōshū
Wan'an Daoyan	卍庵道顏	Wan-an Tao-yan	Man'an Dōgan
Wang Changshi	王常侍	Wang Ch'ang-shih	Ō Jōji
Wang Sui	王隨	Wang Sui	Ō Zui
Weimojie	維摩詰	Wei-mo-chieh	Yuimakitsu
Weituotian	韋馱天	Wei-t'o-t'ien	Idaten
Wenshu	文殊	Wen-shu	Monju
Wolun	臥輪	Wo-lun	Garin
Wumen Huikai	無門慧開	Wu-men Hui-k'ai	Mumon Ekai
Wuzu Fayan	五祖法演	Wu-tsu Fa-yen	Goso Hōen
Wuzu Shijie	五祖師戒	Wu-tsu Shih-chieh	Goso Shikai
Xiang Yu	項羽	Hsiang Yü	Kō U
Xianglin Chengyuan	香林澄遠	Hsiang-lin Ch'eng-yüan	Kyōrin Chōon
Xiangyan Zhixian	香嚴智閑	Hsiang-yen Chih-hsien	Kyōgen Chikan
Xianzong	憲宗	Hsien-tsung	Kensō
Xinghua Cunjiang	興化存獎	Hsing-hua Ts'un-chiang	Kōke Zonshō
Xingjiao Hongshou	興教洪壽	Hsing-chiao Hung-shou	Kōkyō Kōju
Xitang Zhizang	西堂智藏	Hsi-t'ang Chih-tsang	Seidō Chizō
Xiu	秀	Hsiu	Shū
Xuansha Shibei	玄沙師備	Hsüan-sha Shih-pei	Gensha Shibi
Xuanzong	宣宗	Hsüan-tsung	Sensō
Xuedou Chongxian	雪竇重顯	Hsüeh-tou Ch'ung-hsien	Setchō Jūken
Xuefeng Yicun	雪峰義存	Hsüeh-feng I-ts'un	Seppō Gison
Xutang Zhiyu	虛堂智愚	Hsü-t'ang Chih-yü	Kidō Chigu
Yang Danian	楊大年	Yang Ta-nien	Yō Dainen
Yang Yi	楊億	Yang I	Yō Oku
Yangjue Moluo	殃掘摩羅	Yang-chüeh Mo-lo	Ōkutsu Mara
Yangqi Fanghui	楊岐方會	Yang-ch'i Fang-hui	Yōgi Hōe
Yangshan Huiji	仰山慧寂	Yang-shan Hui-chi	Kyōzan Ejaku
Yantou Quanhuo	嚴頭全奯	Yen-t'ou Ch'uan-huo	Gantō Zenkatsu
Yanyang Shanxin	嚴陽善信	Yen-yang Shan-hsin	Gen'yō Zenshin
Ying'an Tanhua	應庵曇華	Ying-an T'an-hua	Ōan Donge
Yongjia Xuanjue	永嘉玄覺	Yung-chia Hsüan-chüeh	Yōka Genkaku
Yongming Yanshou	永明延壽	Yung-ming Yen-shou	Yōmei Enju
Youtianwang	優塡王	Yu-t'ien-wang	Utenō
Yu Di	于頔	Yü Ti	U Teki
Yuanming	圓明	Yüan-ming	Enmyō
Yuanwu Keqin	圜悟克勤	Yüan-wu K'o-ch'in	Engo Kokugon
Yuezhou Qianfeng	越州乾峰	Yüeh-chou Ch'ien-feng	Esshū Kenpō

Yun'an Puyan	運庵普巖	Yün-an P'u-yen	Un'an Fugan
Yunju Daojian	雲居道簡	Yün-chü Tao-chien	Ungo Dōkan
Yunju Shanwu	雲居善悟	Yün-chü Shan-wu	Ungo Zengo
Yunmen Wenyan	雲門文偃	Yün-men Wen-yen	Unmon Bun'en
Zhang Shangying	張商英	Chang Shang-ying	Chō Shōei
Zhang Wujin	張無盡	Chang Wu-chin	Chō Mujin
Zhang Zhuo	張拙	Chang Cho	Chō Setsu
Zhang Zishao	張子韶	Chang Tzu-shao	Chō Shishō
Zhao Biaozhi	趙表之	Chao Piao-chih	Jō Hyōshi
Zhaozhou Congshen	趙州從諗	Chao-chou Ts'ung-shen	Jōshū Jūshin
Zhenjing Kewen	眞淨克文	Chen-ching K'o-wen	Shinjō Kokubun
Zhiyi Daozhe	紙衣道者	Chih-i Tao-che	Shi'i Dōsha
Zhongfeng Mingben	中峰明本	Chung-feng Ming-pen	Chūhō Myōhon
Zhuozhou Kefu	涿州克符	Cho-chou K'o-fu	Takujū Kokufu
Zilin	紫璘	Tsu-lin	Shirin
Ziyu Daotong	紫玉道通	Tsu-yü Tao-t'ung	Shigyoku Dōtsū

Chart of Names in Wade-Giles

Wade-Giles	Characters	Pinyin	Japanese
A-nan	阿難	Anan	Anan
A-shih-feng-chü-sha	阿濕縛窶沙	Ashifujusha	Ashibakusha
Ch'a-ling Yü	茶陵郁	Chaling Yu	Charyō Iku
Chang Cho	張拙	Zhang Zhuo	Chō Setsu
Chang Shang-ying	張商英	Zhang Shangying	Chō Shōei
Chang Tzu-shao	張子韶	Zhang Zishao	Chō Shishō
Chang Wu-chin	張無盡	Zhang Wujin	Chō Mujin
Ch'ang-ch'ing Hui-leng	長慶慧稜	Changqing Huileng	Chōkei Eryō
Ch'ang-ch'ing Lan-an	長慶懶安	Changqing Lan'an	Chōkei Ran'an
Ch'ang-ch'ing Ta-an	長慶大安	Changqing Da'an	Chōkei Daian
Ch'ang-sha Ching-ts'en	長沙景岑	Changsha Jingcen	Chōsa Keishin
Ch'ang-sheng Chiao-jan	長生皎然	Changsheng Jiaoran	Chōshō Kōnen
Ch'ang-shui Tzu-hsüan	長水子璿	Changshui Zixuan	Chōsui Shisen
Chao Piao-chih	趙表之	Zhao Biaozhi	Jō Hyōshi
Chao-chou Ts'ung-shen	趙州從諗	Zhaozhou Congshen	Jōshū Jūshin
Chen-ching K'o-wen	眞淨克文	Zhenjing Kewen	Shinjō Kokubun
Ch'en Ts'ao	陳操	Chen Cao	Chin Sō
Chi Hsin	紀信	Ji Xin	Ki Shin
Chi-yin Tsun-che	寂音尊者	Jiyin Zunzhe	Jakuon Sonja
Chia-na-ti-p'o	迦那提婆	Jianatipo	Kanadaiba
Chia-shan Shan-hui	夾山善會	Jiashan Shanhui	Kassan Zenne
Chia-she Fo	迦葉佛	Jiashe Fo	Kashō Butsu
Chien-fu Ch'eng-ku	薦福承古	Jianfu Chenggu	Senpuku Shōko
Chih-i Tao-che	紙衣道者	Zhiyi Daozhe	Shi'i Dōsha
Ch'in-shan Wen-sui	欽山文邃	Qinshan Wensui	Kinzan Bunsui
Ching-chao Mi-hu	京兆米胡	Jingzhao Mihu	Keichō Beiko
Ching-ch'ing Tao-fu	鏡清道怤	Jingqing Daofu	Kyōsei Dōfu
Ching-shan Hung-yin	徑山洪諲	Jingshan Hongyin	Kinzan Kōin
Ch'ing-liang Tai-ch'in	清涼泰欽	Qingliang Taiqin	Shōryō Taikin
Ch'ing-shui	清税	Qingshui	Seizei
Ch'ing-su	清素	Qingsu	Seiso
Cho-chou K'o-fu	涿州克符	Zhuozhou Kefu	Takujū Kokufu
Ch'ou-yen Liao-yün	稠巖了贇	Chouyan Liaoyun	Chūgan Ryōhin
Chü-chou Pao-t'an	橘洲寶曇	Juzhou Baotan	Kisshū Hōdon

Ch'uan-tzü Te-ch'eng	船子德誠	Chuanzi Decheng	Sensu Tokujō
Chüeh T'ieh-tsui	覺鐵觜	Jue Tiezui	Kaku Tetsushi
Chüeh-fan Hui-hung	覺範慧洪	Juefan Huihong	Kakuhan Ekō
Chung-feng Ming-pen	中峰明本	Zhongfeng Mingben	Chūhō Myōhon
Fan Yen-chih	藩延之	Fan Yanzhi	Han Enshi
Fa-yen Wen-i	法眼文益	Fayan Wenyi	Hōgen Mon'eki
Fa-yun Kao	法雲杲	Fayun Gao	Hōun Kō
Fen-chou Wu-yeh	汾州無業	Fenzhou Wuye	Funshū Mugō
Fen-yang Shan-chao	汾陽善昭	Fenyang Shanzhao	Fun'yō Zenshō
Feng-hsüeh Yen-chao	風穴延沼	Fengxue Yanzhao	Fuketsu Enshō
Fo-chien Hui-ch'in	佛鑑慧懃	Fojian Huiqin	Bukkan Egon
Fo-jih Ch'i-sung	佛日契嵩	Fori Qisong	Butsunichi Kaisū
Fo-yen Ch'ing-yüan	佛眼清遠	Foyan Qingyuan	Butsugen Seion
Fu Ta-shih	傅大士	Fu Dashi	Fu Daishi
Fu-pei	浮盃	Fubei	Fuhai
Han Yü	韓愈	Han Yu	Kan Yu
Han-shan	寒山	Hanshan	Kanzan
Hao-yüeh	皓月	Haoyue	Kōgetsu
Hsi-t'ang Chih-tsang	西堂智藏	Xitang Zhizang	Seidō Chizō
Hsiang Yü	項羽	Xiang Yu	Kō U
Hsiang-lin Ch'eng-yüan	香林澄遠	Xianglin Chengyuan	Kyōrin Chōon
Hsiang-yen Chih-hsien	香嚴智閑	Xiangyan Zhixian	Kyōgen Chikan
Hsien-tsung	憲宗	Xianzong	Kensō
Hsing-chiao Hung-shou	興教洪壽	Xingjiao Hongshou	Kōkyō Kōju
Hsing-hua Ts'un-chiang	興化存獎	Xinghua Cunjiang	Kōke Zonshō
Hsiu	秀	Xiu	Shū
Hsü-t'ang Chih-yü	虛堂智愚	Xutang Zhiyu	Kidō Chigu
Hsüan-sha Shih-pei	玄沙師備	Xuansha Shibei	Gensha Shibi
Hsüan-tsung	宣宗	Xuanzong	Sensō
Hsüeh-feng I-ts'un	雪峰義存	Xuefeng Yicun	Seppō Gison
Hsüeh-tou Ch'ung-hsien	雪竇重顯	Xuedou Chongxian	Setchō Jūken
Hu Ting-chiao	胡釘鉸	Hu Dingjiao	Ko Teikō
Hu-t'ou	虎頭	Hutou	Kotō
Huang T'ing-chien	黃庭堅	Huang Tingjian	Kō Teiken
Huang-lung Hui-nan	黃龍慧南	Huanglong Huinan	Ōryō Enan
Huang-po Hsi-yün	黃檗希運	Huangbo Xiyun	Ōbaku Kiun
Huang-po Wei-sheng	黃檗惟勝	Huangbo Weisheng	Ōbaku Ishō
Hui-k'o	慧可	Huike	Eka
Hui-ming	慧明	Huiming	Emyō
Hui-neng	慧能	Huineng	Enō
Hui-t'ang Tsu-hsin	晦堂祖心	Huitang Zuxin	Maidō Soshin
Hui-yüan	慧遠	Huiyuan	Eon
Hung-chih Cheng-chüeh	宏智正覺	Hongzhi Zhengjue	Wanshi Shōgaku

Hung-jen	弘忍	Hongren	Gunin
Huo-an Shih-t'i	或庵師體	Huo'an Shiti	Wakuan Shitai
Jui-yen Shih-yen	瑞巖師彥	Ruiyan Shiyan	Zuigan Shigen
Ku-lin Ch'ing-mao	古林清茂	Gulin Qingmao	Kurin Seimo
Ku-shan Shih-kuei	鼓山士珪	Gushan Shigui	Kuzan Shikei
Kuan-yin	觀音	Guanyin	Kannon
Kuang-hsiao Hui-chüeh	光孝慧覺	Guangxiao Huijue	Kōkō Ekaku
Kuang-hui Yüan-lien	廣慧元璉	Guanghui Yuanlian	Kōe Ganren
Kuei-shan Lan-an	潙山懶安	Guishan Lan'an	Isan Ran'an
Kuei-shan Ling-yu	潙山靈祐	Guishan Lingyou	Isan Reiyū
Kuei-shan Ta-an	潙山大安	Guishan Da'an	Isan Daian
Kuei-tsung Chih-ch'ang	歸宗智常	Guizong Zhichang	Kisu Chijō
Lang-yeh Hui-chüeh	瑯瑘慧覺	Langye Huijue	Rōya Ekaku
Le-t'an K'o-wen	泐潭克文	Letan Kewen	Rokutan Kokubun
Li T'ung-hsüan	李通玄	Li Tongxuan	Ri Tsūgen
Li Ying	李膺	Li Ying	Ri Yō
Liang	良	Liang	Ryō
Lin-chi I-hsüan	臨濟義玄	Linji Yixuan	Rinzai Gigen
Ling-shu Ju-min	靈樹如敏	Lingshu Rumin	Reiju Nyobin
Ling-yün Chih-ch'in	靈雲志勤	Lingyun Zhiqin	Reiun Shigon
Lo-p'u Yüan-an	洛浦元安	Luopu Yuan'an	Rakuho Gen'an
Lo-shan T'ao-hsien	羅山道閑	Luoshan Daoxian	Razan Dōkan
Lu Ken	陸亙	Lu Gen	Riku Kō
Lung-ch'ing Ch'ing-hsien	隆慶慶閑	Longqing Qingxian	Ryūkei Keikan
Lung-shu	龍樹	Longshu	Ryūju
Lung-t'an Ch'ung-hsin	龍潭崇信	Longtan Chongxin	Ryūtan Sōshin
Lung-ya Chü-tun	龍牙居遁	Longya Judun	Ryūge Kodon
Ma-ku Pao-t'ieh	麻谷寶鐵	Magu Baotie	Mayoku Hōtetsu
Ma-tsu Tao-i	馬祖道一	Mazu Daoyi	Baso Dōitsu
Mi-an Hsien-chieh	密庵咸傑	Mian Xianjie	Mittan Kanketsu
Mi-le	彌勒	Mile	Miroku
Ming-chao Te-ch'ien	明招德謙	Mingzhao Deqian	Myōshō Tokken
Mo-ho Chia-she	摩訶迦葉	Mohe Jiashe	Makakashō
Mo-na-la	摩拏羅	Monaluo	Manura
Mu-chou Tao-ming	睦州道明	Muzhou Daoming	Bokujū Dōmyō
Mu-lien	目連	Mulian	Mokuren
Na-cha	那吒	Nazha	Nata
Nan-ch'üan Pu-yüan	南泉普願	Nanquan Puyuan	Nansen Fugan
Nan-t'ang Yüan-ching	南堂元靜	Nantang Yuanjing	Nandō Genjō
Nan-yang Hui-chung	南陽慧忠	Nanyang Huizhong	Nan'yō Echū
Nan-yüan Hui-yung	南院慧顒	Nanyuan Huiyong	Nan'in Egyō
Nan-yüeh Huai-jang	南嶽懷讓	Nanyue Huairang	Nangaku Ejō
Niao-k'o Tao-lin	鳥窠道林	Niaoke Daolin	Chōka Dōrin

Pa-chiao Hui-ch'ing	芭蕉慧清	Bajiao Huiqing	Bashō Esei
Pa-ling Hao-chien	巴陵顥鑒	Baling Haojian	Haryō Kōkan
Pai Lo-t'ien	白樂天	Bai Letian	Haku Rakuten
Pai-chang Huai-hai	百丈懷海	Baizhang Huaihai	Hyakujō Ekai
Pai-chang Wei-cheng	百丈惟政	Baizhang Weizheng	Hyakujō Isei
Pai-yün Shou-tuan	白雲守端	Baiyun Shouduan	Hakuun Shutan
P'ang Chü-shih	龐居士	Pang Jushi	Hō Koji
P'ang Yün	龐蘊	Pang Yun	Hō On
Pao-feng K'o-wen	寶峰克文	Baofeng Kewen	Hōhō Kokubun
Pao-shou Chao	寶壽沼	Baoshou Zhao	Hōju Shō
Pei-chien Chü-chien	北磵居簡	Beijian Jujian	Hokkan Kokan
P'ei Hsiu	裴休	Pei Xiu	Hi Kyū
P'i-p'o-shih	毘婆尸	Piposhi	Bibashi
P'i-yün	披雲	Piyun	Hiun
Po Chü-i	白居易	Bai Juyi	Haku Kyoi
P'u-hsien	普賢	Puxian	Fugen
P'u-t'i-ta-mo	菩提達磨	Putidamo	Bodaidaruma
San-sheng Hui-jan	三聖慧然	Sansheng Huiran	Sanshō Enen
Seng-chao	僧肇	Sengzhao	Sōjō
Seng-ts'an	僧璨	Sengcan	Sōsan
Shan-ku	山谷	Shangu	Sankoku
Shan-ts'ai T'ung-tzu	善財童子	Shancai Tongzi	Zenzai Dōshi
She-hsien Kuei-hsing	葉縣歸省	Shexian Guixing	Sekken Kisei
She-li-fu	舍利弗	Shelifu	Sharihotsu
Shen-ting Hong-yin	神鼎洪諲	Shending Hongyin	Shintei Kōin
Shih-chia-mou-ni	釋迦牟尼	Shijiamouni	Shakamuni
Shih-shuang Ch'ing-chu	石霜慶諸	Shishuang Qingzhu	Sekisō Keisho
Shih-shuang Ch'u-yüan	石霜楚圓	Shishuang Chuyuan	Sekisō Soen
Shih-shuang Hsing-k'ung	石霜性空	Shishuang Xingkong	Sekisō Shōkū
Shih-t'ou Hsi-ch'ien	石頭希遷	Shitou Xiqian	Sekitō Kisen
Shih-tzu P'u-ti	師子菩提	Shizi Puti	Shishi Bodai
Shou-chou Liang-sui	壽州良遂	Shouzhou Liangsui	Jushū Ryōsui
Shou-k'uo	守廓	Shoukuo	Shukaku
Shou-shan Sheng-nien	首山省念	Shoushan Shengnian	Shuzan Shōnen
Shu-shan Kuang-jen	疎山光仁	Shushan Guangren	Sozan Kōnin
Shuang-shan Yüan	雙杉元	Shuangshan Yuan	Sōsan Gen
Shui-an Shih-i	水庵師一	Shui'an Shiyi	Sui'an Shi'ichi
Ssu-hsin Wu-hsin	死心悟新	Sixin Wuxin	Shishin Goshin
Sung-shan Hui-an	嵩山慧安	Songshan Huian	Sūzan Ean
Sung-yüan Ch'ung-yüeh	松源崇嶽	Songyuan Chongyue	Shōgen Sūgaku
Ta-chien Hui-neng	大鑑慧能	Dajian Huineng	Daikan Enō
Ta-chu Hui-hai	大珠慧海	Dazhu Huihai	Daiju Ekai
Ta-chuan Fu-chi	大川普濟	Dachuan Puji	Daisen Fusai

Ta-hui Tsung-kao	大慧宗杲	Dahui Zonggao	Daie Sōkō
Ta-mei Fa-ch'ang	大梅法常	Damei Fachang	Daibai Hōjō
Ta-yü	大愚	Dayu	Daigu
T'ai-hang K'o-pin	太行克賓	Taihang Kebin	Taikō Kokuhin
T'ai-tsung	太宗	Taizong	Taisō
Tan-hsia T'ien-jan	丹霞天然	Danxia Tianran	Tanka Tennen
Tan-yüan Ying-chen	耽源應眞	Danyuan Yingzhen	Tangen Ōshin
Tao-hsüan	道宣	Daoxuan	Dōsen
Tao-wu Yüan-chih	道吾圓智	Daowu Yuanzhi	Dōgo Enchi
Ta-tao Ku-ch'üan	大道谷泉	Dadao Guquan	Daidō Yokusen
Te-shan Hsüan-chien	德山宣鑑	Deshan Xuanjian	Tokusan Senkan
Te-yün Pi-ch'iu	德雲比丘	Deyun Biqiu	Toku'un Biku
Teng Yin-feng	鄧隱峰	Deng Yinfeng	Tō Inpō
T'ien-huang Tao-wu	天皇道悟	Tianhuang Daowu	Tennō Dōgo
T'ien-t'ai Te-shao	天台德韶	Tiantai Deshao	Tendai Tokushō
T'ien-t'ung Hung-chih	天童宏智	Tiantong Hongzhi	Tendō Wanshi
Ti-p'o	提婆	Tipo	Daiba
Ti-p'o-ta-to	提婆達多	Tipodaduo	Daibadatta
Tou-shuai Ts'ung-yüeh	兜率從悅	Doushuai Congyue	Tosotsu Jūetsu
T'ou-tzu Fa-tsung	投子法宗	Touzi Fazong	Tōsu Hōshū
T'ou-tzu Ta-t'ung	投子大同	Touzi Datong	Tōsu Daidō
Ts'ao-shan Pen-chi	曹山本寂	Caoshan Benji	Sōzan Honjaku
Tsu-lin	紫璘	Zilin	Shirin
Tsu-yü Tao-t'ung	紫玉道通	Ziyu Daotong	Shigyoku Dōtsū
Ts'ui Hao	崔顥	Cui Hao	Sai Kō
Ts'ui Lang-chung	崔郎中	Cui Langzhong	Sai Rōchū
Tung-p'o	東坡	Dongpo	Tōba
Tung-shan Hui-kong	東山慧空	Dongshan Huikong	Tōzan Ekū
Tung-shan Liang-chieh	洞山良价	Dongshan Liangjie	Tōzan Ryōkai
Tung-shan Shou-ch'u	洞山守初	Dongshan Shouchu	Tōzan Shusho
Wan-an Tao-yan	卍庵道顏	Wan'an Daoyan	Man'an Dōgan
Wang Ch'ang-shih	王常侍	Wang Changshi	Ō Jōji
Wang Sui	王隨	Wang Sui	Ō Zui
Wei-mo-chieh	維摩詰	Weimojie	Yuimakitsu
Wei-t'o-t'ien	韋馱天	Weituotian	Idaten
Wen-shu	文殊	Wenshu	Monju
Wo-lun	臥輪	Wolun	Garin
Wu-men Hui-k'ai	無門慧開	Wumen Huikai	Mumon Ekai
Wu-tsu Fa-yen	五祖法演	Wuzu Fayan	Goso Hōen
Wu-tsu Shih-chieh	五祖師戒	Wuzu Shijie	Goso Shikai
Yang I	楊億	Yang Yi	Yō Oku
Yang Ta-nien	楊大年	Yang Danian	Yō Dainen
Yang-ch'i Fang-hui	楊岐方會	Yangqi Fanghui	Yōgi Hōe

Yang-chüeh Mo-lo	殃掘摩羅	Yangjue Moluo	Ōkutsu Mara
Yang-shan Hui-chi	仰山慧寂	Yangshan Huiji	Kyōzan Ejaku
Yen-t'ou Ch'uan-huo	巖頭全豁	Yantou Quanhuo	Gantō Zenkatsu
Yen-yang Shan-hsin	嚴陽善信	Yanyang Shanxin	Gen'yō Zenshin
Ying-an T'an-hua	應庵曇華	Ying'an Tanhua	Ōan Donge
Yü Ti	于頔	Yu Di	U Teki
Yu-t'ien-wang	優填王	Youtianwang	Utenō
Yüan-ming	圓明	Yuanming	Enmyō
Yüan-wu K'o-ch'in	圜悟克勤	Yuanwu Keqin	Engo Kokugon
Yüeh-chou Ch'ien-feng	越州乾峰	Yuezhou Qianfeng	Esshū Kenpō
Yün-an P'u-yen	運庵普巖	Yun'an Puyan	Un'an Fugan
Yün-chü Shan-wu	雲居善悟	Yunju Shanwu	Ungo Zengo
Yün-chü Tao-chien	雲居道簡	Yunju Daojian	Ungo Dōkan
Yün-men Wen-yen	雲門文偃	Yunmen Wenyan	Unmon Bun'en
Yung-chia Hsüan-chüeh	永嘉玄覺	Yongjia Xuanjue	Yōka Genkaku
Yung-ming Yen-shou	永明延壽	Yongming Yanshou	Yōmei Enju

Chart of Names in Japanese

Japanese	Characters	Pinyin	Wade-Giles
Anan	阿難	Anan	A-nan
Ashibakusha	阿濕縛寠沙	Ashifujusha	A-shih-feng-chü-sha
Bashō Esei	芭蕉慧清	Bajiao Huiqing	Pa-chiao Hui-ch'ing
Baso Dōitsu	馬祖道一	Mazu Daoyi	Ma-tsu Tao-i
Bibashi	毘婆尸	Piposhi	P'i-p'o-shih
Bodaidaruma	菩提達磨	Putidamo	P'u-t'i-ta-mo
Bokujū Dōmyō	睦州道明	Muzhou Daoming	Mu-chou Tao-ming
Bukkan Egon	佛鑑慧懃	Fojian Huiqin	Fo-chien Hui-ch'in
Butsugen Seion	佛眼清遠	Foyan Qingyuan	Fo-yen Ch'ing-yüan
Butsunichi Kaisū	佛日契嵩	Fori Qisong	Fo-jih Ch'i-sung
Charyō Iku	茶陵郁	Chaling Yu	Ch'a-ling Yü
Chin Sō	陳操	Chen Cao	Ch'en Ts'ao
Chō Mujin	張無盡	Zhang Wujin	Chang Wu-chin
Chō Setsu	張拙	Zhang Zhuo	Chang Cho
Chō Shishō	張子韶	Zhang Zishao	Chang Tzu-shao
Chō Shōei	張商英	Zhang Shangying	Chang Shang-ying
Chōka Dōrin	鳥窠道林	Niaoke Daolin	Niao-k'o Tao-lin
Chōkei Daian	長慶大安	Changqing Da'an	Ch'ang-ch'ing Ta-an
Chōkei Eryō	長慶慧稜	Changqing Huileng	Ch'ang-ch'ing Hui-leng
Chōkei Ran'an	長慶懶安	Changqing Lan'an	Ch'ang-ch'ing Lan-an
Chōsa Keishin	長沙景岑	Changsha Jingcen	Ch'ang-sha Ching-ts'en
Chōshō Kōnen	長生皎然	Changsheng Jiaoran	Ch'ang-sheng Chiao-jan
Chōsui Shisen	長水子璿	Changshui Zixuan	Ch'ang-shui Tzu-hsüan
Chūgan Ryōhin	稠巖了贇	Chouyan Liaoyun	Ch'ou-yen Liao-yün
Chūhō Myōhon	中峰明本	Zhongfeng Mingben	Chung-feng Ming-pen
Daiba	提婆	Tipo	Ti-p'o
Daibadatta	提婆達多	Tipodaduo	Ti-p'o-ta-to
Daibai Hōjō	大梅法常	Damei Fachang	Ta-mei Fa-ch'ang
Daidō Yokusen	大道谷泉	Dadao Guquan	Ta-tao Ku-ch'üan
Daie Sōkō	大慧宗杲	Dahui Zonggao	Ta-hui Tsung-kao
Daigu	大愚	Dayu	Ta-yü
Daiju Ekai	大珠慧海	Dazhu Huihai	Ta-chu Hui-hai
Daikan Enō	大鑑慧能	Dajian Huineng	Ta-chien Hui-neng
Daiō	大應		

Daisen Fusai	大川普濟	Dachuan Puji	Ta-chuan Fu-chi
Daitō	大燈		
Dōgo Enchi	道吾圓智	Daowu Yuanzhi	Tao-wu Yüan-chih
Dōsen	道宣	Daoxuan	Tao-hsüan
Eka	慧可	Huike	Hui-k'o
Emyō	慧明	Huiming	Hui-ming
Engo Kokugon	圓悟克勤	Yuanwu Keqin	Yüan-wu K'o-ch'in
Enmyō	圓明	Yuanming	Yüan-ming
Enō	慧能	Huineng	Hui-neng
Eon	慧遠	Huiyuan	Hui-yüan
Esshū Kenpō	越州乾峰	Yuezhou Qianfeng	Yüeh-chou Ch'ien-feng
Fu Daishi	傅大士	Fu Dashi	Fu Ta-shih
Fugen	普賢	Puxian	P'u-hsien
Fuhai	浮盃	Fubei	Fu-pei
Fuketsu Enshō	風穴延沼	Fengxue Yanzhao	Feng-hsüeh Yen-chao
Funshū Mugō	汾州無業	Fenzhou Wuye	Fen-chou Wu-yeh
Fun'yō Zenshō	汾陽善昭	Fenyang Shanzhao	Fen-yang Shan-chao
Gantō Zenkatsu	巖頭全奯	Yantou Quanhuo	Yen-t'ou Ch'uan-huo
Garin	臥輪	Wolun	Wo-lun
Gensha Shibi	玄沙師備	Xuansha Shibei	Hsüan-sha Shih-pei
Gen'yō Zenshin	巖陽善信	Yanyang Shanxin	Yen-yang Shan-hsin
Goso Hōen	五祖法演	Wuzu Fayan	Wu-tsu Fa-yen
Goso Shikai	五祖師戒	Wuzu Shijie	Wu-tsu Shih-chieh
Gunin	弘忍	Hongren	Hung-jen
Haku Kyoi	白居易	Bai Juyi	Po Chü-i
Haku Rakuten	白樂天	Bai Letian	Pai Lo-t'ien
Hakuin Ekaku	白隱慧鶴		
Hakuun Shutan	白雲守端	Baiyun Shouduan	Pai-yün Shou-tuan
Han Enshi	藩延之	Fan Yanzhi	Fan Yen-chih
Haryō Kōkan	巴陵顯鑒	Baling Haojian	Pa-ling Hao-chien
Hi Kyū	裴休	Pei Xiu	P'ei Hsiu
Hiun	披雲	Piyun	P'i-yün
Hō Koji	龐居士	Pang Jushi	P'ang Chü-shih
Hō On	龐蘊	Pang Yun	P'ang Yün
Hōgen Mon'eki	法眼文益	Fayan Wenyi	Fa-yen Wen-i
Hōhō Kokubun	寶峰克文	Baofeng Kewen	Pao-feng K'o-wen
Hōju Shō	寶壽沼	Baoshou Zhao	Pao-shou Chao
Hokkan Kokan	北礀居簡	Beijian Jujian	Pei-chien Chü-chien
Hōun Kō	法雲杲	Fayun Gao	Fa-yun Kao
Hyakujō Ekai	百丈懷海	Baizhang Huaihai	Pai-chang Huai-hai
Hyakujō Isei	百丈惟政	Baizhang Weizheng	Pai-chang Wei-cheng
Idaten	韋馱天	Weituotian	Wei-t'o-t'ien
Isan Daian	潙山大安	Guishan Da'an	Kuei-shan Ta-an

Isan Ran'an	潙山懶安	Guishan Lan'an	Kuei-shan Lan-an
Isan Reiyū	潙山靈祐	Guishan Lingyou	Kuei-shan Ling-yu
Jakuon Sonja	寂音尊者	Jiyin Zunzhe	Chi-yin Tsun-che
Jō Hyōshi	趙表之	Zhao Biaozhi	Chao Piao-chih
Jōshū Jūshin	趙州從諗	Zhaozhou Congshen	Chao-chou Ts'ung-shen
Jushū Ryōsui	壽州良遂	Shouzhou Liangsui	Shou-chou Liang-sui
Kaku Tetsushi	覺鐵觜	Jue Tiezui	Chüeh T'ieh-tsui
Kakuhan Ekō	覺範慧洪	Juefan Huihong	Chüeh-fan Hui-hung
Kan Yu	韓愈	Han Yu	Han Yü
Kanadaiba	迦那提婆	Jianatipo	Chia-na-ti-p'o
Kannon	觀音	Guanyin	Kuan-yin
Kanzan	寒山	Hanshan	Han-shan
Kanzan Egen	關山慧玄		
Kashō Butsu	迦葉佛	Jiashe Fo	Chia-she Fo
Kassan Zenne	夾山善會	Jiashan Shanhui	Chia-shan Shan-hui
Keichō Beiko	京兆米胡	Jingzhao Mihu	Ching-chao Mi-hu
Kensō	憲宗	Xianzong	Hsien-tsung
Kidō Chigu	虛堂智愚	Xutang Zhiyu	Hsü-t'ang Chih-yü
Kinzan Bunsui	欽山文邃	Qinshan Wensui	Ch'in-shan Wen-sui
Kinzan Kōin	徑山洪諲	Jingshan Hongyin	Ching-shan Hung-yin
Ki Shin	紀信	Ji Xin	Chi Hsin
Kisshū Hōdon	橘洲寶曇	Juzhou Baotan	Chü-chou Pao-t'an
Kisu Chijō	歸宗智常	Guizong Zhichang	Kuei-tsung Chih-ch'ang
Kō Teiken	黄庭堅	Huang Tingjian	Huang T'ing-chien
Ko Teikō	胡釘鉸	Hu Dingjiao	Hu Ting-chiao
Kō U	項羽	Xiang Yu	Hsiang Yü
Kōe Ganren	廣慧元璉	Guanghui Yuanlian	Kuang-hui Yüan-lien
Kōgetsu	皓月	Haoyue	Hao-yüeh
Kōke Zonshō	興化存獎	Xinghua Cunjiang	Hsing-hua Ts'un-chiang
Kōkō Ekaku	光孝慧覺	Guangxiao Huijue	Kuang-hsiao Hui-chüeh
Kōkyō Kōju	興教洪壽	Xingjiao Hongshou	Hsing-chiao Hung-shou
Kotō	虎頭	Hutou	Hu-t'ou
Kurin Seimo	古林清茂	Gulin Qingmao	Ku-lin Ch'ing-mao
Kuzan Shikei	鼓山士珪	Gushan Shigui	Ku-shan Shih-kuei
Kyōgen Chikan	香嚴智閑	Xiangyan Zhixian	Hsiang-yen Chih-hsien
Kyōrin Chōon	香林澄遠	Xianglin Chengyuan	Hsiang-lin Ch'eng-yüan
Kyōsei Dōfu	鏡清道怤	Jingqing Daofu	Ching-ch'ing Tao-fu
Kyōzan Ejaku	仰山慧寂	Yangshan Huiji	Yang-shan Hui-chi
Maidō Soshin	晦堂祖心	Huitang Zuxin	Hui-t'ang Tsu-hsin
Makakashō	摩訶迦葉	Mohe Jiashe	Mo-ho Chia-she
Man'an Dōgan	卍庵道顏	Wan'an Daoyan	Wan-an Tao-yan
Manura	摩拏羅	Monaluo	Mo-na-la
Mayoku Hōtetsu	麻谷寶鐵	Magu Baotie	Ma-ku Pao-t'ieh

Miroku	彌勒	Mile	Mi-le
Mittan Kanketsu	密庵咸傑	Mian Xianjie	Mi-an Hsien-chieh
Mokuren	目連	Mulian	Mu-lien
Monju	文殊	Wenshu	Wen-shu
Mumon Ekai	無門慧開	Wumen Huikai	Wu-men Hui-k'ai
Musō Soseki	夢窓疎石		
Myōshō Tokken	明招徳謙	Mingzhao Deqian	Ming-chao Te-ch'ien
Nandō Genjō	南堂元靜	Nantang Yuanjing	Nan-t'ang Yüan-ching
Nan'in Egyō	南院慧顒	Nanyuan Huiyong	Nan-yüan Hui-yung
Nangaku Ejō	南嶽懷讓	Nanyue Huairang	Nan-yüeh Huai-jang
Nanpo Jōmyō	南浦紹明		
Nansen Fugan	南泉普願	Nanquan Puyuan	Nan-ch'üan Pu-yuan
Nan'yō Echū	南陽慧忠	Nanyang Huizhong	Nan-yang Hui-chung
Nata	那吒	Nazha	Na-cha
Ō Jōji	王常侍	Wang Changshi	Wang Ch'ang-shih
Ō Zui	王隨	Wang Sui	Wang Sui
Ōan Donge	應庵曇華	Ying'an Tanhua	Ying-an T'an-hua
Ōbaku Ishō	黄檗惟勝	Huangbo Weisheng	Huang-po Wei-sheng
Ōbaku Kiun	黄檗希運	Huangbo Xiyun	Huang-po Hsi-yün
Ōkutsu Mara	殃掘摩羅	Yangjue Moluo	Yang-chüeh Mo-lo
Ōryō Enan	黄龍慧南	Huanglong Huinan	Huang-lung Hui-nan
Rakuho Gen'an	洛浦元安	Luopu Yuan'an	Lo-p'u Yüan-an
Razan Dōkan	羅山道閑	Luoshan Daoxian	Lo-shan T'ao-hsien
Reiju Nyobin	靈樹如敏	Lingshu Rumin	Ling-shu Ju-min
Reiun Shigon	靈雲志勤	Lingyun Zhiqin	Ling-yün Chih-ch'in
Ri Tsūgen	李通玄	Li Tongxuan	Li T'ung-hsüan
Ri Yō	李膺	Li Ying	Li Ying
Riku Kō	陸亘	Lu Gen	Lu Ken
Rinzai Gigen	臨濟義玄	Linji Yixuan	Lin-chi I-hsüan
Rokutan Kokubun	泐潭克文	Letan Kewen	Le-t'an K'o-wen
Rōya Ekaku	瑯瑘慧覺	Langye Huijue	Lang-yeh Hui-chüeh
Ryō	良	Liang	Liang
Ryūge Kodon	龍牙居遁	Longya Judun	Lung-ya Chü-tun
Ryūju	龍樹	Longshu	Lung-shu
Ryūkei Keikan	隆慶慶閑	Longqing Qingxian	Lung-ch'ing Ch'ing-hsien
Ryūtan Sōshin	龍潭崇信	Longtan Chongxin	Lung-t'an Ch'ung-hsin
Sai Kō	崔顥	Cui Hao	Ts'ui Hao
Sai Rōchū	崔郎中	Cui Langzhong	Ts'ui Lang-chung
Sankoku	山谷	Shangu	Shan-ku
Sanshō Enen	三聖慧然	Sansheng Huiran	San-sheng Hui-jan
Seidō Chizō	西堂智藏	Xitang Zhizang	Hsi-t'ang Chih-tsang
Seiso	清素	Qingsu	Ch'ing-su
Seizei	清税	Qingshui	Ch'ing-shui

Sekisō Keisho	石霜慶諸	Shishuang Qingzhu	Shih-shuang Ch'ing-chu
Sekisō Soen	石霜楚圓	Shishuang Chuyuan	Shih-shuang Ch'u-yüan
Sekisō Shōkū	石霜性空	Shishuang Xingkong	Shih-shuang Hsing-k'ung
Sekitō Kisen	石頭希遷	Shitou Xiqian	Shih-t'ou Hsi-ch'ien
Sekken Kisei	葉縣歸省	Shexian Guixing	She-hsien Kuei-hsing
Senpuku Shōko	薦福承古	Jianfu Chenggu	Chien-fu Ch'eng-ku
Sensō	宣宗	Xuanzong	Hsüan-tsung
Sensu Tokujō	船子德誠	Chuanzi Decheng	Ch'uan-tzŭ Te-ch'eng
Seppō Gison	雪峰義存	Xuefeng Yicun	Hsüeh-feng I-ts'un
Setchō Jūken	雪竇重顯	Xuedou Chongxian	Hsüeh-tou Ch'ung-hsien
Shakamuni	釋迦牟尼	Shijiamouni	Shih-chia-mou-ni
Sharihotsu	舍利弗	Shelifu	She-li-fu
Shigyoku Dōtsū	紫玉道通	Ziyu Daotong	Tsu-yü Tao-t'ung
Shi'i Dōsha	紙衣道者	Zhiyi Daozhe	Chih-i Tao-che
Shinjō Kokubun	眞淨克文	Zhenjing Kewen	Chen-ching K'o-wen
Shintei Kōin	神鼎洪諲	Shending Hongyin	Shen-ting Hong-yin
Shirin	紫璘	Zilin	Tsu-lin
Shishi Bodai	師子菩提	Shizi Puti	Shih-tzu P'u-ti
Shishin Goshin	死心悟新	Sixin Wuxin	Ssu-hsin Wu-hsin
Shōgen Sūgaku	松源崇嶽	Songyuan Chongyue	Sung-yüan Ch'ung-yüeh
Shōryō Taikin	清涼泰欽	Qingliang Taiqin	Ch'ing-liang Tai-ch'in
Shū	秀	Xiu	Hsiu
Shūhō Myōchō	宗峰妙超		
Shukaku	守廓	Shoukuo	Shou-k'uo
Shuzan Shōnen	首山省念	Shoushan Shengnian	Shou-shan Sheng-nien
Sōjō	僧肇	Sengzhao	Seng-chao
Sōsan	僧璨	Sengcan	Seng-ts'an
Sōsan Gen	雙杉元	Shuangshan Yuan	Shuang-shan Yüan
Sōzan Honjaku	曹山本寂	Caoshan Benji	Ts'ao-shan Pen-chi
Sozan Kōnin	疎山光仁	Shushan Guangren	Shu-shan Kuang-jen
Shui-an Shih-ichi	水庵師一	Shui'an Shiyi	Sui'an Shi'i
Sūzan Ean	嵩山慧安	Songshan Huian	Sung-shan Hui-an
Taikō Kokuhin	太行克賓	Taihang Kebin	T'ai-hang K'o-pin
Taisō	太宗	Taizong	T'ai-tsung
Takujū Kokufu	涿州克符	Zhuozhou Kefu	Cho-chou K'o-fu
Tangen Ōshin	耽源應眞	Danyuan Yingzhen	Tan-yüan Ying-chen
Tanka Tennen	丹霞天然	Danxia Tianran	Tan-hsia T'ien-jan
Tendai Tokushō	天台德韶	Tiantai Deshao	T'ien-t'ai Te-shao
Tendō Wanshi	天童宏智	Tiantong Hongzhi	T'ien-t'ung Hung-chih
Tennō Dōgo	天皇道悟	Tianhuang Daowu	T'ien-huang Tao-wu
Tettō Gikō	徹翁義亨		
Tō Inpō	鄧隱峰	Deng Yinfeng	Teng Yin-feng
Tōba	東坡	Dongpo	Tung-p'o

Tokusan Senkan	德山宣鑑	Deshan Xuanjian	Te-shan Hsüan-chien
Toku'un Biku	德雲比丘	Deyun Biqiu	Te-yün Pi-ch'iu
Tosotsu Jūetsu	兜率從悦	Doushuai Congyue	Tou-shuai Ts'ung-yüeh
Tōsu Daidō	投子大同	Touzi Datong	T'ou-tzu Ta-t'ung
Tōsu Hōshū	投子法宗	Touzi Fazong	T'ou-tzu Fa-tsung
Tōzan Ekū	東山慧空	Dongshan Huikong	Tung-shan Hui-kong
Tōzan Ryōkai	洞山良价	Dongshan Liangjie	Tung-shan Liang-chieh
Tōzan Shusho	洞山守初	Dongshan Shouchu	Tung-shan Shou-ch'u
U Teki	于頔	Yu Di	Yü Ti
Un'an Fugan	運庵普巖	Yun'an Puyan	Yün-an P'u-yen
Ungo Dōkan	雲居道簡	Yunju Daojian	Yün-chü Tao-chien
Ungo Zengo	雲居善悟	Yunju Shanwu	Yün-chü Shan-wu
Unmon Bun'en	雲門文偃	Yunmen Wenyan	Yün-men Wen-yen
Utenō	優填王	Youtianwang	Yu-t'ien-wang
Wakuan Shitai	或庵師體	Huo'an Shiti	Huo-an Shih-t'i
Wanshi Shōgaku	宏智正覺	Hongzhi Zhengjue	Hung-chih Cheng-chüeh
Yō Dainen	楊大年	Yang Danian	Yang Ta-nien
Yō Oku	楊億	Yang Yi	Yang I
Yōgi Hōe	楊岐方會	Yangqi Fanghui	Yang-ch'i Fang-hui
Yōka Genkaku	永嘉玄覺	Yongjia Xuanjue	Yung-chia Hsüan-chüeh
Yōmei Enju	永明延壽	Yongming Yanshou	Yung-ming Yen-shou
Yuimakitsu	維摩詰	Weimojie	Wei-mo-chieh
Zenzai Dōshi	善財童子	Shancai Tongzi	Shan-ts'ai T'ung-tzu
Zuigan Shigen	瑞巖師彥	Ruiyan Shiyan	Jui-yen Shih-yen

Bibliography

Aitken, Robert
>   1990   *The Gateless Barrier: The Wu-men Kuan*. San Francisco: North Point
>   Press.

Andō Yoshinori 安藤嘉則
>   2002   *"Daitō hyakunijissoku* kara *Shūmon kattōshū* e: Chūsei kara kinsei shotō
>   no Rinzai Zen ni okeru kōanshū no keisei ni tsuite"『大燈百二十則』
>   から『宗門葛藤集』へ―中世から近世初頭の臨済禅における公案集の
>   形成について (From *Daitō-hyakunijissoku* to *Shūmon kattōshū*: On the
>   formation of *kōan-shū* in the Rinzai school, from the medieval to the
>   early modern period). *Komazawa Joshi Daigaku Kenkyū Kiyō* 9:1–24.
>   2011   *Chūsei Zenshū ni okeru kōan no kenkyū* 中世禅宗における公案の研究
>   (Kōans in the medieval Zen school). Tokyo: Kokusho Kankōkai.

App, Urs
>   1994   *Master Yunmen*. New York: Kodansha.

Asahina Sōgen 朝比奈宗源
>   1968   *Rinzairoku* 臨済録 (The record of Rinzai). Tokyo: Iwanami Shoten.
>   1980   *Hekiganroku teishō* 碧巖録提唱 (Lectures on the *Blue Cliff Record*). Tokyo:
>   Sankibō Busshoten.

Blofeld, John
>   1958   *The Zen Teaching of Huang Po: On the Transmission of Mind*. London:
>   Rider.
>   1962   *The Zen Teaching of Hui Hai on Sudden Illumination*. London: Rider.

Blyth, R. H.
>   1966   *Mumonkan: The Zen Masterpiece*. Tokyo: Hokuseido Press.

Buddhist Text Translation Society
>   2009   *The Śūraṅgama Sūtra: A New Translation*. Ukiah, California: Buddhist
>   Text Translation Society.

Chan, Wing-tsit
>   1963   *The Platform Scripture: The Basic Classic of Zen Buddhism*. New York:
>   St. John's University Press.

Chang, Chung-yuan
>   1969   *Original Teachings of Ch'an Buddhism: Selected from the Transmission of
>   the Lamp*. New York: Pantheon Books.

Chen, Kenneth
 1964 *Buddhism in China: A Historical Survey.* Princeton, NJ: Princeton University Press.

Chien, Cheng
 1992 *Sun-Face Buddha: The Teachings of Ma-tsu and the Hung-chou School of Ch'an.* Berkeley: Asian Humanities Press.

Cleary, J. C.
 1999 *Three Chan Classics: The Recorded Sayings of Linji; Wumen's Gate; The Faith-Mind Maxim.* Berkeley: The Numata Center for Buddhist Translation and Research.

Cleary, Thomas
 1988 *Book of Serenity: One Hundred Zen Dialogues.* Boston: Shambhala.
 1990 *The Transmission of Light: Zen in the Art of Enlightenment.* San Francisco: North Point Press.
 1993a *The Flower Ornament Scripture: A Translation of the Avatamsaka Sutra.* Boston: Shambhala.
 1993b *No Barrier: Unlocking the Zen Koan.* New York: Bantam Books.
 1998 *The Blue Cliff Record.* Berkeley: The Numata Center for Buddhist Translation and Research.

Cleary, Thomas, and J. C. Cleary
 1977 *The Blue Cliff Record.* Boston: Shambhala.

Cook, Francis H.
 1991 *The Record of Transmitting the Light: Zen Master Keizan's Denkoroku.* Los Angeles: Center Publications.

Daitō Shuppansha
 1991 *Japanese-English Buddhist Dictionary* 日英佛教辞典. Revised edition. Tokyo: Daitō Shuppan.

Dōmae Sōkan 道前宗閑, ed. and annot.
 2003 *Kaiankoku go* 槐安國語. See *Hakuin Ekaku.*
 2010 *Kōteibon Shūmon kattōshū* 校訂本 宗門葛藤集 (Zen school koan collection: Revised edition). Kyoto: Zen Bunka Kenkyūsho.

Dumoulin, Heinrich
 1988 *Zen Buddhism: A History. Vol. 1: India and China.* Trans. by James W. Heisig and Paul Knitter. New York: Macmillan.
 1990 *Zen Buddhism: A History. Vol. 2: Japan.* Trans. by James W. Heisig and Paul Knitter. New York: Macmillan. English Buddhist Dictionary Committee

Ferguson, Andy
 2000 *Zen's Chinese Heritage: The Masters and Their Teachings.* Boston: Wisdom.

Foster, Nelson, and Jack Shoemaker
  1996   *The Roaring Stream: A New Zen Reader*. Hopewell, NJ: Ecco Press.

Giles, Herbert A.
  1939   *A Chinese Biographical Dictionary*. Shanghai: Kelly and Walsh.

Giles, Lionel
  1993   *The Book of Mencius*. Boston: Tuttle.

Gimello, Robert M., and Peter N. Gregory, eds.
  1983   *Studies in Ch'an and Hua-yen*. Honolulu: University of Hawai'i Press.

Green, James
  1998   *The Recorded Sayings of Zen Master Joshu*. Boston: Shambhala.

Gregory, Peter N.
  1991   *Tsung-mi and the Sinification of Buddhism*. Princeton, NJ: Princeton University Press.
  1995   *Inquiry into the Origin of Humanity: An Annotated Translation of Tsung-mi's* Yüan jen lun *with a Modern Commentary*. Honolulu: University of Hawai'i Press.

Gregory, Peter N., ed.
  1986   *Traditions of Meditation in Chinese Buddhism*. Honolulu: University of Hawai'i Press.
  1987   *Sudden and Gradual: Approaches to Enlightenment in Chinese Thought*. Honolulu: University of Hawai'i Press.

Hakuin Ekaku 白隠慧鶴
  2003   *Kaiankoku go* 槐安國語 (Tales from the land of locust-tree tranquility), Dōmae Sōkan 道前宗閑, ed. and annot. 2 vols. Kyoto: Zen Bunka Kenkyūsho.

Hirata Takashi 平田高士
  1969   *Mumonkan* 無門関. Tokyo: Chikuma Shobō.

Hoffman, Yoel
  1975   *The Sound of One Hand*. New York: Basic Books.

Hori, Victor Sōgen
  2003   *Zen Sand: The Book of Capping Phrases for Kōan Practice*. Honolulu: University of Hawai'i Press.

Huang, Chichung
  1997   *The Analects of Confucius: A Literal Translation with Introduction and Notes*. New York: Oxford University Press.

Hurvitz, Leon
  1980   *Chih-i (538–597): An Introduction to the Life and Ideas of a Chinese Buddhist Monk*. Bruxelles: Institut Belgie des Hautes Études Chinoises.

Iida Tōin 飯田檪隠

　1913　　*Mumonkan sansui* 無門關鑚燧 (Investigations in the *Wumen guan*). Tokyo: Morie Shoten.

　1932　　*Hekiganshū teishōroku* 碧巖集提唱録 (Record of lectures on the *Blue Cliff Record*). Tokyo: Morie Shoten.

Imai Fukuzan 今井福山 and Nakagawa Shūan 中川澁庵

　1935　　*Zengo jii* 禪語字彙 (Zen glossary). Tokyo: Hakurinsha.

Iriya Yoshitaka 入矢義高

　1991　　*Rinzairoku* 臨済録 (Record of Rinzai). Tokyo: Iwanami.

Iriya Yoshitaka and Koga Hidehiko 古賀英彦

　1991　　*Zengo jiten* 禅語辞典 (Zen lexicon). Kyoto: Shibunkaku.

Iriya Yoshitaka, Mizoguchi Yūzō 溝口雄三, and Sueki Fumihiko 末木文美士

　1992–96　*Hekiganroku* 碧巖録 (*Blue Cliff Record*), 3 vols. Tokyo: Iwanami Shoten.

Kajitani Sōnin 梶谷宗忍

　1982　　*Shūmon kattōshū* 宗門葛藤集 (Zen school koan collection). Kyoto: Shōkoku-ji Sōdō.

Katō Totsudō 加藤咄堂

　1939–40　*Hekiganroku daikōwa* 碧巖録大講座 (Lectures on the *Blue Cliff Record*), 15 vols. Tokyo: Heibonsha.

Keijū Dōrin 桂洲道倫, Tandō Reichin 湛堂令椿, and Daizō-in Shu 大蔵院主, comp. (Yoshizawa Katsuhiro 芳澤勝弘, ed.)

　1999　　*Shoroku zokugo kai* 諸録俗語解 (Lexicon of Zen-text slang). Kyoto: Zen Bunka Kenkyūsho.

Kirchner, Thomas Yūhō

　2010　　*Dialogues in a Dream*. Kyoto: Tenryū-ji Institute for Philosophy and Religion.

Komazawa Daigakunai Zengaku Daijiten Hensansho 駒沢大學内禪學大辞典編纂所

　1985　　*Zengaku daijiten* 禪學大辞典 (Zen studies dictionary), new edition. Tokyo: Daishūkan.

Kraft, Kenneth

　1992　　*Eloquent Zen: Daitō and Early Japanese Zen*. Honolulu: University of Hawai'i Press.

Lau, D. C.

　1970　　*Mencius*. New York: Viking Press.

　1979　　*Confucius: The Analects*. Harmondsworth: Penguin.

Luk, Charles (Lu K'uan Yü)

　1961　　*Ch'an and Zen Teaching*, 3 vols. London: Rider.

　1966　　*The Śūraṅgama Sūtra*. London: Rider.

　1972　　*The Vimalakīrti Nirdeśa Sūtra*. Berkeley: Shambhala.

1974   *The Transmission of the Mind Outside the Teaching*. New York: Grove Press.

Mathews, R. H.

1956   *Mathews' Chinese-English Dictionary*. Revised American edition. Boston: Harvard University Press.

McRae, John R.

1986   *The Northern School and the Formation of Early Chan Buddhism*. Honolulu: University of Hawai'i Press.

2003   *Seeing through Zen*. Berkeley: University of California Press.

Minford, John, and Joseph S. M. Lau, eds.

1994   *An Anthology of Translations: Classical Chinese Literature*, Vol. 1. New York: Columbia University Press.

Miura, Isshū, and Ruth Fuller Sasaki

1965   *The Zen Koan: Its History and Use in Rinzai Zen*. New York: Harcourt Brace & World.

1966   *Zen Dust: The History of the Koan and Koan Study in Rinzai (Lin-chi) Zen*. Kyoto: The First Zen Institute of America in Japan.

Morohashi Tetsuji 諸橋轍次, ed.

1960   *Daikanwa daijiten* 大漢和辞典 (Great Chinese-Japanese dictionary), 13 vols. Tokyo: Daishūkan Shoten.

Mujaku Dōchū 無著道忠

n.d.   *Kidōroku rikō* 虚堂録犂耕 (Cultivating the *Record of Xutang*). Unpublished manuscript.

Nakamura Hajime 中村元, ed.

1981   *Bukkyōgo daijiten* 佛教語大辞典 (Dictionary of Buddhist terms). Tokyo: Iwanami Shoten.

Nakamura Hajime et al., eds.

2002   *Iwanami Bukkyō jiten* 岩波仏教辞典 (Iwanami Dictionary of Buddhism). Tokyo: Iwanami Shoten.

Nishitani, Keiji

1983   *Religion and Nothingness*. Jan Van Bragt, trans. Berkeley: University of California Press.

Ogata, Sōhaku

1990   *The Transmission of the Lamp: Early Masters*. Wolfeboro, New Hampshire: Longwood Academic Press.

Ōmori Sōgen 大森曹玄

1994   *Hekiganroku* 碧巖録 (*Blue Cliff Record*), 2 vols. Tokyo: Tachibana Shuppan.

O'Neill, Hugh B.

1987   *Companion to Chinese History*. New York: Facts on File.

Price, A. F., and Wong Mou-lam
   1990   *The Diamond Sutra and the Sutra of Hui-neng.* Boston: Shambhala.

Red Pine
   1989   *The Zen Teaching of Bodhidharma.* San Francisco: North Point Press.

Sadakata, Akira
   1997   *Buddhist Cosmology: Philosophy and Origins.* Gaynor Sekimori, trans. Tokyo: Kōsei Publishing.

Saitō Keikō 斉藤攔香
   1992   *Shōyōroku: Hyakuwa monogatari* 従容録－百話物語 (*Shōyōroku:* Tale of one hundred koans). Tokyo: Iwanami Book Service Center.

Sasaki, Ruth Fuller
   1975   *The Record of Lin-chi: The Recorded Sayings of Ch'an Master Lin-chi Hui-chao of Chen Prefecture.* Kyoto: The Institute for Zen Studies.
   2009   *The Record of Linji.* Honolulu: University of Hawai'i Press.

Sasaki, Ruth Fuller, Yoshitaka Iriya, and Dana R. Fraser
   1971   *The Recorded Sayings of Layman P'ang: A Ninth-Century Zen Classic.* New York and Tokyo: Weatherhill.

Schloegl, Irmgard
   1975   *The Zen Teaching of Rinzai.* Berkeley: Shambhala.

Schumacher, Stephan, and Gert Woerner
   1989   *The Rider Encyclopedia of Eastern Philosophy and Religion.* London: Rider.

Sekida, Katsuki
   1977   *Two Zen Classics: Mumonkan and Hekiganroku.* New York and Tokyo: Weatherhill.

Sheng-yen
   1987   *The Poetry of Enlightenment: Poems by Ancient Ch'an Masters.* New York: Dharma Drum.
   1997   *Complete Enlightenment.* New York: Dharma Drum.

Shibayama, Zenkei
   1974   *Zen Comments on the Mumonkan.* Sumiko Kudo, trans. New York: Harper and Row.

Soothill, William Edward, and Lewis Hodous, eds.
   1937   *A Dictionary of Chinese Buddhist Terms.* Reprint. Delhi: Motilal Banarsidass.

Sutra Translation Committee of the United States and Canada
   2000   *Brahma Net Sutra.* New York, San Francisco, Niagara Falls: http://www.sinc.sunysb.edu/Clubs/buddhism/bns/bnsframe.htm.

Suzuki, D. T.
   1927   *Essays in Zen Buddhism, First Series.* London: Luzac and Company.

1932   *The Lankavatara Sutra: A Mahayana Text*. London: George Routledge and Sons, Ltd.

1933   *Essays in Zen Buddhism, Second Series*. London: Luzac and Company.

1934   *Essays in Zen Buddhism, Third Series*. London: Luzac and Company.

1935   *Manual of Zen Buddhism*. Kyoto: The Eastern Buddhist Society.

1962   *The Essentials of Zen Buddhism: An Anthology of the Writings of Daisetz T. Suzuki*. New York: E. P. Dutton.

1994   *The Zen Koan as a Means of Attaining Enlightenment*. Rutland, VT: Tuttle. (Originally pub. as part of *Essays in Zen Buddhism, Second Series*)

Thurman, Robert A.

1976   *The Holy Teaching of Vimalakirti: A Mahayana Scripture*. University Park, PA: Pennsylvania State University Press.

Waddell, Norman

1984   *The Unborn: The Life and Teachings of Zen Master Bankei*. San Francisco: North Point Press.

Waley, Arthur

1938   *The Analects of Confucius*. London: George Allen and Unwin.

Watson, Burton, trans.

1970   *Cold Mountain*. New York: Columbia University Press.

1993a   *The Zen Teachings of Master Lin-chi*. Boston: Shambhala.

1993b   *The Lotus Sutra*. New York: Columbia University Press.

1997   *The Vimalakirti Sutra*. New York: Columbia University Press.

2002   *The Soka Gakkai Dictionary of Buddhism*. Tokyo: Soka Gakkai.

Watts, Alan

1957   *The Way of Zen*. New York: Vintage.

Wright, Dale S.

1998   *Philosophical Meditations on Zen Buddhism*. Cambridge: Cambridge University Press.

Wu, John C. H.

1996   *The Golden Age of Zen*. New York: Doubleday.

Yamada Mumon 山田無文

1976   *Mumonkan kōwa* むもん関講話 (Lectures on the *Mumonkan*). Kyoto: Zen Bunka Kenkyūsho.

1985   *Hekiganroku zenteishō* 碧巌録全提唱 (Complete lectures on the *Blue Cliff Record*), 10 vols. Kyoto: Zen Bunka Kenkyūsho.

1997   *Rinzairoku* 臨濟録 (Record of Rinzai), 2 vols. Kyoto: Zen Bunka Kenkyūsho.

Yamamoto Genpō 山本玄峰

1960   *Mumonkan teishō* 無門関提唱 (Lectures on the *Mumonkan*). Tokyo: Daihōrinkaku.

Yampolsky, Philip

   1967   *The Platform Sutra of the Sixth Patriarch*. New York: Columbia University Press.

Yanagida Seizan 柳田聖山

   1972   *Rinzairoku* 臨濟録 (Record of Rinzai). Tokyo: Daizō Shuppan.

Yoshikawa Kōjirō 吉川幸次郎

   1978   *Rongo* 論語 (The *Analects* of Confucius), 3 vols. Tokyo: Asahi Shinbunsha.

Yoshizawa Katsuhirō 芳澤勝弘

   2003   *Kōko fūgetsu shū yakuchū* 江湖風月集訳注 (Annotated translation of the *Collection of rivers, lakes, wind, and moon*). Kyoto: Zen Bunka Kenkyūsho.

Index

A fragrant breeze blows from the south, 92

A radiant phoenix dances in the sky, 82

absolute, and relative, 175

activity, 203; and essence, 191

admonitions; of Nantang Yuanjing, 74, 75; of Tettō Gikō, 175

Āgama sutras, 182, 188

ālaya-vijñāna (eighth, seed, or storehouse consciousness), 42, 130

Amitābha Buddha, 43, 215, 279; Pure Land of, 243

Amitābha Sutra, 229

Analects, 45, 97, 111, 134

Ānanda; *bio*, 213; and the flagpole, 119; misc., 227, 251;

Ancestor Zen, 272

Andō Yoshinori, 17–18

Aṅgulimāla; *bio*, 213–14; as arhat, 213; and the difficult delivery, 139–40; as mass murderer, 213

Anthology of the Ancestral Hall, 139

Anthology of Yongjia of the Chan School, 279

Aparagodānīya, 35

Arada Kalama, 259

arhat, 147; killing of, 86, 87; offerings to, 106

arjaka tree, 61

Āryadeva (Kāṇadeva); *bio*, 214; misc., 183, 217

Āryasiṁha; *bio*, 214; paying karmic debt, 141

Aśvaghoṣa; *bio*, 215; misc., 183

attachment; after arrival, 44; to dualistic thought, 15; to food, shelter, and clothing, 63; to liberation, 5; no place for, 62, 63; to no-thought, 35–36; to the relative, 44; and "slaying the mother," 87; to the

teachings, 188; and using things skillfully, 170; to words and concepts, 16

Avalokiteśvara; and Mount Putou, 40; and a sesame cake, 89, 90; misc., 40, 189, 215

Avataṃsaka Sutra; the four dharma realms of, 136–37; "the Great Sea doesn't harbor corpses," 138; and the mind is like an artist, 92; and the six earth-shakings, 148; misc., 40, 90, 135, 168, 185, 188, 218, 230, 232, 255, 257, 267, 269

awareness without thought, marvelous functioning of, 277

awl-point wiles, 128

Azure Palace, 193

Bai Juyi (Governor); *bio*, 215–16; and Niaoke Daolin, 176

Baiyun Shouduan; *bio*, 216; and verse on 'Linji's three-score blows of the stick', 167; and Wuzu Fayan, 201; misc., 219, 271

Baizhang Huaihai; *bio*, 216–17; and the autumn moon turning-phrases, 82; deafened by Mazu's shout, 151, 179; and the fox, 57; and monastic labor, 105, 216; "no work, no eating," 105, 216; and *Pure Rules for the Zen Community*, 216; and teaching through principle, 143; and Mazu's whisk, 150–51; and the wild ducks, 151; misc., 108, 220, 235, 239, 252, 258, 263, 272, 273, 275

Baizhang Weizheng; *bio*, 217; and Nanquan Puyuan, 162–63; and the new rice paddy, 92; misc., 162, 225

Bajiao Huiqing; *bio*, 217; and the staff, 79–80

Baling Haojian; *bio*, 217; and the clear-eyed person falling into a well, 206

bamboo; hit by Xiangyan's tile, 49; moving rocks, 208, 209; shades, 59 bandit, 58; heart of, 171; Yantou killed by, 278; see also *thief*

banner(s); scarlet, 87; signaling a Dharma lecture, 119; in the wind, 86

Baoshou Zhao; *bio*, 217–18; and striking the clear blue sky, 108, 109

Baozang lun, 261

barbarian; and confusion, 70; has no beard, 101; old, 197, 198; from the south, 241

barefoot Persians, 65, 66; as Bodhidharma, 66

basket(s); bottomless, 98, 99; of silk-growers wives, 49

begging (mendicancy), 177, 266; bowl, 139

Beijian Jujian; *bio*, 218; verse, 93

being, 184, 193; is beyond merit, 138

being and nonbeing, 54–56, 184, 193; and Dahui, 55; and Shushan, 54–55; and vines, 54–56

bell; announcing mealtime, 47; b. tower, 69; that resounds throughout the universe, 183; and putting on one's vestment, 130; as a time indicator in the monastery, 159; and Hakuin's enlightenment, 237

Bhikku Meghaśri; *bio*, 218; on Wondrous Mountain, 90

Bhishmottaranirghosha, 90

bhūtatathatā, 132

Big Dipper, 120

Biographies of Eminent Monks, 245

Biographies of Monks of the Zen School, 188, 223, 245, 266

bird(s); alighting in front of the blue cliff, 95; with a broken wing, 198; leaves the clouds, 152; unseen, 152

birth-and-death; escaping from, 36; great matter of, 197; and karma-creating activities, 48; misc., 214, 215, 232, 247, 253, 263, 278, 279

blind ass, and Linji's Dharma, 164

blows; sixty, Huangbo and Linji's, 107; thirty, of Guishan, 105; three-score, 158, 159, 167; misc., 105, 162, 163, 174, 250

Blue Cliff Record, 3, 10, 11, 15, 16, 19, 20, 21, 29, 30, 173, 231, 274, 281; *Case 1*, 75, 197; *Case 4*, 114; *Case 6*, 139; *Case 8*, 91, 184, 246, 264; *Case 9*, 195; *Case 11*, 151, 158, 196; *Case 12*, 74, 159, 173; *Case 13*, 206; *Case 16*, 154; *Case 17*, 169–70; *Case 18*, 76, 203, 256; *Case 19*, 80; *Case 20*, 133; *Case 23*, 90; *Case 24*, 174; *Case 26*, 175; *Case 27*, 107; *Case 28*, 80, 163; *Case 33*, 132, 221; *Case 35*, 180; *Case 36*, 165, 171; *Case 38*, 14, 166; *Case 42*, 48; *Case 43*, 166; *Case 48*, 109, 194, 205; *Case 49*, 164; *Case 51*, 143, 197; *Case 52*, 202; *Case 53*, 151; *Case 55*, 60, 77; *Case 58*, 269; *Case 66*, 98; *Case 76*, 225; *Case 79*, 169; *Case 82*, 195; *Case 84*, 101, 102; *Case 87*, 168; *Case 89*, 137; *Case 90*, 91; *Case 97*, 72, 114; English translations of, 20–21

bo dove, 61

Bo, master craftsman of Lu, 168

board-carrier, 98, 99

bodhi; all the eye perceives is, 178; b. tree, 83, 242, 259; b. meeting, 185

bodhicitta, nature of, 237

Bodhidharma; *bio*, 218; as barefoot Persian, 66; didn't come to China, 103; and Emperor Wu; intention expressed through devices, 142; meaning of coming from the West, 37–38, 45, 142, 172; "no merit," 75; and a pillar tiring, 179; as red-bearded foreigner, 58; true transmission of, 179; misc., 198, 233, 240; see also *Patriarch, meaning of coming from the West*

Bodhisattva Delusion, 68, 89

bodhisattvas, 147; faces, 71

body and mind, distance between, 134

bowl; begging, 139; brittle, 53; Deshan carries his, 70; and Emperor Taizong, 201; of water, 129, 205, 214; misc., 47, 48

boxwood Zen, 55–56

Boyi and Shuqi, not eating the grain of Zhou, 99

Brahma Heaven, 68; Lord of, 187

Brahma Net Sutra, 71

bridge, Zhaozhou's stone, 202

Buddha; and Aṅgulimāla, 139–40; birth verse, 104; Great Purpose of, 125; pointing to the earth and sky at birth, 103; realm of B. versus realm of Mara, 123, 125; relics of, 194–95; relics, light of, 194–95; as represented by garuḍa, 181; requiting the benevolence of, 104; seeking nothing from, 78, 196; supernatural powers, 148; teaching expressed through reason, 142;

in the Trāyastrimśa Heaven, 117, 118;
never turning the Dharma wheel, 80;
misc., 136, 180, 280; see also *Śākyamuni*
buddha(s); becoming a b. by sitting in
zazen, 122; concept of, 194; inherently
perfect b., 146; and "not knowing it," 83;
b. lands, 165; is not limited to any fixed
form, 122; as medicine for sentient beings,
125; is the Mind King, 234; b. names, 165;
offerings to, 106; place from which all b.
come, 92; realm of, 123, 125, 187; seven b.
of the past, 89; shedding the blood of a,
86, 87; of the ten directions, 68; thirty-
two distinguishing characteristics of a,
117, 118, 204; three bodies of a, 43; is this
very mind, 35, 101, 224, 227, 232, 234, 263
Buddha Flower Adornment Samadhi, 185
buddha image, Danxia Tianran's burning
of, 64
buddha nature, 5, 65, 66, 83, 122, 180, 183;
of a dog, 65
Buddha of Great Universal Wisdom Excellence, 69
Buddhadharma, 66, 69, 135, 151, 167; central
teaching of, 176; Huangbo's, 157; is like
the moon in the water, 284; true meaning
of, 156, 157, 167
buddhahood, 72, 81, 101, 189, 199; intrinsic,
146; no thought of seeking, 48; seeing
self-nature and attaining b., 206
buddha-mind, as springless lock, 78
buffalo; and Guishan's rebirth, 73, 75; and
Nanquan's death, 208, 255; Fu Dashi
riding on, 233; passing through a lattice
window, 43; and the "person who knows
it," 91; as symbol of self-nature, 206;
chasing Mañjuśrī and Samantabhadra
into a herd of, 166
bull, white, on the bare ground, 220
Burton Watson, 22
cakravartin (wheel king), 118, 128, 129
Caodong school; and Longya Judun, 133;
Wuzu Fayan's comment on, 86; misc.,
219, 222, 225, 229, 231, 257
Caoshan Benji; *bio*, 219; and the Great Sea
not harboring corpses, 138; and Qingshui, 102; and the snow on the mountains, 42; misc., 229, 266

Caoxi, 94
carp, of the Eastern Sea, 121
Categorized Anthology of the Zen Forest, 204
cats, 83
cause and effect; and people of true
practice, 57–58; as one of Daitō's three
questions, 100
center, hold to the, 72, 73
Chaling Yu; *bio*, 219; enlightenment verse,
201; misc., 216
Changqing Huileng; *bio*, 219; and his staff,
203
Changqing Huileng; *bio*, 219–20; and sitting
like a burnt stump, 219–20; misc., 230
Changqing Lan'an (Guishan Lan'an); *bio*,
220; being and nonbeing, 54–56; and Lu
Gen laughing and crying, 173; and vines
clinging to a tree, 54–56
Changsha Jingcen; *bio*, 220; and "the entire
universe is your body," 221; and the
"Hundred-foot Pole" koan, 49; and the
moon, 171; and Nanquan's death, 208;
and "not knowing it," 83; and original
emptiness, 141; and Yangshan Huiji, 171;
misc., 238, 255
Changsheng Jiaoran; *bio*, 221; and
Lingyun's "a pillar conceives," 41
Changshui Zixuan; *bio*, 221; and pure,
original nature, 180; misc., 247
checking questions, 5
Chen Cao; *bio*, 221; calling to monks from
a tower, 132
chestnut burr, 55, 56
chicken, from Chu, 120
Chinese calendar, eight divisions of, 187
Chouyan Liaoyun; *bio*, 221; on Zhaozhou's
"Wu" koan, 65
Chronicles of the Shin Dynasty, 61
Chuandeng yuying ji (*Precious flowers of
the lamp transmission*), 270
Chuanzi Decheng (Boatman Monk); *bio*,
221; and the dharmakāya is without form,
200; and Jiashan's enlightenment, 244
Ciming, see *Shishuang Chuyuan*
circle-figures, 189–90, 225, 277; six names
of, 190–91; text on, 190
citta, 130
clear eyes, see *eyes, clear*

clear-eyed, 87, 126; master, 143; monk, 184; a c. person falls into a well, 206, 217

clouds; bird leaves the, 152; blocking the valley, 144; marking the Great Pure Sky, 41

Cockfoot Mountain, 175

Collected Poems of Cold Mountain, 205

compassion; Avalokiteśvara as a symbol of, 215; the Buddha's, 228; in demonstrating the Ten Realizations, 199; falling into hell as an act of, 40; of Fu Dashi, 234; as a fundamental aspect of Zen training, 151; of the head monk toward Linji, 156; and the mind of the ancient buddhas, 230; of Nanyuan's stick, 154; of a parent, 152, 171; Samantabhadra as a symbol of, 166

Compendium of the Five Lamps (*Wudeng huiyuan*), 10, 17, 49, 81, 87, 95, 105, 109, 133, 151, 178, 208, 209, 223; and exclamation *ni*, 62

Comprehensive Record of Yunmen, 90

Comprehensive Treatise on the Avataṃsaka Sutra, 247

conduct, four modes of, 129

Confucius, 44, 111; hear of the Way in the morning, 97

consciousness; as apart from Mind-essence, 263; deluded, 65; all dharmas are nothing but, 230; essence of, 64; karmic, 65, 179; levels of, 130; as the Matrix of the Thus-Come-One, 180; as one of the skandas, 93; and the realm of formlessness, 205; storehouse, 42, 130; and Yogācāra, 42

continents (northern, eastern, western, and southern; Pūrvavideha, Aparagodānīya, Uttarakuru, Jambudvīpa), 35, 129, 182

corpses, not harbored in the Great Sea, 138

court monk,141, 142, 205, 238

crimes, five heinous, 86–87; meaning of to Linji, 87

Cui Hao; *bio*, 222; and "The Yellow Crane Pavilion," 165

Cui Langzhong; *bio*, 222; and enlightened teachers falling into hell, 40

Cuiwei Wuxue; hitting Longya with a meditation-brace, 133; misc., 249, 269

Cuiyan Lingcan, 246, 279

Cultivating the Record of Xutang, 21

cultivation, gradual, 235

Dachuan Puji; *bio*, 223; and Lingyun Zhiqin's verse on peach blossoms, 37

Daci Huanzhong, 258, 275, 277

Dadao Guquan; *bio*, 223; and Ciming's tiger roars, 144–45

Dahui Zonggao; *bio*, 223–24; being and nonbeing, 55–56; practicing boxwood Zen, 55; and the Buddha as medicine, 125; on Zen teachings, 184; and Dongshan Huikong, 46; enlightened by poem of Yuanwu, 92; and Shoushan's stick, 118; and silent illumination Zen, 224; verse on veteran general, 184–85; on "*Wu*" koan, 66; on "Xiangyan's up a Tree" koan, 46; and "the walls of Caizhou are demolished," 125; misc. 223, 239, 246, 267, 270, 278, 281, 283

daily activities proclaim the Ancient Way, 50

Daitō, see *Nanpo Jōmyō*

Daitō's One Hundred and Twenty Cases (*Daitō hyakunijissoku*), 10, 17

Daitoku-ji school, 17

Dajue, 109, 110, 273

Damei Fachang, 252; *bio*, 224; and this very mind is buddha, 35; Layman Pang and the plum pit, 76

dāna, 177

Danxia Tianran; *bio*, 224; burning a buddha image, 64; misc., 257

Danxia Zichun, 238

Danyuan Yingzhen; *bio*, 225; and the circle-figures, 189–90; misc., 277

Daoan, 242

Daowu Yuanzhi; *bio*, 225; advises Jiashan to visit Chuanzi, 200; and Shishuang's filling the water bottles, 178; misc., 244, 262

Daoxin (Fourth Patriarch), 238, 260

Daoxuan; *bio*, 225–26; and the greatest of meritorious deeds, 182

dawn, as metaphor for light (duality), 105

Dayu; *bio*, 226; and Linji's awakening, 157

Dazhu Huihai; *bio*, 226; and the six non-Buddhist teachers, 78–79

death; and rebirth as a buffalo after, 91; and going down to the infirmary, 129; koans about, 36, 45, 51–52, 60, 73, 88, 91, 96–97, 98–99, 115, 164, 177, 208; of Layman Pang's daughter, 88; and life, 149; and

Magu, 115; and the seven wise women, 60; see also *Great Death*

debts, karmic, of Venerable Āryasiṁha and the Second Patriarch, 141

Deer Park, 83

defilements (kleśa), 130, 207; becoming one with, 79; mind's subtle flow of, 130

Definitive Chart of the Ancestry for the Transmission of the Dharma in the True School, 233

Delusion (bodhisattva), 68, 89

delusion, 63, 66, 78, 238; bodies and minds are born of, 247; compared to weeds, 36, 137; diamond sword of wisdom cuts off, 148; dusts of, 201; "knowing" is, 97; master cuts off, 91, 217; and Mañjuśrī, 251; root of, 37; subtle, 44; throw off, 129; unity of d. and enlightenment, 247

demons, 47, 128, 129, 175; and the Double Iron-Ring Mountains, 175; drifting to the land of, 60; heads, 71; incantations against, 47, 61; and the scholar, 61–62; spying on Nanquan, 255; and the veteran general of the Dharma assembly, 185; see also *Mara, rakṣasas*

Deng Yinfeng; *bio*, 226; and Mazu Daoyi, 197; and the wheelbarrow, 197

Deshan Xuanjian; *bio*, 227; burns his commentaries, 113; carries his bowls, 70; and a different way of doing things, 133; and the final word, 47, 143; and Longtan's paper torch, 113: and the monk from Silla, 163–64; pushed by Sansheng onto the meditation platform, 108, 109; and where the sages of old have gone, 171; and teaching through devices, 143; misc., 140, 166, 249, 250, 259, 260, 275, 277

Devadatta; *bio*, 227–28; falling into hell, 103; prophecy of becoming a buddha, 228; relation to the Buddha, 213

devices, teaching through, 142–43

Dhammapada, 176

Dharma drum, sound of, 186

Dharma eye, 75; of the mind-ground, 186; is without blemish, 200; see also *True Dharma Eye*

Dharma freedom, 185

Dharma King, body of, 207

Dharma nature, preaching directly from, 185

dharma realms (dharmadhātu), 87, 187, 199, 267; of the emptiness of emptiness, 187; four, of the *Avataṃsaka Sutra*, 100, 136–37

Dharma Sea Sutra, 138

Dharma teaching; five periods of, 187; of the nonsentient, 75; of the sentient, 75

Dharma wheel, 80; in the *Śūraṅgama Sutra*, 187

Dharma, 136; that enlightened teachers never teach, 162; false teaching of the, 64; joy in, 79; nonabiding, 122; seek nothing from the, 196; of supreme perfect enlightenment, 187; transmission to Mahākāśyapa, 119; vessel of, 122; vilifying the, 79; as wondrous lotus-flower, 121

dharmadhātu, see *dharma realms*

dharmakāya, 136; and eating food, 134; divided into a billion, 193; and expounding the Dharma, 81; manifestations of in the natural world, 95; and the three types of sickness, 43, 44; and the two types of light, 43, 44; Vairocana Buddha as, 188, 267; is without form, 200

dharmas (phenomena); and the arising of mind, 224; are dependent on one another, 137; are empty forms, 87; not to perceive any, 135; are nothing but consciousness, 230; and Vairocana and Samantabhadra, 188

Diamond Sutra, 72, 187, 188, 227, 241, 284

diamond sword, see *sword*

difficult to penetrate koans, 43

Discourses of Dahui, 70, 182, 186; and the Flower Adornment samadhis, 185

disease, 155; and the Buddha as medicine, 125; impossible to cure, 150; and Xutang's staff, 155; see also *illness*

do no evil, practice all good, 176

Dōmae Sōkan, 21, 25, 26; *Shūmon kattōshū* of, 25–26

donations, in *Vimalakīrti Sutra*, 78

Donglin, on Avalokiteśvara, 189; see also *Gushan Shigui*

Dongpo; *bio*, 228; misc., 189

Dongshan Huikong; *bio*, 228; and Xiangyan's "Up a Tree," 46

Dongshan Liangjie; *bio*, 228–29, 230; and the earth spirit, 114; and going where there's no grass,137; and the *Heart Sutra*, 101; and the preaching of the sentientless, 229; on suffering illness, 229; and the wasted grain, 114; and the winter solstice fruit, 203; misc., 133, 219, 222, 245, 249, 259, 262, 265–66, 275, 277, 281

Dongshan Shouchu; *bio*, 229–30; and receiving worthy friends, 158; spared the blows of Yunmen's staff, 158–59; and three pounds of hemp, 74; and the visit of Mañjuśrī and Samantabhadra, 166; misc., 244

Dongshan Xiaocong, 233

donkey, in the back garden, 74

Doushuai Congyue; *bio*, 230; and the final word, 123; and the lychee fruit, 123; the three barriers of, 36; misc., 282

Dragon King, 254

Dragon, Heavenly (Musō Soseki), 181

dragon-head, on top of a pole, 120

dragon(s); cloud, 87; heavenly, 186; one-eyed, 55; protectors of Buddhism and rulers of water, 204; taking to water, 160

drop deluded thought, 80

drum, Dharma, 186

Du Fu (poet), 85, 237

duck, wild, 151

dumplings, fried, 77

duty-monk (*weina*), 58, 114, 115, 174, 267; and work, 58, 174

earth, element of, 36, 147

East Mountain, walks on the water, 92

East River, runing uphill, 133

eight phrases of Hongzhi, 193

eight-armed Nalakūvara, 65, 66

eighty secondary characteristics of a buddha, 118

Elder Ding, 275

elements, four, see *four elements*

Elephant King (Samantabhadra), 160

elephant, lordly, 149, 150

Emperor Daizong, 256

Emperor Gaozong, 266

Emperor Go-Daigo, 252, 265

Emperor Hanazono, 265

Emperor Huizong, 281

Emperor Lizong, 271

Emperor Muzong, 196, 274

Emperor Renzong, 275, 284

Emperor Suzong, 256, 285

Emperor Taizong; *bio*, 267–68; and the Sixth Patriarch's bowl, 201; misc., 276

Emperor Wenzong, 92

Emperor Wu, see *persecution of Buddhism*

Emperor Wuzong, see *persecution of Buddhism*

Emperor Xianzong; *bio*, 272–73; and the Buddha's relics, 194–95; misc., 237, 280

Emperor Xizong 262–63

Emperor Xuanzong (Dazhong); *bio*, 274; and Huangbo's bowing, 196

Emperor Yang, 266

Emperor Yingzong, 284

Emperor Zhongzong, 267

emptiness; of all forms, 214; is form, 176; original, 141; and trousers, 126

Encouraging Study of the Zen Barriers, 262

enemy, as referring to true teacher or original face, 71

Enkei Soyū, 285

enlightened teacher (kalyāṇamitra, "good and wise friend"), 40, 71, 94, 145, 162, 163, 208; Ciming as, 145; what they never teach, 162–63

enlightenment (wisdom); of Ānanda, 213; attachment to, 44; and blows with the staff, 163, 165; through breaking a leg, 282; of Chaling, 219; through circumstances, 37; of Dahui, 55, 92; and delusion, 247; and dragons, 204; eye of, 53; and the *Diamond Sutra*, 72, 187; and East River running uphill, 133; by extinguishing paper torch, 113; as a fundamental aspect of Zen training, 151; of Guishan, 235; by hearing a clap of thunder, 256; by hearing the sound of bamboo, 49–50; by hearing sounds and seeing forms, 89–90; by injuring a toe, 63, 103, 274; instantaneous, versus gradual cultivation, 235; of Jiashan, 200; by knowing cause and effect, 58; of Linji, 157; lofty realm of, 152; of Mazu, upon seeing Nanyue polish a tile, 122; and metaphor of the moon, 171; and mortal offenders, 86; by not picking and choosing, 269; as one aspect of bodhicitta, 235; other shore of, 79; pure realm of, 41, 42; relation to cultivation, 235; of Śākyamuni, 259; by seeing plum blossoms, 37; by seeing sweet-olive blossoms, 45; single path to, 103; and stopping thoughts, 202; by swallowing waters of the West River, 48; by thinking not of good or evil, 34, 97; and the three ages of the Buddhadharma, 120; of Xuefeng, on hearing the words of Yantou, 275; of Yangshan, on hearing the words of Guishan, 277; of Yu Di, 279; misc., 36, 44, 58, 63, 69, 79, 81, 83, 126, 136, 139, 145, 151, 166, 180, 188, 191, 199, 230

enlightenment verses; of Lingyun Zhiqin 37; of Laymnan Pang, 48; of Xiangyan Zhixian, 49; of Yuanwu Keqin 94; of Chaling Yu, 201; of Xingjiao Hongshou, 207; of Dongshan Liangjie, 229; of Huineng, 242; of Xiangyan Zhixian, 272

equality and distinction, see *unity and differentiation*

essence, 198, 199; and activity, 191; of consciousness, 64; and function, 105; Guishan lacking in, 105; and Mañjuśrī, 166; all phenomena are lacking in, 232; of wisdom, 43; of Zen, 38; misc., 139, 153, 166, 182, 198, 199

Essential Materials from the Zen School's Successive Lamp Records, 17

essential principle, and clinging to the seated posture, 122

Essentials of Contemplation Sutra, 101

Essentials of Instantaneous Awakening, 226

Essentials of Transmitting the Mind; compilation of by Pei Xiu, 258; and levels of renunciation, 63

Essentials, Three, see *Three Essentials*

evening instruction, 128, 129, 158, 178

existence; as endless blue mountains, 65; phenomenal, 65; provisional, 142; realms of, 75

expedient means, 16, 136, 142, 180, 243

Extensive Record of the Era of Great Peace, 51

extinction, provisional, 142

eye(s); clear, see *clear-eyed*; of the Dharma, see *Dharma eye*; of enlightenment, 53;

of a gnat, 74; of humans and gods, 198; of the mind, 272; of the needle, 182; of practice, 199; World-Honored-One's blue-lotus, 110; of Zen, 143

eyebrows; falling out, 64, 116, 117; entangling, 127; misc., 4, 246, 279

face(s); bodhisattvas', 71; gates of the, 146, 147; Yu Di's, 60; see also *original face*

Fakong Zongben, 271

Fan Yanzhi (Layman Qingyi); *bio*, 230; and Huanglong's Three Barriers, 39

father, 34, 51, 52, 86, 88, 99, 196, 227, 241, 283, 285; meaning of to Linji, 87

Fayan school of Zen, 231, 274, 279; emphasis on the dharmakāya as manifested in nature, 95; Wuzu Fayan's comment on, 86

Fayan Wenyi; *bio*, 230; and the bamboo shades, 59; on Deshan, 163; and Zhaozhou speaking of the juniper tree, 38; and misunderstanding Jiashan's surroundings, 95; and the stone in his mind, 230; and the sutra from which all buddhas issue, 72; misc., 258, 268, 274

Fayun Gao; *bio*, 231; and the ordination certificate, 131

Fenglin Barrier, 206

Fengxue Yanzhao; *bio*, 231; and the end of the Linji lineage, 264; and Nanyuan's pecking and tapping, 154; and Nanyuan's staff of the south, 165, 166; Yangshan's prophesy about, 162; and Shoushan Shengnian's understanding, 110; not transgressing with speech or silence, 84–85; and the World-Honored-One's blue-lotus eyes, 110; misc., 256, 264

Fenyang Shanzhao; *bio*, 231; and koan work, 231; on the ten realizations, 184, 198; misc., 145, 223, 247

Fenzhou Wuye; *bio*, 231–32; and "drop deluded thought," 80

Fifth Patriarch, see *Hongren*

final word; Deshan doesn't know the, 47, 143; Doushuai's expression of and Zhenjing's true medicine, 123–24; and the impassable gate, 123; Wumen's comment on the, 143

fire; and Baizhang's armrest, 93; burns out an old master's grave, 144–145; and

Danxia's buddha images, 64; element of, 36, 147, 187; and Guishan's enlightenment, 235; as metaphor for light (duality), 104–5; and Zhaozhou's "Put out the fire!" 107

fireside, no guest or host by, 177

First Buddhist Council, 213

fish, wooden, 159

five deadly sins, 86–87

five heinous crimes, 86–87

Five Houses of Chinese Zen, 86–87, 263

Five Ranks, 191, 219, 229, 231, 266

flagpole; and Ānanda, 119; with iron dragon-head, 120

flame, as prajñā wisdom, 62

flower(s); of the arjaka tree, 61; in the beaks of birds, 95; fragrant spring f. in Jiangnan, 84; peony, 71; World-Honored One holds up a, 110, 119

Foguo Keqin, see *Yuanwu Keqin*

Fojian Huiqin; *bio*, 232; and the evening turning-phrase, 82; misc., 271

follower of the Way, 48, 63; free of thought, 106

Fori Qisong; *bio*, 233; and the koan collection, 190

form, is emptiness, 176

formless; life from out of the, 139; true form of the, 119

four dharma realms of the *Avataṃsaka Sutra*, 100, 136–37

four elements (earth, water, fire, air), 36, 147

four forms of demeanor, 279

four modes of conduct, 129

four positions of Linji on the person and the surroundings, 125, 173

four propositions and the one hundred negations, 85

Four-Part Vinaya, 168, 226

Foyan Qingyuan; *bio*, 233; the evening turning-phrase, 82; and the monk bitten by a snake, 204; comment on a pillar tiring, 179; misc., 232, 236, 271, 281

Fozhao Deguang, 218

Fozhi Duanyu, 265

friend; good and wise (kalyāṇamitra), 40, 94, 218; true, 140; true, never met a, 55,

140; worthy, 158; see also *enlightened teacher*

fruit, lychee, 123, 124

Fu Dashi; *bio*, 233–34; and service to others, 234; and Vimalakīrti, 84

Fubei; *bio*, 234; and the word that can't be said, 176

Fukuan Sōki, 285

function (compassion), 136, 160, 161, 203; and essence, 105; as fundamental aspect of Zen training, 151; highest, 50; as nondoing, 151; one with f. or separate from, 150; and perception, 160, 161, 174; of the Zen master, 91

Gaofeng Yuanmiao, 284

garuḍa, 181

gate of misfortune, 80

general(s); of the Dharma assembly, 184–85; eight heavenly, 182; Liu Bang, 243; Xiang Yu, 161, 271–72

Genroku edition, *Shūmon kattōshū*, 18–19

ghee, 122

giving life and taking it away, 37, 155, 160, 168, 198, 199

golden-duck censer, 94

gong, 159

good and wise friend, see *friend*

grass; blade of as the body of buddha, 184; no blade of in ten thousand *li*, 137; as kleśa, 137; as medicine, 168

grave, burned out by fire, 144

Great Death, 192; as knowing nothing, 186; and "those who have expired," 138; and the winter solstice, 129, 203

Great King, 195

great man, signs of, 204

Great Matter, 198, 199; of birth and death, 197; of Buddhism, 200; entrusted to Yangqi by Ciming, 152; of Zen, 44

Great Perfect Mirror Wisdom, 42

Great Principle, 92

Great Pure Sky, 41–42; and clouds, 41

Great Sage of India, mind of, 111

Great Sea, doesn't harbor corpses, 138

Guanghui Yuanlian; *bio*, 234; and all evil karma is born of wealth, 120; misc., 276

Guangxiao Huijue; *bio*, 234; and slaughtering cattle, 192

guest, examines the guest, 150; examines the host, 150; no g. nor host by the fireside, 177; in the room of the elder, 162
guest and host, see *host and guest*
Guifeng Zongmi, 258
Guishan Lingyou; *bio*, 234–35; and a grain of rice, 177, 178; and Lingyun Zhiqin's enlightenment on seeing peach blossoms, 37; and rebirth as a water buffalo, 73, 75; misc., 217, 220, 227, 228, 245, 248, 258, 262, 266, 270, 272, 277; see also *Guishan and Yangshan*
Guishan and Yangshan; as founders of the Guiyang line, 190, 217; on Guishan's mirror, 131; on Guishan's rebirth as a buffalo, 73, 75; on Linji's enlightenment, 158; and the man in a well, 76; on the mind's subtle flow of defilements, 130; and function and essence while picking tea, 105; prophecying Fengxue Yanzhao's coming, 162, 231; on Yangshan's headrest, 81
Guiyang school, 235, 277; and the circle-figures, 190; Wuzu Fayan's comment on, 86
Guizong Zhichang; *bio*, 235; resembled Mazu in depth of talent, 108; misc., 226
Gulin Qingmao (Foxing); *bio*, 236; three turning-phrases of, 103
Guo Tianmin, 245
Gushan Shigui; *bio*, 236; as Donglin, 189; seeking his enemy, 71
Haklenayaśas, 214, 251
Hakuin Ekaku; *bio*, 236–37; and the cicada, 154–55; verse on "not entering nirvana," 49; misc., 5, 10, 17, 21, 42, 43, 167, 219, 246, 254
Hakuin Zen; Inzan line, 19; Takujū line, 19
Han Yu; *bio*, 237; and the Budda's relic, 194–95, 237
hand-cloth, Magu's, 115, 116
Hanshan; *bio*, 237–38; and the Three Realms, 205
Haoyue; *bio*, 238; court monk, 141
head of a dragon and the tail of a snake, 163, 164, 204
headrest, of Yangshan, 81
Heart Sutra, 101, 176
Heaven, Brahma, 68; Trāyastrimśa

(Heaven of the Thirty-three Deities), 35, 117, 118, 121
Hekizen hekigo, 18
hell; and Devadatta, 103, 228; Dongshan falling into, 166; enlighted teachers falling into, 40; falling into as an act of compassion, 40; and Maudgalyāyana's mother, 94; and mortal offenders, 86; as one of the six realms, 75, 187; as one of the three evil realms, 79; precept-breaking monks do not fall into, 49; and the single path to nirvana, 103
hemp, three pounds of, 74
Hengchuan Rugong, 236
hermit(s); and the girl, 132–33; checked by Zhaozhou, 160; princes Boyi and Shuqi living as, 99
Heze Shenhui, 242, 256
Hongren (Fifth Patriarch); *bio*, 238; and Huineng, 241–42; misc., 34, 257, 266, 271
Hongzhi Zhengjue; *bio*, 238–39; eight phrases of, 193; and the four uses of activity and essence, 191
horse(s); of Haidan, 120; as metaphor for no-mind, 185; wooden, 184
host; examines the guest, 150; examines the host, 150; neither guest nor h. by the fireside, 177; trying to play the, 153
host and guest, 191; Linji's views on, 109, 135, 136, 149–50
hou; and Yunmen, 132; and Mujaku, 132; as the Sanskrit syllable "hu" (suchness), 132
House Sayings of Confucius, 80
household spirits, 89
Hu Dingjiao; *bio*, 239; and driving a rivet into the void, 109
Huangbo Weisheng; *bio*, 239; and a fierce tiger sits in the road, 69
Huangbo Xiyun; *bio*, 239; and Baizhang, 151; on the bodhisattva mind, 62–63; bowing before a buddha image, 196; and the *Essentials of the Transmission of Mind*, 258; and Linji's training, 156–58; and Linji's pine trees, 161–62; offering Baizhang's backrest and armrest to Linji, 93; on the three levels of renunciation, 63; and Zhaozhou's visit, 107; misc., 110, 217, 235, 248, 252, 253

Huanglong Huinan; *bio*, 240; and Baiyun Shouduan's verse on Linji, 167; and Ciming's "old woman," 159–60; and raising vegetables down by the meditation bench, 69; and receiving Ciming's stick from dawn to dusk, 159; the Three Barriers of, 38–39; and Yunfeng's criticism of his understanding, 159; and Zhenjing's verse on the Yellow Crane Pavilion, 167; misc., 123, 230, 239, 242, 249, 262, 284

Huanglong line, 240

huatou, 4

Huayan school; and Changshui Zixuan, 221; doctrine of the four realms, 100, 136–37

Huike (Second Patriarch); *bio*, 240–41; didn't go to India, 63, 103; mind of, 33; paying karmic debt, 141; misc., 218, 260

Huiming (senior monk); *bio*, 241; original face of, 34; and the Sixth Patriarch's robe and bowl, 33–34, 201

Huineng (Sixth Patriarch); *bio*, 241–42; robe and bowl of, 33–34; verse on "fundamentally not one thing exists," 242; and Wolun's verse on meditation, 202; misc., 238, 241, 256, 257, 263, 278; see also *Sixth Patriarch*

Huitang Zuxin; *bio*, 242; and the sweet-olive blossoms, 44–45; misc., 266

Huiyuan; *bio*, 242–43; and Mount Lu, 242; questions to Kumārajiva, 243; role in establishing Buddhism in China, 242–43; and Sengzhao, 261; and Tiger Creek, 155

Huizhao Qingyu, 265

human birth, loss of, 71

hundred-foot pole, 49, 219, 220

hungry ghosts (preta), 75, 79, 94, 175

Huo'an Shiti; *bio*, 243; misc., 101

Huqiu Shaolong, 223, 278, 281

Hutou (senior monk); *bio*, 243; and Xiangyan's "person up a tree," 45

ignorance, 146, 148; fundamental, 65, 179; as one of three poisons, 44, 130; see also *delusion*

illness; and ghee, 122; of Layman Pang, 88; Liangjie's comments on, 229; the one who suffers no, 229; of Vimalakīrti, 269, 270; of Yuanwu, 280

Imperial Library, 207

In Praise of Identity (poem), 111

Indra (Indian god), 35; nostrils, 121; and the seven wise women, 60

infirmary; and death, 58, 129; "going down to the," 128, 129; Qinshan visits after being hit by Deshan, 200

insentient, preaching of the, 228–29

Inzan lineage, 19

iron; dragon-head, 120; mountains, 35; snake, lying across the ancient road, 82

Iron-Wheel Emperor, 128, 129; see also *cakravartin*

Jambudvīpa, 35, 182

Ji Xin, 161; *bio*, 243

Jianfu Chenggu; *bio*, 244; and the emptiness of emptiness, 187

Jiashan Shanhui; *bio*, 244; and the Central Matter of Zen, 96–97; and the dharmakāya is without form, 200; and enlightenment under "Boatman Monk" Chuanzi, 244; on the dead snake, 98–99; and his surroundings, 95; misc., 222, 250, 266

Jingde-era Record of the Transmission of the Lamp, 10, 17, 173, 208, 214, 226, 235, 247, 249, 255, 256, 270, 276

Jingqing Daofu; *bio*, 244–45; and not perceiving a single dharma, 135; misc., 166, 231

Jingshan Faqin, 257, 268

Jingshan Hongyin; *bio*, 245; and Xuefeng's Dharma, 167–68

Jingzhao Mihu (Qishi); *bio*, 245; and the thousand-year peach pit, 194; and the well-bucket rope, 195

Jue Tiezui; and Zhaozhou's comment on the juniper tree in the garden, 38; see also *Guangxiao Huijue*

Juefan Huihong; *bio*, 245; and Doushuai's "final word," 123–24;

juniper tree in the garden, 37–38, 59, 70, 283; and Kanzan Egen's "works like a thief," 59

Juzhou Baotan; *bio*, 245–46; and the disciples of Mazu and Linji, 108

kalpa; of emptiness, 72, 73; types of, 185

Kānadeva, see *Āryadeva*

Kanakāmuni Buddha, 58

Kanzan Egen; *bio*, 246; as an ancestor of the Ōtōkan lineage, 10, 17; and the Garuḍa King, 181; and the inherently perfect buddha, 146; and "no birth-and-death at my place," 197; and "Zhaozhou's Juniper Tree," 59; misc., 10, 17, 254, 265

Kapimala, 253–54

karmic; consciousness, 65, 179; debts, 241; obstructions, 141, 157; seeds, 42, 130; ties, 126

Kāśyapa Buddha; *bio*, 246–47; and the seven wise women, 60; verse of, 247; misc., 57, 58

kenshō, 5

kill; mother and father, 52, 86, 87; Buddha, 52, 104, 122; arhat, 52, 86; a dead snake, 98, 99; Wu Yuanji, 125, 126; cattle, 192; and give life, 155, 160, 168, 198, 199; a white elephant, 227

King Bimbisāra, 227

King of Dharma, 279

King Udayana, 117, 118

kleśa, 16, 130, 207

koans; and language, 12–13, 16; and texts, 12–13; unfinished, 77

koan-introspecting Zen, 224, 239

koan work; and checking questions, 5; definitions of, 1; entanglements, 5; and logic, 2; meaning of, 1–5, 11–13; metaphors for, 1–2; and Rinzai sect, 5; secret records of (*missan roku*), 17–18; and the Sōtō sect, 5; as upāya, 143; and Westerners, 3; Zen masters' comments on, 2, 4, 5

Kogetsu Zenzai, 49

Kōhō Kennichi, 181, 253, 264

Kosen Ingen, 285

Krakucchanda Buddha, 58

Kṣitigarbha; and Mount Jiuhua, 40; as Yanmo, 61

Kumārajiva, 205; and Huiyuan, 243; and Sengzhao, 260, 261

Kuzō kattōshō, 15

labor; see *monastic labor*

Langye Huijue; *bio*, 247; and the great bell, 183; on Linji's perception and function, 160; and pure original nature giving rise to the great earth, 180; and Yunmen's

requiting the benevolence of the Buddha, 104; misc., 50, 221

Laṅkāvatara Sutra, 255

Lanxi Daolong, 254

Latter Age of the Dharma, 120

lay brother, 34

Layman Pang (Pang Yun); *bio*, 257; and daughter's death, 88; illness of, 88; and swallowing the water of the West River, 48; and the plants, 87–88; and the plum pit, 76; verse on drawing water and carrying firewood, 257; and Yu Di, 88; misc., 224, 225, 280

li (unit of measurement), 131

Li Bo (poet), 165, 222, 237

Li Tongxuan; *bio*, 247; and the wisdom-waters of the Dharma realm, 187

Li Ying (Governor); *bio*, 247; and Zhaozhou's stone bridge, 202

Li Zunxu, 280

Liang, of Wufeng; *bio*, 248; and his koan collection, 190

liberation; of other beings, 40, 44, 73, 74, 75, 89, 114, 126, 152, 215, 237, 266; through sudden awakening, 226

life, giving and taking away, 37, 155, 160, 168, 198, 199

light; beam of wondrous, 193; of the Buddha's relics, 194–95; of the buddhas' wisdom, 90; of the eyes, 36; of a lamp, 154; as a metaphor for duality, 105; of the mind turned inward, 34; of an old buddha, 116; shining forth, 201; two types of, 43, 44

Lingshu Rumin; *bio*, 248; retained supernatural powers, 139; misc., 282

Lingyun Zhiqin; *bio*, 248; and awakening through circumstances, 37; and peach tree blossoms, 36–37; and a pillar conceiving, 41; misc., 219, 235

Linji Yixuan; *bio*, 248–49; and begging in the capital, 177; comments on the guest and host, 149; and Dayu, 157; and a different way of doing things, 133; the Four Perceptions and Functions of, 161, 174; and the four positions on the person and the surroundings, 125, 173; and the four realms of no-form, 147; and the four shouts, 148; and hitting Longya with a cushion, 133; and the hunk of red flesh, 146; on life and death, 149; and a man atop a solitary peak, 83–84; Memorial Tower Inscription of, 218; and planting pine trees, 161–62; and the qualities of his disciples, 108–10; and refusing Baizhang's backrest and armrest, 93; and Sansheng the blind ass, 164; and teaching through devices, 143; seven steps beyond, 208; and the Three Statements, 135–36; and the three vehicles' twelve divisions of teachings, 181; training under Huangbo, 156–57; and the true meaning of Huangbo's three-score blows, 179; and the true person of no rank, 191; the true teachings of, 145; and Zhaozhou, 172, 173; misc., 17, 166, 217, 218, 227, 239, 249, 250, 256, 260, 273, 275, 285

Linji school; end of, 264; Wuzu Fayan's comment on, 86; misc., 231, 257, 276

Linji's Dharma, true transmission of, 207

Lion of West River, 145, 146, 262

lion, 149, 150, 160; golden-haired, 120, 148; and Mañjuśrī, 150, 161; riding a, 149; true cub of a, 38

Little Jade, Wuzu's poem on, 95

Liu Bang (General), 243, 271–72

Liu Gongquan, 92

lock, springless, as buddha-mind, 78

Longqing Qingxian; *bio*, 249; and Huanglong's three statements, 38

Longtan Chongxin; *bio*, 249; and the paper torch, 113; misc., 200, 227, 268

Longya Judun; *bio*, 249; and no meaning to the Patriarch's coming from the West, 133; misc., 268

Lotus Sutra; and the arjaka tree, 61; and Buddha of Great Universal Wisdom Excellence, 69; "Earning a living and producing things," 111; and the land of the rakṣasas, 60; and the one great [purpose] of the buddhas, 125; samadhi in, 68; misc., 188, 228, 231, 233, 267

lotus, blooming in the twelfth month, 116, 117

Lu Gen (Governor); *bio*, 249–50; laughs and cries at Nanquan's funeral, 173; misc., 255

Lu Xiujing, 155

Luohan Guichen, and the stone in Fayan's mind, 230

Luopu Yuan'an; *bio*, 250; and a single follower of the Way free of thought, 106

Luoshan Daoxian; *bio*, 250; comments of Shushan's memorial tombstone, 116; misc., 252

Lushan Huguo, 188

Ma Fang; *bio*, 250; and the remaining shout, 148

Madhyamaka school, 254, 255

Magu Baotie; *bio*, 251; and digging weeds with a spade, 141; the hand-cloth and the question of death, 115; misc., 258, 264

Mahākāśyapa; *bio*, 251; and Ānanda lowering the flagpole, 119; Buddha's transmitting the Dharma to, 93, 119; smiles, 119; transmitting the Dharma to Ānanda, 175; misc., 213

Mahāparinirvāṇa Sutra, 232

Mahāprajñā Sutra Preached by Mañjuśrī, 49

Mahā-prajñā-pāramitā Sutra, and the six earth-shakings, 148

Mahāvyutpatti, 118

Maitreya; *bio*, 251; descending to this world, 175; as Fu Dashi, 234; as someone's servant, 34; and Yangshan given the second seat, 85; misc., 267

man; atop a solitary peak, 83, 84; at a busy crossroads, 83–84

manas, 130

Mañjuśrī; *bio*, 251; asking the Buddha to turn the Dharma wheel, 80; and Buddha Flower Adornment Samadhi, 185; and the lion, 160; and Mount Wutai, 40, 136, 251, 282; and Samantabhadra, 40, 44, 150, 160–61, 166, 174–75; and Sudhana gathering herbs, 168; symbolic meaning of, 40, 166; and Vimalakīrti, 117; and the woman in samadhi, 67–68, 89; and Wuzhuo's questioning, 136; misc., 150, 218, 260, 270, 282

Manora; *bio*, 251; transmission verse, 50

mano-vijñāna (seventh consciousness), 130

Mara, realm of, 123, 125

marvelous principle, 279

Master, Ruiyan Shiyan calling to the, 39

Maudgalyāyana; *bio*, 251–52; and the Buddha image, 117; mother in the realm of the hungry ghosts, 94; the supernatural powers of, 94, 117; misc., 228, 260

Mazu Daoyi; *bio*, 252; and according with the samadhi of formlessness, 186; and the autumn-moon turning-phrase, 82–83; deafening Baizhang with a shout, 179; and Deng Yinfeng, 197; not lacking salt or sauce, 70; this very mind is buddha, 35, 224, 232; not mind, not buddha, 35, 224; and Nanyue polishing a tile, 122; on the nature of ordinary mind, 97; qualities of his disciples, 108–10; and swallowing the West River, 48; and teaching through principle, 142–43; and the wheelbarrow, 197; and the whisk, 150–51; and the wild duck, 151; misc., 216, 217, 224, 225, 226, 228, 232, 234, 235, 239, 251, 255, 257, 268, 273, 285

medicinal herbs, 168

meditation; seated, 122; in monastic life, 69; and thought, 35, 202

meeting a buddha, slay the buddha, 52

Meghaśrī, Bhikku, 90

melon, Shūhō Myōchō and the, 265

memorial tombstone, 116, 117

Mencius, 152

merit; no attachment to, 62–63; being is beyond m., 138; of donating to the sangha, 182; of Emperor Wu's good actions, 75; of the follower of the Way, 106; offerings yield no, 78, 179; and the revolving sutra library, 234

Mian Xianjie; *bio*, 252; and the brittle bowl, 53; and Deshan carrying his bowls, 48; and the single path to enlightenment, 103; misc., 264, 267, 278

midnight, 174, 175; lost the ox at, 104–5; Mañjuśrī and Samantabhadra formulating views at, 174–75; as metaphor for darkness (equality), 105, 175; moonlight shone on the window at, 91

millstone, eight-sided, 120

Mind King, 234

Mind Seal, 122

mind; arises again and again, 202; and the banner in the wind, 86; and body, distance between, 134; as buddha, 35, 101, 224, 227;
232, 234, 263; ceaselessly produces the five skandhas, 92; as citta, 130; as the eighth consciousness (ālaya-vijñāna), 130; grasping m. with m., 184; of the Great Sage of India, 111; misuse of, 81, 236; of nirvana, 119; ordinary, 97; original, 234, 235; past m. is unobtainable, 227; peace of, 33, 72, 250, 275; phantom-person's, 139; returning to its source, 277; is the root, 226; is the source of all, 224; no striving with, 214; thief has no peace of, 37

mind-essence, 263

mind-ground, 186; Dharma eye of the, 186

mind-nature, is not produced and cannot be destroyed, 232

mind-seal, secretly transmitted from the West, 232

mind-to-mind transmission, 4, 66, 75, 119

Mingzhao Deqian; *bio*, 252; on "being" and "nonbeing," 55

mirror; ancient, 65; as symbol of buddha nature, 65; and enlightenment, 41; smashing the m. of infinite luminosity, 41; smashing Guishan's m., 131

Miscellany of the Mūlasarvāstivāda Vinaya, 104

monastic labor, 58, 105, 174, 207, 246; and Baizhang, 105, 216; in the fields, 99; in the garden, 69, 165; in the mountains, 57, 127; see also *work*

mondō (questions-and-answers), 16, 166

money, 72, 73, 115, 120

monkeys, clasping their young, 95

monument, broken, across an old road, 86

moon; autumn, 82; crosses the nighttime sky, 193; illuminates the clear pool, 135; isn't full, is full, 169; as a metaphor for the enlightened mind, 171; pushing carts under the, 128; reflected in water, 263, 284; supported by branches of coral, 217

moonlight; playing a lute in the, 38; shining on the window at midnight, 91; and the well-bucket rope, 194

mortal offenders, 86, 87

mother, 34, 52, 86–87, 104, 117–18, 140, 196, 214, 241, 253, 261, 280; Maudgalyāyana's, 94; meaning of to Linji, 87

Mount Emei; and Samantabhadra, 40; symbolic meaning of, 40
Mount Jiuhua, as abode of Kṣitigarbha, 40
Mount Lu, 155, 201, 218, 226, 235, 241, 242, 244, 265, 284; Zen monks of, 201
Mount Putou, 40, 189; as abode of Avalokiteśvara, 40
Mount Shaohua, collapse of, 131
Mount Sumeru, 35, 129, 175; five in the eye of a gnat, 74; using for a brush, 59
Mount Tai (Wutai), 39–40; as abode of Mañjuśrī, 40; and Deng Yinfeng, 227; and the old woman, 39–40; symbolic meaning of, 40; misc., 136, 251, 282
mountains; Double Iron-Ring, 174, 175; endless blue, 65; m., rivers, and the great earth, 180, 199, 207
Mujaku Dōchū, 21; on the board-carrier, 99; on the broken monument and the watchman, 87; on Ciming closing the gate and the fire in the grave, 145; on confusion, 70; on Dadao, 145; on Daitō's comment about Musō, 181; on demolishing the walls of Caizhou and killing Wu Yuanji, 126; on Deshan as a bandit, 171; on the function of the whisk, 151; on a half-sheet of paper, 89; on household spirits, 89; on Jiashan, the monk, and the pit, 96–97; on Jiashan's dead snake, 99; on leaving confusion behind, 70; on Magu's hand-cloth, 115; on the monk bitten by a snake, 204; on peach brooms, 52; on Qiannu and her spirit, 52; on the walls of Caizhou, 126; on the word *hou*, 132; on Xutang's "This old monk blundered," 98; on Zhaozhou and the well, 98
Mūla-madhyamaka-kārikā (*Fundamental Verses on the Middle Way*), 254
Musō Soseki; *bio*, 252–53; 246; and Daitō, 181; and the Garuḍa King, 181; and Kanzan Egen, 181; on teaching through principle, 142–43; misc., 10, 284
Muzhou Daozong (Daoming); *bio*, 253; and Governor Wang, 178–79; and Yunmen Wenyan, 282; misc., 221, 270
Myōan Eisai (Yōsai), 240
Myōshin-ji, 246
Myōshin-ji school, 17–19; Tōkai lineage of, 18

Myōsō Saitetsu, 285
Mysterious Gates, three, of Linji, 136
Nāga King, draws his sword, 138
Nāgārjuna; *bio*, 253–54; misc., 183, 196, 214, 255, 260, 261,
Nalakūvara; *bio*, 254; eight-armed, 65, 66; misc., 196
Nanpo Jōmyō (Daitō Kokushi); *bio*, 254; and iron, 142; and Musō Soseki, 181; and his two turning-phrases, 127; and his three questions, 100; misc., 10, 17, 181, 224, 246, 264, 265, 276, 281
Nanquan Puyuan; *bio*, 254–55; and the autumn-moon turning-phrases, 82; and King Udayana's Buddha image, 117; and the fried dumplings, 77; and his greatness of mind, 108; losing both the ox and the fire, 104; and Lu Gen, 173, 249–50; mind is not buddha, 101; and "not knowing it," 83; not-mind, not-buddha, [not-things], 162–63; rebirth as a water buffalo, 91, 255; and his sickle, 57; and the views of Mañjuśrī and Samantabhadra, 174; visited in his hermitage by a monk, 127; on where he went after death, 208; and the word beyond wisdom, 192; misc., 17, 220, 228, 252, 273, 283
Nanshan Vinaya school, 225–26
Nantang Yuanjing; *bio*, 255; and demon, 61; ten admonitions, 74–75
Nanyang Huizhong; *bio*, 255–56; and the circle-figures, 189–90; and the court monk Zilin, 205; let down by his attendant, 53; and the seamless tower, 256; misc., 225, 228, 273
Nanyuan Huiyong; *bio*, 256; on simultaneous pecking and tapping, 154; and the prophecy on Fengxue, 162; and the staff of the south, 165, 166; misc., 231
Nanyue Huairang; *bio*, 256–57; and polishing the tile, 122; on practice and realization, 106; and according with the samadhi of formlessness, 186; verse on the mind-ground, 186; misc., 171, 242, 252, 256, 267
nature, see *original nature, true nature, self-nature*
needle; eye of, 182; tiptoe on the point of, 126

nenbutsu, 237, 279
New Treatise on the Avataṁsaka Sutra, 188, 247
ni (exclamation), 61, 62
Niaoke Daolin; *bio*, 257; meditating in a pine tree, 176
Nikāyas, Pali, 182
Nine-Dragon Carriage, 161, 243
nirmāṇakāya, 136; Śākyamuni as example of, 44
Nirvana Sutra, 188, 217, 277; on buddha nature, 65
nirvana, 49, 78, 79, 89, 187, 205; ineffable mind of, 119; of Nanyang, 256; and repaying debts, 142; single road to, 121; virtuous practicers not entering, 49; misc.
no-birth, 247, 278
Noble Voice, 117, 118
no-form, four realms of, 147
nonbeing, 184, 193
non-Buddhists, 78, 187
non-Buddhist teachers, 78–79, 214, 252
nondoing, 48, 123, 151
nonduality, 120, 205; of body and mind, 100
Northern school, 238
nostrils, of Indra, 121
nothing to do, people with, 158
no-thought, person of, 106
not-knowing and not-understanding, 186
not-mind, not-buddha, [not-things], 163
ocean; and the four continents, 35; o. of meaning, o. of writing (in the circle figures), 190, 191; throwing a drop of water into the, 113
officially even a needle is not permitted, 152
old woman; burns down a hermitage, 132–33; and Ciming, 144, 159–60; and Deshan at the teahouse, 227; and Linji on his begging rounds, 177; on the road to Mount Wutai, 39–40
On Believing in Mind, 184, 260, 269
one-word barriers, Yunmen's, 35, 46, 47, 52, 132, 282
ordaination, and nine generations of ancestors reborn in heaven, 94
ordinary mind is the Way, 97
ordination certificate, 131

original emptiness, see *emptiness*
original face, 12, 71, 83, 156; before your parents were born, 34; is right before you, 184, 199
original nature, 72, 75, 81, 180, 220, 272
Ōtōkan lineage, 10, 11, 17, 246, 254, 265
ox; through a lattice window, 43; as metaphor for darkness (equality), 105; lost at midnight, 104, 105; cart, 122; tending an, 220
oxen; cats and, 83; cannot pull a word from a government office, 81
palm fronds, 71
Pang Yun, see *Layman Pang*
paper; curtain, 115; half-sheet of, 89; torch, 113, 114
Parinirvāṇa, Buddha's, 80
Parrot Island, 167
partridge, 84; song, 46; as symbol of homesickness, 46
Patriarch, meaning of coming from the West, 59, 76, 133, 232; see also *Bodhidharma, meaning of coming from the West*
peace, 187; mind is at, 33, 238; of mind, 37, 72, 250, 275; sitting in, 43; world is at, 104
peach; blossoms, 36–37, 90, 172, 173, 248; branches, 51–52; pit, thousand-year, 194
peak; of another mountain, 90; Dayu P., 33, 116, 201; Eagle P., 126; of Mount Wutai, 227; purple, 95; rugged, 152; solitary, 83, 84, 110, 113; Vulture P., 93, 119; one is not white, 42; of Wondrous Mountain, 90
pearl(s); bright, in the dusts of delusion 201; in the purple-curtained room, 108, 109
pecking and tapping, 154
peddlers, pushing carts under the moon, 128
Pei Xiu, 54; *bio*, 258; and the *Essentials of the Transmission of Mind*, 258; misc. 239, 280
perception, 93, 102; and function, 160, 161, 174
periods; five, of the Buddhist teachings, 187–88; ten, of past, present, and future, 175; three, of time, 106
persecution of Buddhism; under Emperor Wuzong, 140, 222, 227, 229, 258, 274, 275, 279; under Emperor Wu, 260

person, 60, 81, 91, 178–79; awakened, 148; at a busy crossroads, 84; clear-eyed, 206, 217; liberated, 143; of no rank, 146–47, 191; of no-thought, no-abiding, no-cultivation, and no-attainment, 106; and surroundings, Linji's views on, 125, 126, 173; on top of a solitary peak, 84

phantom-person, 139

phoenix, 82; of Danshan, 120

pillar; conceiving, 41, 42; in Daitō's turning-phrases, 127; "does a p. tire?" 179; monk from Silla runs into a, 164; and not perceiving a single dharma, 135; as a symbol of no-mind, 42, 127, 135, 164, 179

pine trees; Linji plants, 161; thousand-foot, 208, 209

Piyun; *bio*, 258; and Magu's hand-cloth, 115

plants, Layman Pang's comment on, 88

Platform Sutra of the Sixth Patriarch, 202, 241

Poems of Venerable Longya Judun, 249

Pointing at the Moon Record, 235

Poison-painted Drum (Zudokko), 19

polo, 178

Prajñā Is Not Knowledge, 261

prajñā (wisdom), 62, 193, 198, 251, 261

prajñā-pāramitā; sutras, 176, 188, 242; texts, 254

Prajñātara, 218

pratyekabuddha, 180; offerings to, 106

Precious Flowers of the Lamp Transmission, 270

preta (hungry ghosts), 75, 79, 94, 175

Priests Do Not Bow before Kings, 243

primordial chaos, 41, 42, 142

Prince Nata, 196, 254

principle, 136; abstruse, 36, 168; essential, 122; great, 92; Mañjuśrī as symbol of, 166; marvelous, 279; realm of, 100, 136–37; relation with phenomena, 100, 136–37; of the teaching, 206; teaching through, 142–43; transcendent, 117

Punyayaśas, 215

puppet(s); of Linji, 136; show, 143

Pure Land tradition, 243

Pūrvavideha, 35

Qianfeng, see *Yuezhou Qianfeng*

Qiannu, 51, 52

Qingliang Taiqin; *bio*, 258; and the unfinished koan, 77

Qingshui; *bio*, 258; and best wine of Qingyuan

Qingsu; *bio*, 258; and the lychee fruit, 123; and the final word, 123; misc., 230

Qingyuan Xingsi, 208, 209, 242, 256, 257, 263, 275, 277

Qinshan Wensui; *bio*, 258–59; struck and injured by Deshan, 199–200

quietism, 50

rabbit, pushing a cart, 193

rakṣasas, land of the, 60, 280

reality, 56, 84, 136, 184, 198, 199

realizations, ten, 198

realm(s); of the animals, 208; of Buddha, 123, 125; of the dead, 51, 52; of desire, 117, 205, 251; of emancipation, 79; of existence, 75; of form, 205; of formlessness, 205; four dharma r., 100, 136–37; heavenly, 94; of hungry ghosts, 94; infinite, 175, 94; of Mara, 123, 125; of no-form, 147; of nothingness, 99; of phenomena, 100, 136; of principle, 100, 136; of pure clarity, 150; of the universe, 100; of the unobstructed and mutual interpenetration of principle and phenomena, 100, 137; of the unobstructed and mutual interpenetration of phenomena and phenomena, 100, 137; see also *three realms*

reason, in the Buddha's teaching, 67, 142

rebirth, 232; of Devadatta as a buddha, 228; endless r. of the deluded, 232; as a fox, 58; after the Great Death, 129; in the heavenly realms, 94; of Maitreya, 251; in the Pure Land, 243; as a sage, 63; and the supernatural powers of Yunmen, 139; in the Three Realms, 205; as a water buffalo, 73, 208

Record of Ciming, 193

Record of Daitō, 21

Record of Dongshan, 94, 166

Record of Equanimity, 10, 239; and the three types of sickness, 44; *Case 13*, 164; *Case 14*, 171; *Case 18*, 65; *Case 38*, 147; *Case 44*, 181; *Case 47*, 38; *Case 57*, 36; *Case 79*, 49, 220–21; *Case 87*, 56; *Case 89*, 137; *Case 100*, 180

Record of Foyan, 179
Record of Langye, 183
Record of Layman Pang, 88
Record of Linji, 10, 15, 16, 19, 20, 21, 29, 52, 84, 86–87, 136, 147, 148, 149, 150, 158, 161, 162, 164, 172, 173, 180, 225, 250, 260, 273; English translations of, 20–21; and exhausting karma, 48; on slaying the Buddha, 52
Record of Songyuan, 173
Record of the Source Mirror, 279
Record of the Transmission of the Dharma in the True School, 233
Record of the True School of Linji, 56
Record of Xutang, 10, 17, 21, 80, 128
Record of Yunmen, 169–70
Recorded Sayings of Muzhou, 16
Recorded Sayings of the Ancient Worthies, 17
Recorded Sayings of Xutang, "Alternate Answers," 276
red flesh, hunk of, 146, 147
red threads, 126
red-bearded foreigner, 58
relics (śarīra); and Danxia, 64; and Emperor Xianzong, 194–95
Rentian yanmu, 161
renunciation, Huangbo's three levels of, 63
rice; gruel, 38; importance of one grain of, 177, 178
rivers, the birds, the trees…, all chant the name of Dharma, 229
Rivet-and-Shears Hu (Hu Dingjiao); *bio*, 239; driving a rivet into the void, 109; misc., 108
robe, 93, 98; of Buddha, 74, 175; of Ciming, 145–46; monk's, 93; paper, 170, 285; purple, 131, 223, 233, 263, 267, 281, 285; of the Sixth Patriarch, 33–34, 201, 242; smelly, 158; split in two, 182
robe and bowl of the Sixth Patriarch, 33–34, 201, 242
Ruiyan Shiyan; *bio*, 259; calling to the Master, 39
Śākyamuni; *bio*, 259; and Devadatta, 103, 227–28; and the Golden-Millet Tathāgata, 100; holds up a flower, 110, 119; as the Old Foreigner, 51, 52; as the skillful weaver-

woman, 206; transmission of the Dharma to Mahākāśyapa, 93, 119; and a woman in samadhi, 67–68, 89; misc., 34, 58, 139, 198, 227, 228, 233, 247, 251, 269; see also *Buddha*
salt; or sauce, 70; selling privately on a public highway, 183
samadhi, 64, 79; Flower Adornment, 185; formless, 186; of the infant, 192; Jeweled-mirror, 266; of the Joyful Play of the Lion, 148; light of, 44; in the *Lotus Sutra*, 68; and Maitreya, 251; and "ocean of meaning," 191; of perfect freedom, 45; in the *Śūraṅgama Sutra*, 64; of a woman, 67–68, 89
Samantabhadra; *bio*, 259–60; and the attainment of Dharma freedom, 185; as the Elephant King, 160; and the function of teaching and practice, 188; and the light of wisdom, 44; and Mañjuśrī, 44, 150, 161, 166, 174, 251, 259; and Mount Emei, 40; losing his domain, 188; riding a white elephant, 150; and Vairocana, 188; misc., 251, 267
samāpatti, 121
śamatha-vipaśyanā, 231, 278
saṃbhogakāya, 43, 136; Amitābha Buddha as example of, 43
samsara, 52, 205, 280; see also *birth-and-death*
sangha; destroying the harmony of, 86, 87, 103, 228; and Devadatta, 103, 228; do not join the, 78–79; expulsion from the, after breaking the precepts, 138; government control of, 131, 243; merit of donating food to, 182; ordination certificates and, 131; seek nothing from the, 79, 196
Sanghadeva, 243
Sanjaya Belatthiputta, 252, 260
Sanlun school, 255
Sansheng Huiran; *bio*, 260; and Linji's Dharma, 164; and Nanquan's death, 208; misc., 108, 109, 273
sanzen, 104, 118
Śariputra; *bio*, 260; misc., 183, 228, 252
Sarvāstivāda school, 243
seal of realization, 135, 136
seamless tower of Nanyang, 256
Second Patriarch (Huike), see *Huike*

secret koan records (*missan roku*), 17–18

seeing self-nature and attaining buddhahood, 206

Seiryō-ji (Kyoto), 118

self-nature, 81, 206, 264; see also *original
nature, true nature, mind-nature*

Semblance Dharma, age of, 120

Sengcan (Third Patriarch); *bio*, 260; and no
duality in the Dharma, 184; misc., 240

Sengzhao, 84; *bio*, 260–61; treatises of, 261

senses, six, as 'the six teachers', 78

separate teaching transmitted outside the
sutras, 66, 75, 111, 119

service for others; Huike, 241; koans on;
"Guishan's 'Water Buffalo,'" 73; "Nan-
quan's 'Water buffalo,'" 91; "Nantang's
'Other Realms,'" 74–75

sesame rice-cakes, 89, 90

Seven Buddhas of the Past, 58, 139, 203;
transmission verses of, 139

seven destinations, 187; see also *six realms
of existence*

seventh consciousness, 130

Shangu (poet Huang Tingjian); *bio*, 261;
and the sweet-olive blossoms, 44–45

Shanguo Yue'an, 265

Shending Hongyin; *bio*, 261; and his
encounter with the Lion of West River,
145–46; misc., 233

Shenxiu, 238

Shexian Guixing; *bio*, 261; and Shoushan's
stick, 118

Shide, 237

Shinchi Kakushin, 271

Shishuang Chuyuan (Ciming); *bio*, 262;
and the bowl of water, 129; and Dadao
Guquan, 144; eccentricities, 100, 128, 129,
144, 145–46; as enlightened teacher, 14;
entrusting the Great Matter to Yangqi, 152;
foolish or wise, 100; Huanglong receiving stick from dawn to dusk, 159; and
"Hundred-foot Pole" koan, 49; Lion of
West River, 145–46, 262; and the original
face, 134; and the single word, 134; and his
tiger's roar, 145; on the Way, 193; and his
woman, 144, 159–60; and a wild, uncut
meadow, 152; and the winter solstice
signboard, 128, 129; and Yangqi's turning-

phrase, 144; misc., 123, 223, 231, 236, 240,
258, 276

Shishuang Qingzhu; *bio*, 262–63; and a
grain of rice, 178; and the grass by the
monastery gate, 137; and the springless
lock, 78; misc., 238, 250, 282

Shishuang Xingkong; *bio*, 263; and the man
in a well, 76

shit, dry piece of, 46

Shitou Xiqian; *bio*, 263; and advice from
the Sixth Patriarch, 208; "In Praise of
Identity," 111; misc., 225, 226, 257, 268

Shōchū Debate, and Shūhō Myōchō, 265

Shoukuo; *bio*, 264; and the sages of old, 171;
misc., 231

Shoushan Shengnian; *bio*, 264; and the
Buddha's lotus-blue eyes, 110; and the
Noble Voice, 118; and the skillful weaver-
woman, 206; and his stick, 118; and the
sutra from which all buddhas issue, 72;
misc., 231, 234, 261, 270

shout(s), 184, 203; blind and wild, 109;
consecutive s. by Ciming and Yangqi, 152;
that deafened Baizhang for three days,
151; and guest examining host, 150; Linji's,
109, 148, 157, 227, 249; and Sansheng's
blind ass, 164; and the stick, 66, 108, 142,
249, 252, 283; by Linji's two head monks,
149; and the word *ni*, 62; by Xinghua and
the blind-oaf monk, 153; by Yantou at his
death, 278

Shouzhou Liangsui; *bio*, 264; at Magu's
gate, 141

shrine, earth-spirit, 114

Shuangshan Yuan; *bio*, 264; and the wind-
bleached signpost, 53

Shūhō Myōchō (Daitō Kokushi); *bio*,
264–65; and his doubts about Musō, 181;
and Gojō Bridge, 264–65; and "iron,"
142; and his three questions, 100; and his
three turning-phrases, 127; misc., 10, 17,
246, 254, 268

Shui'an Shiyi; *bio*, 265; and the barbarian
with no beard, 101

Shūmon kattōshū; Ansei edition, 18–19;
additional koans in Ansei edition, 18;
Daitoku-ji school and, 18; Genroku edition, 18, 26; Hakuin Zen and, 19; *Hekizen*

hekigo and, 18; history of, 10–11, 15–19; Japanese koans in, 10; Japanese Rinzai school and, 11; Kajitani Sōnin edition, 19–20; *kinshishū* and, 18; koans from the *Blue Cliff Record*, 16; koans from the *Record of Linji*, 16; koans from the *Record of Xutang*, 17; koans from the *Wumen guan*, 16; and the *Kuzō kattōshō*, 15; meaning of the title, 15–16; Myōshin-ji school Tōkai lineage and, 18; Ōtōkan lineage and, 10–11, 17–18; Sōtō school and, 18; Xutang Zhiyu and, 17

Shushan Guangren; *bio*, 265–66; and Dongshan's transmission of the Dharma to Caoshan Benji, 266; 56; "being" and "nonbeing," 54–56; and paying for the memorial tombstone, 116–17

sickle, Nanquan's, 57

sickness; three types of, 43, 44; see also *illness*

signpost, broken, 53

Śikhin Buddha, 58

silence and speech, 85

silent illumination Zen, 224, 237, 239, 262

Silla, 217; monk from, 163–64

sin(s), 192; five deadly, 86–87

single road to nirvana (enlightenment, liberation), 100, 103, 121

sitting cloth, 59, 109, 115, 217; to spread, 59

Śiva, 182

six earth-shakings, 147–48

six realms of existence (six paths, six ways), 75, 187 205, 263

Sixin Wuxin; *bio*, 266; and the fragrance of the sweet-olive blossoms, 45

Sixth Patriarch (Huineng); and the banner in the wind, 86; and the circle-figures, 190; criticizing Wolun, 202; and any explanation is off the mark, 106; wise friend and teacher, 94; misc., 225; see also *Huineng*

Skanda, 182

skandhas; five, 92, 93; ceaselessly produced by the mind, 92

sky; Baoshou's applying the staff to, 108, 109; cloudless, 64; empty, 59; Great Pure, 41, 42; radiant phoenix dances in, 82

sleeves, shaken, 82, 83, 110, 152, 172

smile, of Mahākāśyapa, 119

snake; biting a monk, 204; dead in the road, 98, 99; iron s. across the ancient road, 82; tail of a, 163, 204; well-bucket rope mistaken for, 194

snow; covers a thousand mountains, 42; a silver bowl filled with, 217; and a snowy egret, 38

snowy egret, 38

solitary peak, 83, 84, 110, 113

Song of Enlightenment, 184

Songshan Hui'an; *bio*, 266–67; misc., 106, 257

Songyuan Chongyue; *bio*, 267; on Langye Huijue, 183; on Linji and Zhaozhou's "washing my feet" *mondō*, 172; and his three turning-phrases, 126; misc., 93, 252, 281

Southern Cross, 120

Southern school of Zen, 238, 242

special transmission outside the teachings, 66, 75, 111, 119

spirit(s); earth, 114; existence of, 61–62; household, 89; of Qiannu, 51–52

śrāvaka, 89, 180

staff, 58, 64, 105, 107, 109, 110, 118, 129, 145, 153, 159, 161, 225, 227, 283; applied to the clear blue sky, 108, 109; Bajiao giving and taking away, 79–80; Channgqing and completing a lifetime's practice, 203; Nanyuan and the s. of the south, 165, 166; Qianfeng drawing a line with, 121; Xutang's big-talking, 155; Yunmen killing the Buddha with his, 104

Statements, Three, of Linji, 135–36

stick, 8, 113, 118, 154, 167–68, 174, 181, 250; Deshan's use of, 227; Huangbo beats Linji with, 156; Linji's use of, 249; Mazu's use of, 252; Nanyuan's, 154; Shoushan's "If you say it's a stick," 118; and the shout, see *shout, and the stick*; thirty blows with, 162, 163, 174; three-score blows with, 158, 167; Yunmen spares Dongshan three-score blows, 158, 159; Zhaozhou's nonuse of, 283

stone bridge of Zhaozhou, 202

suchness, 132, 190, 199, 277

sudden awakening, 49, 179, 180, 219, 226, 229

Sudhana; *bio*, 267; seeks herbs for Mañjuśrī, 168; visit to Bhishmottaranirghosha, 90; visit to Meghaśri, 90; misc., 218

sulu, sulu! 47

Sumeru Seat, 181; see also *Mount Sumeru*

sunlight, shining through a window, 162

śūnyatā, 42, 44, 142, 191, 205, 214, 217; philosophy, 254; see also *emptiness*

supernatural powers; of the Buddha, 148, 206, 214; of Layman Pang, 257; of Lingshu, 139, 248; of Mañjuśrī, 68; of Maudgalyāyana, 94, 117, 251–52; of Prince Nata, 196; of Vimalakīrti, 102; of Yunmen, 139

Supplementary "Biographies of Eminent Monks, 226

Supplementary Biographies of [Mount] Qingliang, 282

Śūraṅgama Sutra, 121, 180, 187, 221, 236; and requiting the benevolence of the Buddha, 104; and skill in turning things around, 170; on staying awake, 64

surroundings, 95; Jiashan's, 95, 244; mind turning with, 50; aren't outside things, 207; and person, 125, 126, 173

Sushu, 282

Sutra in Forty-two Sections, 106

Sutra of Complete Enlightenment, on inherently perfect buddhas, 146

Sutra of the Collection of the Original Acts of the Buddha, 104

Sutra of the Seven Women, 60

Sutra of the Thousand Buddha-Names, 165

Sutra Preached at the Request of Brahmadeva, 205

sutra, from which all buddhas issue, 72

sweet-olive blossoms, 45

sword, 129; of Bingzhou steel, 189; s. blade, 81; Blown-hair, 217, 265; that deters unrest, 164; Dharma general's, 185; diamond s. of the Vajra King, 148; fangs like a row of, 113; general's, 164, 185; s. master, 37; of the Nāga King, 138; of Mañjuśrī, 251; of wisdom, 37

Taihang Kebin; *bio*, 267; and the rice-and-vegetable dinner, 114–15

Takujū lineage, 19

Tales from the Land of Locust-tree Tranquility (Kaiankokugo), 21

tathā," 199

Tathāgata, 146, 175; Golden-Millet T., 100, 101, 102; skill in turning things around, 170; T. Zen, 272

tathāgata-garbha, 188

teacher(s), 149, 150, 157, 159; ancestral, 2; excellent, 150; fifty-three of the *Avataṃsaka Sutra*, 90; non-Buddhist, 78–79, 214; true, 71; Zen, 136; see also *enlightened teacher*

teaching; importance of, 77, 150; true, 65, 66

ten admonitions of Nantang, 74, 75

ten realizations of the same reality, 184, 198–99

Tenryū-ji, 181

terrapin, becomes a softshell, 62

tests; Daitō's three questions, 100; Daitō's two turning-phrases, 127; Doushua's three barriers, 36; Foxing's three turning-phrases, 103; girl hugs a hermit, 133; Huanglong's three barriers, 38–39; Songyuan's three turning-phrases, 126; three questions on the dharmakāya eating food, 134; three turning-phrases of Baling, 217; Wuzu's Mount Sumeru for a brush, 59; Xutang's three questions, 126

Tettō Gikō; *bio*, 268; *Admonitions*, 175; misc., 10, 17, 18

The Song of Enlightenment, 278

thief; has no peace of mind, 37; red-bearded foreigner as, 58; "Zhaozhou's 'Juniper Tree'" functioning as a, 59; drawing the bow after the departure of, 107; see also *bandit*

think not of good, think not of evil, 34

Third Patriarch, see *Sengcan*

thirty-two distinguishing characteristics of a buddha, 117, 118

this very mind is buddha, 35

thorn forest, 46, 47

thought(s), 81, 101, 107, 130; break through the single t. of not-knowing, 186; deluded, 80, 126, 226; of enlightenment, 191; every t. is buddha-mind, 234; follower of the Way free of t., 106; Linji's views on, 87, 147–48; marvelous functioning of awareness without, 277; the master cuts of the student's t., 91; a moment of t. penetrates the three worlds, 90; obstructive, 36; one t.—ten thousand years, 262; stopping, 62, 202; not a single t. of seeking buddhahood, 48; when not a single t. arises, 35

thousand-year peach pit, 194

three barriers of Huanglong, 38–39

three barriers of Doushuai Congyue, 36

Three Essentials, of Linji, 135–36, 136; seal of, 135, 136

Three Mysteries and Three Essentials, 184; pointing to this very moment, 184

Three Mysterious Gates, 136, 184

three poisons (attachment, aversion, and ignorance), 44, 130

three realms (desire, form, formlessness), 205, 263; are nothing but mind, 230; three evil r., 78, 79, 179

Three Statements, of Linji, 135–36

three vehicles, 187, 188; and the twelve divisions of teachings, 180

three worlds, 263, 285

Thus-Come-One, Matrix of, 180, 188

Tianhuang Daowu; bio, 268; misc., 200, 249, 263

Tiantai Deshao; bio, 268–69; misc., 207, 273, 279

Tiger Creek, 155, 242

tiger; head of, 158; in the middle of the road, 69; roar of (Ciming's), 145; tail of, 158; whiskers of, 157; Yangsha as, 171

tile, hitting bamboo, 49; polishing of to become a buddha, 122; no t. to cover his head, 244

time, 39, 90; of death, 52; of primordial chaos, 41, 42; three periods of, 106; timeless t., 184, 185; without beginning, 170

Tipo school, 217

Tōkai lineage, Myōshin-ji school, 18

torch, paper, 113, 114

tortoise's tail hairs, 116, 117

Toutou Temple Stele Inscriptions, 101

Touzi Datong; bio, 269; and buddha is the Way, 169; misc., 268, 275, 277

Touzi Fazong; bio, 269; and his straw sandals, 96

tower; Chen Cao calling to monks from, 132; Huanglong reciting sutras in, 69; memorial t. of Linji, 218; memorial t. of the Sixth Patriarch, 232; Nanyang's seamless t., 256; of Vairocana Buddha, 267; Yellow Crane T., 222; of Zhao Sheng, 181; Zhaozhou calling for help from, 98

training season, 54, 137, 155, 158, 246, 284

transcendence, 41, 42, 74, 134; and functioning, 84, 85

Transmission of the Lamp, 10, 17, 151, 173, 175, 200, 208, 214, 226, 236, 247, 249, 255, 256, 270, 276

transmission verses; of the Buddhas of the Past, 138–39; of Manora, 50

tray of sticky glue, 149

Trāyastrimśa Heaven, 35, 117, 118; and Yunmen's fan, 121

Treasury of Bright Light, 108

Treasury of Great Light, 246

Treasury of the True Dharma Eye, 119, 164, 175

Treatise on Awakening Faith in the Mahayana, 257

Treatise on the Transmission of the Dharma in the True School, 233

tree(s); arjaka, 61; boxwood, 56; dead, 61; giving shade to people, 157; juniper, 37–38, 59, 70, 283; hanging from by teeth, 45; Linji plants pine t., 161; Niaoke Daolin meditating in, 176; and vines, 54–55

true adept, 193

true ascetic, 63

True Dharma Eye, 53; Linji's, 108, 164; Treasury of the, 119, 164, 175

True Dharma, age of, 120

true friend, see friend

true nature, 36, 194, 206; see also original nature

true person of no rank, 146–47, 191

true teaching, 65, 66

turd, dried, 147

turn your own light in upon yourself, 34

turning-phrase, 54, 56, 58; and Bajiao's staff, 79–80; Baling's three, 217; Daitō's two, 127; Foxing's three, 103; Songyuan

Chongyue's three, 126; on the tiger sitting in the road, 69; of Wuzu Fayan's Three Buddhas, 82; of Yangqi at Ciming's woman's house, 144

turtle, black, 181

Tushita Heaven, 251

Udayana (King); *bio*, 269; and the buddha image, 117, 269

Unborn, 179

unity (equality, oneness) and differentiation (discrimination, distinction), 38–39, 41–42, 104–5; 174–75; 217; see also *snow*

upāya, 117, 118, 143; see also *expedient means*

Uttarakuru, 35

Vairocana Buddha, 43, 188, 267

vajra, 55, 56

Vajra King, diamond sword of, 148

Vasubandhu, 251

verses; on Avalokiteśvara, 189; on the birds in front of the blue cliff, 95; on the Blown-hair Sword, 265; on the bodhi tree and bright mirror, 242; the Buddha's birth v., 104; on Chaling Yu's bright pearl, 201; on the cold clouds and hidden rock, 135; on a dead tree on a cold cliff, 133; on the eight-sided millstone, 120; on the final word, 143; on the fragrant southern breeze, 92; on the golden-duck censer, 94; on Hongzhi's eight phrases, 192; on Jiangnan in the third month, 84; of Kāśyapa Buddha, 247; on last year's poverty, 272; on Linji's Four Functions, 174; on Linji's three-score blows, 167; on Layman Pang's drawing water and carrying firewood, 257; on Layman Pang's enlightenment, 48; on Little Jade, 95; of Manora, on the mind, 50; on mind arising, 202; on the mind-ground, 186; on the Noble Voice, 117; on original emptiness and repaying karmic debts, 142; on peddlers in the capital, 128; on Penetrating-the-Mystery Mountain, 269; on peony flowers, 71; on a pillar tiring, 179; on the pink peach blossoms, 172, 173; on the preaching of the sentientless, 229; on the princes reveling in the spring breeze, 53; on Qiannu and her spirit, 51; on seeing it in the twinkle of an eye, 272;

on the single road to nirvana, 121; on the sound of the falling firewood, 207; on the sword-master and peach blossoms, 37; on a tile hitting a bamboo, 49–50, 272; on the veteran general of the Dharma assembly, 185–86; Vipaśyin's transmission v., 139; on white clouds blocking the valley, 106; on Wolun's stopping thoughts, 202; of Xutang on the board-carrier, 98; of Xutang on cold clouds and the frosty moon, 135; on Zhaozhou's "*Wu*," 65

vestment, 93, 181; Mahākāśyapa's brocade, 119; Musō covering his head with, 181; putting on at the sound of the bell, 130; Touzi's straw sandals in, 96

vijñāna, 130

Vimalakīrti Sutra, 146, 179, 187, 188, 196, 205, 260, 269; and the six non-Buddhist teachers, 78–79; and the ten-foot-square chamber, 118

Vimalakīrti; *bio*, 269–70; and Fu Dashi, 84, 234; as the Golden-Millet Tathāgata, 100, 101, 102; illness of, 269–70; and lay Buddhism, 269–70; and his ten-foot-square room, 102; and Mañjuśrī, 117; supernatural powers of, 102

vines, and being and nonbeing, 54–55

Vipaśyin Buddha; *bio*, 270; yet to attain the Mystery, 203; transmission verse of, 138–39; misc., 58

void; breaking through the, 103; casting a single hair into, 113; driving a rivet into, 109; empty, 265; Great, 187; mind is v. from the start, 139; all states are originally v., 232

Vulture Peak; holding up a flower on, 119; transmission of the Dharma to Mahākāśyapa on, 93

Wan'an Daoyan; *bio*, 270; comment on Ciming's signpost, 128

Wang Changshi (Jingchu); *bio*, 270; and the polo game, 178–79

Wang Jin, Toutou Temple Stele Inscriptions, 101

Wang Sui; *bio*, 270; and the emperor holding up the bowl, 201

"Watch where you step!" 82

water buffalo, see *buffalo*

water; Ciming's bowl of, 129; dirty, 172; dragon taking to, 160; drenching oneself with, 117; drinking w. and carrying firewood, 257; drop of in the great ocean, 113; East Mountain walks on the, 68, 92; element of, 36, 147, 187; eloquence like flowing, 183; flow of the, 284; fresh, 35; Huizhong's bowl of, 205; like the moon in the, 263, 284; of a mountain stream, 71; Nāgārjuna's bowl of, 214; pure, 135; too shallow for a ship to moor, 160; stagnant, 171, 207; standing on, 206; still as the w. of the autumn river, 238; tasting for oneself, 34, 108; throwing baby into, 140; of the West River, 48

Watson, Burton, 20

Way; affinity with the, 186; ancient, 50; of all buddhas, 240; doesn't anger, 193; entering the, 70, 140, 279; follower of the, 48, 63, 106; friend of the, 140; great, 279; as the Great Pure Sky, 42; hear sound and realize the, 89; hear of the W. and die content, 97; in the Latter Age, 120; master of the, 37, 50; mind that seeks the, 70; the mind-ground can perceive the, 186; ordinary mind is the, 97; in seeking the W. there is no striving with the mind, 214; wisdom is not the, 101; the W. is without form; misc., 136, 169, 214

wealth, 111; as the source of all evil karma, 120

weeds; as kleśa, 36; Magu digging, 141; shadowy, 148; wild, 180

West River, 48

what is buddha? 35, 46, 74, 80, 169

what is that! 232

what is the dharmakāya? 200

what is the Way? 97, 169, 193, 206, 217

what is Zen? 169

wheel king, see cakravartin

wheel of the Dharma, see Dharma wheel

wheelbarrow, 197

whisk, 80, 150, 151, 228

White Lotus Society, 243

wind; black, 280; element of, 147, 187; fierce w. blows a ship off course, 60; Sixth Patriarch's banner in the, 86; violent, 72;

watch the w. and set the sails accordingly, 143; misc., 162

window; lattice, 43; moonlight on the, 91; sunlight through the, 162; watching through a narrow, 184

wine; of Qingyuan, 102; Mr. Zhang drinks, 70

winter solstice, 128, 129; and Great Death, 129, 203

wisdom (enlightenment); bodhisattva of, 40; dharmakāya as the essence of, 43; dragons as symbols of, 204; as a fundamental aspect of Zen training, 151; Great Perfect Mirror W., 42; like flowing water, 183; and its function, 79; light of, 44, 90; and Mañjuśrī, 89, 136, 161, 166, 251, 270; mind is, 263; sameness of, 198, 199; and Śāriputra, 260; sword of, 37, 81, 148; is not the Way, 101; where w. cannot reach, 192; misc., 125, 136, 187, 188, 214

wise friend and teacher, see enlightened teacher

Wolun, 202; bio, 270

woman; bowing in the manner of, 190, 191; Ciming's, 144, 159–60; Qiannu, 51; and samadhi, 67–68, 89; seven wise, 60; and Zhaozhou, 39–40;

Wondrous Mountain, 90

wood, sound of, 207

wooden fish, 159

word(s); Buddha never preached a single, 143; that can't be said despite the greatest effort, 176; living and dead, 229; oxen cannot pull from a government office, 81; do not seek for anything within, 179; single w. and a four-horse team, 134; spoken from where wisdom cannot reach, 192; see also final word

work; cancellation of, 174; and the duty-monk, 174; "no work, no eating," 105; see also monastic labor

World-Honored One; "above the heavens and below, I alone am the," 104; blue-lotus eyes of the, 110; holds up a flower, 110, 119

Wu koan, 65–67; functioning of, 66; Zhongfeng's question on, 66

Wu Yuanji, 125, 125–126, 227

Wujin, Layman; *bio*, 282; and the final word, 123–24; misc., 245, 280, 284

Wumen guan (*Gateless Barrier*), 3, 10, 11, 15, 16, 19, 20, 21, 29, 30, 271; *Case 1*, 65; *Case 2*, 58; *Case 4*, 101; *Case 5*, 45; *Case 6*, 119; *Case 9*, 69, 197; *Case 10*, 102; *Case 11*, 160; *Case 12*, 39; *Case 13*, 47, 143; *Case 15*, 159; *Case 16*, 130; *Case 17*, 53; *Case 18*, 74; *Case 19*, 97; *Case 20*, 126; *Case 22*, 119, 203; *Case 23*, 34; *Case 24*, 84; *Case 26*, 59; *Case 27*, 163; *Case 28*, 114; *Case 29*, 85; *Case 30*, 35; *Case 31*, 40; *Case 33*, 35; *Case 34*, 101; *Case 36*, 195; *Case 37*, 38; *Case 38*, 43; *Case 41*, 33; *Case 42*, 68; *Case 43*, 118; *Case 44*, 80; *Case 45*, 34; *Case 46*, 49; *Case 47*, 36; *Case 48*, 121; postscript, 39; English translations of, 20–21

Wumen Huikai; *bio*, 271; on "Deshan Carries His Bowls," 143; and "Zhaozhou's 'Wu,'" 271

Wuxie Lingmo, 101

Wuyong Jingquan, 281

Wuzhuo, and Mañjuśrī, 136

Wuzu Fayan; *bio*, 271; and the *bo* dove, 61; and the demon, 61; and the evening turning-phrase, 82; comments on the Five Houses of Zen, 86; lineage of, 204; and meeting an accomplished wayfarer, 195; and painting with sky, sea and Mount Sumeru, 59; and the poem on Little Jade, 95; and someone's servants, 34; and the talk of complete and incomplete, 37; misc., 216, 232, 233, 255, 280

Wuzu Shijie; *bio*, 271; and Guishan's mirror, 131

Xiang Yu (General); *bio*, 271–72, 161, 243

Xianglin Chengyuan; *bio*, 272; as Yunmen's attendant, 169; misc., 62, 265

Xiangyan Zhixian; *bio*, 272; enlightenment verses, 49–50, 273; and the everyday samadhi of the infant, 192; and the person up a tree, 45; and the sound of a tile hitting bamboo, 49–50; misc., 235

Xingchan Weikuan, 273

Xinghua Cunjiang; *bio*, 273; and the blind-oaf monk, 153; and the blind shouts, 109; and further study under Sansheng and Dajue, 109–10; and holding to the center,

72–73; and the rice-and-vegetable dinner, 114–15; scattering pearls, 108, 109; waves his hand twice, 108, 153; misc., 249, 256, 264, 267

Xingjiao Hongshou; *bio*, 273; and the sound of the falling firewood, 207

Xingyang Pou, 181

Xitang Zhizang; *bio*, 273; and the autumn-moon turning-phrases, 82; and the teaching of Daoyi, 273

Xiu; *bio*, 274; and Nanquan's death, 208

Xuansha Shibei; *bio*, 274; and Bodhidharma not coming to China, 63, 103; on Lingyun's peach blossoms, 37; not perceiving a single dharma, 135; on stumbling and hurting his toe, 103; misc., 219, 275, 276

Xuanzang, 226

Xuanzong (emperor); *bio*, 274; and Huangbo's bowing before a buddha image, 196

Xuedou baize songgu, 275

Xuedou Chongxian; *bio*, 274–75; comment on Deshan and the monk from Silla, 163; comment on the person up a tree, 45; misc., 247, 269

Xuefeng Yicun; *bio*, 275–76; and Deshan carrying his bowls, 47; enlightenment during pilgrimage with Yantou, 275; and monk leaving to visit Jingshan, 167–68; and Xuansha's "Bodhidharma didn't come to China," 63; misc., 199, 219, 221, 244–45, 258–59, 260, 274, 277, 282

Xutang Zhiyu; *bio*, 276; and his big-talking staff, 155; on the chalk line by Bo of Lu, 168; on Ciming's signpost, 128, 129; on Ciming's two shouts, 152; commenting in place of Nanquan, 98; on Deshan's fastening tethers in the stagnant water, 171; lineage in Japan, 17; on the monk's visit to Nanquan's hermitage, 127–28; a penniless scholar in the Imperial Library, 207; on raising the old sail, 74; on Shoushan uttering wild fox cries, 207; and the *Shūmon kattōshū*, 17; as teacher of Nanpo, 254; and his three questions, 126; verse on peddlers pushing carts, 128; verse on "Qiannu and Her Spirit," 51; on the woman in samadhi, 89; on Xuansha's single dharma not perceived, 135; misc., 10, 15, 17, 19, 21, 27, 118, 281

Yan, 61

Yang Danian; *bio*, 276, and the problem of wealth, 120; misc., 280

Yangqi Fanghui; *bio*, 276–77; visiting Ciming's woman, 144; shakes sleeves, 152; and the unseen bird, 152; misc., 216, 219, 262, 271

Yangqi line, 240, 276

Yangshan Huiji; *bio*, 277; and Changsha the tiger, 171; and the circle-figures, 189–90, 191, 225; function and essence, 105; and Guishan's buffalo, 73; and Guishan's mirror, 131; lecturing at Maitreya's place, 85; and the man in a well, 76; picking tea, 105; pushing forward his headrest, 81; and Xiangyan's enlightenment verses, 272; misc., 108, 109, 217, 235, 245, 260, 275, 277; see also *Guishan and Yangshan*

Yangzhou (town), going down to, 72, 73

Yantou Quanhuo; *bio*, 277–78; and the baby, 140; death at the hand of bandits, 278; and the final word, 47, 143; and the old sail, 74; visiting Deshan with Qinshan and Xuefeng, 199–200; and Xuefeng's enlightenment, 275; misc., 250, 258–59

Yanyang Shanxin; *bio*, 278; coming to Zhaozhou with nothing, 35–36

Yao Yuanming, 155

Yaoshan Weiyen, 221, 225, 263

Yellow Crane Pavilion, 167, 222; poem on, 165

Yellow River, flows north, 74

yin and yang, 129, 175, 203

Ying'an Tanhua; *bio*, 278; and misuses of the mind, 81; and taking shelter in an old mausoleum, 72; and the True Eye of the Dharma, 53; misc., 252, 267

Yogācāra school; philosophy of mind, 42; and the three modes of perceiving existence, 194

Yongjia Xuanjue; *bio*, 278–79; on Zen practice, 279; misc., 21, 142, 245, 256

Yongming Yanshou; *bio*, 279; misc., 207

Yu Di (Governor), 258; *bio*, 279–80; exchange with Ziyu Daotong, 60, 279–80; and land of the rakṣasas, 60; and Layman Pang's illness, 88

Yuan Zhan (scholar), 61

Yuanjian Fayuan, 271

Yuanming; *bio*, 280; on Deshan, 163

Yuanwu Keqin; *bio*, 280–81; being and nonbeing, 55; and the *Blue Cliff Record*, 95, 244; and boxwood Zen, 55; and Dahui Zonggao, 55, 92; enlightenment verse, 94; and the evening turning-phrase, 82; and the gate of misfortune, 80; and the place from which all buddhas come, 92; on the Patriarch's coming from the West, 133; praising the Sixth Patriarch, 94; misc., 204, 217, 223, 232, 271, 278, 282

Yuelun Shiguan, 271

Yuezhou Qianfeng; *bio*, 281; and the three types of sickness, 43; and the single road to nirvana, 121; and "Take up the One," 174

Yun'an Puyan; *bio*, 281; returning Baiyun Shouduan's vestment, 93; comment on Linji's begging rounds, 177

Yunfeng Wenyue, and criticism of Huanglong's understanding, 159, 240

Yunju Daojian; *bio*, 281; on Vimalakīrti as the Golden-Millet Tathāgata, 100

Yunju Daoying, 281

Yunju Shanwu; *bio*, 281; and the monk bitten by a snake, 204

Yunmen Wenyan; *bio*, 282; and his attendant Xianglin, 169; and the dharmakāya eating food, 134; and East Mountain, 68; enlightenment upon breaking leg, 282; and "Exposed!" 52; and the eye of the needle, 182; hearing sound and realizing the Way, 89; and Jianfu Chenggu, 244; on killing the Buddha, 104; and loss of supernatural powers, 139; and Mount Sumeru, 35; and "one-word barriers," 52; and the place from which all buddhas come, 92; and poking Indra with a fan, 121; and putting on one's vestment, 130; spares Dongshan three-score blows, 158, 159; and his three statements, 91; and the twenty-fifth day of the twelfth month, 107; "What is that?" 169; where to repent for killing buddhas, 52; and the word *hou*, 132; and Yuezhou Qianfeng, 43, 174; misc., 17, 46, 159, 217, 221, 229, 246, 248, 253, 266, 272, 276, 280, 284

Yunmen school, 275; Wuzu Fayan's comment on, 86

Yunmen's Extensive Record, 70

Yunyan Tansheng, 222, 225, 228, 245

Zen Forest Records, 173, 245

Zen Phrase Lexicon, 66, 107

Zengyi ahan jing, 118

Zhang Wujin (Prime Minister; Layman Wujin); *bio*, 282; and Doushuai's "final word," 123–24; misc., 245, 280, 284

Zhang Zhuo; *bio*, 282; and the buddha-names, 165

Zhang Zishao (Zhang Jiucheng); *bio*, 282–83; and Dahui, 125; and Linji's four positions, 125

Zhao Biaozhi (official), 55; *bio*, 283

Zhao's Treatises, 261

Zhaozhou Congshen; *bio*, 283; and the blade of grass as the body of a buddha, 184; and Cui Langzhong, 40; and dog's buddha nature, 65; and "drawing the bow after the thief has left," 107; and dropping nothingness, 35–36; falling into hell, 40; and the Great King, 195; neither guest nor host by the fireside, 177; "Juniper Tree" koan, 37–38, 59, 70, 283; and karmic

consciousness, 65; and Linji, 172, 173; and Mañjuśrī and Samantabhadra, 174; and Mount Tai, 39–40; and Nanquan Puyuan, 91, 97, 98, 174; and the stone bridge, 202; and the two hermits, 160; and washing his feet at Linji's place, 172; and the well tower, 98; and the "*Wu*" koan, 65–67, 271, 283; misc., 17, 59, 234, 255, 269, 278

Zhenjing Kewen; *bio*, 283; and Baiyun Shouduan's verse on Linji, 167; and the final word, 124; and the verse on "Linji's three-score blows of the stick," 167; and Layman Wujin, 123; on Manora's transmission verse, 50; as Qingsu's teacher, 123; misc., 230, 231, 245

Zhiyi, 268

Zhongfeng Mingben; *bio*, 284–85; on the "*Wu*" koan, 66

Zhuozhou Kefu; *bio*, 285; and Linji's "person and surroundings," 125

Zilin (court monk); *bio*, 285; and Huizhong's bowl of water, 205

Ziyu Daotong; *bio*, 285; and Yu Di's rakṣasas, 60; and Yu Di's persecution of mendicant monks, 279–80

Zutang ji, 219

About the Translator

THOMAS YŪHŌ KIRCHNER, a native of Connecticut who has resided in Japan since 1969, is an ordained Rinzai Zen monk and a graduate of Ōtani University in Kyoto with an M.A. in Buddhist studies. After practicing for ten years in Japanese monasteries he worked on the editorial staff at the Nanzan Institute for Religion and Culture in Nagoya. He presently serves as priest at the temple Rinsen-ji in the Arashiyama area of Kyoto, and is a researcher at the International Research Institute for Zen Buddhism at Hanazono University. Kirchner's other publications include the *Record of Linji* (editor) and Musō Soseki's *Dialogues in a Dream* (translator).

What to Read Next
from Wisdom Publications

Dialogues in a Dream
The Life and Zen Teachings of Musō Soseki
Musō Soseki and Thomas Yuhō Kirchner

"An astonishing book in its depth and breadth. This is a treasure of Buddhism."—Joan Halifax, author of *Being with Dying*

Dogen's Extensive Record
A Translation of the Eihei Kōroku
Eihei Dōgen
Translated by Taigen Dan Leighton and Shohaku Okumura
Foreword by Tenshin Reb Anderson

"Taigen and Shohaku are national treasures."—Norman Fischer, author of *Sailing Home*

Mud and Water
The Collected Teachings of Zen Master Bassui
Translated by Arthur Braverman

"This sparkling translation fully captures Bassui's unique vigor and insight and throws new light on an often neglected period of Zen's history."—Peter Haskel, author of *Bankei Zen*

Zen's Chinese Heritage
The Masters and Their Teachings
Andy Ferguson
Foreword by Reb Anderson and Steven Heine

"This is an indispensable reference for any student of Buddhism. Ferguson has given us an impeccable and very readable translation."—John Daido Loori, late abbot, Zen Mountain Monastery

About Wisdom Publications

Wisdom Publications is the leading publisher of classic and contemporary Buddhist books and practical works on mindfulness. To learn more about us or to explore our other books, please visit our website at wisdompubs.org or contact us at the address below.

Wisdom Publications
199 Elm Street
Somerville, MA 02144 USA

We are a 501(c)(3) organization, and donations in support of our mission are tax deductible.

Wisdom Publications is affiliated with the Foundation for the Preservation of the Mahayana Tradition (FPMT).